POLAND DAILY

POLAND DAILY

ECONOMY, WORK, CONSUMPTION AND SOCIAL CLASS IN POLISH CINEMA

Ewa Mazierska

berghahn
NEW YORK · OXFORD
www.berghahnbooks.com

First published in 2017 by
Berghahn Books
www.berghahnbooks.com

© 2017, 2022 Ewa Mazierska
First paperback edition published in 2022

All rights reserved. Except for the quotation of short passages for the purposes of criticism and review, no part of this book may be reproduced in any form or by any means, electronic or mechanical, including photocopying, recording, or any information storage and retrieval system now known or to be invented, without written permission of the publisher.

Library of Congress Cataloging-in-Publication Data
A C.I.P. cataloging record is available from the Library of Congress

British Library Cataloguing in Publication Data
A catalogue record for this book is available from the British Library

ISBN 978-1-78533-536-5 hardback
ISBN 978-1-80073-209-4 paperback
ISBN 978-1-78533-537-2 ebook

Contents

List of Illustrations	vi
Acknowledgements	viii
Introduction	1
Part I: Interwar Cinema: Striving for Social Promotion	27
1 The 1920s: The Cult of the Body and the Machine	35
2 The 1930s: The Beauty and Sadness of the Room at the Top	46
Part II: The Cinema in People's Poland: Taking a Great Leap	81
3 The 1950s: Holy Work?	103
4 The 1960s: Industrial Expansion and Small Stabilization	144
5 The 1970s: Bad Work and Good Life	181
6 The 1980s: Between Refusal to Work and Alienation of Labour	223
Part III: Postcommunist Cinema: From Triumphant Neoliberalism to Accumulation by Dispossession	255
7 The 1990s: Heroic Neoliberalism or Everybody Can Be a Winner	265
8 The 2000s and Beyond: Accumulation by Dispossession	287
Bibliography	309
Index	329

Illustrations

Illustration 1.1	Strong passions in *The Strong Man*, directed by Henryk Szaro	40
Illustration 1.2	Lachowicz in *Souls in Bondage*, directed by Leon Trystan	42
Illustration 1.3	Polish woman forced into prostitution in *A Trail of Disgrace*, directed by Mieczysław Krawicz and Alfred Niemirski	43
Illustration 2.1	Jan and Jadzia in *Jadzia*, directed by Mieczysław Krawicz	52
Illustration 2.2	Girls from Nowolipki in the film directed by Józef Lejtes	64
Illustration 2.3	Young ballet dancers dreaming about success in *The Ghosts*, directed by Eugeniusz Cękalski and Karol Szołowski	73
Illustration 3.1	Hanka and Janek building Warsaw in *An Adventure at Marienstadt*, directed by Leonard Buczkowski	116
Illustration 3.2	Adolf Dymsza in *Matter to Be Settled*, directed by Jan Fethke and Jan Rybkowski	122
Illustration 3.3	Work in the mine in *The Stars Must Burn*, directed by Andrzej Munk	132
Illustration 3.4	Life at the end of the world in *The Depot of the Dead*, directed by Czesław Petelski	135
Illustration 4.1	Kazik among the industrial sublime in *Gold*, directed by Wojciech Has	153
Illustration 4.2	Andrzej admiring Joanna's picture in *Marriage of Convenience*, directed by Stanisław Bareja	169
Illustration 4.3	Franek in *The Year of Franek W.*, directed by Kazimierz Karabasz	176
Illustration 5.1	Michał Roman in *Brunet Will Call*, directed by Stanisław Bareja	192
Illustration 5.2	Romek Januchta and his work pals in *Personnel*, directed by Krzysztof Kieślowski	197
Illustration 5.3	Lutek Danielak as Estrada employee in *Dance Leader*, directed by Feliks Falk	199
Illustration 5.4	Bugdol tending to his medals in *A Story of a Man Who Filled 552% of the Quota*, directed by Wojciech Wiszniewski	208
Illustration 5.5	Krystyna in *Krystyna M.*, directed by Kazimierz Karabasz	215

Illustration 6.1	Karol Szostak in *Dignity*, directed by Roman Wionczek	235
Illustration 6.2	The hard work of a female worker in *Day after Day*, directed by Irena Kamieńska	242
Illustration 6.3	Polish guest workers in London in *Moonlighting*, directed by Jerzy Skolimowski	248
Illustration 6.4	Ewa investing in her appearance in *Without Love*, directed by Barbara Sass	250
Illustration 7.1	An Intellectual turned into a businessmen in *Capital, or How to Make Money in Poland*, directed by Feliks Falk	268
Illustration 8.1	Franz Maurer in *Dogs*, directed by Władysław Pasikowski	289
Illustration 8.2	Lucjan looking for a corpse in *Bailiff*, directed by Feliks Falk	295

Acknowledgements

This book would not be possible without the help of many colleagues and friends, to whom I wish to express my gratitude. Elżbieta Ostrowska, Mirosław Przylipiak, Anna Mrozewicz and Eva Näripea read parts of this manuscript and offered insightful comments. Grażyna Grabowska and Adam Wyżyński from the Polish Film Archive and Barbara Gierszewska provided me with much of the secondary material used in this book. I am also grateful to my university, the University of Central Lancashire, which awarded me a one-semester long study leave to complete the manuscript.

Part of chapter 3, about the 1970s films of Krzysztof Kieślowski, was published in *Studies in Eastern European Cinema*, vol. 6, nr 1, under the title 'The Ideal and Reality of Work in the 1970s Films of Krzysztof Kieślowski'. Part of chapter 7, on the documentary films about state farms, was published in the *Hungarian Journal of English and American Studies*, volume 22, nr 2, under the title 'Representation of Slow Violence in the Films about Collapsed East European State Farms'. Permissions were granted to re-publish these articles.

Introduction

Economy, Social Class and the Everyday in Polish Cinema

In this book I analyse Polish cinema from the perspective of the representation of political economy, social classes and the everyday. Given that from 1945 to 1989 in official ideology class took precedence over other markers of human identity, such as gender, age and ethnicity, one might expect that the existing histories of Polish cinema would also prioritize this aspect. However, this is not the case. The issue of class is present, but rarely given centre stage. The existing histories of Polish cinema privilege problems pertaining to Polish society as a whole, what can be described as the issue of Polishness in Polish cinema.[1] With the passage of time, class is losing rather than gaining in prominence in such studies, reflecting global trends and some specifically Polish factors. While in the 1960s and 1970s western academics had privileged class and ignored other categories, affecting human social position and identity, in the subsequent decades sociologists and historians have become wary of class as a category of analysis (Meiksins Wood 1986; Jameson 1992: 48; Rowbotham and Beynon 2001: 3; Mazierska 2015a). Ellen Meiksins Wood, who was among the first thinkers to observe this 'retreat from class', explains this phenomenon by the disappointment caused by the defeat of the western working class in the struggle with capital, which took place in the late 1970s (Meiksins Wood 1986: 3–24) as well as a 'certain fastidious middle-class distaste for – not to say fear of – the working class' (ibid.: 10–11). I will risk a statement that a 'certain fastidious middle-class distaste for the working class' can also be identified in the existing histories of Polish cinema, as demonstrated by their scornful attitude to socialist realism and neglect of popular cinema. Yet, it does not mean that class differences, namely differences which determine our place in the social hierarchy, ceased to matter. On the contrary, under neoliberal capitalism class matters more than ever, because the development of capitalism renders other differences between humans, for example those pertaining to religion, ethnicity, gender and sexual orientation, less important than under earlier systems. For David Harvey the rejection of this category in current debates is a means of obfuscating the class character of neoliberal politics: 'Class is the foundational inequality necessary to the reproduction of capitalism. So the answer of existing political power is either to deny that class exists, or to say that the category is so confusing and complicated (as if the other categories like race and gender are not) as to be analytically useless' (Harvey 2010b: 231–232). Harvey's argument espouses a wider idea, eloquently presented by Pierre Bourdieu: 'The struggle of classification is a fundamental division of class struggle' (Bourdieu 1990a: 138).

The Polish postwar hostility to class as a category of social inquiry might be attributed in part to the cause Harvey identifies, especially if we modify his statement, adding that class is the foundational inequality necessary to the reproduction of any system based on inequality, which also includes state socialism. Another reason is linked to the specificity of Polish history. In the nineteenth century, which in Europe gave birth to the nation states, Poland did not exist as a state, but was partitioned among Russia, Prussia and the Habsburg Empire. And even later, when it regained independence, its existence was fragile and not quite independent. Poles thus saw their country as always at risk of being swallowed by their more powerful neighbours. They also believed that to survive, they had to keep together, rather than struggle among each other to advance the position of a specific class or modernize their social structure. As Adam Bromke argues, in Poland national independence took precedence over social reforms, and social reform was often advocated less as an end in itself than as a means of strengthening Poland against external enemies (Bromke 1962). The conviction that national unity is of paramount importance was particularly strong after Poland regained statehood in 1918. The most important Polish politician of the interwar period, Józef Piłsudski, famously said 'I have left the streetcar called "socialism" at the stop called "independence"' (quoted in Starski 1982: 6).

Although during the period of state socialism Marxism became the official ideology of the state, at the time the authorities and historians were again reluctant to tackle the issue of class. The official line was that Polish people were on the way to create one class: the working class. The other classes, such as peasants and small capitalists, were left over from the interwar system, and in due course would disappear. Such an approach was meant to obscure the fact that this system in fact bred a new ruling class, the nomenklatura, made up of the higher echelons of the Party, confirming the rule identified by Harvey that the best way of preserving class inequalities is to pretend that they do not exist. Even those historians (and by extension filmmakers) who recognized and criticized the existence of the nomenklatura adopted a somewhat myopic vision of Polish society as that of (almost) the whole nation united in its opposition against the ruling elite. The divisions between workers and peasants, workers and the intelligentsia or within different categories of workers were played down. The Marxist terminology, increasingly used by the ruling elites as free-wheeling signifiers, awoke in society hostility to phrases such as the 'working class' or 'class struggle'. This hostility has not been eradicated even a quarter of a century after state socialism fell in Poland, putting the researchers willing to engage with such concepts on the defensive, as they risk being seen as followers of a disgraced tradition. My ambition in this book is to demonstrate that these categories can be used productively in the study of Polish cinema and Polish history at large; the challenge is not to take them for granted, not to see them as essential and static, but dynamic. Rather than asking what is the working class and 'class struggle', I will describe what characters depicted in Polish films do for their living and how their advancement or demotion affects other class structures.

Polish filmmakers and film critics also eschew the everyday. The most critically acclaimed Polish films show Poles fighting against external enemies, rather than dealing with everyday problems and enjoying the small pleasures of life. Examples include the patriotic films of the interwar period, such as *Cud nad Wisłą* (*The Miracle on the Vistula*, 1921) by Ryszard Bolesławski, the films belonging to the Polish School of the late 1950s and early 1960s, or heritage films, based on Henryk Sienkiewicz's novels, produced by Jerzy Hoffman from the late 1960s onwards. While Polish films about fighting are usually serious and are met with critics' appreciation, work and the everyday is the stuff of genre films, which until recently have been brushed aside by historians as low quality entertainment. There are tens of dozens of book-length studies and hundreds of articles devoted to the films about the Second World War, which constitute the canon of Polish cinema (on the Polish canon, see Mazierska 2014a; Zwierzchowski and Kornacki 2014), while studies about the 'everyday' are rare. In part, this reflects how art or even history is created by most nations. Georges Perec observes, 'What speaks to us, seemingly, is always the big event, the untoward, the extra-ordinary: the front-page splash, the banner headlines. Railway trains only begin to exist when they are derailed, and the more passengers that are killed, the more the trains exist' (Perec

2002: 177). However, this also testifies to the Polish preference to see themselves as martyrs, always suffering at the hands of others.

Finally, although the bulk of studies acknowledge the fact that Polish films reflect Polish reality, including economic reality, this general opinion is rarely supported by a more detailed investigation into how specific economic situations or economic programmes of respective Polish governments affected what we see on screen. Finally, we barely see any studies analysing how the state of the country's economy and, especially, its transformation, affected representations, except for some general remarks.

It is not my intention here to criticize the aforementioned tendencies as I see them as productive ways of conducting the history of Polish cinema. Nevertheless, the results are histories in which Polish national interest takes precedence over other aspects, and leaves many issues unexplained. In particular, shunning the everyday equals neglecting the very core of human life. This point was made many times by the leading philosopher and cultural theorist researching this concept, Henri Lefebvre, who proposed to construe the everyday as fertile humus, which is a source of life-enhancing power as we walk over it unnoticed. As he puts it, 'A landscape without flowers or magnificent woods may be depressing for the passer-by, but flowers and trees should not make us forget the earth beneath, which has a secret life and a richness of its own' (Lefebvre 1991: 87). Similarly, as Ben Highmore observes, downplaying the everyday brings the risk of neglecting the voices from below, of the dominated, for the sake of listening to the dominating elites (Highmore 2002: 1). Indeed, this project has much to do with listening to the voices from below, or finding out why they are silenced or represented in one way rather than another. Yet, as noted by the same author, there is no 'everyday' as such, there is always 'somebody's everyday' (ibid.: 1–2); most importantly, it belongs to those who have power to represent it. One of my aims is to establish to whom this power belongs.

The fall of state socialism and with it the removal of direct censorship allowed for a re-examination of class politics and class identity as portrayed on the Polish screen during the state socialist period. Another factor conducive to such exploration is the changes in film studies, especially the growing interest in popular cinema, at the expense of the auteurist paradigm. The last two decades or so saw the publishing of several book-length studies devoted to Polish popular films, which touch on the problem of class and the everyday (for example Skotarczak 2004; Talarczyk-Gubała 2007; Zwierzchowski and Mazur 2011), and several others are in production. Moreover, there is a growing interest in the economy in relation to film, but the focus of such studies is typically on the politics and economy of film production rather that its reflection in the film's text (Adamczak 2010). The continuous preoccupation with the country's history as national history in the official discourses in Poland, as reflected, for example, in the agenda of state television and the politics of commemoration,[2] in part used as a means to obscure and smooth over the real class divisions effected by the shift to neoliberalism and the global rise of identity politics, associated with postmodernism, means that the eyes of film historians still tend to be set on questions other than social class, economy and the everyday.

Capitalism, True Communism and State Socialism

My study is inspired by Marx's writings, because there we can find descriptions of two systems, which prevailed in Poland in the period covered by this book, as well as of the system to which Polish society (or at least some of its sections) aspired. The first is capitalism, whose analysis fills the bulk of Marx's most famous works, *Capital* (1965, 1967, 1974), *The Communist Manifesto* (Marx and Engels 2008), *Economic and Philosophic Manuscript of 1884* (1977) and *The German Ideology* (Marx and Engels 1947). This system dominated in Poland during the interwar period and returned, albeit in a modified form, after 1989. The second system is state socialism, which ruled in Poland after the Second World War until 1989. Marx presented such a system, albeit briefly, in *Economic and Philosophic Manuscripts of 1844*. Finally, the ideal system of 'true' communism is evoked in *The German Ideology* and *The Communist Manifesto*. I will describe them briefly, as it will help in establishing how much the reality in Poland of different periods had in common with these models.

Capitalism develops thanks to the production of surplus value, which can be described schematically as the difference between what the capitalist invests in the production of specific goods, including the wages he (as it is usually him) pays to his workforce, and what he receives when selling these goods in the market. If the capitalist is successful, this difference is bigger than is necessary to sustain his lifestyle and he is able to expand his activities by investing the accumulated surplus value, known as capital, into new ventures. Because profit is the main objective of the capitalist, he tries to reduce his costs by increasing the productivity of his workforce. In the past this led to such phenomena as building factories, because when accumulated in one place workers were more productive than when they were dispersed, forcing labourers to work in shifts, so that no hour of potential production is lost, prolonging the working day, as well as replacing more expensive workers by cheaper ones, for example men by women and children, and local workers by immigrants (Marx 1965; Harvey 2010a, especially 109–134). The affluence and comfort of the worker is never the capitalist's objective. On the contrary, it is in the capitalist's interest that the worker is poor, because his/her poverty and need to buy their daily bread forces the worker to get up in the morning and stand in front of the machine, producing surplus value for his employer. Marx put it in not unambiguous terms in *The Communist Manifesto*:

> *In proportion as the repulsiveness of the work increases, the wage decreases. Nay more, in proportion as the use of machinery and division of labour increases, in the same proportion the burden of toil also increases, whether by prolongation of the working hours, by the increase of the work exacted in a given time or by increased speed of machinery, etc. (Marx and Engels 2008: 43)*

As the above quote indicates, the character of capitalism affects the social position and experience of the worker. The richer the capitalist is, the poorer the worker. Their interests are antagonistic and lead to struggle, as manifested by the creation of workers' unions and strikes. Moreover, capitalist work leads to the 'alienation' (estrangement) of the worker. The term conveys the fact that work under capitalism exhausts the worker and reduces him to an animal-like existence. Moreover, the worker becomes lonely in the world he created – this world is alien to him and the more he produces, the more alienated he becomes. Alienation has several dimensions, reflecting four types of relations of man: to his productive activity, to his product, to other men and to the species. Alienation towards one's labour is the most important as it is the root of other forms of alienation (Marx 1977: 71). The only limit to the exploitation of workers by the capitalist system is the need to renew the workforce: 'The cost of production of a workman is restricted, almost entirely, to the means of subsistence that he requires for maintenance, and for the propagation of his race' (ibid.: 43). Marx writes, quoting Adam Smith, that the wage the labourer receives is always a minimum wage, 'the lowest compatible with common humanity, that is, with cattle-like existence' (ibid.: 21). In a situation where there is no limit to the workforce (which is usually the case), the capitalist has no incentive even to ensure that his labourers, real and potential, will physically survive. Should supply greatly exceed demand, a section of the workers sinks into beggary or starvation (ibid.: 21).

The more advanced capitalism is, the more it is disembedded from national institutions and traditions. Cold calculation replaces any other motivation, such as ensuring national cohesiveness. This is a situation which especially characterizes neoliberal capitalism, which in the 1980s in the West began to replace 'embedded liberalism', understood as a system which attempted to combine capitalism with the protection of national interests and ensuring a degree of equality (Harvey 2005a: 11). Eastern Europe also adopted neoliberalism, with varying zeal, after the fall of state socialism, partly due to the conviction of its leaders that this was the best system to overcome the problems of an inefficient economy, inherited from the previous system, and partly through international pressure, exerted by institutions such as the World Bank and the International Monetary Fund (see part 3).

Marx also envisaged two systems which are different from capitalism. They can be described as 'true communism' and 'crude communism'. Under both surplus value is not collected by individual capitalists, but by a community or its representatives. In the first one, which was meant to be introduced under conditions of advanced capitalism, when everybody can enjoy affluence, division of work is abolished, alienation disappears and people, more or less, engage in activities which bring them personal fulfilment. This is presented in a fragment from *The German Ideology*, where, borrowing from the utopian socialist, Charles Fourier, Marx muses on a possible society of the future, where

> nobody has one exclusive sphere of activity but each can become accomplished in any branch he wishes, society regulates the general production and thus makes it possible for me to do one thing today and another tomorrow, to hunt in the morning, fish in the afternoon, rear cattle in the evening, criticize after dinner, just as I have a mind, without ever becoming hunter, fisherman, shepherd or critic (Marx and Engels 1947: 22)

The examples used by Marx are obviously dated, but the message is not. Democracy and affluence are crucial features of true communism. In such circumstances people lose interest in having private property, because what belongs to the community fulfils their needs and the majority does not allow a minority to accumulate excessive wealth at their expense. Under crude communism surplus value is collected by the state. The author of *Capital* pointed to the similarity of this system to (ordinary) capitalism:

> *(For crude communism) the community is simply a community of labor and equality of wages, which are paid out by the communal capital, the community as universal capitalist. Both sides of the relation are raised to an unimaginary universality – labor as the condition in which everyone is placed and capital as the acknowledged universality and power of the community... The first positive abolition of private property – crude communism – is therefore only a manifestation of the vileness of private property trying to establish itself as the positive community. (Marx 1977: 95)*

This fragment points to Marx's distaste towards crude communism as a system burdened with the same problems as capitalism, including high levels of alienation and uniformization of the worker, and a danger (although it is only suggested by Marx) that a privileged minority will amass property and power at the expense of the majority. At the same time one can conjecture that crude communism might under some circumstances be a necessary step to achieve true communism. Such a view was adopted in Russia, following the victory of the Bolshevik revolution, which took place not under conditions of the abundance of consumer goods, but their scarcity, with the leader of the revolution, V.I. Lenin, being its chief espouser (Lenin 1989: 120–161).

The system introduced in Poland after the Second World War was also of a crude communism type, as it was introduced in the situation of scarcity rather than abundance, in a country devastated by war, whose social structure was practically feudal. Moreover, it was in part a consequence of Poland becoming subordinate to its Eastern neighbour, the Soviet Union. I describe its version as 'state socialism' to emphasize the role of the state in collecting the surplus value and deciding what to do with it; such a term is also favoured in the literature on Eastern Europe during the Cold War (for example Berend 1996). The fact that the ultimate guarantor of state socialism was the Soviet Union does not mean that Poles were intrinsically antisocialist or inegalitarian, far from it. Most likely, if they had had a choice to participate in free elections after the Second World War, in their majority they would have voted for the parties of socialist programme or those combining socialism with Catholicism. Although state socialism fell short of the Marxist ideal of true communism, it included some of its elements, such as granting all citizens the right to welfare through the policy of full employment and a system of benefits, such as child support, incapacity benefit, as well as universal healthcare and free education (Narojek 1991; Szumlewicz 2010). The socialist state also went some way towards granting privileges to the groups which were previously disadvantaged. I shall mention here such policies as dividing the aristocratic estates among petty peasants, giving managerial positions to ordinary workers (Narojek 1991: 23–24), building in the centre of Warsaw a large estate for working class people (Crowley 2002) and special privileges for students from working class and peasant backgrounds (Narojek 1991: 24). They were moderate in comparison with some western democracies during a similar period, but significant in the context of the Polish devastation, backwardness and political marginality after the Second World War. One can ask the question of whether the standard of living of the underprivileged and especially of those at the bottom (as their situation should always be the measure of socialism of any system) would have been any better if the political system from the interwar period had persisted after the Second World War. In my opinion, it would not. Hence, one of the objectives of this book is to defend the socialist dimension of state socialism, while illuminating when and why it fell short of socialist values. It is also from such a leftist perspective that I will look at Polish cinema. I do not pretend that it is unbiased, but every study of cultural product is biased, either explicitly or implicitly.

Everyday Polish Style

Everyday life existed and was a topic of investigation through all periods of Polish history covered in this book, but it raised particularly interesting questions during the period of state socialism.

As Ben Highmore observes, 'it would be impossible to understand fully the importance of everyday life in social and cultural thought in the twentieth century without taking into consideration the Russian Revolution of 1917' (Highmore 2002: 85). There are two tendencies pertaining to the everyday under state socialism. One reflects a desire to turn everyday life into a work of art; the other to organize the everydayness of revolutionary society from the centre. Highmore singles out Leon Trotsky as holding a pivotal position in regards to ideas about reconfiguring everyday life in both of these ways (ibid.: 85). The famous revolutionary also claimed that to achieve this goal the everyday had to become an object of legitimate research.

In his work, Trotsky draws attention to the invisibility of ordinary life and to the fact that people are more the products of accumulated experience than its creators. It is easier to transform these aspects of human life which are public and refer to industrial relations than those which concern private life. To demonstrate it, he uses the term 'Rasteryaevism', whose origin lies in the novel by Gleb Uspensky, *The Morals of Rasteryaev Street,* published in 1866, about the life of workers in Tula in the second half of the nineteenth century, which is very conservative. Trotsky writes:

> *The brutal treatment accorded to apprentices, the servility practiced before employers, the vicious drunkenness, and the street hooliganism has vanished. But in the relations of husband and wife, parents and children, in the domestic life of the family, fenced off from the whole world, Rasteryaevism is still firmly implanted. We need years and decades of economic growth and culture to banish Rasteryaevism from its last refuge – individual and family life – recreating it from top to bottom in the spirit of collectivism. (Trotsky 2002: 85)*

Although Trotsky's words refer to a specific situation in post-revolutionary Russia, they have a wider resonance and can be applied both to Poland after its various political transformations, especially after the Second World War and to the fall of state socialism. On each occasion there was a sense that everyday life lags behind political and public life: the new cannot defeat the old. In the period post-1989 this view was conveyed by the widespread use of the term 'homo sovieticus' in the most pejorative way, referring to people whose morals and manners are frozen in the old, disgraced, state socialist system.

The important point made by Trotsky is that socialist politicians and ideologues should not leave everyday life 'in peace', but attempt to change it, to ensure liberation of the lower classes, including women trapped in patriarchal relations. The changes in industrial relations are a necessary step to change morals, but they are not sufficient. Popular culture, in common with high art, was given the task of assisting politicians in this respect by showing people what is wrong with their behaviour and how to change it. But it was difficult to fulfil because, as Trotsky observes, 'art, by nature, is conservative'. Artists often share the same prejudices as the 'backward masses' and, rather than advance new ideas, promote and normalize the old ones. Hence the role of communist parties is to influence artists to produce art which advances socialist goals, most importantly the creation of a classless society.

Trotsky's arguments are examined by Raymond Williams in his essay 'Culture Is Ordinary', even though the British author does not refer specifically to Trotsky, only to Marxism at large. Williams shares with Trotsky the view that ordinary everyday life should be researched, because it equals culture. He also argues that this culture must be interpreted in relation to its underlying system of production. Where Williams parts with Trotsky (no doubt in part due to representing a different culture) is that 'the advocacy of a different system of production is in some way a cultural directive, indicating not only a different way of life, but new arts and learning' (Williams 2002: 96). Instead he claims that 'a culture is common meanings, the product of a whole people', therefore 'it is stupid and arrogant to suppose that any of these meanings can in any way be prescribed; they are made by living, made and remade, in ways we cannot know in advance' (ibid.: 96). Of course, by pronouncing that culture should not be prescribed, Williams indirectly opposes such projects as the Soviet avant-garde and socialist realism, which today are seen as utopian and naive (the former) and philistine and inhuman (the latter). My own position is somewhere between these two thinkers. On the one hand, I am against prescribing culture to the people, but at the same time I do not think it should be left entirely to natural forces. Again, popular culture plays a role in shaping everyday culture and it can be seen as progressive or regressive.

Here it is worth mentioning Michel de Certeau and his concepts of 'strategy' and 'tactics', with 'strategy' relating to forces coming from above. 'Political, economic, and scientific rationality has been constructed on this strategic model' (de Certeau 2002: 69). By contrast, 'the place of the tactic belongs to the other... Whatever it wins, it does not keep. It must constantly manipulate events in order to turn them into "opportunities"' (ibid.: 70). It can be argued that both the functioning of state socialism and its eventual collapse was to a large a result of the strength of the tactics used by the citizens to circumvent policies and rules coming from the top.

When discussing the everyday it is difficult to ignore probably the best known author of this topic, Henri Lefebrve. In common with Trotsky and Williams, but to a larger extent, Lefebrve equals culture with the everyday, with the mundane, and is an advocate of researching it, not only for the sake of pure knowledge but for its political transformation. With Trotsky and Williams he also observes that such research is never neutral, but always conducted from a specific class position: 'The criticism of everyday life was in fact *a criticism of other classes*, and for the most part found its expression in contempt for productive labour; at best it criticized the life of the dominant class in the name of a transcendental philosophy or dogma, which nevertheless belonged to that class' (Lefebrve 2002: 226, emphasis in original). From this perspective Lefebrve criticizes one movement associated with socialism, surrealism, observing that 'surrealism rendered triviality unbearable' (ibid.: 226).

One part of Lefebrve's investigation of the everyday concerns the value of work and the relationship between work and leisure. He writes that

> Historically, in real individuality and its development, the 'work-leisure' relation has always presented itself in a contradictory way. Until the advent of bourgeois society, individuality, or rather personality could only really develop outside productive labour... Bourgeois society reasserted the value of labour, above all during the period of its ascendancy; but at the historical moment when the relation between labour and the concrete development of individuality was emerging, labour took on an increasingly fragmented character... Thus at the same time a distinction was made between man 'as man' on the one hand and the working man on the other... Family life became separate from productive activity. And so did leisure. (ibid.: 227, emphasis in original)

Lefebrve's observations raise interesting questions in relation to society under state socialism. There is no doubt that the socialist ideology, following Marxist ideas about 'amateurism' as an ideal of human life, tried to bring unity between work and leisure. In reality, however, this unity was never achieved. Moreover, at the time when work felt like leisure, this was because of the perception that the socialist workers do not work hard enough or even use their working time for leisure. This opinion was typically voiced by the intelligentsia, resentful about various privileges enjoyed by manual workers and it is notable that while during the period of state socialism studies of everyday life in Poland were relatively rare, in the last two decades we have observed an upsurge (for example Szpakowska 2008; Kienzler 2015). Most likely, they reflect the growing distance from the state socialist past, its transformation into history and, to some extent, nostalgia for bygone days.

Polish Popular and Arthouse Films

The everyday is almost synonymous with 'ordinary': ordinary events and common people. By the same token it contrasts with 'extraordinary' and 'elitist'. If we map these categories onto cinema, then we can conjecture that this book will be concerned largely with popular cinema, as this is a cinema addressed at the 'masses' or 'common people', as opposed to elites. This is indeed the case here. However, different national cultures in different periods project their 'common people' differently and thus the concept of popular cinema and its realization is culture- and time-specific.

In western literature, until recently, popular cinema was routinely equated with genre cinema, whose principal domain is Hollywood. Barry Keith Grant, in an often repeated definition, states that 'genre movies are those commercial feature films which, through repetition and variation, tell familiar-stories with familiar characters in familiar situations'. Such films were 'exceptionally significant in establishing the popular sense of cinema as a cultural and economic institution, particularly in the United States, where Hollywood studios early on adopted an industrial model based on mass production' (Grant 2003: xv).

Art or arthouse films are usually perceived as 'non-Hollywood' through their attempt to avoid stereotypes, challenging the audience and being produced outside the film 'factories' in a more artisanal, individualized way. Steve Neale argues that

> *Art films tend to be marked by a stress on visual style (an engagement of the look in terms of a marked individual point of view rather than in terms of institutionalised spectacle), by a suppression of action in the Hollywood sense, by a consequent stress of character rather than plot and by interiorisation of dramatic conflict... It is also true that Art films are marked at the textural level by the inscription of features that function as marks of enunciation – and hence, as signifiers of an authorial voice (and look). The precise nature of these features has varied historically and geographically, as it were, since it derives in part from another, simultaneous function that these features perform: that of differentiating the text or texts in question from the texts produced in Hollywood. (Neale 2002: 103–104)*

Neale also observes that 'the mark of the author is used as a kind of brand name, to mark and to sell the filmic product' (ibid.: 105). We tend to go to the cinema to see Jean-Luc Godard's new film and the new Batman movie.

Can we map these categories onto Polish cinema? To some extent we can. In particular, the division of cinema into popular and arthouse existed throughout the whole of Polish film history, and Hollywood films were an important point of reference for filmmakers of different generations. However, these categories were also blurred and complicated by various factors. First, in the interwar period, the weakness of the Polish industry led to a great pressure to make commercial films according to the genre formulas. In such circumstances art film had little chance to develop and even those directors who had the talent and ambition to make arthouse films, such as Józef Lejtes or filmmakers linked to START (Stowarzyszenie Miłośników Filmu Artystycznego [Society for Devotees of Artistic Film]), had to conform to the demands to make genre films. After the Second World War we can notice a changing approach to the popular/art divide. Under Stalinism this divide seems to be almost obliterated thanks to the power of the state to decree what is popular and to demand that filmmakers follow the prescribed formula. After the end of Stalinism popular and art cinema took somewhat different paths; it is more or less the case, as in the scheme described by Neale, that Poles will go to see a comedy or a Has or Kieślowski film. However, there are certain specificities pertaining to the Polish situation. One concerns the unprecedented hostility of Polish critics to genre films, especially genres seen as un-Polish, such as science fiction, with the career of Marek Piestrak perfectly illustrating this approach (Näripea 2014).

The second was the expectation that Polish art films will be popular. It is worth mentioning here Aleksander Jackiewicz, the creator of the term 'Polish School' (Szkoła polska), referring to the critically most successful movement in Polish cinema. This very term equates a certain number of films with a strong authorial stamp with what is typically Polish, namely made for ordinary Poles (Jackiewicz 1954: 9). For Jackiewicz the problem was not how to make popular genre cinema à la Hollywood in Poland, but how to make art cinema popular (Mazierska 2015b: 98). This objective was, to some extent, achieved, as proven by the fact that some films by Wajda, Ford or Kawalerowicz reached mass audiences. This was in part thanks to the willingness of the most celebrated Polish filmmakers, such as Andrzej Wajda, Roman Polanski or Wojciech Has, to engage with genre, particularly war and heritage films. However, this popular bias of Polish arthouse cinema is largely unrecognized. At the same time, some directors of popular films, especially comedies, were seen as auteurs. In Poland during the state socialism period, people often went to see not just a Polish comedy but Bareja, Piwowski or Kondratiuk's comedy. Their directors were seen as a brand in the same way that directors of art films are.

The fall of state socialism led to the combining of two tendencies in relation to art and popular cinema. On the one hand, the high status of the film director is preserved. On the other hand, the pressure to produce popular films increased. The result is a two-tier approach to genre cinema, with more established directors turning to genres which are seen as more prestigious, such as melodrama and heritage films (Ostrowska 2016) and the less established left to make comedies, horrors or criminal films. However, this situation is expected to change, with the pressure to produce 'popular arthouse cinema' growing, mirroring the situation in western European countries.

When critics talk about popular and art cinema, they normally exclude documentary films from such discussions; it is seen as beyond this divide. However, numerous Polish documentary films can be seen as both popular and art: popular, because many of them were shown in cinemas before the main programme, hence enjoyed mass audience (even if this audience did not choose to see them); and art, on account of the high status of their directors, such as Kazimierz Karabasz or Wojciech Wiszniewski.

Cinema, Ideology and the Artists' and Viewers' *Weltanschauung*

My book does not concern Polish economy, class system and the everyday as they exist objectively (if this can be established at all), but their filmic representations. I will treat films as historical documents, from which we can learn how people at a specific time looked, what they ate, where and how they lived and worked, and even what they thought.[3] In many ways, films are more convincing documents than historical books or drawings, because they mechanically reproduce the world in front of our eyes, as André Bazin and his followers argued. They are particularly useful tools in capturing the everyday, the ordinary stuff of life, which historical books and statistical accounts tend to neglect. Throughout this book I will compare films with other types of documents, such as books and articles on the political and economic history of Poland.

Although films reproduce the world, they do not do so indiscriminately, but make specific choices and transform the material they use to send a message; hence they are a terrain of ideology. This view was put succinctly by Jean-Luc Comolli and Jean Narboni, who wrote

> *Clearly, the cinema 'reproduces reality': this is what a camera and film stock are for – so says the ideology. But the tools and techniques of filmmaking are a part of 'reality' themselves, and furthermore 'reality' is nothing but an expression of the prevailing ideology. Seen in this light, the classic theory of cinema that the camera is an impartial instrument which grasps, or rather is impregnated by, the world in 'concrete reality' is an eminently reactionary one. What the camera in fact registers is the vague, unformulated, untheorized, unthought-out world of the dominant ideology. Cinema is one of the languages through which the world communicates itself to itself. They constitute its ideology for they reproduce the world as it is experienced when filtered through the ideology. (Comolli and Narboni 1992: 684–685)*

I agree with Comolli and Narboni that the world offered to the cinemagoer is filtered through ideology, but so is the world proposed in other types of historical documents and ordinary speech. There is no escape from ideology, as there is no escape from language. The only thing we (the professional and amateur film historians) can do is to identify what values and opinions the films transmit and the reasons for that.

It is also argued that different types of films have different relationships to the dominant ideology (which is almost always regarded by the authors as a bad thing). For example, the higher a film's budget and the more it is geared towards the mass audience, the more likely it is to accord with the dominant ideology. Such a view chimes with the opinions of many filmmakers who are credited with successfully breaking its chains, such as Jean-Luc Godard and Raul Ruiz. The latter said:

> *I gradually came to understand that every spectator of the movies today is really a 'connoisseur', that is, the opposite of a spectator. I take the expression of 'connoisseur' in Benjamin's sense: in cinema as in sports, the spectators understand what's going on, to the point where they can anticipate what happens next, because they know the rules, by learning or by intuition... That's*

why commercial cinema presupposes an international community of connoisseurs and a shared set of rules for the game of social life. In that sense, commercial cinema is the 'totalitarian social space par excellence'... The spectator/connoisseur compares the scenes less with his private life than with other scenes watched in other movies. (Ruiz 2005: 58–59)

The opinion that commercial and non-commercial cinema have different relationships to the dominant ideology also prevails among historians of Eastern European cinema. The latter, arthouse, auteurist films are typically regarded as being more critical of the state and hence granted more attention than popular and genre films. However, not all critics agree with the view that mainstream cinema is conformist while non-mainstream is not. In their discussion of ideology Comolli and Narboni do not differentiate between 'commercial' and 'mainstream' films on the one hand and 'arthouse' and 'auteurist' films on the other in respect to ideology, claiming:

The majority of films in all categories are the unconscious instruments of the ideology which produces them. Whether the film is 'commercial' or 'ambitious', 'modern' or 'traditional', whether it is the type that gets shown in art houses, or in smart cinemas, whether it belongs to the 'old' cinema or the 'young' cinema, it is most likely to be a re-hash of the same old ideology. (Comolli and Narboni 1992: 685)

This category is contrasted by Comolli and Narboni with films which attack their ideological assimilation on two fronts: either by direct political action, on the level of the 'signified', that is, when they deal with a directly political subject; or on the level of form, on the 'signifiers', when they break down of the traditional way of depicting reality. They also stress that 'only action on both fronts, "signified" and "signifiers", has any hope of operating against the prevailing ideology. Economic/political and formal action have to be indissolubly wedded' (ibid.: 686).

In this context it is also worth mentioning Jacques Rancière, who in his essay 'The Paradoxes of Political Art' recognizes that there are different types of political art or types of pedagogy attributed to critical art, which he describes as representational mediation, ethical immediacy and aesthetic distance. Rather than arguing in favour of any of them as most efficient in challenging the dominant ideology, Rancière singles out that which disrupts the consensus (introducing dissensus) by 'breaking with the sensory self-evidence of the "natural" order that destines specific individuals and groups to occupy positions of rule or of being ruled, assigning them to private or public lives, pinning them down to a certain time and space, to specific "bodies", that is to specific ways of being, seeing and saying' (Rancière 2013: 139). Politics, including political art, is that which breaks with the existing order (which Rancière describes as the order of police) by inventing new subjects, most importantly bringing into visibility those who remained hidden.

If we use such rigid criteria, then we shall conclude that the vast majority of films produced in Poland complied with the dominant ideology, not least because the films conveying oppositional political messages tended to use traditional form and films engaging in formal experiments tended to contain little political content. However, the majority of films, produced in Poland and elsewhere, are not in a simple relation to dominant ideology. They pick and mix elements from different ideologies, often in an incoherent fashion. Or, to put it differently, the meaning of a film, as that of other media, results from the juxtaposition of different discursive codes. Ideological ambiguity might be a consequence of a film being a product of the collaboration of people with different political agendas, such as scriptwriters, directors and actors, as well as censors, who might neutralize each other in the course of film production. Films also end up being ambiguous for other reasons, such as the conscious desire of their makers to render them less obvious and more interesting for the audience and to appeal to a wider pool of viewers than those following a specific political agenda. In Poland, where mainstream films made in the interwar period and under state socialism had a particularly bad press largely due to their ideological transparency, the urge to make ideologically ambiguous films was particularly strong. We shall also add that interpretations of films are not passive, but active. The spectator not only decodes what is put in the film, but often transforms the message intended by the film's author, drawing on her/his knowledge and adjusting the film's messages to his/her opinions. Interpretations by the same viewer might also change with the passage of time. In summary, although I agree that the dominant ideology leaves its distinct mark on films and there exists an 'international community of connoisseurs' able to decipher some of the film's messages, as Ruiz claims, there are also messages which can be picked up or created only by a narrower pool of viewers.

Claiming that films reflect the dominant ideology raises the question of what ideology is and when a specific ideology becomes dominant. Ideology is typically defined as a system of ideas governing the behaviour of a specific group of people in a specific area. We encounter terms such as 'feudal', 'capitalist', 'socialist', 'religious', 'patriarchal' or 'feminist' ideology. When the majority of people accept a given ideology, then it becomes dominant. In the Marxist discourse, dominant ideology is linked to the issue of power, which arises from possessing material things: slaves in the times of slavery, feudal estates in medieval times, money under capitalism:

> *The ideas of the ruling class are in every epoch the ruling ideas: i.e. the class, which is the ruling material force of society, is at the same time its ruling intellectual force. The class which has the means of material production at its disposal, has control at the same time over the means of mental production, so that thereby, generally speaking, the ideas of those who lack the means of mental production are subject to it. (Marx and Engels 1947: 89)*

Stuart Hall adds:

> *The concept ideology... entails the proposition that ideas are not self-sufficient, that their roots lie elsewhere, that something central about ideas will be revealed if we can discover the nature of the determinacy which non-ideas exert over ideas. The study of 'ideology' thus also holds out the promise of a critique of idealism, as a way of explaining how ideas arise. (Hall 1978: 10–11)*

The domination of a particular ideology is reflected in the parameters of discourse, in what appears to be a natural subject of discussion and what an unfashionable or taboo topic. This affects, for example, the way histories are written; each epoch has a predilection to certain perspectives and 'buzzwords' expressing them. Again, Marx identified this rule, claiming that:

> *during the time that the aristocracy was dominant, the concepts honour, loyalty, etc., were dominant, during the dominance of the bourgeoisie the concepts freedom, equality, etc. ... For each new class which puts itself in the place of one ruling before it, is compelled, merely in order to carry through its aim, to represent its interest as the common interest of all the members of society, put it in an ideal form; it will give its ideas the form of universality, and*

> *represent them as the only rational, universally valid ones. (Marx and Engels 1947: 40–1)*

Ideology also speaks (metaphorically) through silences. This aspect of ideology was discussed at length by Pierre Macherey and Terry Eagleton. In his introduction to Macherey's seminal works, *A Theory of Literary Production,* Eagleton observes that, according to Macherey, literature represents ideology, but it does not mean that it passively reflects it, but rather that it 'stages' or 'produces' it. In doing so, 'it highlights those limits, absences and contradictions in the ideology which are not so visible to us in everyday life, where ideology is, so to speak, too close to the eyeball to be objectified' (Eagleton 2006: ix). In order to establish what the text says, we have to find out what it does not say, capture the text's 'symptomatic repressions, evasions, slippages, self-contradictions and eloquent silences' (ibid.: viii). Eagleton refers to the silences, repressions and absences in the individual art works, but we can also talk about them in relation to movements and periods.

Although the dominant class attempts to impose its worldview on the rest of the society, there is no direct translation between the interests of the dominant class and the ruling ideas. The concept of the dominant ideology is particularly thorny in relation to state socialism. This is because state socialism was meant to be based on the principles of Marxism, most importantly egalitarianism and abolishing alienation of labour. Polish society under this system was indeed more egalitarian than in the interwar period and after the fall of state socialism. However, it fell short of these ideals. As a result, the ruling elite were reluctant to discuss them, fearing that they risked exposing their hypocrisy or incompetence. I will also argue that they were too weak politically and intellectually to create an ideology which would effectively keep hold of people's minds and defend their class interests. This 'ideological void' 'at the top' was increasingly covered with the 'communist speak' of the sort George Orwell mocked. At the bottom, it was filled, to a large extent, by the anti-communist messages promulgated by the Catholic Church. The overall result was the co-existence of a plethora of competing ideologies circulating in Poland at the time, some unofficially, but many officially, including in films.

Paradoxically, although Poland during the state socialism period, in common with other countries belonging to the Soviet bloc, is often described as 'totalitarian' (for example Świda-Ziemba 1998; on the criticism of this approach, see Geyer and Fitzpatrick 2009; Majmurek and Szumlewicz 2010), which implies that the state tightly controlled all aspects of citizens' lives and their artistic production, the films produced in this period, especially in the 1970s and the 1980s, reveal a critical attitude to state socialism, to the extent that some critics use the term 'dissident cinema' to describe part of the official film production of this period. The existence of such cinema was also explained by factors such as the porous character of socialist censorship, with some censors being 'liberal', the ability of some directors to write 'innocuous scripts', into which subversive messages were smuggled during the shooting (Adamczak 2012), and a desire on the part of the authorities to project to the West an image of Poland as a country which allows or even encourages ideological pluralism (Ostrowska 2012). Such factors have to be considered when accounting for the representation of the everyday.

The Content and Structure of This Book

The purpose of this book is twofold. First, I want to find out what we can learn about the Polish economy, class structure and its everyday experience by studying Polish films. I treat films as historical documents; the better we use them, the more we are able to compare them with other historical documents, most importantly those related to Polish politics and economy. Second, I will try to identify whether Polish films reveal a specific class bias by, for example, privileging the representation of specific classes and under-representing others, and assessing their members in certain ways, as victors or victims, people who contribute to the country's wealth or who act as parasites on other classes. I will thus treat Polish films as political works which I will compare with other political works. Of specific interest for me is the relationship between the ruling class and the subordinate classes. I want to find out how it changed over the decades and what were the main factors precipitating these changes.

Talking about class cannot be separated from discussing other aspects of human identity, most importantly gender, because the division of labour, practically as long as humankind has existed, has been organized along gender lines, with some positions reserved for men and some for women. This results in part from the differences in human biology. Women give birth and hence are attributed the task of looking after children to a greater extent than men. Men are physically stronger, therefore have traditionally been expected to engage in heavy work, such as hunting and later working in the mines and on construction sites.

However, throughout the course of history, this simple division of labour has been complicated. For example, following the end of the Second World War, which resulted in Poland losing a large chunk of its menfolk and the country embarking on an ambitious programme of industrialization, women were encouraged to take upon themselves masculine tasks. In my study I will show how the changing position of women as workers was depicted in Polish films. Another aspect of identity affecting class position is age. It is assumed that with age comes authority, as during their lifetime people are expected to climb the social ladder. However, during times of political transformation, this rule tends to be reversed: the older people are thrown from their pedestals to make space for the young ones. I will investigate whether the films chosen for my analysis follow this pattern. Class structure is not static. It is affected by major political events and itself affects the course of history. This rule is reflected in the Marxist saying that human history is the history of class struggle. On the smaller scale of Polish history, we also have to take into account other factors whose class character is less obvious, such as the two world wars.

I decided to divide my book into three parts, each reflecting on a different economic and political system which ruled in Poland in a specific time. The first part is devoted to the interwar period, when Poland became an independent country after over one hundred years of partition, and which was accompanied by the suppression and censorship of indigenous culture. During this period Poland also built its own film industry. Poland of the interbellum was a capitalist country, dominated by small industry, and the Polish film industry also fits this description. Its main objective was to attract as large an audience as possible, which explains the fact that the majority of films produced during this period is genre cinema. Although film production and distribution were at this time in private hands, the state played a significant role in stimulating film production and distribution by a system of subsidies and tax regulation, as well as in direct censorship. The films of this period both flattered its audience and attempted to respond to a certain 'call from above' by helping to build a cohesive, harmonious and modern society.

The second and longest part of my book deals with the postwar period, up to the fall of state socialism in 1989. During this period the largest chunk of the economy, including cinema, was nationalized. The state directly affected the production and exhibition of films and took advantage of its monopolist position. However, politics and the economy changed significantly during this period and cinema engaged with these transformations. The overall trend, although applied unevenly, was towards increased liberalization and leaving important decisions in the hands of filmmakers. In the last period of the existence of People's Poland, we can observe a tendency towards a capitalist mode of producing and exhibiting films and an important reduction of the state's censoring function. The relatively weak requirement that the films should be profitable and the strong expectation that they would play a cultural and educational role led to the domination of a certain version of auteurist paradigm in the cinema of state socialism. The privileging of auteurist cinema is even more noticeable in film criticism and film history concerning this period, with historians treating popular cinema with neglect and contempt. It should be added that a similar phenomenon pertains also to the European West, reflecting the fact that state socialism and embedded liberalism have much in common, in particular a strong state which is willing and able to shape the country's culture.

The third part discusses the postcommunist period, which coincides with the introduction of western-style parliamentary democracy and neoliberal rules into the Polish economy. This shift means, primarily, privatization, financialization and commodification of all spheres of the economy, including culture. In line with this general rule, many film institutions which belonged to the state, including film studios and cinemas, were privatized. However, cinema has remained a protected good in Poland, especially since the setting up of the Polish Film Institute in 2005, which heavily subsidies film production and has a significant influence on the type of films produced and distributed in Poland.

Of course, it is impossible to cover all Polish films engaging with the problems of economy, class and the everyday in a book of a standard length. Therefore, in my selection I privilege films which I suspect of representing mainstream views, chiefly full-length fiction films produced for a cinema audience, which attracted popular and critical attention. One could describe them as canonical films if not for the previously mentioned fact that Polish canon is dominated by historical films. I also consider a number of documentary films. This is because in Poland, especially during the period of socialist rule, documentary films enjoyed a high status, exceeding that in the West, and at times also a large audience. Hence they cannot be seen as occupying the margin of national film production.[4] At the same time, the format of documentaries, namely short films – less expensive and quicker to produce than their feature film counterparts – make them an ideal medium for capturing the everyday (for example the specificity of different professions) and reacting quickly to changes in the country's politics and economy. A documentary can be seen as a corrective of the fiction film, by offering the viewer less manicured images of reality and focusing on characters whom fiction films are unwilling to represent, such as victims of adverse circumstances (Winston 2008: 46–54) or 'others' (Nichols 2001: 3–13), as well as simply ordinary people, as opposed to heroes. While fiction films tend to have individual protagonists, documentary films more often focus on group protagonists. This aspect is taken up by Harun Farocki, who observes in relation to the film by the Lumiere Brothers: 'Immediately after the workers hurry past the gate, they disperse to become individual persons, and it is this aspect of their existence which is taken up by most narrative films. If, after leaving the factory the workers don't remain together for a rally, their image as workers disintegrates' (Farocki 2002). This is important to me because, whenever possible, I would like to capture the moments when a class is presented as a class, namely as a group of people.

Although in my work I try to detect wider tendencies, I do so through in-depth analysis of selected examples rather than offering a broad survey, focusing on the film's characters and narratives. In each chapter I also briefly present the state of Polish cinema at the time, so that the reader can locate my examples in a larger framework. Following Eagleton's and Macherey's advice, I devote some attention to what is un- or under-represented, such as peasants, who constituted the largest class in the interwar period but hardly feature in the cinema of this period, and try to account for specific omissions and silences. I account for what was specific in a cinema in a given decade, drawing attention to the motif of shock workers in the 1950s, strikes in the cinema of the 1980s and unemployment in the films made in the interwar period and after 1989. Simultaneously, I organize my material in a way which allows the reader to compare the decades. For this reason, in each chapter I not only consider economy, class, work, consumption and leisure but, as much as available material allows, I also look at the same types of characters, such as miners, peasants and sex workers. Throughout I also attempt to identify how the role and self-perception of filmmakers has changed over the course of Polish history.

Each part of the book and each chapter also includes a discussion of the political and economic situation of Poland in a given period, presented against some wider trends. This is more extensive than in other histories of Polish cinema known to me, amounting to about 30 per cent of the entire book. The reason is that this part serves me not only as a context, but as a principal hypotext, with which I compare my hypertext[5] – the chosen examples of films. I am interested in whether these texts match each other. To put it differently, I want to find out where, to use Marxist categories, there is a fit between the base and the superstructure or rather a fit between a certain discourse about the base and that of the superstructure.

Throughout this book, openly or implicitly, I employ Marxist categories. This is because I regard them as useful in analysing the topics which interest me, including that of class. Moreover, during a large chunk of twentieth-century history the Polish state was officially Marxist; the state was meant to implement Marxist principles and the artists to convey Marxist ideology. In contrast, after 1989 the authorities rejected the previous period *tout court* on the grounds that the system was forced upon Poles by the Soviets, its economic principles were irrational, and it precluded personal freedom. The new system was meant to eradicate the economic and social pathologies, and purging it of its Marxist bias was one way to achieve this. Writing this book is for me an opportunity to assess the tangled relationship between Poland and Marxism during the period of People's Poland, as well as before the Second World War and after the fall of state socialism. By the same token, I want to engage in a debate about the viability of communism as a political and economic system, or what Alain Badiou names the 'communist hypothesis' (Badiou 2010) and about the immorality and irrationality of capitalism. Inevitably, to achieve this goal, I will focus on some historical processes and neglect others that might be regarded by some readers as more important. But, as I already mentioned, there is no way to write an unbiased history of cinema; we can only acknowledge this bias or try to hide it.

Notes

1. The interest in how Poles see themselves as Poles is conveyed by the titles of the histories of Polish cinema, published in Poland and abroad: Bolesław Michałek and Frank Turaj's *The Modern Cinema of Poland* (1988), Marek Haltof's *Polish National Cinema* (2002), Paul Coates's *The Red and the White: The Cinema of People's Poland* (2005) and Tadeusz Lubelski's *Historia kina polskiego: Twórcy, filmy, konteksty* (2009a).
2. A poignant example of this preoccupation is the lavish commemorations of the Warsaw Uprising, usually presented as the fight of the united nation against its foreign enemies, as opposed to the event in which the Polish intelligentsia played a crucial role.
3. I omit from my discussion the problem of film as a historical document, because I deal with it at length in one of my earlier books, *European Cinema and Intertextuality: History, Memory and Politics* (Mazierska 2011).

4. A testimony of the importance of the documentary genre in Poland is the large number of publications devoted to this genre (for example Janicka and Kołodyński 2000; Jazdon 2009; Hendrykowska 2015).
5. In my understanding of the terms 'hypotext' and 'hypertext' I follow Robert Stam (Stam 2000: 65–66).

PART I
Interwar Cinema
Striving for Social Promotion

Polish Economy in the Interbellum

In 1918 the First World War ended and Russia, Prussia and the Habsburg Empire, who had ruled Poland since the end of the eighteenth century, ceased to exist. In this way the great Polish dream of living again in one independent country could be fulfilled. It was officially achieved in June 1919, when Poland's right to sovereignty was confirmed by the victorious powers through the Treaty of Versailles, even though the borders of Poland were not finally established until 1923. For Poles the regaining of statehood was a great cause for celebration. Other aspects of their situation, however, provided grounds for concern. Poland had a large proportion of ethnic minorities and some of these minorities harboured ambitions to possess their own state. The borders of Poland were fragile, due to the conflicts with its neighbours about regions with mixed populations (Ukrainian, Czech, Lithuanian and German) and Soviet Russia's initial ambition to export communism to the whole of Europe. Transportation, communication and administration were difficult because of the legacy of Poland being divided between three states. Politically Poland was divided too, with several centres of power and different visions of Poland, of which the strongest were offered by conservative nationalists (led by Roman Dmowski) and moderate socialists (gathered around Józef Piłsudski). However, for both the nationalists and the socialists the question of national unity was a priority. There also existed the communist party of Poland (the KPP), but it had only modest support in the interwar years. This was not because Poles were opposed to social revolution, but because communism was viewed as a disguised form of Russian domination (Bromke 1962). This was not without reason as the KPP supported Russia in the Polish-Bolshevik war. In the 1920s even the future communist leader, Władysław

Gomułka, joined the socialist party (the PPS) rather than the communists (Bethell 1972: 8).

While the parties at the centre and on the left wanted to introduce social reforms, especially land reform, to alleviate poverty in the countryside, those on the right opposed them. Those in the centre and on the left wanted Poland to respect the rights of ethnic and religious minorities; those on the right wanted to privilege the rights of ethnic Poles and Catholics. An indication of the deep political divisions was the assassination in 1922 of the first Polish president, a representative of the moderate left and a favourite of ethnic minorities, Gabriel Narutowicz, by an extreme Polish nationalist. Difficulty in finding compromise between different political factions and the threat of extremism led in 1926 to a coup, masterminded by Józef Piłsudski, and the suspension of democratic institutions. Piłsudski established himself as the strong man in charge, leader of the political movement known as Sanation (Sanacja), whose programme included fighting corruption and high inflation. Despite not holding an office, Piłsudski was effectively the political leader of Poland till his death in 1935. The Poland of Sanation had many of the negative markers of a totalitarian state, such as the monopolization of power, ruthless elimination of political opponents (labelled 'terrorists') by internment or forced emigration, as well as nepotism and corruption. Under such circumstances free expression was thwarted. By the time Piłsudski consolidated his power, his camp had shed its socialist character.

Following the First World War industry was paralysed and in 1918 over four-fifths of industrial workers were unemployed. Agricultural production had fallen dramatically, and poverty and malnutrition stalked the land. According to the census of 1921, the geographical distribution of the population put 25 per cent in the towns and 75 per cent in the countryside; the occupational structure was made up of manual workers (27 per cent, of which almost half were agricultural labourers), peasants (65 per cent), intelligentsia and professionals (5 per cent), entrepreneurs (2 per cent) and landowners (under 1 per cent) (Davies 2005: 304). Polish industry was mostly of a small scale, with the majority of enterprises employing less than fifty people. A large proportion of the firms were in foreign hands, mostly German. According to the main standards of modernity, namely urbanization and industrialization, Poland during this period was one of the most backward countries in Europe, somewhat suspended between feudalism and capitalism, not unlike Russia before the Bolshevik revolution. However, while in Russia there was a revolution, which dramatically transformed class relations across the entire country, in Poland this did not happen. Another problem for the Polish economy was its bad relations with its neighbours. Poland practically lost its eastern market due to the autarkic tendencies of Soviet economic policy. In the West the German government tried to use its economic strength to bring about Poland's economic collapse (Brodziński 1971: 111).

The economic and political problems culminated in 1923, in the collapse of the centre-right coalition government and a general strike. From that moment, however, the economic situation started to improve and kept improving till the end of the 1920s, thanks to the financial stability introduced by the non-party government of Władysław Grabski and the state taking an active role in reinvigorating the economy. Another significant factor was the general strike in Britain in 1926, which gave a precious opening to Poland, thanks to which it almost doubled its export of coal (ibid.: 111). This improvement was marked by some ambitious investments, such as the construction of a new port and city in Gdynia. The same period saw the expansion of elementary education, press and periodicals, and the ownership of radios, which increased from 120,000 in 1927 to 246,000 in 1930 (Lukowski and Zawadzki 2001: 214). Not surprisingly, radios feature heavily in Polish films of the 1930s, with the leading star of this period, Eugeniusz Bodo, playing the roles of inventor of a new type of radio and celebrity radio presenter. The modest economic improvements, however, were reversed in the 1930s, due to the world economic crisis which started with the Wall Street Crash in October 1929. The crisis was felt particularly strongly in Poland, because rather than stimulating effective demand (as happened in Germany under Hitler), the Polish government prioritized fighting inflation by maintaining the high value of the Polish currency. By 1932 industrial production had fallen to 54 per cent of the 1929 level. The difficulty in selling inevitably affected the condition of Polish firms. Many went bankrupt; others had to lay off workers which, again, led to high unemployment. In mining, steel production and manufacturing the number of people employed went down 37 per cent, from 844,000 in 1929 to 531,000 in 1933. Outside agriculture, there were about 70,000 unemployed in 1929. Four years later this number had grown to 780,000 people, more than the number of people employed in this sector. This situation was exacerbated by partial employment, resulting from shortened working hours and, consequently, lower wages. While in the majority of European countries during the interbellum industrial production went up, despite the crisis, in Poland it remained static. The situation in agriculture, which suffered from over-population during the whole interwar period, was even more precarious, as testified by the fact that only two per cent of Polish farms had electricity. One consequence of the poverty of Polish peasants was a high level of emigration, especially to the United States and France, where Poles often became small farmers, factory workers and miners. When the economic situation started to improve again, the rise of German militarism hit Poland; in 1939 Poland fought and lost the war with its western neighbour.

The economic system which dominated in the interwar years or rather the one the young country aspired to achieve was that of 'embedded liberalism' (on the definition of embedded liberalism, see Harvey 2005a: 11) by stimulating the economy centrally and embedding it in state institutions. This was seen as the only way to modernize the country, which at the time meant lifting it from poverty and backwardness, of which the clearest indicator was the high proportion of the rural population living in conditions close to serfdom. The state took this route because it inherited many institutions from the partitioning powers, such as the railways and post office. Another reason was the previously mentioned weakness of the indigenous class of entrepreneurs, also testified by the fact that many private factories went bankrupt at various times of Polish interwar history. The state took over from them as a means of producing vital commodities and fighting unemployment. It also introduced relief programmes (which can be compared to the American New Deal of the 1930s, introduced under Roosevelt), embarking on large investments, such as the previously mentioned Gdynia shipyard and later the Central Industrial Region which took responsibility for producing military supplies. All in all, it rendered the state the main Polish employer and an important purchaser of goods produced by Polish business (Landau and Tomaszewski 1985: 33). Piłsudski's coup can be seen as an attempt to deepen the system of embedded capitalism by extending the role of the state. As a country opting for embedded capitalism Poland was not unique in the interwar years. This system was also adopted by Germany under Hitler and, after the Second World War, by the majority of western democracies in Europe. Contrary to dominant opinion, the Poland of state socialism continued this politics by extending the nationalization of industry and attempting to nationalize agriculture.

Polish Film Industry in the Interwar Years

Although the economic and political situation in Poland in the interbellum oscillated between bad and mediocre, even against the backdrop of other European countries hit by the crisis, this was not reflected in a simple way either in the state of the Polish film industry or in the images projected by films of this period. As in other capitalist countries, the bulk of Polish films were produced and distributed by private companies, and exhibited in privately owned cinemas. In the existing literature the Polish interwar film industry is presented as a cottage industry, but also as a somewhat speculative, even wild enterprise. With few professionally equipped studios, the majority of enterprises were starved of capital and were geared towards making immediate profit (Banaszkiewicz 1966: 124; Madej 1994: 22–23; Hendrykowska 2009: 12; Lubelski 2009a: 41). A third of companies managed to produce only one film and few studios flourished during the entire interwar period; one of these was Sfinks, set up by Aleksander Hertz in 1908, which lasted till 1936 (Stradomski 1988: 21; Maśnicki and Stepan 2007: 24–26). The cinema owners were important players in the film industry. They received a large percentage of the state subsidies available and had a major influence on the choice of themes, actors and songs used in the films (Zajiček 1992: 11).

The authorities, in line with the wider rule of embedded liberalism, intervened in the operations of the Polish film business indirectly, introducing specific customs and tax regulations applied to film production and distribution and on occasions directly investing in the production and promotion of films. In the years 1919–1920 imported films were classified as luxury products, along with cognac, champagne, caviar, diamonds and silk (Banaszkiewicz 1966: 120). At a similar time, cinema tickets in Warsaw were heavily taxed, in part to subsidize the rebuilding of the Rozmaitości Theatre in 1921 (ibid.: 121). The autarkic character of the Polish economy had an even greater effect on film production in the 1930s. During this period, to spare foreign currency the government limited the import of foreign films and introduced tax relief for cinemas showing Polish films (Stradomski 1988: 20). Given that cinema-going was one of the cheapest forms of entertainment (Madej 1994: 62) and cinemas were centres of cultural life, the Polish film industry in the interwar period was flourishing. One sign of this was the appearance of cinemas not only in Warsaw but also in other cities, such as Lviv, where one critic claimed that local cinemas looked as good as in the greatest metropolises (quoted in Gierszewska 2006: 215). The Polish state also recognized the importance of film in projecting a certain image of Poland for domestic and foreign consumption. Initially, the state commissioned the production of newsreels from the frontiers, such as the Polish-Bolshevik war and plebiscites, as well as films promoting specific economic strategies, such as state borrowing schemes. The Ministry of Propaganda also commissioned and subsidized films, offering viewers a positive image of Poland, which were sent to Polish diplomatic outposts. First, this was an image of a ruined and starving Poland, awaiting foreign sympathy and charitable help; then a Poland full of natural resources (including human resources), overcoming unemployment, developing industry and open to foreign investment. Such images were conveyed mostly in documentaries (Banaszkiewicz 1966: 126). Although private film producers were not obliged to follow such an agenda, it inevitably affected them, not least because they were also interested in receiving state commissions and subsidies. This translated into a tacitly accepted requirement to avoid controversial issues and work towards achieving national unity in the face of disunity along class, ethnic, religious and political lines. The problems concerning national unity and identity are central to this cinema, as is testified by the large number of films presenting high points in Polish history, with the bulk of them adding to anti-Russian sentiments and conflating Polish with Catholic identity (Madej 1994: 137–169; Hendrykowska 2009: 10–11; Ostrowska and Wyżyński 2006; Lubelski 2009a: 46–60; Skaff 2008).

However, the filmmakers' main objective in this period was to attract viewers. Polish films had to repay their costs for the film producers, distributors and exhibitors to survive. This fact accounts for a certain conservatism in the film fare, most importantly its adherence to the rules of genre cinema and favouring of those genres which have an immediate effect on the viewers, causing their bodily reactions: melodrama (tears) and comedy (laughter).[1] Other consequences include a reliance on stars (Madej 1994: 58–62); adaptation of the most popular books, authored by, among others, Stefan Żeromski, Helena Mniszkówna and Tadeusz Dołęga-Mostowicz, sometimes more than once during the twenty interwar years (Madej 1994: 33–52; Lubelski 2009a: 50–60; Gierszewska 2011); and a predilection for certain settings, such as music halls, cabarets, ballrooms and high-class restaurants, which can be seen as a way of offering the film audience expensive entertainment in an ersatz form. The pressure to produce profit quickly resulted in the most successful filmmakers making several films per year. The most prolific director of the interwar period, Michał Waszyński, was shooting on average three to four films per year, inevitably many of them according to the same scheme (Jagielski 2013: 76–131). All in all, Polish cinema of this period conforms to the idea of 'kitsch', as defined by Clement Greenberg (Greenberg 1973: 10) and the 'culture industry', as elaborated by Theodor Adorno (Adorno and Horkheimer 2002). It was a cinema of the 'conveyor belt': quickly produced and geared towards the urban masses 'insensible to the values of genuine culture, yet hungry nevertheless for the diversion that only culture of some sort can provide' (Greenberg 1973: 10). This opinion also prevails in the existing studies of Polish interwar cinema, past and present.

Unlike Adorno, who condemns the culture industry *tout court* as stylistically homogenous, ideologically conservative and generally trite, without paying attention to the subversive and utopian potential of popular cinema and culture at large (on this potential, see Dyer 2002; Wayne 2014), I will examine its variations and account for its development over the years. I shall mention that to a larger extent than in the two remaining parts of this book, my study of this period is limited to what is available, rather than what best exemplifies my argument. This is because many films from the first decade after Poland regained its independence – such as the adaptations of Władysław Reymont's *Chłopi* (*The Peasants*, 1922) directed by Eugeniusz Modzelewski and *Ziemia obiecana* (*Promised Land*, 1927), directed by Aleksander Hertz and Zbigniew Gniazdowski, or *Tajemnica przystanku tramwajowego* (*A Mystery of a Tram Stop*, 1922), directed by Jan Kucharski – are lost. There are also no surviving films of arguably the first auteur of Polish cinema, Wiktor Biegański (Stepan 2009), nor the early avant-garde artist, Feliks Kuczkowski. The majority of these films perished during the Second World War. To an even larger extent this is true of documentary films from this period. Polish film historians overcome the problem of the lack of primary material by basing their studies on film reviews (for example Hendrykowska 2009; Stepan 2009) and on some occasions I will do the same. However, as much as possible I will try to avoid such a strategy, because my goal is to assess how the invisible class relations are represented in the film and for that I need a visible document.

It makes sense to divide Polish interwar cinema into two parts: the first covering the years 1918–1930 and the second 1931–1939. Although the first period is longer, only around twenty films survived in whole or in fragments (Lubelski 2009a: 46), which explains the fact that my discussion is unbalanced: I devote much more space to the cinema of the 1930s than to the 1920s. In terms of politics and economy, the most important events in the first period, apart from Poland regaining independence, was the war with the Bolsheviks in 1919–1921, won by

Poland, and the relative prosperity of the second half of the 1920s. This part also coincides with the building of the Polish film industry, which includes the establishment of its infrastructure and development of a specific idiom of filmic expression. By that I mean a dramatic film with a fair amount of unlikely or fantastic events, partly to account for the tragic character of Polish history and partly to make up for the lack of sound, which required bolder gestures. The second part covers the crisis years, when the Polish economy crumbled and Poland became an authoritarian state with Marshall Piłsudski and his circle accumulating all political power. During this period, in 1930, Polish cinema made the transition to sound. This date is allegedly a reflection of the technical and mental backwardness of the Polish film industry (Maśnicki and Stepan 2007: 30–32), but it is worth mentioning that it was only one year after Alfred Hitchcock made the first British sound film, *Blackmail* (1929).[2] By and large, my view is that the Polish cinema of the interbellum was more technologically advanced and of higher artistic quality than critics have led us to believe and, at any rate, to assess it, we should not compare it with the masterpieces of Murnau, Lang, Hitchcock and Eisenstein, but with the average fare produced in Europe at the time.

Notes

1. Linda Williams describes such films as 'films of excess' or 'jerkers' (Williams 2000: 207).
2. There are interesting parallels between the beginnings of the sound in Poland and Britain, for example, in the first sound films made in the respective countries, the main roles were given to foreign actresses: Any Ondra in *Blackmail*, and Dela Lipińska in the Polish *Moralność pani Dulskiej* (on the introduction of sound in Polish cinema, see Maśnicki and Stepan 2007; Wyżyński 2009).

CHAPTER 1
The 1920s
The Cult of the Body and the Machine

During the whole interwar period the main social and political role of Polish cinema was to boost patriotism and create national unity. It played this role most vigorously during the First World War and the first years after its end, due to the instability of Poland's borders, which culminated in the Polish-Soviet War of 1919–1921. At this time, the film industry fed the viewers with stories which documented the injustices carried out by the old partitioners (Russia, Prussia and the Habsburg Empire) against the Polish people. Most of these films condemned the Russian and then Soviet empire, and began to be produced even before the First World War ended. This upsurge of anti-Russian films was caused by the Russian authorities leaving Warsaw in 1915, and subsequently all of the Polish territories coming under German and Austrian occupation. This encouraged the agents of German and Austrian film studios, such as Projektions A.G. Union and UFA, to arrive in Warsaw with their fare, and to offer support to Sfinks, to make films on such subjects as the persecution of Poles by the Tzar's army and bureaucracy, and Polish resistance against its Russian neighbours (Ostrowska and Wyżyński 2006). *Cud nad Wisłą* (*The Miracle on the Vistula*, 1921), by Ryszard Bolesławski, about the Polish victory over the Bolsheviks at the Battle on the Vistula river in August 1920, a film almost concurrent with the historical events it depicted, is the most famous of this group (Lubelski 2009a: 48).

In due course, the films about the injustices suffered by Poles from the Russian oppressors were joined by films about Polish-German relations, where Poles, again, were represented as victims of colonial oppression. These unashamedly nationalistic films were intermingled with films about love. Some of them were ostensibly set in contemporary times, but they played down their contemporary setting to portray love as an eternal and all-consuming passion. For this reason, I will not categorize them as melodramas but dramas concerned with love, in contrast to proper melodramas of the 1930s (on the difference between drama and melodrama, see the next chapter). The whole silent period in the history of Polish cinema is usually treated with disdain, both by critics whose writings were concurrent with their production and by those writing about them from a later perspective. For example, a well-known Polish writer and intellectual from the interwar period, Antoni Słonimski, in a review of the (lost) film *Iwonka* (1925), directed by Emil Chaberski, which Słonimski treats as representative of the entire film production of this period, muses on the most embarrassing sins of the Polish cinema, mentioning its lack of realism and excessive dependence on the conventions of literature, as opposed to elaborating its own idiom of expression (Słonimski 2012), a criticism which we also find in the writings of the leading Polish film theoretician, Karol Irzykowski (Irzykowski 1982: 190–202). Słonimski also mentions that this film projects Polish society as being obsessed with military traditions and lacking any decent or rationally thinking people; all Poles, who are not in the army, are presented in *Iwonka* as drunkards, occupying themselves with seducing women and duels (ibid.: 73). Stefania Zahorska, the most respected film critic of the interwar period, writes in an article published in 1928 that Polish films project the image of a nation enthused by military idealism, and unable to transform this enthusiasm into modern life (Zahorska 1928: 4). Both Słonimski and Zahorska are very concerned about how foreigners might imagine Poles after watching these films,[1] worrying that they come across as backward, irrational and not focused on working and building, but on destroying. Alina Madej in her study of Polish interwar cinema as a whole and Tadeusz Lubelski in his discussion of Polish silent cinema point to the fact that it offered the viewers a simplified version of the Polish romantic tradition (Madej 1994). Lubelski puts this idea in unambiguous terms: 'Romanticism trivialised' (Lubelski 2009a: 41),[2] which means reduced to clichés and empty gestures, including excessive worship of symbols, and focusing on the relationships between chaste, angelic, faithful and patriotic girls and equally faithful and patriotic boys.

Although, as Zahorska laments, economy, work and social class are neglected in the patriotic films of the 1920s, indirectly they are tackled by this very neglect, according to the rule that ideology speaks through silences. One example is *Dla Ciebie, Polsko* (*For You, Poland*, 1920), directed by Antoni Bednarczyk and co-produced by the Polish government. Its subject is the Soviet invasion of the Eastern territories of Poland. The film shows the Soviet army as barbarous, trying not so much to gain Polish territory as to destroy what is there and rape or kill the civil population. Bolshevism is reduced to barbarity and its egalitarian political programme is neglected. The boorishness of the Soviet side is contrasted with the civility of Poles, both the gentry and peasants. There is no sign of class conflict, because members of the Polish gentry are presented as good masters, treating the poor peasants and agricultural workers (effectively the serfs) well and educating them in the spirit of patriotism. Such a negative portrayal of Bolshevism and its ideology was exacerbated by censorship. Distribution of *Bronenosets Potemkin* (*Battleship Potemkin*, 1925) by Sergei Eisenstein and many other masterpieces of Soviet Formalism during the interwar years was forbidden.

Another interesting example is *Bartek Zwycięzca* (*Bartek the Winner*, 1923), directed by Edward Puchalski and based on a short story by Henryk Sienkiewicz. Both the literary original and the film are set during the Franco-Prussian War of 1870. Polish peasant Bartek Słowik, who lives in the territory belonging to Prussia, is drafted into the Prussian army to fight the French. He is even awarded a medal for his bravery in the battle of Gravelotte. Unfortunately, his service to the Prussians is not appreciated back home by the German authorities. He is sent to prison following his beating up of a German teacher who insults his son, and loses his farm. The situation is exacerbated when a local Polish aristocrat loses an election to the Prussian parliament. Destitute and disappointed, Słowik has to look for a new occupation, joining the growing mass of proletariat, made up of ethnic Germans and other nations. However, the film does not call for the proletarians to unite against capitalism, colonialism and militarism, but only for Poles to unite, because without their own country there will be no social justice for them. The film thus intermingles class and national conflict to promote nationalism. Not without reason, as gaining independence led to Poles taking over many positions which were previously reserved for the occupiers, especially in state administration (Narojek 1991: 17).

In the second half of the 1920s more films were set in contemporary times, and were less preoccupied with Polish national interest pitted against Russian or German interests. This shift points to the greater stability of Polish politics and economy in this period and a certain viewer fatigue with films documenting the suffering of the Polish gentry, peasants and women under the Russian or German occupiers. Inevitably, these films, even if they did not want to engage with the everyday, as Zahorska complained, had to show people of specific occupations and social positions. The privileged milieu portrayed is that of wealthy people. Typically, we are not sure where this wealth comes from, which seems to be a deliberate strategy on the part of filmmakers: to create a certain mystique around wealth, to fetishize it as opposed to showing that it involves exploitation of the labouring classes. Wealth in these films equals beauty, refinement and charity, and a nonchalant attitude to one's wealth, which can be linked to the effect of Romanticism. This is because the Romantics encouraged Poles to fight for their country in uprisings, at the risk of losing their estates and personal wealth. In these films the rich support the poor by their charitable work and the poor, on the other hand, worship the rich and try to join their ranks by hook or by crook. Poverty is presented not as a problem for society, but one for the individual to solve, and often takes the form of debt. We see people threatened with eviction or losing their place at school. In such circumstances only a miracle can help – and the miracle happens. *Mocny człowiek* (*The Strong Man*, 1929), directed by Henryk Szaro, and *Dusze w niewoli* (*Souls in Bondage*, 1930), directed by Leon Trystan, well illustrate this trend.

Their characters engage in two types of work: artistic production (for men) and prostitution (for women). Artists are the main characters in *The Strong Man*, *Kult ciała* (*The Cult of the Body*, 1930), directed by Michał Waszyński, and *Souls in Bondage*; and prostitutes in *O czem się nie mówi* (*What Should Not Be Mentioned*, 1924), directed by Edward Puchalski (this film would be remade in the 1930s), and *Szlakiem hańby* (*A Trail of Disgrace*, 1929), directed by Mieczysław Krawicz and Alfred Niemirski. The cult of the body (as enunciated in the title of one the abovementioned films) and of artistic production can be attributed to the effect of the philosophical, literary and artistic influences of the early twentieth century, such as Neoromanticism (and Romanticism, as argued earlier) and Decadence, which edified the artist as the ultimate creator, searching for a model to create an ideal object. These films are about crimes of passion, such as excessive and promiscuous love, envy and betrayal. Usually they refrain from showing them in a wider social and cultural perspective. It appears that pure love and hatred provide the characters with enough reason to cheat, kill or commit suicide. This foregrounding of passion can be additionally explained by the fact that cinema was silent, therefore it had to focus on what was easiest to communicate by gestures: great love and uncontrollable animosity. Presenting too many factors affecting human behaviour meant running the risk that the film would become incomprehensible. In this sense Polish cinema was no different from what dominated in Europe, with the exception of Soviet Russia. Even the bulk of films belonging to German Expressionism, although they were later interpreted, most importantly by Siegfried Kracauer (2004), as foretelling the victory of Hitler, avoided showing the connection between the neurosis, madness and crimes of its characters and the economic and political situation of their country.

Of the films which survived, the best known is *The Strong Man*, based on a novel by Stanisław Przybyszewski, one of the most influential authors belonging to the 'Young Poland' movement (Młoda Polska), which was close to western Symbolism and Decadence. Przybyszewski not only wrote books, but set the tone for Polish bohemia and a section of the Polish intelligentsia; he advocated living in tune with one's desires, as opposed to social conventions – an ideal which he himself followed. What stands out in this film is the mix of melodrama (understood as a story of great love) and the theme of social promotion to be achieved at any price. The film also takes issue with Poland's attempts to modernize itself, a subject developed further in the cinema of the 1930s. This is conveyed by the choice of main character, a mediocre journalist and writer Henryk Bielecki, who dreams about a career defined in a 'modern way', as prosperity and fame. To achieve this goal, he visits a more famous writer than him, Jerzy Górski, who undergoes a crisis. Bielecki encourages Górski to commit suicide by providing him with a lethal dose of morphine. The motif of morphine clearly belongs to the idiom of Decadence with its blasé attitude to life by people furnished with unusual talent and sensibility. Bielecki is the opposite of a decadent, having his feet firmly on the ground. He steals Górski's manuscript, and using money from a falsified cheque publishes Górski's book, *The Strong Man*, under his own name. The book proves a bestseller, is adapted for the theatre (and, we can conjecture, also for film), ensuring Bielecki fame and wealth. In step with these successes Bielecki's social aspirations grow, as testified by his love affair with the elegant wife of his aristocratic friend. However, the moment of Bielecki's greatest triumph, when the ecstatic audience applaud 'his' play after its premiere, is also the moment of his downfall, as he shoots himself, tormented by taking Górski's place. Such a combination of triumph, suffering and downfall, or even representing downfall as ecstatic, is in the style of Przybyszewski, an author not particularly sensitive to social issues. However, the first part, which shows Bielecki's push for success and the methodical way in which he fulfils his plans, introduces us to a different reality, where people behave in a pragmatic way and where even love is closely linked to social promotion – a situation more common in the films of the 1930s, especially *Doktór Murek* (*Doctor Murek*, 1939) by Juliusz Gardan. The ideal promoted in this part is that of 'being strong', which means being ruthless. *The Strong Man* also shows how success breeds success, in the case of literature, how it is franchised into different media and, to use contemporary language, goes 'viral'. This reflects on Przybyszewski's own career, who was both a writer and playwright, but also on the mechanics of the media under capitalism. In a manner which might be seen as being influenced by *Ballet Mécanique* (1923–1924) by Dudley Murphy and Fernand Léger and *Metropolis* (1927) by Fritz Lang, *The Strong Man* points to the role of machinery in the production of cultural commodities. A rapid montage illuminates the speedy process of production, trade and promotion of books. The director even creates a split screen effect to show how different stages of production are connected with each other and how time under capitalism is accelerated. The theatrical production of what is taken for Bielecki's novel comes across as an expressionistic spectacle. We see dancers and actors wearing masks, conveying an idea – present also in *Das Kabinett des Dr. Caligari* (*The Cabinet of Dr Caligari*, 1920), directed by Robert Wiene, and *Metropolis* – that people are not who they appear, that true identity is elusive, perhaps does not even exist. In a manner which will set the tone for the films of the 1930s, Warsaw of the interbellum comes

Illustration 1.1: Strong passions in *The Strong Man*, directed by Henryk Szaro

across as a site of carnival. The theatres and restaurants are full of people enjoying themselves and everywhere we see affluence. The conspicuous consumption produces a specific moral climate, in which poverty is a source of shame.

Another film with an artist in the main role is *The Cult of the Body*, a Polish-Austrian co-production, with the Hungarian star Victor Varkoni in the main part of Czesław, a sculptor who falls in love with his model, Hanka. Unfortunately for Czesław, Hanka is engaged to another man, Baron Stumberg, and to make her forget her beloved, her wealthy fiancé takes her to Vienna, where they enjoy luxurious hotels and trips to the theatre. Hanka, however, cannot forget her artist lover and in the end returns to him. For her the artist's charisma is worth more than money, which is a romantic idea. Yet, true to its title, the film concerns not only the cult of art, but also that of the body. Czesław falls in love with Hanka not because she is intelligent, talented or patriotic (this we never learn), nor chaste (she is obviously not, as she cheats on her fiancé), but because she is very attractive, a contemporary incarnation of Venus. The search for physical perfection is underscored in the episode of Hanka and Baron Stumberg visiting a theatre in Vienna, when they admire a show of bodybuilders, displaying their over-developed muscles. At the same time, not unlike in *The Strong Man*, the film celebrates modernization of which one sign is mobility – travelling quickly across Europe thanks to railways and cars.

Souls in Bondage concerns the tragic effects of alcohol abuse, as demonstrated by the fate of the Lachowiczs, a young man and woman of upper-class origins, who suffer financial problems due to their father's alcoholism. The solution comes, again, in the form of good luck. The man, who is an artist, gains the heart of a rich woman who is also the sponsor of a competition for artists which he wins with a picture entitled 'Souls in Bondage' about the problem of alcoholism. Conveniently, what is a problem turns out also to be the solution. *Souls in Bondage*, despite its 'spiritual' title, is also filled with beautiful bodies, this time female bodies happily giving themselves to the dashing painters who consume them. Here the act of painting acts as a substitute for sexual intercourse, which at the time was impossible to show directly due to censorship.

The search for, if not perfect, then at least attractive bodies, is also presented in the films dealing with prostitution. The immense interest in this phenomenon of the filmmakers from the entire interwar period reflects the commerce-driven character of this cinema because sex always sells, as well as the fact that for a cinema devoid of voice it was easier to show bodies than ideas. Yet, it also testifies

Illustration 1.2: Lachowicz in *Souls in Bondage*, directed by Leon Trystan

to the social reality of many women in Poland making their living from prostitution, as much in their own country as abroad. This fact points to the limited professional opportunities for women, especially from peasant and working-class backgrounds, general poverty and overpopulation of rural Poland and emigration as a means of alleviating the problem. Especially interesting in this context is *A Trail of Disgrace*, devoted to the trafficking of Polish women to South American brothels. In reality they were mainly Jewish women from shtetls in the territories of the previous Austro-Hungarian partition, lured by the promise of good work in the houses of wealthy Argentinian or Brazilian men. It is estimated that in some years as many as 3000 women were trafficked by ship, typically via Hamburg (Kapica 2012). Their traffickers pioneered many of the 'tricks' which are still used today in the trafficking of women from poor regions, including Eastern Europe, to brothels in richer countries, except that Western Europe, Dubai and Turkey are nowadays more common destinations than South America.

    A Trail of Disgrace is based on an idea by Antoni Marczyński, who later wrote the book *In the Claws of the Women Traffickers*, subsequently adapted as *Kobiety nad przepaścią* (*Women on the Abyss*, 1938), directed by Michał Waszyński, which I will discuss in the next chapter. *A Trail of Disgrace* tells the story of Marysia Żurkówna, a peasant girl who leaves her boyfriend and goes to Rio de Janeiro, to get an 'honest' job there and instead ends up in one of its brothels. Luckily she is saved by a Polish sailor and returns to her village to be reunited with her faithful fiancé. Although unashamedly sentimental and very coy in presenting the lives of prostitutes (this inevitably being the result of the censorship of this period), it nevertheless points to the connection between poverty, emigration and sex work. As with the films about the artists, *A Trail of Disgrace* shows Polish people, in this case women, believing that social promotion can only be achieved in a radical way, in this case by emigrating. However, unlike *The Strong Man* and *Souls in Bondage*, *A Trail of Disgrace* denounces the myth of a speedy climb-up the social ladder, showing that it only leads to greater misery for those on the receiving end. By and large, the fiction films of this period show society as being polarized between those who worshipped perfect bodies and those who had to sell them to survive,

Illustration 1.3: Polish woman forced into prostitution in *A Trail of Disgrace*, directed by Mieczysław Krawicz and Alfred Niemirski

which can be seen as a metaphor of class-driven and poverty-ridden Poland of the 1920s. The films of the next decade would also include this motif, but would enrich it by other themes.

The production of documentary films in the interbellum was steadily growing. From 1925 there were more films of this type produced in Poland than fiction films, peaking in the years 1927–1929, when Poland was celebrating the tenth anniversary of the regaining of independence (Witczak 1966: 210). Documentary films, although mostly privately produced, responded to a specific state requirement: to project Poland favourably for both internal and external consumption. Many of them concerned rebuilding Poland and expanding its industry, as in *Praca Polski na morzu* (*Polish Work at the Sea*, 1928), produced by Sea and River League (Liga Morska and Rzeczna) about the building and work of the Gdynia shipyard; *Śląsk – źrenica Polski* (*Silesia – the Pupil of Poland*, 1927), directed by Włodzimierz Wyszomirski, and whose title spoke for itself; *Łódź – miasto pracy* (*Łódź – The City of Work*, 1927), directed by Stefan Grodzieński, focusing on the Łódź textile industry; *Nafta – źródło energii w Polsce* (*Oil – The Source of Energy in Poland*, 1929); and *Szlakiem Polskich Kolei Państwowych* (*On the Trail of the Polish State Railway*, 1929) (ibid.: 211–212). These films, whose titles bring to mind British documentaries of the slightly later period from the Grierson school, ignore class relations, show Polish citizens working together for the sake of making their country strong and prosperous, and foreground the role of the state in achieving this task. Individuals do not matter much in these films; work itself appears to be disconnected from human effort; it is a product of modernization, of attaching the right machinery to the right material.[3]

Notes

1. The issue of how the other nations, especially westerners, see 'us' is a strong undercurrent of Polish life, particularly for the Polish elites. A typical Pole appears to be more concerned with the perception of him/her of those from outside than his/her self-perception. Such obsession can be attributed to living among more powerful neighbours (as much in terms of culture as in military might) and the long periods of partition, when Poles had to constantly compare themselves to Russians and Germans.
2. There are some attempts to look with a less caustic eye at Polish popular cinema of the interbellum. Artur Górski in his discussion of two interwar melodramas, *Znachor* (*The Quack*, 1937) and *Profesor Wilczur* (*Professor Wilczur*, 1938), both directed by Michał Waszyński, postulates to treat melodramas differently than auteurist films by focusing on their social function rather than purely aesthetic value (Górski 1980: 50). Aleksander Jackiewicz

provocatively compares the screenings of Mniszkówna's novels to *L'Année dernière à Marienbad* (*The Last Year in Marienbad*, 1961), directed by Alain Resnais, claiming that they are similar in their theatricality and arguing that the sense of claustrophobia and the passage of time ennobles the Polish films (Jackiewicz 1968: 331–332). Sebastian Jagielski examines Polish interwar cinema from the perspective of conveying a gay sensibility. Consequently, these features which put off other critics, such as a penchant for exaggeration, characters who perform rather have a stable identity, and the lack of psychological realism, are valorized positively (Jagielski 2013).

3. Such an approach was even stronger in Polish theories of the avant-garde film of this period, which gave rise to some films of the 1930s. Their authors postulated that films show work as if abstracted from its human character. Such a formalist element can be found in the writings of Anatol Stern (paradoxically one of the most prolific scriptwriters in the interwar period, whose scripts were largely to blame for the slavish adherence to genre cinema) and Jalu Kurek. Kurek wrote that 'Cinema should not illustrate the everyday, but be an optic poetry, transcending the human element' (quoted in Witczak 1966: 217–218). At best, we can see such avant-garde ideas as neutral in relation to the socialist ideology; at worst as reactionary.

CHAPTER 2
The 1930s
The Beauty and Sadness of the Room at the Top

In 1930 Polish cinema acquired sound. This resulted in a distinct change in the films' style and especially acting, which became more naturalistic, because words could express what before had to be transmitted through exaggerated body language. Certain types of films declined, others flourished. Historical patriotic films lost their privileged place in film production. 'High dramas' à la Stanisław Przybyszewski, with improbable events, violent crimes and ghosts, which were meant to reveal the eternal contradictions of human nature, were replaced by more ordinary melodramas. The technical possibility of shooting more realistic films also led to realism (understood mostly as psychological probability and historical accuracy) being upgraded to the main criterion of assessing the overall value of film. The critics of this period (quoted in Gierszewska 2012), in common with those writing about interwar cinema from a postwar perspective (Madej 1994; Lubelski 2009a: 73–108), chastise the films of the 1930s for being exaggerated or formulaic. This assessment goes hand in hand with criticisms of the dominant commercial mode of producing films of this period and the group of filmmakers who succeeded in this mode. They were described as 'tradesmen' or 'professionals' (*branża*). In a different context the label might have positive connotations, emphasizing professionalism, but in Poland it was a derogatory term. It stands for producing kitsch and for the domination of the film industry not by creative people but by businessmen: producers, distributors and owners of cinema theatres (Starski, quoted in Lubelski 2009a: 79). The most ambitious initiative of reinventing Polish cinema of this period, the left-leaning Society for Devotees of Artistic Film (Stowarzyszenie Miłośników Filmu Artystycznego, START), a film club set up at the beginning of the 1930s, conspicuously distanced itself from the 'tradesmen'. Its programme included the creation of films which would be at the same time realistic, useful and artistic: a set of requirements which normally would not be put together (Armatysowie 1988: 161–187)

The years 1930–1939 saw a flourishing of romantic comedy with a musical element, although usually not musicals in the ordinary sense. The possibility of showing people singing or dancing to the rhythm of the music was one reason that common settings of the interwar films were music halls, music theatres, skating rinks and large restaurants whose guests were entertained by music or dance performances. Such settings were also common in films from the previous decade, but then they were usually set abroad, in Vienna or Paris, and frequented by members of the privileged classes. In the films of the 1930s even members of the lowest stratum could afford this form of entertainment. This gives the impression that Poles in the 1930s participated in a neverending carnival, rather than striving to survive in the harsh economic climate. This paradox can be explained by the tendency to link carnival with a crisis and approaching catastrophe (Hodgin 2014), as in the case of the sinking of the Titanic. In the Polish case the carnival balances the economic crisis of the early 1930s and the proximity of the Second World War (Jagielski 2013: 89). Carnival may constitute a liminal space between one state (both political and mental), and another, and express a desire to remain in this nowhere land rather than to face the brutal reality. Such a desire is often expressed openly by female characters asking their partners not to leave the music hall or the restaurant, where they are having a good time.

After comedy, the second most popular genre of this period was melodrama. Finally, I shall mention historical and religious films. They were less numerous, but often prestigious productions, attempting to project a specific image of the nation. There was overlap between these genres, most importantly historical films utilized melodramatic conventions. In this chapter I will focus on romantic comedies and melodramas, as they overtly deal with class divisions concurrent with the period of their production.

Happy Ending in an Unchanged World

There is controversy about the relationship of comedy to the dominant ideology, with some authors regarding comedy as subversive and progressive, while others see it as normalizing the status quo, hence conformist and regressive. The first approach is attributed to Mikhail Bakhtin, who draws attention to the liberating potential of laughter and its ability to create a parallel, utopian universe, where the old hierarchies are overthrown and a more democratic order is introduced: 'Laughter liberates not only from external censorship but first of all from the great interior censor; it liberates from the fear that developed in man during thousands of years: fear of the sacred, of prohibitions, of the past, of power... Laughter opened men's eyes on that which is new, on the future' (Bakhtin 1979: 300). We can find a similar attitude in the writings of Ernst Bloch. Bloch criticized Hollywood cinema for offering its viewers a 'happy end within a completely unchanged world' (Bloch 1986: 410), but also argued that, thanks to using such means as montage and music, films can give us a glimpse into a better future, creating utopian moments. Drawing on this idea, Johan Siebers points to the scene in Chaplin's *City Lights* (1931), in which the tramp, on the run from the police, jumps into the car of a millionaire from one side, to get out of it on the other. That montage of rich and poor, which would be unconvincing if staged in a theatre or opera because it requires a hint at a rupture of the unity of action, time and place, sets off the action in which a blind girl mistakes the tramp for a millionaire. The tramp's jump through the car is the leap of imagination, where the dialectic of rich and poor can be unravelled (Siebers 2014: 53). Bloch notes that the utopian moment might be encountered in the gap between image and sound, or in the fragment, in the surplus, in that which escapes order, in the carnivalesque, as noted by Bakhtin. The progressive laughter provokes a break in our perception and discloses some secret connection of things hidden behind the everyday reality.

Other authors or even the same authors, however, warn that the bulk of mainstream comedies are regressive. Theodor Adorno, the most ardent critic of the capitalist 'culture industry', while agreeing with Bakhtin that laughter releases us from fear and can be aligned with a critical self-reflection and a possibility of emancipation from power, argues that in most cases it plays the role of a 'medicinal bath which the entertainment industry never ceases to prescribe' (Adorno and Horkheimer 2002: 112), responsible for deadening uniformity and a liquidation of critical thinking. This is the laughter of the alienated masses who attempt to overcome their fear by identifying with power and violently ridiculing deviations from the social norm in a way that resembles the imaginary logic of fascism (ibid.). This laughter serves to externalize the fear and pain arising from man's alienation by transferring it to an object of sadistic ridicule: 'In wrong society ... Laughter [Lachen] about something is always laughing at it [Verlachen: ridicule]' (ibid.; see also Ladegaard 2014). In line with this thinking, the authors discussing American comedy point to the fact that it is based on exaggerated stereotypes, and in this way its role is to ingrain capitalist values in the minds of the public, as well as reassuring the audience in their ethnic, racial and sexual prejudices. Moreover, the fact that comedy tends to be based on repetitions (repetitions within individual films and also repetitions within the genre, due to the films recycling narrative schemes and characters), rather than opening a utopian future to the audience, it locks it in the present. My own view is that comedies can be both progressive and regressive and this largely depends on the context of their viewing.

On first sight, Polish comedies from the 1930s commit all the sins attributed to the culture industry by Bloch and Adorno. They recycle settings, narrative patterns, characters and stars, the last to such an extent that sometimes it is difficult to establish whether the actors play specific characters or just play themselves playing stereotypes they invented earlier. In this sense, their main use for my study is through providing material allowing a reconstruction of the dominant ideology. They are set in two distinct milieus: the class of Polish capitalists; and their employees and servants, the shop assistants, maids, waiters and waitresses. The bulk of them are based on the premise of mistaken identities.[1] Many follow the Jane Austen formula, famously presented in *Pride and Prejudice*, when a rich man meets a poor but pretty, proud and clever girl. Each of them is prejudiced against the other, but eventually they warm to the alleged enemy. The happy ending occurs when the couple is properly reunited, by a marriage or its promise. This usually happens because the person, disadvantaged by her or his class position, reveals such large erotic and cultural capital that it overcomes his or humble origin. At the same time, the person who occupies a supposedly higher position turns out not to be as rich as was expected, therefore what looked like a misalliance turns out to be a union of almost equal partners. Alternatively, the one in the position to choose is so wealthy that he can marry below him, purely for love. Marriage across class boundaries is presented as highly desirable, yet very difficult to achieve. It is so sought after because for many it is the only way to lift them out of their predicament, as talent and hard work are not sufficient to achieve social promotion. Such an idea is presented openly in *Piętro wyżej* (*One Floor Above*, 1937), directed by Leon Trystan, when the protagonist, Henryk Pączek, discusses debts with his friend, Kulka Kulkiewicz. It turns out that Kulkiewicz has to borrow more and more money in order to pay his old debts (a situation which brings to mind management of debts under neoliberalism). 'When will it be over?', asks his friend. 'When I get married; my rich father-in-law will pay all my debts', is Kulka Kulkiewicz's answer. 'I'm already compiling a list of dowries with women; sorry, women with dowries'. However, finding a wealthy spouse is unlikely because, like in a lottery, many chase this rare commodity and those perceiving themselves as highly desirable are on guard not to end up as prey to unscrupulous hunters or simply want to prolong their pleasure of having many followers. Polish romantic comedies thus concern the pursuit of true love or social promotion, depending on whether we look at them with a romantic or cynical eye. Both goods are possible to find only in exceptional circumstances.

Such a scenario is proposed in *Panienka z poste restante (Miss from Poste Restante*, 1935) by Jan Nowina-Przybylski, where Marysia, a female postal clerk, is unexpectedly asked to pretend to be the wife of a wealthy industrialist, Adam Olszewicz, on a business trip from Warsaw to the Balkans via Vienna, and by the end of the trip becomes his real wife. Olszewicz makes such a decision because he falls in love with her, but this love is facilitated by him discovering her value as a potential secretary. Marysia is able to type and cook, discreetly offers Olszewicz business advice and impresses his foreign guests with her impeccable appearance and manners. Ultimately, she turns out to be a good investment. The requirement to get married pertains to Olszewicz's specific circumstances, but can also be seen as a condition tacitly imposed on Polish industrialists and aristocrats to be seen as 'mature' and respectable. In this case one can see a parallel between patriarchy as a principle organizing the micro-economy of the family and the macro-economy of a factory or the state, as pointed out by Marx and Engels.

Patriarchy in the family and the workplace is also a motif of *Czy Lucyna to dziewczyna? (Is Lucyna a Woman?*, 1934), directed by Juliusz Gardan, although on this occasion the point is that it is possible to overcome it. The film begins with a celebration of the titular character gaining an engineering diploma in Paris. The choice of Paris might reflect on Lucyna's elevated material status, the higher standard of French technical schools than those in Poland, or on the fact that studying technical subjects was easier for a woman in France than in Poland. All these possibilities are indeed hinted at. Upon returning home Lucyna is, somewhat illogically, expected to settle in the family home and get married. This prospect does not appeal to her, therefore she puts off prospective husbands from her upper-class milieu first by passing around a rumour that her father is bankrupt, and then by working in his factory wearing a masculine outfit. This factory, conveniently, produces engines. The fact that Lucyna does not try to start working in her father's firm under her own name suggests that he would oppose it, although he does not seem the type who wants to suffocate his daughter's ambitions. At work, rather than trying to expand her knowledge about engines, Lucyna busies herself in gaining the heart of a young engineer, Stefan. After some trials and tribulations, her plan works and the couple are united, for the sake of marital happiness and the prosperity of the family business. This union is presented as being much more in the spirit of modernity than Lucyna marrying an aristocrat. This fact is also recognized by the people around Lucyna, such as her aunt, a fake baroness, who falls for Stefan, and aristocratic family friend, Baron Amadeusz Maria de Witz, who would like to marry Lucyna. The society in Gardan's film is thus divided between the professional class, whose members are young, energetic, fit and independent, as evidenced by the fact that they drive their own vehicles and include a strong female element, and the aristocrats (real or fake), who are old, slow, idle and static, dominated by patriarchal values.

Jadzia (1936) by Mieczysław Krawicz offers another variation of the motif of mistaken identities, which, when eventually revealed, leads to a match of monetary, cultural and erotic capital. In common with *Miss from Poste Restante*, the film centres not on a damsel in need of a knight, but rather on a businessman in distress, desperate to be saved by a damsel proficient in business matters, and Jadzia fits the bill. She is a young woman of modest, petit bourgeois background, who works in the family business which consists of a workshop and a shop selling sports equipment. Although small, the business is thriving, thanks to the high quality of goods produced by Malicz and to Jadzia's extraordinary talent for commerce, as shown in an episode when a customer who comes to Maliczs's shop to buy a ball for his son leaves with more equipment than he is able to carry. Jadzia Malicz is also able to convince Polish tennis champion, Jadzia Jędruszewska,[2] to play with her tennis rackets. The Maliczs's success annoys the Okszas, their competitors, whose company, although large and not lacking in capital, as demonstrated by the fact that they invest in advertising, fails to match the quality of the Maliczs' product. The Okszas suggest to the Maliczs that they merge their businesses, but Jadzia rejects their offer, seeing it as a hostile takeover masterminded by the firm's mighty chairwoman. The situation changes when Jadzia meets the heir to the Oksza's 'sports' empire', Jan, allegedly a playboy who recently returned from abroad. The couple are attracted to each other and, after overcoming the obligatory numerous obstacles, such as Jan taking Jadzia the businesswoman for Jadzia the tennis player, come together as lovers and business partners. The fact that Jadzia has more to offer Jan than her erotic capital renders

Illustration 2.1: Jan and Jadzia in *Jadzia*, directed by Mieczysław Krawicz

her a perfect match for him. The case of mistaken identity only adds a pinch of romanticism to what otherwise would be a marriage of convenience.

The consolidation of the two firms can be seen as an encouragement for Polish industry to unite, making it stronger against foreign competitors, and for women to venture into places previously occupied solely by men. As Iwona Kurz observes, this rendered *Jadzia* modern and attracted praise from Stefania Zahorska, a leading fighter against the parochialism of Polish cinema and of Poland at large (Kurz 2009: 17). However, *Jadzia*'s supposed feminism is undermined by the fact that the businesswomen work not so much for themselves as for the men who use the surplus value these women create for their enjoyment, as is the case of Jan, or for the men who are so deaf and senile that they cannot lead the business themselves, like Jadzia's father. Jadzia and Jan's mother working for the family businesses when the men are physically or metaphorically away can be seen as a repetition of the sort of situation arising in the times of partitions, when Polish men were fighting in wars and uprisings far from home and women had to ensure the material survival of their families. They also foretell the postwar situation, when the shortage of men would force the women to try their hand at male professions, such as mining. As if to confirm the view that a successful business means prosperity for the whole country, both *Is Lucyna a Girl?* and *Jadzia* portray a pacified social order, in which employees and servants come across as naughty, yet happy children, who need gentle discipline to stay on the right track.

Both Lucyna and Jadzia are played by Jadwiga Smosarska, who started her career in silent films as a tragic heroine who lives and dies solely for love (on Smosarska's career, see Haltof 2002: 6–9; Hendrykowska 2007a). By contrast, in sound films she specialized in the roles of professional, financially independent women. Smosarska's heroines succeed in overcoming patriarchal prejudices, although often thanks to their ability to charm the men rather than defeat them in an open contest. Smosarska's trajectory encapsulates the changes in the representation of women in Polish interwar films, which granted them more autonomy and a greater role to play in public life. It can be seen as a sign of modernization, of moving from a feudal system, where an accident of birth is the main factor in one's place on the social ladder, to capitalism, where personal qualities are more important.

Two films with the romantic comedy leading actor, Eugeniusz Bodo, *Jego ekscelencja subiekt* (*His Excellency the Shop Assistant*, 1933) and *Jaśnie pan szofer* (*His Highness the Chauffeur*, 1935), both directed by Michał Waszyński, also deal with closing the gap between people of different economic status. The very titles of these films point to the deep social divisions which permeated Polish interwar society and the desire of those at the bottom to break them. 'His Excellency' and 'Your Highness' are inherited titles; they cannot be 'earned' by hard work or commitment. 'Shop assistant' and 'chauffeur' are service jobs, common among urban working-class males of this period. The films ask what will happen if working-class men achieve positions attributed to the upper classes (in *His Excellency the Shop Assistant*) or if upper-class people are degraded to the position of servants (in *His Highness the Chauffeur*). This situation can be seen as a glimpse into what would happen after the Second World War, when aristocratic titles were abolished and the gentry lost their properties and had to take more mundane occupations. *His Excellency the Shop Assistant* begins with images of Jurek, a super-successful seller of female clothes, working in a large department store, in reality Jabłkowski store in Warsaw, the largest and most popular of its type in Poland. Such an image, to a British viewer, might awaken associations with *Kind Hearts and Coronets* (1949), the famous Ealing comedy directed by Robert Hamer about a mistreated aristocrat who was reduced to selling ladies' underwear. The story of Jurek is similar in that he also attempts to leave his milieu by taking shortcuts, arriving in a suit borrowed from his shop at a ball for the cream of Warsaw society, where he is taken by the well-known lawyer Chełmoński. Jurek decides to play the identity game, because he falls in love with Ania, the beautiful daughter of the hosts of the ball. The truth about his background is revealed, but the suitor of the upper-class girl is accepted when it turns out that the girl's parents are bankrupt and Jurek proves to be the better candidate than the cheat who wants to marry her merely for her presumed wealth. It transpires that there are too many people chasing too few dowries, not unlike too many chancers trying to get lucky lottery tickets. Jurek's attractiveness increases when he is wooed back to the department store with the offer of a large increase in his wages. As in *Jadzia*, the coming together of lovers is achieved not merely by the power of love, but also by the levelling out of their cultural and economic capital: the girl becomes poorer (or rather has her poverty exposed), the boy gets richer, thanks to proving his ability to create extra profit for the capitalist. *His Excellency the Shop Assistant* belongs to a larger group of films whose characters ultimately do not need inherited wealth because they earn enough to afford a decent living. Their situation is summarized by a radio announcer, Henryk Pączek, in *One Floor Above*, who boasts in a song that he does not need a woman's dowry because he earns 600 zloties per month.

These new financially independent people, such as Jadzia, Henryk Pączek and Jurek, as well as Paweł in *Paweł i Gaweł* (*Paweł and Gaweł*, 1938), directed by Mieczysław Krawicz, tend to work in the new industries, such as the media and leisure industry. This fact points to the gradual replacing of feudalism by capitalism, as marked by the emergence of the upper strata of the middle class, who usurped the place of the old gentry. In cinema this process of social modernization happens much faster than in reality; rather, it projects the desired (capitalist) future. In these films, commerce and advertising are furnished with an almost magical power; the person who knows how to praise his or her fare can mesmerize a customer. This is reflected in the style of episodes set in their workplaces, such as the department store in *His Excellency the Shop Assistant*, with a dynamic montage to emphasize the extraordinary speed with which Jurek sells underwear to the ladies.[3] This edification of commerce also reflects the fact that the bulk of romantic comedies were set in Warsaw, where commerce was most developed, and many wealthy customers came from the provinces to buy luxury products there.

The numerous bankruptcies, to which Polish comedies of the 1930s refer, apart from providing a perfect solution to the romantic trials and tribulations of their characters, reflect the problems suffered by the Polish economy at this period. These films also show the immense pressure of keeping up the appearance of possessing wealth and cultural capital among the 'high society' and those who aspired to find themselves in this group. In the 1930s the level to which one was able to consume luxury goods was the main factor in establishing one's social position (Górski 1980: 52). Those who once managed to climb the social ladder preferred to commit crimes and 'sell' their daughters to men they did not love than admit to the world that they were no longer upper class. Such a requirement to keep up appearances is an important feature of the capitalist order practically everywhere. It allows capitalism to flourish by speeding up the process of capital's accumulation, because dispossessed people succumb to the capitalist rules more easily than affluent ones.

While in the films discussed so far bridging the gap between rich and poor is shown as desirable, in *Będzie lepiej* (*Things Will Get Better*, 1936) and *Włóczęgi* (*Vagabonds*, 1939), both directed by Michał Waszyński, social promotion is presented as preposterous. The films feature a popular comedy duo from Lviv, Szczepko and Tońko, a kind of Polish Laurel and Hardy, who gained great popularity thanks to their radio programme, (*Na lwowskiej fali* (*On Lviv's Wave*). In *Things Will Get Better* the couple begin their adventure with working in a factory producing toys, such as singing dolls and miniature musical instruments. The factory is owned by Julian Dalewicz, a man obsessively focused on his work. His motto is 'Work and silence, silence and work' and he expects everybody to follow this rule. Such representation renders the capitalist not as an unscrupulous bloodsucker, ruthlessly extracting surplus value from the workers, while himself living in luxury, but as the most diligent worker of all, leading by example his infantilized, noisy workforce.[4] Yet, there is a contradiction between the commodity produced in Dalewicz's plant, which is noisy, and the demands to respect the boss's need for peace and privacy, this being one of the sources of humour in the film. In contrast to the most famous cinematic rendering of factory work of the interwar period, *Modern Times* (1936) by Charles Chaplin, where the movement of the objects down the conveyor belt is frantic, the belt in *Things Will Get Better* moves slowly, indeed too slowly, making the workers lethargic and bored. This difference points not only to Chaplin's left-wing leanings, which he was not shy to reveal in his films, contrasting with Waszyński's unwillingness to reveal his *Weltanschauung*, but also to the different position of capitalism in the United States and Poland. In the first country, where it had ruled for a long time, it was taken for granted, while in backward Poland it was seen as a new and progressive order.

Szczepko and Tońko break the rule of silence (which also means working slowly) and start singing. Their singing proves contagious and soon the whole hall is taken up by their singing, holding dolls in their hands, playing the miniature instruments and dancing. Such a scene can be regarded as a perfect advert for the factory, but Dalewicz, alerted by the noise, enters the hall; he is outraged by the behaviour of the workers and sacks Szczepko and Tońko on the spot, despite their protestations that they acted in good faith. The rest of the film is filled with the adventures of the two men from Lviv, who find an abandoned baby and then lose it again, when it is appropriated by Wanda, the well-off heiress of a toy shop. Wanda uses the baby as a means to put off the geeky and morbid Dalewicz, whom her family wants her to marry. When Szczepko and Tońko come to Warsaw to recover their baby, Wanda announces that Tońko is her husband and for a while the two men enjoy the privileges of belonging to a higher class. For the first time in their lives they use a bathroom with running water, sleep in pyjamas, have a professional haircut and eat fine food. Their inability to comprehend the lifestyle of well-off people (which by this point were taken for granted even by the working classes in many parts of the world), even if it is meant to be humorous, testifies to Poland's backwardness and social inequality. One of the perks of Szczepko and

Tońko's unexpected move to Warsaw is that they are promoted to the position of managers in Wanda's shop. This decision proves very fortunate, as their reversal of Dalewicz's rule of labouring in silence and instead dancing and singing at work makes their customers merry and helps to sell toys. However, it turns out that their fortune is merely a carnivalesque reversal of the normal state of things: a glitch in a stable class system. In the meantime, Dalewicz changes his appearance and enchants Wanda by singing and playing the piano. The film finishes with Wanda and Dalewicz's reunion, which paves the way to their joining their businesses through combining manufacture with trade, not unlike in *Jadzia*, where a romantic union was combined with a business merger. Although not spelt out, Wanda and Dalewicz's coming together means that the couple from Lviv are no longer needed as shop managers. They have to return to Lviv, leaving behind 'their baby', persuaded that they lack the material resources needed to look after it properly, unlike Wanda's well-off uncle. Ultimately, they end up with nothing, except the memory of their adventure, unlike the rich who gain everything, multiplying their fortune and finding love, and even having a beautiful child without having to undergo the pain of pregnancy and birth.[5]

Vagabonds is based on a similar premise to *Things Will Get Better*. Szczepko and Tońko again take upon themselves the duty of looking after an orphan. This time, however, the orphan, named Krysia, is not a child, but a seventeen-year old woman. The couple take care of her because she lost her parents and her only living relative, her grandmother baroness von Dorn, is a tyrannical old woman who broke all connections with Krysia's parents. The narrative is filled with the vagabonds trying to provide for the disinherited aristocrat in line with the requirements fitting her class. For this purpose, they put the girl in a boarding school, where she has a chance to socialize with people of her own background. There she also meets her future husband, a relative of her new best friend. At the same time, the girl's wealthy grandmother, who has a better heart than she shows, is trying to pass on her inheritance to Krysia. Despite the appearances of the conflict of interests, the attempts of Szczepko and Tońko and baroness von Dorn go in the same direction, to ensure that the girl achieves a lifestyle fitting her birthright. This goal is eventually reached and the film finishes with the wedding of Krysia to her wealthy suitor. For this occasion Szczepko and Tońko are released from jail, where they were put for breaking the law, all in their attempt to help the 'poor' girl. The implication of the story is that after doing their duty by making sure that their 'child' is put into good (rich) hands, they will carry on their poor, vagabond life.[6] Szczepko and Tońko's story is thus a perfect case of the 'Hollywood scenario', summarized by Bloch as 'happy end within a completely unchanged world'.

The film not only finishes in Hollywood style, but also suggests that there are two types of happiness: one for the rich and one for the poor. The rich must have immense material resources to achieve happiness; they cannot be left, like the orphaned Krysia, to fight for themselves. The poor can content themselves with fresh air, fresh water and dry bread. As one reviewer commented at the time of the film's premiere in 1939:

> *Szczepko and Tońko's humour results from the eternal joy of life. These two 'troubadours from Lviv' simply enjoy the fact that they are alive, that there are stars above them which are their property. 'Why do you need money, stupid Tońko, better jump on the roof and see how much gold is on the sky. Who has as much gold as us?' They are even happier if they can help somebody, even at their own expense. (Sobolewski 2012: 316)*

The idea that the poor need little to be content brings to mind the opinion of Tadeusz Peiper, the poet and literary critic, close to futurism and presented with derision, that affluent people suffer most of all; the reason for their suffering might change, but the depth and intensity of that suffering remains (Peiper 1972: 126). According to the same logic, poor's people misery is superficial and can be easily alleviated, as *Things Will Get Better* demonstrates.[7]

In the comedies from the interwar period class is underlined not only by the actual material status of people belonging to specific strata, but by such markers as their titles and manner of speaking. Titles, referring either to aristocratic or professional status, such as 'His Excellency' (Jego wysokość) or 'Mr. Chairman' (Panie prezesie), point to the undemocratic character of Polish society and the great desire of those at the top to preserve their exclusive status. At the same time, these films make fun of Polish title-mania, either by making the characters pronounce them too conspicuously or making fun of people who pay attention to titles but are unable to differentiate between their true and fake bearers. The emphasis on the titles and their frequent emptiness highlight two contrasting social tendencies: one towards preserving the quasi-feudal status quo, represented by the nationalists; the other towards modernization, represented by moderate socialists.

Modernization in Polish comedies of this period always means moving towards capitalism, when one's individual efforts, as opposed to one's inheritance, ensures his or her success or downfall. The sympathy of the directors is for modernization which is not surprising given that they themselves were at the forefront of the modernist drive; also, many of them were Jews, hence it was in their interest to undermine the privileges of the ethnic Polish aristocracy. A group effort to promote socialism is never on the agenda (unless we count Szczepko and Tońko as a proto-communist 'cell'). The success is ultimately measured by one's place on the social ladder, as is put succinctly by one of the characters in *His Highness the Chauffeur*: 'Happiness is when your friends are dying of envy'.

Paradoxically, Polish comedies also show that honest work and commitment play a negligible role in ensuring social promotion. The best way to climb the social ladder is to pretend that one is already at the top. 'Fake it till you make it' is the motto of the most successful characters of this period, especially in the comedies of Michał Waszyński. Waszyński's chameleon characters try to be somebody or somewhere else and their dressing-up game frequently pays off. Even when their 'original' identity is revealed, the very act of performing well affects how they are later seen by others and by themselves. Something important from their fake identities remains when they return to their true selves. In this sense, the films of the Polish director prefigure the concept of identity as performed, rather than fixed, most famously identified with the writings of Judith Butler (1999). The role of faking, dressing up in helping one to climb the social ladder is reflected in the life story of Waszyński himself, a Jew from a working-class background who changed his identity many times, in step with changes in his circumstances, including pretending to be a Polish prince (Jagielski 2013: 79–80).

The motif of faking, cheating, playing might also point to the fact that comedies underscore the unusual moments in human life, the breach in the mundane, and the general lack of psychological realism of Polish interwar cinema. The prominence of this motif also tells something about the crisis years when these films were made. As theorists of the economic crises observe, including Marx himself, crisis is a response to a falling rate of profit. The capitalists try to counteract this phenomenon by depressing the wages below the value of labour power, which leads to high unemployment and desperate measures undertaken by the working classes to survive, and often also by the capitalists facing bankruptcy (Marx 1974: 232–266). In line with this rule, the crisis of the 1930s led to widespread pauperization. The response of the many affected was to take great risks, for example leaving their home in search of employment and engaging in criminal activities, such as smuggling and selling counterfeited goods, organizing robberies or frauds. For the majority of the real and metaphorical gamblers, such a solution led to an even greater pauperization, because most gamblers lose. However, mainstream cinema tends to focus on exceptional cases – the winners in the capitalist game.

I mentioned earlier that the romantic comedies of the 1930s have a strong musical element. At some point the main male character starts to sing about his love, either addressing his confession directly to the object of his affection or to us, the spectators, in a kind of inner (even if externalized) monologue. On the first hearing, the songs are in tune with the narrative, because both concern the pursuit of love. However, there is a dissonance between the order of things conveyed in the song and that of the main action of a film. The songs are about the 'democracy of love', for example 'Everybody is allowed to love' (*Każdemu wolno kochać*), or a special logic of love which cuts across the logic of everyday existence, as in 'I have a date with her at 9 o'clock' (*Umówiłem się z nią na dziewiątą*) in *One Floor Above*, when at nine o'clock everything ceases to matter so that love can take its course. The question arises whether such songs normalize the status quo by providing viewers with a temporary escape from the harsh reality, as did the carnival in medieval times, or provide a glimpse into a better future which can be achieved if the ordinary regime is subverted. This question has long haunted popular music and popular culture and continues to do so.

Everybody is Allowed to Love, but Not to Live

The second most popular genre in the 1930s was melodrama, with the most outstanding examples being produced in the second half of the decade. In Poland, before as well as since the Second World War, melodrama has been seen as a conservative, low-brow and unrealistic genre (Madej 1994: 33). It was reproached by critics for watering down high art themes and problems, recycling characters and narrative patterns, and being geared towards an uneducated audience, made up of 'female cooks and shopping assistants' searching for an escape from ordinary existence.

However, in western film criticism, 'melodrama' is frequently seen as a realistic and progressive genre, on account of its democratic character, its focus on women (marginalized in genres such as the Western or the gangster film) and its drawing attention to the contradictions and injustices of patriarchal and capitalist society (O'Shaughnessy 2007: 131–159). Robert Bechtold Heilman in his classical text differentiates melodrama from tragedy by claiming that drama is 'polypathic' because it arouses a multitude of contrasting feelings, whilst melodrama is 'monopathic' because the emotion it awakens is strong and points in one direction. Tragedy and melodrama are used for different purposes: the first serves to depict timeless conflicts, the second themes specific to a particular period of history, focusing on the external circumstances of a person's situation. Melodrama is an ally of history; tragedy has affinities with myth (Heilman 1968: 92–101). Geoffrey Nowell-Smith argues that

> *melodrama, like realism, supposes a world of equals, a democracy within the bourgeois strata (alias bourgeois democracy); it also supposes a world without the exercise of social power... The characters are neither the rulers nor the ruled, but occupy a middle ground, exercising local power or suffering local powerlessness, within a family or small town... In this world of circumscribed horizons patriarchal right is of central importance... In their struggle for the achievement of social and sexual demands, men may sometimes win through, women never. (Nowell-Smith 1987: 71–72)*

Thomas Elsaesser points to the fact that melodramas flourish in times of political upheaval, for example before revolutions, and convey the conflict between an extreme and highly individualized form of moral idealism in the heroes and a thoroughly corrupt yet seemingly omnipotent social class (Elsaesser 1987: 45). He also argues that melodrama can function either subversively or as a form of escapism, with the films by Griffith fitting both categories (ibid.: 47).

Many of these insights pertain to Polish films, such as *Dziewczęta z Nowolipek* (*Girls from Nowolipki*, 1937) by Józef Lejtes, *Kłamstwo Krystyny* (*Krystyna's Lie*, 1939), directed by Henryk Szaro, *O czem się nie mówi* (*What One Does Not Talk About*, 1939), directed by Mieczysław Krawicz, *Strachy* (*The Ghosts*, 1938) by Eugeniusz Cękalski and Karol Szołowski, *Trędowata* (*The Leper*, 1936) and *Wrzos* (*Heather*, 1938), both directed by Juliusz Gardan.[8] However, unlike in American or British melodramas, which are set in a bourgeois milieu, in the Polish interwar melodramas the main site of events is the lower stratum of society – the working class, petit bourgeois or the impoverished gentry – and the action frequently switches between the lower and upper class. The greater focus on the lower class might be explained by the fact that (as the abovementioned statistics show) Poland at the time had a less developed middle class than countries such as the United States, Great Britain or Germany, and that its viewers were recruited largely from the lower classes, such as the industrial proletariat and petit bourgeoisie.[9] The conflicts in Polish melodramas revolve not around the middle-class heroine's inability to reconcile her personal desire with the bourgeois moral code imposed on her, but rather on the lower-class heroine's difficulty in joining a higher class, or at least the impossibility of her doing so on her own terms. The story of great love is frequently intermingled with a story of class advancement (or lack thereof). Love, almost always of a woman for a man, proves to be stronger than her ambition to climb the social ladder. Such great love can be seen as a hysterical reaction to the situation when a woman's professional ambition cannot be fulfilled. Thus these films, as in the scheme described by Heilman, can be seen as social dramas, taking issue with the position of working-class women in undeveloped capitalist society.

Several films from the aforementioned group are based on novels written by some of the best Polish authors of the twentieth century, including female writers with feminist or left-wing agendas, such as Zofia Nałkowska, Pola Gojawiczyńska and Maria Ukniewska. Even if the choice of these books was dictated merely by the producers' wish to capitalize on well-known literature (Madej 1994: 24–25, Lubelski 2009a: 93–98; Gierszewska 2011), the very fact of choosing them encouraged filmmakers to translate some of their social content onto screen. Women in these films can be seen as epitomizing the whole of the proletariat. This is because, as Engels observed, the shift towards capitalism disadvantaged women more than men (Engels 1902: 191–217), and the intensification of capitalism (which happens at the times of capitalist crises, as in the 1930s) puts a greater burden on women's shoulders than on men's. David Harvey's assessment of the position of women under the 'crisis capitalism' of the late twentieth century captures well that of Polish women in the 1930s:

> *Accumulation by dispossession typically undermines whatever powers women may have had within household production/ marketing systems and within traditional social structures and relocates everything in male-dominated commodity and credit markets. The paths of women's liberation from traditional patriarchal controls in developing countries lie either through*

degrading factory labour or through trading on sexuality, which varies from respectable work as hostesses and waitresses to the sex trade (one of the most lucrative of all contemporary industries in which a good deal of slavery is involved). (Harvey 2005a: 170)

The problems facing ambitious women from the lower social strata in a capitalist society are foregrounded in *Girls from Nowolipki*, based on the semi-autobiographical novel by Pola Gojawiczyńska. The title of the book and the film refers to a street in Warsaw, which was inhabited by members of the working class and the petit bourgeoisie, and where Gojawiczyńska's father had his workshop. The film follows four girls, Bronka, Franka, Amelka and Kwiryna, who live on this street and share a similar economic background, but who have different interests and temperaments. Nevertheless, their fate, with the exception of Kwiryna, is similar. All of them want to improve their lot and have romantic dreams. They cannot, however, achieve their goals because they cannot provide for themselves. Their only road to social advancement is via men. This proves difficult because the men in whom they locate their hopes do not offer them a secure and prosperous existence. All these problems leave the girls in a precarious position, culminating in Franka's suicide.

Although Lejtes's film is faithful to the basic stories of the four girls, it introduces a meaningful change in relation to the book, by granting each girl a different amount of screen time, in contrast to Gojawiczyńska, who was at pains to treat her heroines in a 'democratic' way.[10] The main character in the film is Bronka. Played by Elżbieta Barszczewska, who encapsulates the 'girl from the Polish manor', she fits perfectly the image of a melodrama heroine. She is in love with her childhood friend, Ignaś, but when he goes to war, she starts to work as a typist in a large establishment, owned by Różycki, who earlier tried to gain her heart by discreetly helping her family. Initially Bronka resists Różycki's advances, but eventually gives in and becomes his lover. Yet, rather than enjoying the privileges of high life, she behaves in a masochistic way, adopting the posture of a 'fallen woman'. In this way she attempts to punish her lover who 'bought her' with his money, unlike Ignaś, who did not need any monetary capital to win her heart. Ignaś returns from the war with the victorious Polish army and Bronka sees him among the soldiers, in an image foretelling a later Soviet film, *Letyat zhuravli* (*The Cranes are Flying*, 1957) by Mikhail Kalatozov. However, by this point Bronka, due to her choice of 'soft prostitution', has lost the chance for a happy life, not least

Illustration 2.2: Girls from Nowolipki in the film directed by Józef Lejtes

because Ignaś expected 'chaste behaviour' from her during the time of their separation (although without providing her any means to live such a way). Bronka's case suggests that a working-class woman cannot have a career and love. Career precludes love and the lack of love renders her career meaningless.

While Bronka steals the show with her contradictory behaviour, Kwiryna, who inherits a grocery shop and finds a boyfriend of her own class, is the least important of the four girls in Lejtes's film. She is reduced to the stereotype of a 'simple' girl, overweight, lacking the elegance of Bronka and Amelka, and Franka's spirituality. Kwiryna's attitude to life is always very matter of fact, even in the face of great tragedy, such as the murder of her parents. Although she is the only one who achieves relative success, her success practically does not matter within the diegesis. If anything, the film suggests that hard work and ambition is unwomanly; it strips a woman of her erotic allure.[11] Lejtes's film finishes with an image of four girls, playing at the Nowolipki street, the younger versions of Bronka, Franka, Amelka and Kwiryna. This repetition points to the lack of prospects for the women of working-class backgrounds. They are locked in an 'eternal fate' from which their only temporary refuge is female support and friendship.[12]

Barszczewska also plays the main character in a number of melodramas about 'working girls', such as Stefcia in *Trędowata* (*The Leper*, 1936), directed by Juliusz Gardan, the most popular melodrama of the interwar years, and in *Krystyna's Lie*. In the latter film we meet the eponymous character, when, smartly dressed, she invades the office of the owner of a salon selling cars. It turns out that she sells advertising space in a magazine aimed at affluent readers and asks the businessman to put an advert there. He tries to shrug her off, but she persists, eventually starting to complain about her fate as somebody who finds it very hard to earn money and who has to keep up appearances of a well-off professional woman despite the reality of poverty. Her candour impresses the businessman and he offers her the position of his secretary. Soon Krystyna becomes an object of the erotic attention of her boss and one of his customers, Jan Marlecki, an heir to a family of wealthy industrialists who buys a car there. Jan asks her to become his wife and she agrees, but his parents do not want him to marry below his status. Their refusal becomes even stronger when, thanks to a series of coincidences (coincidences are common in melodramas and Polish ones tend to overuse them), Marlecki comes to the conclusion that Krystyna has had an affair with her boss. To save Marlecki from a marriage his parents would disapprove of and at the same time to save herself from a loveless, even if affluent life with her boss, Krystyna attempts suicide, but Marlecki rescues her at the last moment. The last episode shows her married to Marlecki and pregnant, surrounded by her in-laws who by this point have accepted her, moved by her devotion to their son. Krystyna thus ultimately makes the transition to the upper class and finds love, but at the price of risking her own life. In this respect she is similar to Stefcia in *The Leper*, whose similar trajectory ends in death. Stefcia's death and Krystyna near-death thus can be seen as a measure of the almost impossible distance a woman from a modest background has to bridge to reach a higher-class position. And yet films like *The Leper* and *Krystyna's Lie* fed on a widespread desire for social promotion, for entering opulent houses not as servants but as partners of their owners.

Granica (*The Border*, 1938), based on the acclaimed novel by Zofia Nałkowska and directed by Józef Lejtes, offers a somewhat different role for Barszczewska, because in this film she plays a distinctly upper-class girl, Elżbieta, and is therefore much more in control of her life than her heroines in *The Leper* and *Girls from Nowolipki*. Nevertheless, the film conforms to the scenario in which a poor girl tries to climb the social ladder by seducing an upper-class man, only this time the girl, named Justyna, is a servant in an aristocratic estate in love with Zenon, the

Paris-educated son of its owner. Their affair has no chance of surviving due to their class differences, encapsulated by the title of the film, and the fact that Zenon's true love is Elżbieta, not Justyna. However, on this occasion the man pays a heavy price for his sin. As is often the case with melodrama, all the characters are treated with sympathy, including the young members of the upper classes, Elżbieta and Zenon, who strive to improve the lives of the poor. Nevertheless, the only chance of changing the lives of the poor is by acts of charity; revolution or any other communal action is not on anybody's agenda. Reviewers writing about this film drew attention to the fact that the most powerful character was created by Lena Żelichowska, who in her role as Justyna overshadowed Barszczewska's Elżbieta (Zahorska 2012c: 300). This role and some others by female characters demonstrated that even if Polish cinema of the 1930s did relatively little to further the socialist or feminist agenda, it at least made working-class characters visible.

While *Girls from Nowolipki* and *The Border* only allude to prostitution as a way in which Polish women could earn their living between the wars, among melodramas of this period we also find films which deal with this subject directly, such as *What One Does Not Talk About* and *Kobiety nad przepaścią* (*Women on the Abyss*, 1939) directed by Michał Waszyński and Emil Chaberski. The first film, based on a novel by Gabriela Zapolska, is set in Warsaw circa 1910, and is about love between a prostitute, whose real name is Frania, but who is nicknamed the Morning (Poranek), and Krajewski, a Polish clerk whom Poranek nicknamed Daddy (Tatuńcio). Krajewski is unaware of Poranek's true profession, thinking that she is a seamstress, working at night for her rich female clientele. Krajewski's ignorance of her true identity, his contempt for 'fallen women' and Poranek's inability to leave her profession, render their love doomed. In such circumstances death proves the only solution and indeed Poranek commits suicide, leaving Krajewski devastated and forever mourning his only true love. *Women on the Abyss*, a remake of the previously discussed film *A Trail of Disgrace*, tackles the problem of women trafficking through the case of Marysia Żurkówna, who is saved from her despicable predicament by Polish sailors before she is inculcated into her new profession in South America. This is because it is assumed that as a prostitute, even against her will, she has no value for 'decent men', as is the case of Poranek for Krajewski. These films, while showing sympathy for women forced into prostitution either by physical force or by economic circumstances, uphold the patriarchal moral code which requires a woman to be faithful to one man and have no sexual experience prior to marriage.

In both films, as in the works of Marx and Engels, prostitution is linked to female poverty. Women resort to it because they have no other way to earn a living. Hence, cities like London, Manchester and Warsaw, where Krawicz's film is set, are 'awash with whores'. Prostitutes are punished twice, by having to perform dangerous and alienating work, and having to endure moral indignation, including from representatives of their own class, which internalized the moral code of the bourgeoisie more deeply than the upper classes. In *What One Does Not Talk About*, the issue of class is intermingled with that of national identity. This is conveyed in Poranek's attitude to her client, described as a wealthy merchant from Odessa. This man with a jolly character and affinity for alcohol does not treat Poranek as a sex slave, who can be exchanged for another prostitute, but as a lady for whose affection he strives, not unlike other older upper-class men trying to woo their female secretaries. Yet, paradoxically, Poranek resists him with greater force than these women; according to Mariusz Guzek, this is because he represents the colonial oppressor, forcing himself on an innocent Polish girl (Guzek 2011: 30). By the same token, prostitution in this film is presented not only as a class issue, but also as a legacy of Russian colonialism.

While Bronka, Krystyna, Teresa (in *The Ghosts*, discussed below) and other working-class women who resist or accept reluctantly the advances of their older bosses are treated with sympathy in the films, women who take advantage of their bosses' interest, embarking on the task of seducing and marrying them, are denigrated within the narrative. Take, for example, Amelka, the secretary and lover of a wealthy businessman or banker in *Moi rodzice się rozwodzą* (*My Parents Are Divorcing*, 1938) by Mieczysław Krawicz. She comes across as a cunning, haughty and materialistic woman, trying to drive a wedge between her lover, his wife and their daughter, treating badly his servants and having dreams limited to possessing fashionable dresses and fur coats. Amelka's harsh make-up, kitschy clothes and coarse manners poignantly contrast with her boss's wife's refined, mature elegance and her suffering, caused by her inability to reconcile her dream for erotic fulfilment (with her dashing actor lover) and her sense of duty toward her daughter. Predictably, Amelka does not get the reward she dreams of. Her boss remains married to his wife, for the sake of saving their only (and conveniently) sick child from mental torment and perhaps death. We are to believe that even if Amelka succeeded in her plan of marrying her boss, she would not succeed in bridging the class barrier, which is marked not merely by money but also the age of this money, with old money associated with refinement and a civilizing influence on the lower classes, and new money with kitsch, lack of morals and callousness.

The rule of putting a woman at the centre of melodrama was not without exceptions in this period. The most notable cases are adaptations of the novels by Tadeusz Dołęga-Mostowicz, such as *Znachor* (*Quack*, 1937), directed by Michał Waszyński, and *Doktór Murek* (*Doctor Murek*, 1939) by Juliusz Gardan. While the former has an almost fairy-tale narrative and timeless feel, the latter is more firmly embedded in contemporary reality. It concerns the economic and moral downfall of a man of essentially good character, the eponymous Doctor Murek, a lawyer with a doctorate, working in a business firm. Perhaps due to the large amount of material to be put on screen, the action of the film is very condensed and one event leads immediately to the next. This provides Gardan's film with a fatalistic feel, bringing to mind Rainer Werner Fassbinder's *Angst essen Seele auf* (*Fear Eats the Soul*, 1974), where the characters (except the main couple) behave in the most rational way from the perspective of capitalism, always following their economic interest.

The story begins during the crisis of the 1930s, which resulted in grave problems in businesses, especially in the provinces (as provinces always suffers more than the centre during economic downturn), and the declassation of many previously successful people. Murek, who is a diligent and honest worker, is offered a bribe which he refuses to take and consequently loses his job, as honesty in a time of crisis is seen as weakness. The doors of other firms are closed to him, because his little town is built on corruption. Unemployed, destitute, abandoned by his upper-class fiancée, who is in fact as impoverished as he, he moves to Warsaw. There he eventually makes a career, and in the last part of the film is about to marry the daughter of his wealthy employer. His career, however, is based on crime and deception – all things he tried to resist in his youth, only to embrace them in his later life. Eventually, he starts to suffer from delusions, being haunted by all the people whom he has harmed. In the last scene we see him heading into a fog, which might either stand for death or redemption.

Not unlike some films by Fassbinder, in Gardan's film physical attractiveness and sexual liaisons, what Catherine Hakim labels 'erotic capital' (Hakim 2011), are reduced to a factor in achieving social promotion. The rule is that when one climbs up the social ladder, s/he becomes sexually attractive and, conversely, beauty and sex is used to extract money from fellow human beings. The most extreme case is Karolka, Murek's one-time servant who convinces him that he got her pregnant and subsequently extracts money from him to support his non-existent child. If we apply here Heilman's definition of melodrama, then *Doctor Murek* is a melodrama at its purest, as it renders a man completely dependent on external circumstances. Murek not only accepts his fate but identifies with the roles society has attributed to him. The work he performs defines him entirely. At one point he asks rhetorically: 'What is a man without employment, without wages?' When he is reduced to the position of a rubbish collector, he feels like a man from the bottom of the human pile. Given that *Doctor Murek* is one of the last films produced and premiered before the Second World War, it offers a grim diagnosis of interwar Poland.

Although at the level of the narrative many Polish melodramas are saying that money is not the most important good (with *Doctor Murek* being an exception) and that only love is worth one's struggle, their mise-en-scène, as in western melodramas, tells otherwise. A great part of the pleasure yielded by these films lies in their opulence: the texture and elegant cut of dresses, the generous size of boudoirs, and bunches of flowers decorating the dining rooms of upper-class people. The ideal is to have all these 'entrapments of wealth' but pay no attention to them, even be bored with them, which is a typical attitude of 'old money' toward money. The upper-class women, frequently played by Maria Gorczyńska, who reveal a blasé attitude to their luxuries, provided by their busy, dull, yet well-meaning husbands, tend to be the unhappiest of all the characters. It is worth mentioning that women of this type would metaphorically be punished in postwar films, where they are represented as old-fashioned, petty, snobbish and, most importantly, as an obstacle to their husbands working successfully for their country. 1930s melodramas put the audience in the somewhat impossible position of wishing to achieve social promotion, yet at the same time suggesting that such promotion is impossible or might only be achieved by extraordinary sacrifice, such as risking one's life. Most likely this gap did not put the viewers off the cinema but, on the contrary, made them eager to watch another film.

In Search of Real Life

The films discussed so far, encapsulating the style of the 'professionals', were and still tend to be dismissed as having little to do with the Polish reality of the time. A much higher opinion is held of the films made by members of the left-leaning

START, of which the most prominent member was Aleksander Ford, who managed to shoot a number of documentaries before moving to fiction cinema. In his documentary productions Ford presents what is typically marginalized in fiction films of this period: work experience and the relation between work, state politics and class system. By the same token, as Barbara and Leszek Armatys argue, his production marked the upper limit of tolerance of the authorities to cinema which was critical of the status quo (Armatys 1988: 168). Ford's interests are conveyed by the very titles of his documentaries, such as *Tętno polskiego Manchesteru* (*The Pulse of Polish Manchester*, 1930) and *Narodziny i życie gazety* (*The Birth and Life of a Newspaper*, 1931). The first film shows one day of work in a textile factory in Łódź (known as the Polish Manchester). As well as presenting how the cloth is produced, Ford draws attention to the working conditions in the textile industry and life in the industrial centre. The idea is to show people under capitalism as reduced to a machine, when they are fit to work, and disposable, when no longer able to operate the machine (ibid.: 168–169). Inevitably, *The Pulse of Polish Manchester* had problems with censorship; the author had to delete controversial scenes, such as those showing personal searches of female workers leaving the factory. The apogee of Ford's critical work was *Droga Młodych* (*Children Must Laugh*, 1936) about a sanatorium in Miedzeszyn which treated children suffering from tuberculosis, run by Jewish specialists. The film contrasts the state of the art sanatorium with the despicable conditions of the children's lives, which is the cause of their contracting the illness. Moreover, it refers to strikes in the mines and uses a soundtrack based on *The Internationale*. The censors did not allow the distribution of Ford's film. Similar ideas to those in Ford's films were conveyed in the works of some avant-garde artists of this period, most importantly Janusz Maria Brzeski, who created an apocalyptic version of civilization and culture destroyed by the technological advancements in his photomontages, *Narodziny robota* (*The Birth of a Robot*, 1933). However, in Brzeski's work (like the bulk of the avant-garde work of this period), technology is disconnected from politics; in Ford's work technology serves the ruling class.

While START's documentary films were truly subversive, their fiction films were less so, as demonstrated by *Ludzie Wisły* (*The People of the Vistula*, 1938), directed by Ford and Jerzy Zarzycki. On the surface the film introduces a new subject: the quotidian existence of working-class people. It is set entirely in the milieu of the 'people of the Vistula', who own or rent small boats, *berlinkas*, to carry cargo along the Polish river. Such a setting should provide excellent material to present class relations in 1930s Poland, as transport is the artery of capital, as we also learn from the opening titles. However, any conflict presented in the film is purged of its class dimension, and from a Marxist perspective the film can be seen at best as ideologically innocuous and at worst reactionary.[13] *The People of the Vistula* runs two parallel stories together. One concerns a love affair between Anna and Aleksy, a handsome yet dispossessed man who makes his living by thievery on the route of the Vistula carriers. The protagonist of the second is Matyjaska, who owns an old *berlinka*. She is threatened with unemployment and possibly destitution due to her advanced age and that of her boat, deemed no longer fit to carry goods. Both these stories, however, are reduced to private affairs without any wider political significance. Aleksy is presented as an ordinary crook, preying on naive women who fall for him, rather than a product of specific historical circumstances, such as poverty and the economic crisis. Although he genuinely loves Anna, everybody tells her that he is not suitable for her and this opinion is confirmed by his death in a scuffle. After this incident Anna can take care of a more decent man – her recently widowed brother-in-law. Matyjaska's problem is solved when she receives her ex-husband's money. By and large, rather than presenting the carriers' lives as a reflection on the country's economy (as they promise to do in the initial titles), Ford and Zarzycki underscore their exoticism, not unlike the way in which gypsies or sailors tend to be presented in mainstream films. Moreover, although the film is supposed to concern the everyday toil of the Vistula carriers, almost no actual work is shown. Instead, the camera ponders on the river and picturesque Toruń and its surroundings where the film is set, rendering *The People of the Vistula* a touristy film. Anna, played by Ina Benita, one of the greatest Polish stars of the interbellum, in her impeccable dresses, heavy make-up, made-up hair and high heels, hardly looks as if she is suffering from overwork.[14] *The People of the Vistula* reveals the same shortcomings as those which members of START located in the works of the 'professionals'. The only aspect of the film which links it to socialist aesthetics is the frequent use of certain camera angles which render the characters monumental, in the style of socialist realism, by this point well developed in Soviet art. For example, on several occasions Matyjaska is shot from below which makes her appear super-human, confirmed by the dramatic acting style of Stanisława Wysocka (Armatys 1988: 271). In the last scene, Anna, at the front of the speeding *berlinka*, looks like a 'Warsaw mermaid', the symbol of Warsaw and Poland. It is worth mentioning that unlike in the fairy tale by Hans Christian Andersen, the Warsaw mermaid does not connote fragility, but rather strength and resilience.

The Ghosts turned out to be a more successful START film, with Zahorska regarding it as the most accomplished Polish film of the 1930s (Zahorska 2012a: 303). Its success can be explained in part by its being not only directed but also produced by members of START, who had by this point set up Spółdzielnia Autorów Filmowych (SAF, the Cooperative of Film Authors).[15] It is based on a novel by Maria Ukniewska, which can be compared to the works of Jean Rhys, with both authors drawing heavily on their own life stories.[16] The main character, Teresa Sikorzanka, is a chorus girl trying to make a career in the unstable world of the Warsaw music hall and theatre. Teresa's origin is working class; she is the main breadwinner in a family consisting of her parents and younger sister. She seems to have only two options in her life: either to work in a music hall or become an apprentice with a hairdresser. One can also think of a third option, prostitution, which here is not included, perhaps because at the time a career in show business was regarded as a cover for or a gateway to prostitution. Teresa chooses the music hall not because it pays better or because it offers more stable employment, as the opposite is the case, but because she has a vocation. She loves theatre and would like to be famous. Thus Teresa is probably the only heroine of Polish melodrama of the 1930s who can be described as a natural 'career woman', because for her, unlike Bronka, Krystyna or Stefcia, professional success is more important than love. This is despite the fact that, following Ukniewska, Cękalski and Szołowski present the music hall as a patriarchal world, where men occupy positions of power, acting as the theatre's directors, producers and solo singers and dancers, while women are ordinary employees labouring in a Fordist way, as chorus girls, rarely entrusted with solo parts. This professional order along gender lines is underscored by the division of space. Men have their own offices; women have to share a common dressing room. Men earn enough to afford elegant apartments; Teresa returns after work to a one-room apartment shared with her parents and younger sister. In the music hall the boundary between the professional and private lives of the dancers is blurred, because men control women's sexuality, by luring them to bed with promises of promotion. Both Teresa and her best friend, Linka, have such liaisons with senior men in the theatre, respectively the leading singer Modecki and the producer Radziszewski, and become pregnant by them. Their fate, however, could not be more different. Linka is not only abandoned by her lover, but has an abortion and is blackmailed by him. However, Modecki enjoys

Illustration 2.3: Young ballet dancers dreaming about success in *The Ghosts*, directed by Eugeniusz Cękalski and Karol Szołowski

the prospect of becoming a father and proposes to Teresa. In a sense the film thus finishes with a happy ending. And yet, the ending is not entirely happy, because Teresa, unlike female characters in other Polish melodramas, does not see marriage as a proper career for her. She prefers working in theatre.

The Ghosts show that in theatre one can escape alienation. Seen through the camera of a young cinematographer, Stanisław Wohl, the theatre is a magic place, where the dancers not only show their acrobatic skills, but create illusions of a train moving, a man flying in the sky, or a gigantic black and white ball made of moving female legs. In this sense, *The Ghosts* is also one of the first Polish meta-cinematic films, and can be seen as a commentary on Polish interwar cinema, which was impoverished, provincial and amateurish, yet still able to produce magical spectacles. On stage Teresa is radiant and she is not just a chorus girl, but a creative artist who has original ideas. This is also the reason that in the end she chooses Modecki over an affluent man who proposes marriage to her, as with

Modecki she has a chance of continuing her career and remaining an artist, while with the other man this option would be closed to her. By contrast, Linka's ultimate goal is marriage, therefore she falls prey to unscrupulous men.

Between Feudal and Gangster Capitalism: Class, Nation and Work in Polish Interwar Cinema

We can easily establish a social and moral hierarchy of characters in Polish films from the interwar period. The most decent and hard working are women from the working class or impoverished gentry, and older capitalists (industrialists, bankers or unspecified 'chairmen'), as both types work for commendable reasons. Women support their families, especially their poor, demented, depressed, alcoholic or simply unfit or lazy fathers. Such representation reflects the patriarchal character of Polish society of the time, and can be seen either as a criticism of the way in which Polish families worked or a means of normalizing the patriarchal status quo. The conclusion depends largely on the film at hand. The protagonist of *Krystyna's Lie* does not question her duty to support her inept and embarrassing father. We witness a somewhat different situation in the more left-leaning *The Ghosts*, where Teresa does not hide her exasperation that her father squanders the money she earns. If we agree that working-class women stand for the proletariat as a whole, then the sympathy shown to women in these films can be translated into a veiled sympathy on the part of filmmakers to the working class at large. However, this sympathy never translates into encouraging women to fight collectively to change their social position, nor for the working class to become a class for itself, as Marx put it – aware of its interests.

Older capitalists spend whole days in their offices, dictating business correspondence, answering phones or meeting important customers. They are portrayed as 'good masters' who labour for the benefit of the entire country as well as for their employees and customers, rather than for themselves. Making money is never their main objective, as is demonstrated by the fact that they do not indulge in a lavish lifestyle; if anything, their wealth enables the comfortable lives of their spouses and children. These men often have their offices in the same houses in which they live and have a personal attitude to their employees, knowing them by name. Sometimes this attitude is a bit 'too personal', as they embark on love affairs with their secretaries, but this can also be seen as a means of integrating their life into their work. A further marker of the decency of the older Polish capitalists is their charity work. Charity events, such as balls to support orphanages, feature heavily in films of this period. They project an image of a caring capitalist, who sets himself the task of eradicating poverty and misery in his country. On the other hand, this testifies to the social problems troubling Poland of this time which were not dealt with sufficiently by a state that was too weak.

The aforementioned representation does not fit the depiction of capitalists offered by Marx, but rather his description of feudal lords. Marx argued that in feudalism land was regarded 'as the inorganic body of its lord' (Marx 1975: 318). After feudalism, the relation between the land and its owner became abstract and reduced to 'the economic relationship between exploiter and exploited' (ibid.: 319). The feudal landowners became capitalists dealing in abstract relations. Land and man, wrote Marx, then sank 'to the level of a venal object' (ibid.: 319). To this we should add that the worker under capitalism is 'free', bound to the capitalist merely by a need to earn money. The capitalist, however, has the right merely to his/her labour, as opposed to his/her body.

Older Polish capitalists are represented as good feudal lords, which might be explained by the fact that Polish industrialists were merely one or two generations away from their roots in the countryside and retained close relations to the Polish gentry. Hence, their attitude to their employees was more feudal than in those countries where capitalism had deeper roots. These paternalistic capitalists can also be seen as a metaphor of the state, which tried to play the role of a caring capitalist. One can even see a certain similarity between busy and responsible capitalists played by Kazimierz Junosza Stępowski and Józef Piłsudski, who since his coup played the role of father of the nation, and even epitomized the state. While older capitalists come across as hardworking and responsible for their businesses and the country, their offspring fit this depiction less. Among them we find careless men who think more about their pleasure than duty. Take, for example, Jan Oksza in *Jadzia*, who at the beginning of the narrative returns from abroad where he lived an idle life, Jan Marlecki in *Krystyna's Lie*, who is disengaged from his father's business and whom we meet for the first time when he is buying a car, or Andrzej Sanicki in *Heather*, nominally a lawyer, who spends his life at parties, entertained by women of dubious reputation. The frivolity and incompetence of these young men confirms the view that Poland needs good, old masters; feudal or embedded capitalism is the best system for this country.

While the older upper-class men are well equipped to carry great responsibility on their shoulders, the same cannot be said of their counterparts from the lower classes. Older working-class men are unsuitable due to illness, detachment from reality and, most commonly, drunkenness. The younger men of humble background are often prone to an even greater sin than their fathers: that of choosing a path of crime as a means of enriching themselves. In Polish films of the 1930s we frequently find gangsters and embezzlers who do not simply cheat, but try to cheat the cheaters. Such men are presented, for example, in *Doctor Murek*, and in *Co mój mąż robi w nocy? (What Is My Husband Doing at Night?*, 1935), directed by Michał Waszyński. A common way of cheating is marrying a rich woman. I read this motif as testimony to the capitalist crisis which befell Poland in the 1930s, as crises tend to lead to 'casino capitalism',[17] namely taking risky paths to achieve success.

The appetite for social promotion concerns not only the lower classes, but also those who are already at the top. In their case it is conveyed by their desire to travel and do business abroad, because it is 'cooler' to be a rich American, Briton or Austrian than a Polish businessman. Such a conviction reflects Polish colonial history, the long period of living not only under foreign rule but on the peripheries of foreign empires, most importantly far from Vienna, which is presented as the place where Poles would most like to be. By the same token, they bear witness to a sense of Polish inferiority towards the colonial nations. On this occasion we should talk about postcolonial mimicry, as defined by Homi Bhabha, when characters in postcolonial texts imitate the behaviour of the colonizers as a way to gain cultural capital (Bhabha 1994). Postcolonial mimicry also applies to filmmakers, who borrow heavily from western cinema, as much from Hollywood as from German and Austrian films. However, while in the 1920s filmmakers identified with a desire to mimic the (ex)colonizers, in the films of the 1930s they mocked Poles who speak with foreign accents, after allegedly forgetting Polish during a period of living abroad, as if suggesting that by this point Poles should speak their own language and achieve modernity on their own terms. The drive towards modernization can also be detected in the type of industries presented in the films, such as producing and selling tennis rackets, selling cars, producing toys, radios and working in radio (Kurz 2009: 17). Judging by the films, one can even conjecture that in the 1930s Polish industry was moving from feudalism straight into post-Fordism, bypassing completely the industrial phase. Fordism would return to Polish reality and Polish cinema with a vengeance after the Second

World War, with factories producing coal and oil refineries, and employing thousands of people.

I mentioned in the introduction to this volume that ideology affects not only what is said and shown, but also what is silenced. In films of this period the most remarkable 'white spot' is the life and work of the largest social stratum in interwar Poland: the peasantry. We barely see peasants on screen and they are never cast in the main parts. If anything, they provide the background for the activities of the upper classes, being almost invisible servants of the Polish gentry. Such invisibility can be explained by two interconnected factors. First, unlike the urban proletariat, it was a socially marginalized class, sentenced to either extinction or transformation through emigration to the cities and abroad. This phenomenon is sometimes present in the films, although never put at the centre of the narrative. For example, in *Heather* a male servant follows his mistress when she moves from the country to the city to marry an affluent man. The second reason why we see so few peasants on screen was that the life of peasants was regarded as 'uncinematic'; they were poor but not in an interesting way, as is the life of the urban poor, especially those who chose the path of gangsters or imposters. Moreover, the vast majority of filmgoers in the period discussed lived in the cities, and wanted to see their new lives, even if portrayed in a distorted way, rather than the type of existence they left behind. Polish directors and scriptwriters of this period (many of them Jewish, hence urban to the core) also came from cities. Not surprisingly, in the rare cases when the filmmakers tried to show life in the countryside, it looks unconvincing, as in the previously mentioned *Women on the Abyss* about selling Polish women into sex slavery in South America. Stefania Zahorska notes that the tragedy of the Polish peasant woman from the Łowicz region is the worst part of the film: 'The dialogue of the peasants encourage laughter, although the scenes, when they are uttered, were meant to be most tragic' (Zahorska 2012b: 285). What is also missing in the interwar cinema is any sense of Polish workers acting as a group against their employers, despite the fact that the interwar period was punctuated by numerous strikes and communists were visible on the political scene. This lack points to the fact that this cinema promoted national unity. Given that in 1939 Poland's national interests were threatened by Nazi Germany, such an attitude appears to be natural.

Finally, I would like to repeat my comment about the lack of interest of this cinema in work and the everyday. From the films at hand we learn relatively little about how ordinary people worked and what were the relations in the family, most importantly between a wife and her husband. Work is often only a pretext to examine something else. Take *Za zasłoną* (*Behind a Curtain*, 1938), directed by Tadeusz Chrzanowski, which begins promisingly with images of men working on a construction site, only to move to the typical spaces of leisure, such as restaurants, and the problems resulting from men visiting such places, namely catching sexually transmitted diseases. By and large, the prevailing impression from watching films of this period (especially comedies) is that they simply try to entertain the viewers rather than proselytize. They also give the impression that work is easy and not really important. There are better ways to improve one's lot than through work. This changes in Polish postwar films, which are ideologically more transparent and emphasize the need to work.

Notes

1. This fact is noted by a number of authors writing about Polish interwar cinema, but the existing studies underscore confusion around gender and sexual identity rather than class identity (Kurz 2009; Kosińska 2009).
2. This is a reference to the real Polish tennis player, Jadwiga Jędrzejowska, who reached the Wimbledon final in 1937.
3. These episodes remind me of the film *King, Queen, Knave* (1972), by another Polish director, Jerzy Skolimowski, in which the owner of a department store shows his nephew magical tricks he needs to learn to sell ties.
4. According to Sebastian Jagielski, by producing dolls, which in the interwar jargon meant 'homosexual', this workforce is also in danger of becoming gay (Jagielski 2013: 95–96).
5. In a contemporary context this reminds us of the common practice of rich, older or gay people 'buying' their children from surrogates or impoverished people from the Third World. As I previously mentioned, Szczepko and Tońko come across as a gay couple, although it is not openly acknowledged in the film due to the self-censorship of the cinema of this period (Jagielski 2013: 88). Szczepko and Tońko's homosexuality might explain why neither of them tries to be the 'real' husband of Wanda, but this does not exclude their class as a possible reason.
6. Again, the necessity for them to carry on this way might be explained by their closeted homosexuality.
7. A similar reasoning will return in some of the films made after the fall of communism, most importantly *Edi* (2002) by Piotr Trzaskalski (Mazierska 2012b: 62–63).
8. I am treating these films as contemporary melodramas, in contrast to historical melodramas, such as *Księżna Łowicka* (*Łowicz Princess*, 1932), directed by Mieczysław Krawicz and Janusz Warnecki, and *Kościuszko pod Racławicami* (*Kościuszko*, 1938), directed by Józef Lejtes, even though not all of them are set in the 1930s, but often at the beginning of the twentieth century, when Poland was still partitioned. However, this fact does not impact much on the depiction

of the characters and narratives. They can be seen as reflecting the 1930s or at least the interbellum period with its typical problems.
9. In a study about the viewing patterns of audiences from the Kieleckie region in the 1920s and 1930s, Monika Bator observes that melodramas exceeded the popularity of comedies. She attributes this fact to the need of female workers to find 'feelings' on screen which were not allowed in the workplace (Bator 2011: 39–41). Without dismissing such explanations and the high artistic standard of some Polish interwar melodramas, I will suggest that they were also chosen because of their realist dimension, namely the use of family to reflect on larger social issues.
10. By virtue of having no central character, but treating all four in the same way, Gojawiczyńska's book can be seen as an exercise in feminism and socialism.
11. In 1985 the leading creator of Polish women's film, Barbara Sass, made a new, two-part version of *Girls from Nowolipki*, where the proportions are reversed, so to speak, because in this film Kwiryna steals the show. This is in part thanks to the casting of charismatic Ewa Kasprzyk as Kwiryna in Sass's film, who overshadows the other actresses, but also because she is granted more 'space', so to speak, to reveal her personality. This shift can be attributed to Barbara Sass' penchant for casting strong women in her films, but is also a reflection on the 1980s, when Poland, although still under communist rule, took the first steps towards neoliberalism, and private producers (*prywaciarze*) gained in status as the champions of the approaching order (see chapter 6).
12. In this sense *Girls from Nowolipki* is not a melodrama, but a drama.
13. This could be in part a result of the hostility of Polish film exhibitors to this project. They demanded extensive changes, making it more melodramatic and hence more attractive to viewers (Armatys 1988: 270–271).
14. This aspect of the film was picked up by the reviewers (for example Korczyński 2012).
15. A thorough discussion of the background to the production of *The Ghosts* and its critical reception is offered in Gierszewska 2010.
16. However, Ukniewska did not participate in writing the script for this film. Among their scriptwriters, however, were some of the most distinguished authors of the 1930s, Konstanty Ildefons Gałczyński and Władysław Broniewski, who were also famous postwar poets. On the language of *The Ghosts*, see Siatkowski 1980.
17. I'm borrowing this term from Jean-Luc Godard, who used it in the context of his 1980s films (Morrey 2005: 172). I will return to this concept in the third part of my book.

PART II
The Cinema in People's Poland
Taking a Great Leap

Economy, Work and Consumption in Poland in 1945–1989

In 1945 the Second World War ended. Its effect on Poland was in many ways similar to that of the First World War: the country was again destroyed. Poland was at the time the most devastated country in Europe; it lost about 38 per cent of its wealth, which was many times more than Germany's loss. Poland also lost the bulk of its intelligentsia. To exist, it had to rebuild its infrastructure, the factories, the housing stock, the roads and railway lines and its cultural capital. Poland also entered this period from a position of economic backwardness, with the vast majority of its citizens living in the countryside, lacking basic facilities. Its borders also changed, moving westward. Poland gained a large part of what previously belonged to Germany (so called regained territories, on account of the fact that they belonged to Poland hundreds years previously), but lost a large chunk of its eastern part, which was incorporated into the Soviet Union. In total, its size was reduced by 20 per cent, but it acquired a 300-mile-long Baltic coastline and the part it regained was economically more developed that the one it lost, to some degree making up for the losses inflicted on it by the German occupier (Landau and Tomaszewski 1985: 184).

Around the same time Poland underwent a profound political and economic change: from capitalism to state socialism. This was not a consequence of political choice by a majority of Polish citizens (even if they identified with the main goals of state socialism), but of a new political order, imposed at the Yalta conference in February 1945 by the victorious powers – Britain, the United States and the Soviet Union – which agreed to incorporate part of Poland directly into the Soviet Union and the rest into the Soviet sphere of influence. The Polish state had to cede a large part of its sovereignty towards Moscow or risk a 'friendly' military invasion (as happened in Hungary in 1956 and Czechoslovakia in 1968), and follow the Soviet economic model. Political power in Poland was to be concentrated in the hands of the Polish communist party.

However, in contrast to Russia after the October Revolution, the authorities in Poland decided not to press on with the collectivization of land. This decision was favoured by Władysław Gomułka, who was Deputy Prime Minister in the Provisional Government of the Republic of Poland, responsible for the regained territories. According to the land reform of 6 September 1944, estates of over one hundred hectares as well as those in the regained territories were redistributed among the small peasants and those living in the country who had no land (Landau and Tomaszewski 1985: 187; Crampton 1997: 219). The average size of a farm was 6.9 hectares (Landau and Tomaszewski 1985: 190). In the years 1948–1956 the authorities attempted to collectivize the Polish countryside but without success, and individual farming remained the basis of Polish agriculture till the fall of state socialism and beyond this period.

The bulk of the existing literature emphasizes the backwardness of Polish agriculture under state socialism and the unfairness with which the state treated Polish peasants by introducing compulsory deliveries, requiring farmers to sell their produce to the state at fixed prices. However, if we compare this with the situation before the Second World War, when hunger was not uncommon, as well as such signs of backwardness as the lack of electricity (in 1945 only 2 per cent of households had it), it will look like a success story. During the period of state socialism in Poland production of milk and grain increased by four to five times, and that of pork almost ten times. From a country which could not feed itself, Poland even became an exporter of food. This happened at the same time as the country was losing its surplus of peasants. In 1946 the percentage of peasants in Poland was 68.2; in 1990 it was only 38.35; still high by western standards, but low compared to the starting point (Ciborowski and Konat 2010: 29–31).

Land reform was followed by the nationalization of industry. The nationalization decree of 3 January 1946 had placed in public ownership all enterprises employing more than fifty workers per shift and all but two of the country's banks (Landau and Tomaszewski 1985: 198; Crampton 1997: 218). Not unlike the land reform, this reform was driven as much by sheer pragmatism as by ideological principles. This was because many factories lost their owners during the war or were so devastated that they could not be rebuilt without state support (Landau and Tomaszewski 1985: 196). Although after 1989 it is easier to find a negative assessment of Polish industry than a positive one, in many ways it was a success story. Industrial production of the postwar period increased thirty-eight times (Ciborowski and Konat 2010: 29–31) and in some periods grew faster than in the West. The geography of industry also changed, being more balanced at the end of the state socialist period than before the Second World War thanks to the construction of many industrial centres in regions which were previously underdeveloped.

Under state socialism strategic decisions had to conform to grand ideological designs and the Party was determined to keep all power within its own control. The authority of the Party equalled the authority of the state. The First Secretary of the Party was de facto the head of state, more important than the Prime Minister. This is one reason that people's democracies are often described as totalitarian.[1] On a lower level, factory managers could hold their posts only if they were cleared under the nomenklatura system (Crampton 1997: 251). Next was the preference for planning over spontaneous economic activities. The postwar history of Poland can be divided into various economy plans, based on the Soviet model with its preference for a five-year plan. Another principle was the fetishism of large-scale industry and Fordist organization, in which every job is divided into smaller components. These aspects are closely connected: the larger the enterprise, the more difficult it is to grasp its parts, hence the need to break down the tasks and divide responsibilities. Under state socialism there was also a marked distinction between 'productive' and 'unproductive' work, with the former being officially valued higher than the latter.

Rapid industrialization, particularly in the first decade after the end of the war, had two positive effects, which can be seen as the greatest achievements of the socialist state, particularly from today's vantage point. One was eradicating unemployment, especially in the countryside, and its many negative side effects, such as poverty, hunger and high mortality rates. The second was providing its citizens with welfare. The socialist state took care of many of its citizens' needs, such as education, health and leisure (Narojek 1991: 21–35). This allowed many Poles of modest background (including myself), to achieve social promotion which their ancestors could only dream of, largely through education, whose level was comparable or even higher than in the West, especially for women. These characteristics of state socialism point both to the difference and similarity of Poland post-1945 with Poland of the interbellum. In the interwar period the channels of social promotion were limited, especially for the peasantry, the economy was marred by high unemployment, and the level of welfare provided by the state was very low. At the same time, as I indicated in the previous part, the state attempted to intervene in the economy to fight unemployment, reduce economic inequalities and provide welfare. This, however, proved very difficult due to the internal and international situation.

The economic and social programme of state socialism was quite similar to that of European western countries, which after the war introduced what is termed 'social liberalism' (Hobsbawm 1995: 274), 'Keynesianism' or 'embedded liberalism', namely capitalism controlled by and embedded in state institutions (Harvey 1990: 121–140; 2005a: 11). Such an agenda included the policy of near full employment, high taxes for the rich, free education and healthcare, and various programmes aimed at eradicating class divisions, as well as speedy industrialization. Jakub Majmurek, in his perceptive study of Polish economic history, uses the World-System theory of Immanuel Wallerstein (1984) and Ivan Berend's construction of Eastern European postwar history as a 'detour from the periphery to the periphery' (1996) to argue that the path Poland took after the Second World War can be seen as a typical project of peripheral modernization, pertaining to many countries and regions which over the years and even centuries attempted to overcome their marginal status (Majmurek 2010). One of the markers of this type of modernization was that it came from above rather than from below, being introduced by the local elites who in this way attempted to strengthen their position in the world system (ibid.: 75). Majmurek regards the state socialist project as the most successful of those on which Poland embarked over the centuries, not least because without it Poland would not only have failed to catch up with more advanced countries, but would have increased its distance with the West.[2]

I agree with this diagnosis. Nevertheless, it raises a number of questions. One concerns whether the system could have worked better and what prevented it from such improvement. The second relates to the reasons why it collapsed. Finally, the question is why it attracts such negative assessment in postcommunist times. The answer to the first question should be, predictably, 'yes'. Many authors point to two interrelated flaws of state socialist economy. One concerns Poland's dependence on the Soviet Union, which provided Poland with raw materials and machines, and dictated its economic priorities. As a result Polish industry was biased towards heavy and even military industry, at the expense of producing consumer goods. The Polish economy can even be seen as developing in cycles, when after mass discontent and a change of leadership (in the years 1945 to 1947, 1956 to 1958, 1970 to 1973) it embarked on improving the quality of living by increasing production of consumer goods, only to return to expanding heavy and military industry when some improvement was achieved (Ciborowski and Konat 2010: 41). According to the popular perception, the Soviet Union cheated Poland by not paying market prices for its products, such as coal and ships. On the other hand, however, it could be argued that it was thanks to the Soviet Union that Poland had no problems with exporting them. Hence the Soviet Union was an important factor in Poland enjoying full employment, as acknowledged even by the then leader of Solidarity, Lech Wałęsa.[3] The emphasis on heavy industry became particularly problematic in the 1970s and the 1980s, when Western Europe embarked on the fifth industrial revolution, based on the development of electronics (Berend 1996: 226–230).

Privileging heavy industry and with that a tendency towards excess, to 'Magnitogorsk mentality' (the term taken from the rapid development of the town which was a flagship of Stalin's Five-Year Plan), led to high wastage of material and human resources. For example, smelting plants were built where local ores were inadequate for steel production and became unprofitable and in due course abandoned (Crampton 1997: 250–251). The fetishization of the plan meant that little thought was given to whether it is worth fulfilling the plan, when there was no obvious market for specific goods. There was also little coordination between different production units. For example, cars would be produced, but not spare parts for them or even suitable roads to use them. Too much was left to central planning; leaving a larger margin for spontaneous economic activity would have rendered the system more efficient. However, a high level of waste also pertains to capitalist productions because capitalism's goal is maximizing surplus value, irrespective of human or ecological costs (Marx 1977: 40). Abandoned factories are as frequent in the West as in the East and people are disposed of by their employers even more often in the West than they were in the socialist East.

Spontaneous economic activity did take place across the whole of Eastern Europe and in Poland it was of significant size, being one of the largest countries in Eastern Europe (Aslund 1985: 2; Wedel 1992; Kurz 2008a). It consisted of the illegal production and trade of privately produced goods for domestic and foreign consumption, trading in goods brought from abroad, selling and buying foreign currencies, working abroad without informing the Polish tax office, as well as stealing tools and material from the workplace for private consumption and reselling them for profit. A mild, yet very common form of the second economy was 'exchanging favours', for example keeping 'under the counter' some pairs of stockings, in short supply, to be exchanged for sausage or shoes (Pawlik 1992; Firlit and Chłopecki 1992; Kurz 2008a). The inventiveness of Poles in circumventing the official economy appeared to be limitless and is a favourite subject of Polish comedies of the whole socialist period. The private sector was a merciless mirror of the flaws of a socialized economy (Aslund 1985: 1; Mazurek 2013). However, following authors such as Elemér Hankiss (1990), I argue that the existence of the second economy also prolonged the existence of the official economy by plugging gaps in the state socialist system. It also skewed the class system in Poland, because those who were able to benefit from it, for example by having easy access to goods in short supply, were effectively higher on the social ladder than those on higher salaries but with no access to scarce goods. Over the years the authorities recognized the importance of the second economy and from the 1970s attempted to integrate it into the official system.

Let's move now to the reasons why state socialism collapsed. This had as much to do with the internal as with the external situation. We should list factors such as lagging behind in the technological race with the West, greater reliance on imports from capitalist countries, which led to crippling debt, cutting back on investments and then the deterioration of the standard of living in the later 1970s and 1980s (Berend 1996: 222–253). Another reason was Mikhail Gorbachev's unwillingness to preserve socialism in the Eastern bloc and the Soviet Union, and the global shift towards neoliberalism. Following authors such as Joseph Berliner, Ivan Berend, and in the Polish context Jakub Majmurek and Piotr Szumlewicz, I shall emphasize my conviction that the fall of state socialism had mainly to do with this late period (Berliner 2010; Berend 1996; Majmurek and Szumlewicz 2010), rather than its being doomed from the start due to its alleged internal contradictions and immorality.

The Nomenklatura and the 'People', or the Class System in Poland of State Socialism

Although I'm using here the term 'state socialism', behind the abstract term 'state' were people who made political and economic decisions in the name of the whole society and allegedly for its welfare. They were first chosen by the authorities in the Soviet Union, who recruited them from people who proved loyal to the Soviet authorities. In due course the leaders tried to be more independent from the

Kremlin and even emphasized Polish national interest as a means of legitimizing their position; Władysław Gomułka at the beginning of his rule was a prime example of this attitude.

The main group which opposed Poland becoming a socialist state consisted of the elites which had dominated the country between the wars, such as the gentry, the officers and the metropolitan intelligentsia. However, Polish communists were strengthened by the Warsaw uprising, which resulted in the virtual destruction of the leadership of the historic political forces. A large proportion of peasants were also distrustful of the new government, being anxious that the land reform was only an introduction to collectivization based on Soviet patterns (Landau and Tomaszewski 1985: 188). During the first years after the Second World War the legal opposition was eliminated, and the existing parties were merged or dismantled. The popular leader of the Polish Peasant Party, Stanisław Mikołajczyk, was forced to leave Poland in 1948. The end of the process of 'political cleansing' saw the formation of the Polish United Workers' Party (Polska Zjednoczona Partia Robotnicza, PZPR)[4] in December 1948. Its First Secretary and effectively the most important person on the Polish political scene became Gomułka's chief rival, Bolesław Bierut, who held this function till his death in 1956. As a communist trained in Moscow and an NKVD (Soviet secret police) agent, he contributed significantly to the PZPR's unpopularity. It is worth noting that the word 'communist' did not feature in the name of the PZPR. According to Włodzimierz Choroszewski, this omission testifies to the depth of anti-communist sentiments among ordinary Poles (Choroszewski 1971: 56), reflecting the fact that during the Polish-Bolshevik war, following the end of the First World War, Polish communists supported Soviet Russia (seeing it as a force of progress), rather than their own country. They were thus seen not as internationalists fighting for social justice but as traitors of their own country (Bromke 1962; see also chapter 1).

The leaders of the PZPR were not chosen democratically by ordinary members of the Party, but by those already in power who opted for those comrades whom they could trust (the choice of the First Secretary thus had much in common with voting for the Pope). This group of Party officials effectively ruled the country, as the government consisted of the top members of the Party and was subordinated to the Party executive, and the high positions in the economy were also either filled by members of the Party elite or their associates. This initially small group in due course expanded and became a ruling class. Today, we tend to use the term 'nomenklatura' to describe it. A large proportion of the studies devoted to state socialism in Eastern Europe and to Poland specifically is devoted to this stratum, even if their authors do not use the term 'nomenklatura' (Djilas 1965; Kuron and Modzelewski 1982; Starski 1982: 13–24; Burawoy and Lukács 1992; Staniszkis 1992).[5]

Probably the first study devoted to the phenomenon of the nomenklatura as pertaining to state socialism at large, and still one of the most perceptive, was offered by Yugoslav dissident writer and politician Milovan Djilas, author of an essay 'The New Class', published in 1957, where the 'new class' can be identified as the nomenklatura. Djilas argued that Stalin was the principal creator of the nomenklatura, which was made up of 'those who have special privileges and economic preference because of the administrative monopoly they hold' (Djilas 1965: 321). The new class has its base in the communist party, but the party and the new class are not identical:

> *As the new class becomes stronger and attains a more perceptible physiognomy, the role of the party diminishes. The core and the basis of the new class is created in the party and at its top, as well in the state political organs. The once live, compact party, full of initiative, is disappearing to become transformed into the traditional oligarchy of the new class, irresistibly drawing into its ranks those who aspire to join the new class and repressing those who have any ideals. (ibid.: 321)*

The strengthening of the nomenklatura is at the expense of the rest of the party and society. This is because the main objective of the nomenklatura, like that of the nobility under feudalism and the bourgeoisie under capitalism, is the preservation of class power, not the welfare of the rest of society. This does not mean that the nomenklatura in Poland and elsewhere was not willing to make any concessions to the rest of society. The history of Poland of state socialism can be seen as a history of people getting such concessions, usually as a result of strikes and demonstrations, hence in the classical acts of class struggle. The important dates in Polish postwar history – 1956, 1970, 1980 – are the dates when these concessions (higher pay, lower prices, greater freedom of the media, gentler censorship and even the restructuring of industry) were won. These dates also coincide with changes in the leadership of the Party and by the same token of the composition of the nomenklatura.

The nomenklatura was not particularly popular among the rest of society, although some leaders of the Party were almost loved at the beginning of their rule: Władysław Gomułka in 1956 and Edward Gierek in the first half of the 1970s.

Increasingly, the nomenklatura was labelled 'them', as opposed to 'us', to emphasize the distance between the rulers and the ruled.⁶ An important reason was its behaviour as a new aristocracy, securing for itself excessive bonuses, and privileged access to scarce goods and services. In relation to that Djilas writes, 'discrepancies between the pay of workers and of party functionaries are extreme; this could not be hidden from persons visiting the U.S.S.R. or other communist countries in the past few years' (ibid.: 320; see also Burawoy and Lukács 1992: 146–147). In the Polish context the typical privileges enjoyed by the nomenklatura were special shops 'behind yellow curtains', where they could buy goods in short supply, easier access to housing, better healthcare, better working conditions and free foreign travel for themselves and their families (Leszczyński 2000: 25–35). These benefits were comparable to those enjoyed by the economic and political elites in the capitalist world at that time and seem even modest compared with those of the neoliberal elites, but in the state socialist context they were annoying because a socialist state was meant to be egalitarian and because for many decades the rulers demanded from the rest of the society hard work, sacrifice, asceticism and idealism.

As time passed, the nomenklatura's privileges became more extensive. Stanisław Starski mentions, for example, that in 1973 a special act of parliament was passed 'on pensions granted to individuals who render particularly important services to the state', through a 'rigid hierarchy which measured services rendered in terms of the post achieved and the length of time ... held' (Starski 1982: 23). Starski describes the bill as a 'plain outrage' (ibid.: 23), but it only confirms Djilas's observation that 'he who grabs power grabs privileges and indirectly grabs property' (Djilas 1965: 327). The fact that the nomenklatura was guaranteed material privileges does not mean that all communist rulers in Poland built palaces for themselves and transferred millions of dollars to Swiss bank accounts, taking advantage of their privileged position. Again, the case in point is Gomułka, whose ascetic lifestyle was famous, rewarding him with the respect even of his political enemies (Bromke 1971; Bethell 1972). Although the nomenklatura enjoyed a lot of power, it was not unlimited. On the one hand, it had to take orders from the Kremlin, and on the other, it had to ensure that the economy was working sufficiently well to prevent a large-scale crisis. One should also not underestimate the internal power struggle inside the upper echelons of the Party. All these factors played a part in introducing economic and social reforms. The general trend, following the death of Bierut and the end of Stalinism, was towards appeasing the people, yet without introducing parliamentary democracy with a multi-party system. The trend of wooing the population was particularly visible during Gierek's rule in the 1970s, partly due to the Helsinki accord which required the countries of the Soviet bloc to respect human rights (Berend 1996: 234–237).

On the opposite side of the nomenklatura or 'them' were the 'people' or 'us'. Both sides of the political divide tried to present this group as homogenous and united and indeed it was at times, especially in the early 1980s, during the triumphs of the (first) Solidarity. However, it was heterogeneous due to the different ways in which the members of specific groups earned their living and in terms of their different styles of consumption, as well as fractured by competing class interests. This was further exacerbated by a complicated system of rewards, introduced by the socialist welfare state. The main classes within 'us' were the industrial working class, the peasants and the intelligentsia. The importance of the first was acknowledged in the official ideology of state socialism, as this was the class which was meant to build socialism through physical effort and political leadership. However, although industrial workers were an object of official adulation, their material status and their position vis-à-vis other classes was lower than was officially claimed. Their life was particularly hard during the period of the most intensive industrialization in the 1950s, due to the poor state of the factories and the machines, the disregard for health and safety, a lack of proper working clothes and shoes, poor organization of work, the pressure to fulfil unrealistically high quotas, and low wages. The distinguished Polish writer, Maria Dąbrowska, described working in a factory producing train engines as being like living in hell and paying for the sins which one did not commit (Dąbrowska, quoted in Brzostek 2002: 37). This hardship can be linked to postwar poverty and backwardness, for which the manual workers had to pay more than any other social strata. But there were also other factors which made the life of a Polish worker particularly hard, such as the state limiting workers' rights, most importantly the right to organize free unions and strikes. Unions nominally existed under state socialism, but they acted not as workers' representatives but as transmitters of the orders from above, hence additional agents of oppression, along with the management and the Party (Brzostek 2002: 43–55). Strikes were forbidden on the grounds that there was no need for them under the conditions of the dictatorship of the proletariat. If they took place, they were dismissed as expressing the interests of forces antagonistic to the proletariat, such as foreign agents who had infiltrated the factory and had to be extinguished at all costs, even at the price of using weapons against the striking workers.[7] One frequently encounters the opinion that it was harder to work under state socialism than capitalism (Norman 1955: 8). However, with the passage of time the conditions of work improved and the pressure to fill quotas eased. In the 1970s in Poland a common opinion, frequently expressed in comedies, was that workers in Poland had a better life than other classes, most importantly the intelligentsia, and even better than in the West. This was because state socialism led to a certain nonchalance on the part of the workers, which their counterparts, labouring under capitalism and threatened with unemployment, could not afford (Narojek 1991: 22). The apparent advantage of Polish workers was demonstrated, among other things, by their lack of respect for their superiors, low quality of work, lack of initiative and theft of state property with impunity.

The working class was also internally divided, according to such criteria as occupation, age, gender and traditions. For example, coalminers, metalworkers and shipbuilders had higher salaries, better healthcare and entitlements for holidays than the rest of the workers on the grounds that their work was especially important for the economy. At the opposite end of the spectrum were those who worked in services, for example in cargo transport or factory canteens. Older workers usually fared better than younger workers, reflecting a wider rule that Poland of state socialism was a gerontocracy, despite its praise of youth in songs and political speeches. Female workers were paid less than male workers. This was reflected in the wages women took home for the same work as that done by men, in their harsher treatment in the workplace (Brzostek 2002: 79–88; Fidelis 2010), and in the division of occupations into typically male and female, with the latter, usually in service, being paid at a lower rate than typical male occupations. Workers from a working-class background were treated better by the management and occupied higher positions in factories than newcomers from the countryside, so called 'storks' or 'hares' (Brzostek 2002: 72–79). This was also reflected in their housing situation; the former used to live in their own (council or cooperative) apartments; the latter had to content themselves with a place in the workers' hostels. These general rules were modified by time, because each leader had a special affinity with certain professions. For example, Gomułka placed the chemical industry higher than metalwork.

The second class comprising 'us' was that of the intelligentsia, namely people earning their living by performing mental work. This can be seen as the equivalent of the western salaried middle class. This group was, like the working class, heterogeneous. At one extreme, it included low-ranking clerks, who, in the opinion of their critics, acted as parasites on the healthy body of the workers. At the other extreme, there were artists and intellectuals, who were expected to represent and guide the nation, and mould the socialist 'new man'. The state, at least initially, attempted to lower the position of the intelligentsia in order to upgrade that of the industrial proletariat, by paying a lower wage to most of them, especially teachers and clerks, in comparison with the wages of miners and steelworkers. There were also occasional anti-intelligentsia campaigns, most importantly in 1968. And yet, the bulk of Poles, including those from the working class, aspired to join the intelligentsia, while it rarely happened that the children of the intelligentsia wanted to become blue-collar workers. This hierarchy of Polish workers reflected a higher level of alienation of manual toil over intellectual work and a conviction that manual labour can be performed by practically everybody, while intellectual work requires significant cultural capital. Moreover, the members of this stratum were not subjugated to the same harsh regime as factory workers. The managers had higher salaries, more flexibility at work and longer holidays (Mazurek 2005) and teachers enjoyed many non-monetary privileges, such as the right to early retirement. The socialist state further inflated the value of certain intellectual professions, such as doctors, artists or actors, by introducing highly competitive university entrance exams, which reflected the authorities' views on the needs of the state for specific professions. In this way those who managed to pass them were rewarded twice: by joining the exclusive club of educated people and by having their professional future ensured.[8] Moreover, after Gomułka's rule, the intelligentsia rather than ordinary workers provided the bulk of the cadres for the nomenklatura (Władyka 2009: 116).

Poland of state socialism also included peasants. Their material status and prestige was lower than that of the working class and the intelligentsia. This was an outcome of the convergence of various factors. One was the despicable position of Polish peasants in the interwar period, which the land reform of 1944 only partly addressed, and the continuous overpopulation of the Polish countryside, which has lasted practically till today. The onslaught on the peasantry, especially on the richer section of this group (known as *kulaks*), after the Second World War, their strange status as a leftover from bourgeois times and as private producers yet highly dependent on the state which was the main buyer of their products, compounded their low status. The majority of Polish peasants were of the opinion that the only way for them to achieve social promotion was by moving to the city. As noticed by Eugenia Jagiełło-Łysiowa as early as the 1960s, when the paths of social promotion are open for everybody, it is assumed that a young person becomes a farmer not because he is sentenced to such a fate by his peasant background, but because he is a loser (quoted in Narojek 1991: 61). My own experience confirms this diagnosis. My father, who inherited a family farm as a result of the death of his father during the Second World War, was seen by his two siblings who moved to the city as a loser and he internalized this perception. My parents did not wish their children to stay on the farm. Returning there after completing my education would have been seen as a sign of failure on my part, and so I never returned.

One special group of peasants were workers-peasants (*chłoporobotnicy*), whose income from farming was so low that they had to earn extra income in the city. Although they were often materially better off than peasants, their social standing was lower than that of either peasants or workers due to their lacking a distinct place in the social structure.

Finally, we should list a small group of people who were self-employed, mostly artisans and small capitalists. Their material status and prestige was low, as conveyed by the contemptuous term *prywaciarz* (meaning 'private producer', but with a sneer). Not unlike the peasants, they were treated as remnants of the old system and worked in adverse circumstances, facing numerous bureaucratic barriers and working on the verge of illegality. Not surprisingly, many were geared towards a quick profit and were associated with low-quality production. The higher living standard of some of the Polish capitalists was also a source of envy for the rest of society who lacked the entrepreneurial spirit. But in this case the attitudes evolved over time. As Narojek observes, in the 1980s the economic and political circumstances became more conducive to this form of work and the prestige of *prywaciarz* went up. Many young people chose to earn their income this way as a kind of political gesture, a refusal to work in a state enterprise (ibid: 39).

We can observe two tendencies in postwar Poland, promoted by the state: towards greater egalitarianism and towards singling out and rewarding certain groups of workers and exceptional individuals and, of course, conferring privileges on the nomenklatura. At the same time, those who achieved social promotion, granted by education or just by moving from the country to the city, wanted to differentiate themselves from those who were below them. Such an attitude is often explained by human nature: people do not want to be economically and socially equal; they would always like to be 'more equal', as observed by George

Orwell. Nevertheless, it is safe to say that support for egalitarianism was rather high in socialist Poland and it remained so even after the demise of state socialism.

Production of Subjectivities

Among the challenges which the new Polish authorities faced in 1945 was the creation of a new socialist man (as it was typically a man mentioned in the literature), living in tune with the new economic and political reality. The new man was meant to be selfless and focused on building socialism, rather than fulfilling his private needs. He should achieve his objectives not by following his nature (which in fact was not natural, but a product of bourgeois culture), but by fighting against it and 'working on oneself'. The authorities were meant to assist him or her in the transformation, as suggested by Trotsky in 'Habit and Custom' (discussed in the introduction), by first learning about what really happens on the shop floor and eradicating behaviour which was harming the working population. The change in morals was meant to make people happier by being more reconciled to the new social reality and increasing material production. As Trotsky put it, 'even the slightest success in the sphere of morals, by raising the cultural level of the working man and woman, enhance our capacity for rationalizing production, and promoting socialist accumulation' (Trotsky 2002: 89). The importance attributed to cinema under state socialism had much to do with the expectation that film would play a major role in producing such a person.

The question arises whether state socialism succeeded in producing a new personality type. The common answer today is that it did, but not in the way envisaged by socialist ideologues. State socialism rather led to the birth of 'homo sovieticus'. This concept was introduced in 1981 by the Russian dissident writer Aleksander Zinoviev, who published a satirical novel under this title (Zinoviev 1985). Zinoviev's 'Homo sovieticus' is a selfish and conformist man, who, unlike a western man, has no convictions, only a 'stereotype of behaviour' (ibid.: 11) and is used to living in a bureaucratic maze, where a large part of people's lives is spent writing reports, because 'the Report is a powerful way of integrating people into the Communist system' (ibid.: 16), rendering them anxious and docile.

The idea of 'homo sovieticus' did not disappear altogether with the state socialist system. On the contrary, it gained in vitality, being used as a shorthand for pathologies pertaining to state socialism which made it difficult for people living under this system to adjust to a new, neoliberal democracy. For example, in 2011, following parliamentary elections in Russia, 'The Economist' published an article entitled 'The long life of Homo sovieticus', which attributed the results of the elections to the legacy of the system which ruled the country since the October revolution, transforming not only the economy but also hearts and minds.

It was transplanted to Polish soil by Catholic philosopher and priest Józef Tischner (2005), who likewise used it to explain the difficulties experienced by Poles in adjusting to the new, neoliberal democracy. Tischner describes 'homo sovieticus' as somebody who lived under state socialism for so long that s/he became addicted to it. He avoids personal responsibility and attempts to 'escape from freedom' (Tischner 2005: 141). Other authors add that 'homo sovieticus' suffers from a lack of initiative and personal responsibility in the workplace, indifference toward the preservation of common property, the habit of using one's professional position for private advantage, and the fierce rivalry for deficit goods, often by proving that one is more deserving than others, what Mirosława (Mira) Marody describes as 'small individualism' (quoted in Narojek 1991: 29). On the one hand, 'homo sovieticus' is regarded as a conformist who wishes to adapt to and merge with the majority. In this sense s/he is 'sovieticus'. On the other hand, however, he is an egoist who uses and abuses the system for his/her own advantage. These characteristics can be traced to the structural features of state socialism, most importantly the relatively weak link between one's achievements at work and what one is paid. However, it would be a mistake to assume that only under state socialism can we find people revealing the aforementioned traits. These are also typical of western welfare states and were routinely used by right-wing politicians, such as Margaret Thatcher in Britain, to reduce state welfare provision as a means of making their recipients more active and entrepreneurial.

The sociologists, however, are wary of the 'homo sovieticus' concept because of its shifting meaning, its highly judgemental character and the fact that, as I already mentioned, traces of 'homo sovieticus' behaviour and mindset can also be found outside the Eastern bloc. As Marody claims, after 1989 the term is used 'as a tool of stigmatizing certain deplorable behaviour which resembles behavioural patterns from the communist period. It has become an equivalent of adjectives such as "unadjusted", "unmodernized" and "conservative"' (Marody 2010: 89; see also Swader 2010).

However, what interests me in my investigation is not whether Poland in the period of state socialism was populated with heroic 'new men' or lazy and conformist 'homini sovietici', but rather whether these types found their way to Polish films, how and why films modified their meanings and whether we find other personality types in Polish cinema. I am also interested in the mechanics of production of subjectivities, as shown in the films, most importantly who is given the task to mould the new personalities. My argument is that the 'new man' can be found in relatively few Polish postwar films, while 'homini sovietici' appear to be eternal and the closer we come to the present day, the more they proliferate, reflecting on the growing opposition towards state socialism and filmmakers' boldness in articulating this opposition.

Polish Cinema under State Socialism

The situation of Polish cinema after the Second World War was not much better than that of Polish industry at large. The interwar film industry had been practically destroyed by the occupier. All film studios were in ruins, together with film labs and distribution offices. Poland also lost a large proportion of its filmmakers. Many perished in the fight with the Nazis, others in camps, and many emigrated. In 1947, when the first union of filmmakers was created, it comprised only twenty-eight people (Zajiček 1992: 42–43). Without nationalization the film industry would not have survived and the state took upon itself the responsibility of rebuilding it and supporting it by financing and distributing films. Polish cinema of the period of state socialism is widely seen as a success story, both in terms of quantity and quality. With the exception of the first years after the Second World War and Stalinism, Poland produced on average between thirty and thirty-five films per year, placing it close to France. In the Eastern European context Poland was seen as a mini- cinematic 'empire' and its films penetrated this region quite deeply, a fact which was appreciated only after 1989, when the country lost this position (Mazierska and Goddard 2014). Some Polish directors, such as Wanda Jakubowska, Andrzej Wajda, Jerzy Kawalerowicz, Andrzej Munk, Wojciech Has, Krzysztof Kieślowski, Krzysztof Zanussi and Agnieszka Holland, reached worldwide fame, setting the standards of arthouse cinema in Europe at large.

As the state paid for films, it was only natural that it also sought to influence the products it paid for through overt and covert censorship, the character and severity of which kept changing, usually following the larger political conjunctures which brought with them either liberalization or a tightening of filmmakers' belts.

In general, it was a two-tiered process. First, scripts were pre-approved by industry internal censors and then the completed films were assessed by Party representatives (Michałek 1988: xiii; Iordanova 2003: 33–36; Adamczak 2012: 178–179). It was difficult to stop a film once it had been approved for production.[9] This allowed the filmmakers to depart from the script by including politically 'unsafe' material during shooting (Adamczak 2012: 79). Once such material was included, the censors had two options: accept it or shelve it, namely withdraw the contentious film from distribution. The second barely happened in the 1950s, but became common in the 1970s and 1980s, which should not be regarded as a sign of increased censorship but, on the contrary, its easing (ibid.: 179). In the 1950s, films which diverted from the official line were not allowed to be produced. In the 1970s and the 1980s, such practice of diverting from the agreed script was common, which resulted in the making of many films which were critical of the socialist state, such as *Człowiek z marmuru* (*Man of Marble*, 1977) by Andrzej Wajda or *Barwy ochronne* (*Camouflage*, 1977) by Krzysztof Zanussi. One form of censorship was the narrow distribution of contentious films: few copies, for special cinemas (*kina studyjne*). A by-product of this approach was the state abetting development of a certain type of audience, which was both arthouse and politically minded, consisting largely of students and the urban intelligentsia.

The filmmakers themselves knew that in order to pass the final examination by Party officials, a certain degree of self-censorship was necessary (ibid.: 179–180). The combination of the censors' fluctuating tolerance and the filmmakers' calculated compromises makes it impossible to draw a clear line between 'conformist' and 'dissident' films and filmmakers, although some filmmakers at a certain point of their career were so unhappy about the way in which the film industry operated in Poland that they decided to leave. One such was Jerzy Skolimowski, who refused to excise a contentious episode showing a poster of Stalin with two pairs of eyes in his *Ręce do góry* (*Hands Up!*, 1966, premiered in 1985) and moved abroad. Other examples are Roman Polanski and Walerian Borowczyk, whose cinematic interests were not in tune with the subjects favoured by the Party or by fellow filmmakers. We should also mention here the temporary relocation abroad in the 1980s of such filmmakers as Andrzej Wajda, Agnieszka Holland and Krzysztof Zanussi, and also the large number of filmmakers of Jewish origin who left Poland in the wake of an anti-Semitic campaign in 1968 (Zajiček 1992: 196–197). However, on the whole the proportion of Polish filmmakers who followed in their footsteps was low in comparison with those who remained in

Poland. This is one indicator that, despite numerous unofficial and sometimes official complaints about the lack of freedom experienced by Polish filmmakers, they saw in the socialist system more advantages than disadvantages. The conviction that working in the socialist film industry was a privilege, not a burden, was especially felt by those who remembered the interwar years, when the pressure to produce profit was paramount and the margin of artistic experimentation was narrow. For members of START, the nationalization of the film industry was like a gift from heaven. As many of them, such as Eugeniusz Cękalski and Wanda Jakubowska, had leftist sympathies, the requirement to make films advocating the socialist ideology was also not a problem and many of them were rewarded with high positions in the film industry. For example, Aleksander Ford became the head of Film Polski (Polish Film), the institution in charge of most of the activities of the Polish film industry after the war.

Political events not only affected the type of films made in Poland, but also the organization of the film industry and the number of films produced. Political liberalization was followed by the increase in autonomy for the film industry. This was reflected in setting up semi-autonomous film units, with prominent directors as their heads. Over the course of time these included directors such as Wanda Jakubowska, Aleksander Ford, Jerzy Kawalerowicz, Andrzej Wajda, Krzysztof Zanussi and Juliusz Machulski, to list just a few. Some of these people, such as Wanda Jakubowska, were put in their positions because they were seen as both accomplished filmmakers and loyal to the regime. Others, like Wajda or Machulski, were granted this role mostly due to their artistic achievements and, albeit more rarely, the popularity of their films. Liberalization also went hand in hand with the increase in film production and Polish successes in the international arena, which was also an important goal for Polish filmmakers. Centralization, by contrast, meant fewer films of mostly lower quality. Such organization affected the status of film directors in Poland. As Bolesław Michałek and Frank Turaj maintain, under state socialism

> *the creative position of a director is considerably enhanced. [He] is no mere manipulator of mise-en-scène, nor simply an executor of a producer's projects, nor yet a combination technician-businessman-organizer (a paradigm familiar to Americans). He is nothing less than an exponent of universal aspirations and concerns, a creator who has gained the status heretofore reserved for poets, writers, and artists. (Michałek and Turaj 1988: xi)*

Under such circumstances, Polish cinema under state socialism was dominated by auteurism. Another specificity of the state industry was that, as Michałek and Turaj put it, 'the threat of unprofitability was of no concern' (ibid.: xii; see also Adamczak 2012). This explains why at times Poland embarked on super-productions which were able to compete in their lavishness with Hollywood products, as exemplified by *Rękopis znaleziony w Saragossie* (*The Saragossa Manuscript*, 1965), directed by Wojciech Has, *Faraon* (*Pharaoh*, 1966) by Jerzy Kawalerowicz, or *Ziemia obiecana* (*The Promised Land*, 1974) by Andrzej Wajda (Adamczak 2010: 229–235). On many occasions, the more expensive the film, the higher the bonus for its director. By contrast, the profit made by films had little impact on the financial or critical standing of their makers. Box office hits were routinely derided by critics as conformist and pandering to the low taste of the audience. This is reflected in the histories of Polish cinema which tend to marginalize Polish popular and genre cinema: a trend which this book attempts to rectify to some extent.

The relative neglect of profit also affected the star system. Polish cinema had many stars, such as Zbigniew Cybulski, Daniel Olbrychski, Elżbieta Czyżewska and Krystyna Janda, but it lacked the 'star system' of the type operating in Hollywood or even western Europe (Skwara 1992), because the value of a star as the creator of extra profit was of little relevance to the film producers.

The changes in cinema mirrored the political junctures, such as the end of Stalinism and the ascent of Władysław Gomułka's rule in 1956, the fall of Gomułka and his replacement by Edward Gierek in 1970, Gierek's fall in 1980, the first victory of Solidarity in 1980–1981, the imposition of martial law in 1981, and finally the fall of state socialism in 1989. However, there was usually some delay before a new political situation was reflected in cinema. This particularly affected full-length fiction films, whose production is lengthy, especially under the socialist system, when the script and the film required acceptance by the political authorities. Therefore, in my discussion the boundaries between specific periods are 'soft'. My main concern in classifying a specific film as belonging to this or that period is its subject, ideology and style, rather than the date of its production or premiere.

Work-centred films and films concerned with the everyday were produced in all of these periods, although less frequently than one might expect in a country whose leading force had 'workers' in its name. This was in part due to the fact that under the conditions of censorship it was harder to make films about the present day than the past. Yet films about work and the everyday often fulfilled more functions than their western equivalents, because they not only represented work relations and experiences, but substituted for films about macro-politics. This was because in Poland, where free debate on contentious subjects was not possible in public, such discussion had to be conducted in a coded way. What was represented in a film about a factory or an office could be read as pertaining to the country at large. For example, when in Andrzej Munk's film *Człowiek na torze* (*Man on the Tracks*, 1956) the viewers heard at the end of the film the words 'It is stifling here' (*duszno tu*), they were probably aware that they refer not only to the specific place where these words are uttered, but to the country at large. As Michałek and Turaj observe, 'this phrase entered the colloquial language as an expression that typified, in its understated way, life during the Stalinist era' (Michałek and Turaj 1988: 118). In my discussion I will try to capture such moments, without losing sight of their literal meaning.

Notes

1. In the Polish context such an opinion is held, for example, by Hanna Świda-Ziemba (1998). However, rather than defending or refuting such claims, which would require a major investigation, including a discussion of the situation of Poles at different moments of Polish postwar history and comparing the Poland of state socialism with other countries of the eastern bloc, as well as those from the West and the 'global South', I am interested here primarily in how state socialism worked 'on the ground', according to filmic representations. I am leaving it to the viewers to decide whether these representations testify to totalitarianism or the lack thereof in the Poland of state socialism.
2. The current difficult economic situation of Greece, which like Poland is a peripheral country, but which after the Second World War took a different path than Poland, might be seen as an indicator that state socialism was a better route than embracing capitalism Greek style.
3. Wałęsa does so in an omnibus film *Solidarność, Solidarność* (*Solidarity, Solidarity...*, 2005), to which I will return in the last chapter of my book.
4. Subsequently I will use the word 'Party' (with the capital P) to indicate that I am referring to the PZPR, as opposed to any other party.
5. Kuron and Modzelewski use the term the 'central political bureaucracy' (Kuron and Modzelewski 1982: 15), Starski 'the class of state owners' and 'the Polish ruling class' (Starski 1982: 13–24).
6. The term 'they' is used in the title of the book of interviews with prominent communists conducted by Teresa Torańska (1989) and in the titles of two chapters in a book analysing letters of complaint sent to the important, although short-lived, post-October 1956 journal, *Po Prostu* (Leszczyński 2000).
7. Such a claim can be dismissed as a propagandistic lie perpetuated by the nomenklatura, concerned only about its position or anxious not to provoke Soviet intervention. That said, the

most successful series of workers' strikes in the early 1980s ultimately led to the demise of the Polish working class.
8. Symptomatic in this respect is Andrzej Wajda, who confessed that he is not only proud to belong to the intelligentsia, but to be a second-generation member (Mazierska 2002a).
9. In Poland it happened only once, in 1978 during the production of *Na srebrnym globie* (*On the Silver Globe*), Andrzej Żuławski's science fiction super-production. However, even on this occasion the main reason was not political, but economic, namely the fact that the director had significantly exceeded his budget in a situation of financial crisis. The film was eventually finished in 1987.

CHAPTER 3
The 1950s
Holy Work?

As already indicated, after the end of the Second World War Poland embarked on two principal tasks: rebuilding the country from the war devastation and changing its economy through nationalization, or state-ization, as it was described by its critics (Starski 1982: 10) and intensive industrialization. These objectives were implemented at the same time, but at different speeds. Initially the rebuilding was the priority, then nationalization and industrialization. The first ten to fifteen years of the People's Poland were also greatly affected by the rapidly changing international situation.

It is worth dividing this period into two parts. The first is marked by the Three-Year Plan (1947–1949), whose main purpose was to rebuild the country; its chief architect was a renowned economist, Czesław Bobrowski, who started his career in the prewar period. This plan was achieved and is regarded as the most efficient plan in the history of Polish socialism, which accounts for the acceptance, if not enthusiasm, of the population for the new order. This period also coincided with the upward mobility of a large part of the population, including the peasants who emigrated from the country to the cities and the new industrial centres (Starski 1982: 11–12; Narojek 1991: 5–33; Koryś 2007: 443–445). Unlike in the interwar period, which was marred by the lack of opportunities for social promotion for the proletariat and peasantry, after 1945 such opportunities were immense. The state embarked on a programme of training young people without any qualifications to become the new leaders of Polish industry. In 1949, the Party postulated that 15,000 ordinary workers should be promoted to managerial positions and special short training 'courses for a thousand' were organized to facilitate this goal. By 1954, 2,888 ordinary workers achieved this goal (Szczepański, quoted in Sobotka 1985: 38).

The Three-Year Plan partly coincided with the rule of Władysław Gomułka as leader of the Party. With his moderate stance in relation to collectivization and no close links to Moscow, he was seen as a Polish 'national communist'. This was in contrast to his successor, the Stalinist hardliner, Bolesław Bierut, to whom Gomulka lost his position in 1948. The reason for this shift was Stalin's concern about his loss of control over the satellite countries, not irrational in the light of the decision of the leader of Yugoslavia, Tito, to disobey Stalin and go along its own path to communism the same year. Stalin reacted to his loss of Yugoslavia by demanding purges from the communist parties across the whole socialist bloc which resulted in numerous executions or long-term prison sentences for real or suspected enemies of Stalin. Poland fell under the same rule, but it was distinctive for the mildness of the purge. Gomułka was denounced as a right-wing deviant and arrested, but his life was spared. The Soviets were possibly so indulgent because they remembered such events as the Polish-Soviet War of 1919–1921 and many other examples of Polish resistance to its eastern colonizers (Crampton 1997: 266). Poland was the largest of the Soviet satellites and conflict with this country, even if it carried only a small risk of overthrowing the communist system, might have drained the Soviet military, economic and human resources. The result of imprisoning Gomułka, at the same place where the leader of the Polish Catholic Church, Cardinal Stefan Wyszyński, was detained, was that when Stalinization in Poland finished in the mid-1950s, Poland had a 'new' leader ready, one who was seen as a national hero.

The purges at the top were mirrored by those on the lower rungs of the social ladder: in the factories, at the universities and in the army. Hundreds of thousands of people were imprisoned and many were executed. Factors such as having a family in the West, possessing private land or small business, or belonging to non-Leninist left-wing parties before the war rendered one especially vulnerable to the accusation of being an enemy of the state. The need for purges was justified by the Stalinist doctrine that the class struggle intensifies in the immediate aftermath of the socialist revolution and in the first stages of the construction of socialism. Furthermore, extra vigilance was required because of the danger of an attack from the West; the Cold War meant that the real war was expected any time.

The second postwar economic plan, the Six-Year Plan of 1950–1955, designed by a hardline Stalinist Hilary Minc, was implemented under these martial-like conditions. It was most ideologically driven of all Polish economic plans and its purpose was 'total modernisation' (Koryś 2007: 443), achieved through speedy industrialization, centralization and the eradication of the remnants of the market economy in trade and agriculture. The metaphor of fight was widely used at that time. Poles had to fight to fulfil the plan and prevent others from sabotaging their efforts. This metaphor was also widely used in film. Priority was given to heavy and military industry, symbolized by the building of Nowa Huta, the steelworks and the city near Kraków, which was meant to be a new type of city, inhabited by people free from religious prejudices and working in a new way. For the plan to be fulfilled, all spare labour had to be mobilized, most importantly the female workforce. The idea of gender equality, promoted by the classics of Marxism, turned out to be a convenient tool for extracting more work from society (Scott 1976; Fidelis 2010). Both men and women were expected to work overtime, indeed devote their entire life to work: work was rendered the new god.

Despite this immense pressure, the economic objectives of the Six-Year Plan were not achieved in full. The performance of the Polish economy during this period fell far below the performance level of not only capitalist countries but also its own performance during the Three-Year Plan. For example, in Nowa Huta steelworks, the planned output for 1955 was 750,000 tons of steel, whereas the actual output was 327,000 tons, i.e. 42 per cent of the target. In Nowy Targ shoe factory, the planned output for 1955 was 1.2 million pairs of shoes, but the actual output was only 8 per cent of the target (Zielinski 1973: 4). The relatively low production, especially of consumer goods, and the focus on heavy industry was reflected in the standard of living, which did not increase as much as people hoped. This led to widespread social unrest, culminating in the Poznań riots in 1956 (see chapter 4).

The state failed to collectivize agriculture, although it succeeded in considerably reducing private trade. However, as Piotr Koryś argues, despite all these failures, the Six-Year-Plan achieved its main ideological objective: it eradicated from the social consciousness an attachment to the market economy: 'In 1956 Polish society consisted of workers, fighting for their rights in the framework of the socialist economy and intellectuals, fighting for socialism with a human face. It lacked those who contested the economic and political foundations of the socialist state' (Koryś 2007: 36). It could be argued that it was during the Six-Year Plan that the socialist man was born.

Socialist Realism Polish Style

Film production in the first decade after the war was dominated by filmmakers active before 1939. As Bolesław Michałek observes, they represented two approaches to interwar cinema: broadly speaking those who saw cinema as a commercial institution whose main function was providing entertainment for the audience and those disdainful of commercial cinema. Representatives of the second approach strove to make artistic films, which would both express the individual vision of the filmmaker and actively shape the audiences' interests and tastes, and it was not immediately obvious whose vision would prevail (Michałek 1981: 119–120). Michałek suggests, however, that these two approaches can be mapped into two sub-periods of the first decade. The first period, dominated by the aim of innovating or even revolutionizing the cinema, is represented by films such as *Zakazane piosenki* (*Forbidden Songs*, 1947) by Leonard Buczkowski, and *Ostatni etap* (*The Last Stage*, 1948) by Wanda Jakubowska, and some 'butchered' projects, such as *Robinson warszawski* (*Warsaw Robinson*, 1950) by Jerzy Zarzycki, and *Dom na pustkowiu* (*The Lonely House*, 1949), directed by Jan Rybkowski (ibid.: 120–121). These films were concerned largely with the Second World War, therefore I omit them from my analysis. In the second period contemporary subjects dominate (ibid.: 121–122), and arguably they are made according to the tenets of socialist realism. They are exemplified by *Przygoda na Mariensztacie* (*An Adventure at Marienstadt*, 1954), directed by Leonard Buczkowski, *Sprawa do załatwienia* (*Matter to Be Settled*, 1953), directed by Jan Fethke and Jan Rybkowski, and *Irena do domu!* (*Irena Go Home*, 1955), directed by Jan Fethke. They were usually made by the filmmakers who in the interwar period belonged to the so-called prewar 'establishment' (*branża*) (Toeplitz 1964: 7; Hendrykowski 2002: 123–124; Zwierzchowski 2005: 119–150; Marszalek 2006: 47; Ostrowska 2006a: 59), namely those who specialized in producing popular, commercial films.

Given the highly ideological, pro-communist bias of these films, it might seem paradoxical that they were made by such un-ideological filmmakers. However, as the aforementioned authors argue, making them required the ability to adapt to the requirements of the financial backers (be it prewar commercially driven producers or postwar Party ideologues) and fill the imposed formula with attractive content. The ambition of socialist realism was the production of popular films, or rather socialist realism did not differentiate between popular and avant-garde films; all were meant to be popular (Taylor 1983). Given that the state had a monopoly on the production and distribution of films, this was a realistic goal. Finally, their approach to ideology, namely hiding it rather than laying it bare, was in tune with Stalinist culture, which was 'interested in the means by which the subconscious could be shaped without revealing the mechanism of the process' (Groys 1992: 43–44).

Socialist realism was created in the Soviet Union and from there it was exported to other socialist countries, where it was meant to develop into local variations. Its creation is attributed to Andrei Zhdanov, who was influenced by some Marxist thinkers such as Georg Lukacs. Zhdanov proclaimed in 1934, at the first all-union Congress of Soviet Writers, that

> *Socialist realism is the basic method of Soviet literature and literary criticism. It demands of the artist the truthful, historically concrete representation of reality in its revolutionary development. Moreover, the truthfulness and historical concreteness of the artistic representation of reality must be linked with the task of ideological transformation and education of workers in the spirit of socialism.* (quoted in Kenez 2001: 143)

The creators of socialist realistic films were required to focus on a typical (wo)man. However, 'typical' in this context does not mean 'average'; on the contrary, as expressed by Georgii Malenkov:

> *The typical is not that which is encountered most often, but that which most persuasively expresses the essence of a given social force. From the Marxist-Leninist standpoint, the typical does not signify some sort of statistical mean... The typical is the vital sphere in which is manifested the party spirit of realistic art. The question of the typical is always a political question.* (Malenkov, quoted in Groys 1992: 51–52)

The typical character of socialist realist art had to be above average and synthesize the most important aspects of his/her times, like a perfect prism, refracting the salient features of the current political and social situation. S/he should also show others a new direction either through fight or work, undertaken for the benefit of the collective. Because socialist art was required to focus on what was historical in the character's situation and personality, and most importantly in his/her class's position, it demanded that the other aspects of his/

her life be underplayed. Despite the popular opinion that socialist realist films were practically all the same, they varied, ranging from those who were truly novel in their content, form and spirit, such as East German *Roman einer jungen Ehe* (*Story of a Young Couple*, 1952) by Kurt Maetzig (Parvulescu 2015: 44–69), to others which conveyed a new ideology in an old package. The consensus is that the majority of Polish films felt short of novelty and distinctiveness. They have much in common with western films and interwar films. Their characters are constructed as in classical Hollywood cinema, which present psychologically defined individuals who struggle to solve a clear-cut problem or to attain specific goals. In the course of this struggle, the characters enter into conflict with others or with external circumstances. The story ends with a decisive victory or defeat, a resolution of the problem and a clear achievement or non achievement of the goals (Bordwell et al 1985: 16–17).

The dominant socialist realistic style is a version of neoclassicism, marked by 'restraint, stasis, clarity and rigidity' (Hanáková 2011: 148). Distinct seasons, such as summer and winter, are chosen over spring or autumn, because the world had reached its goal of 'becoming', and hence did not need to change (Margolit 2001: 31–32). Because of its classicism and the generally positive attitude to bourgeois artistic tradition, socialist realism is seen as conservative, as a step back in comparison with the Soviet avant-garde which preceded it. However, according to Boris Groys, it was in fact more revolutionary than the avant-garde. This is because, by comprehensively rejecting bourgeois art, the avant-garde recognized its importance as its main point of reference. By contrast, 'the absolute novelty of socialist realism needed no external, formal proof, for it followed from "the absolute novelty of the Soviet socialist order and the party agenda". Thus the novelty of Soviet art derived from the novelty of its content rather than any "bourgeois" novelty of form, which merely concealed an old, "bourgeois" content' (Groys 1992: 41).

One can thus observe a certain mismatch between the style and content of the majority of socialist realist films: the content is dynamic, the form is static. Thematically, the films 'deal with certain forms of emancipation, especially of three kinds: the establishment of equality between the city and the country (the workers and the peasants), between the manual and intellectual workers and between men and women' (Hanáková 2011: 148). In Polish socialist realist films common characters are incomers from the countryside who find employment on building sites, in steel production and coalmining, inevitably in large factories.

Work is thus their main subject. Usually young characters are cast in principal roles because they are not contaminated by the values and working practices of capitalist times and embody opportunities for social advancement (Sobotka 1985: 39–40). As Katerina Clark observes, a typical socialist realist film follows the tradition of *Bildungsroman*; it shows character's maturation by achieving harmony within himself and in relation to his society (Clark 1981: 17). However, it is not only young people that mature but older people too, and the roles of the mentor/pupil are often reversed, with the young teaching the old about the advantages of socialism. Women are represented roughly as often as men, but they tend to be endowed with a more important role within the narrative than their male counterparts, to point to the opportunities for women's emancipation brought about by socialism, and their role as the educators of their conservative spouses and fellow workers.

Socialist realism in Polish cinema lasted from the end of the 1940s till the mid-1950s. Its beginning is marked by such events as Bolesław Bierut's speech during the opening of the radio station in Wrocław, in 1947, and the Congress of Polish writers in Szczecin and Polish filmmakers, in Wisła, both in 1949 (Sobotka 1985: 27; Madej 1997). However, socialist realist films did not appear in 1949 or 1950. Some filmmakers anticipated the new trend before it was pronounced official, as in *Stalowe serca* (*Hearts of Steel*, 1948), directed by Stanisław Januszewski. Neither did socialist realist films disappear suddenly, but were produced practically throughout the whole of the state socialist period. However, their status shifted from the hegemonic to the residual by the mid- to late 1950s and their style, characters and ideology mutated in step with the political, economic and cultural changes in Poland. This is reflected in their contamination by other styles, such as existentialism, romanticism and surrealism, as in Andrzej Wajda's *Pokolenie* (*A Generation*, 1954), *Baza ludzi umarłych* (*The Depot of the Dead*, 1959) by Czesław Petelski, and Wojciech Has's *Złoto* (*Gold*, 1961). This poses the question of where to locate such socialist realist hybrids. I decided to discuss *The Depot of the Dead* in this chapter and *Gold* in the next, partly on account of chronology, as the first film was made in the 1950s, the second in the 1960s, and partly because more connects Petelski's film with socialist realist tenets than with the cinema of the 1960s, while *Gold* is stylistically closer to the New Wave.

Socialist realism was meant to adapt to the local specificities. According to Jerzy Toeplitz this did not happen either in Poland or elsewhere; if an outsider watched a socialist realist film without sound, s/he would not know whether the film came from Poland or Bulgaria (Toeplitz 1964: 8–9). This is a huge exaggeration and the perceived similarities in socialist realist films reflected on the similarities between the situation in different socialist countries and the Soviet Union, such as the general backwardness, the privileging of heavy industry, and the mobilization of women into the workforce. For example, Victoria Bonnell notices that a blacksmith (and by extension a steelworker) occupied a privileged position in Soviet posters because he belonged to the workers' elite in capitalist times, merged contemplation with action and acted as a metaphor for the forging of the new socialist man (Bonnell 1997: 24–32). Not surprisingly, steelworkers also feature heavily in Polish socialist art.

Although work was exalted in the official ideology of state socialism, and even became seen as 'holy', it posed a challenge to representation. After all, work can be painful, exhausting or at best boring. By and large, as Jean-Luc Comolli observes, work does not excite viewers (quoted in O'Shaughnessy 2012: 156). This is confirmed by the fact that during the period of socialist realism in the Soviet Union, only twelve 'construction dramas' were produced (Kenez 2001: 148). The same situation applied to Polish cinema. As Tadeusz Lubelski notices, from 1950 to 1954 only twenty-three new Polish films had their premiere (Lubelski 2009a: 145). Their makers' answer to the question of how to present work in a positive and exciting way to the viewers was to merge the 'boring' (work) with the 'exciting' (non-work), either by showing work and non-work side by side or by rendering work as non-work, as an adventure or pleasure. Viewers were also lured by using popular genres, such as musicals, criminal stories, comedy or melodrama (Talarczyk-Gubała 2007: 37–58; Stachówna 2008). The blatant way in which the films attempted to do this, combined with their political conformism, ensured that their status was lower among Polish film critics than film viewers. Their low status is conveyed by their label: *produkcyjniaki*. The closest translation is 'production films', but with an added layer of scorn, suggesting that not only do they depict material production, but they are themselves mass produced. This is despite the aforementioned fact that the cinematic conveyor belt did not work very effectively, as proven by the modest output of 'production films'.

Socialist realist films were meant not only to promote state socialism, but more specifically to assist the state in fulfilling the Six-Year Plan. For this reason the films commend the value of specific enterprises in heavy industry, such as building the steelworks in Nowa Huta (the most common subject of documentary films), and extol specific working practices, promoted by the authorities, such as socialist competition.

Building the New Poland

I shall begin my discussion with *Dwie brygady* (*Two Teams*, 1950), a socialist realist film about socialist realist art which not only reflects on the lives of workers but also transforms their lives. The idea of breaking the division between art and life applies not only to socialist realism, but also to the avant-garde (Bürger 1994: 57–58). Consequently, it is argued that socialist realist art fulfils some of the crucial ambitions of the avant-garde and in the Soviet context can be even seen as a continuation of the avant-garde of the 1920s (Groys 1992: 36).[1]

The film was scripted and directed by a group of students from the Łódź Film School under the supervision of Eugeniusz Cękalski. Its subject is the staging of a theatre play, *Brygada szlifierza Karhana* (*The Team of the Grinder Karhan*, 1949) by Czech playwright Vašek Káňa, regarded at the time as one the greatest achievements of socialist realist art.[2] The play and the film are concerned with the conflict between a team of young workers and their older foreman, Karhan. At the same time, it is about the conflict between working old style, fast enough to fulfil one's duty and earn one's living, and working in a socialist way, at a frantic pace, to fulfil one's quota early so that more can be achieved in a shorter time. The same conflict exists in the theatre. The actor who is meant to play Karhan also works old style, delivering his lines in an exaggerated, theatrical way, disrespecting the way in which real workers speak and behave. Like the older workers, he needs persuasion to act in the new way. This only happens when he starts visiting the factory and observing productive work. At the same time, the blue collar workers go to rehearsals and observe the actors' work. In this way they learn to appreciate 'unproductive' work, noticing that people who work in the theatre encounter similar problems to those working in a factory, such as the requirement to produce a complex commodity at short notice. The manual workers face the challenge of the plan; the theatre employees must be ready for the premiere. Up until the last moment the latter lack their most important prop, the grinding machine, not unlike the socialist workers who suffer from the lack of material and tools. Even the manner of obtaining this machine turns out to be very 'real socialist': the theatre director phones the cabinet minister, asking him to use his personal authority to ensure that the precious commodity is sent on time. Watching the rehearsals also allows the workers to better understand their own work and their place in the wider scheme of things. This applies especially to the older foreman who is chosen by the older actor as his model. Similarly, like the older actor who initially feels humiliated by the criticism of his younger colleagues and does not want to change his ways, the older factory worker does not want his attitude to be exposed and criticized publicly. All ends well, because the older workers realize that learning from the young does them good and the young convince the older workers that they are still useful and able to innovate. What ultimately matters is not who has the upper hand in the factory or the theatre, but the joint work for the common good. The supremacy of the young is thus presented not as a means of changing the structure of power in a factory, but of furthering the country's economic and social development. The ethos of working in the factory and the theatre is anti-individualistic; individual success matters only inasmuch as it furthers the success of the community.

The generational dynamics presented in *Two Teams* reflects the relationships in the production of the film. Eugeniusz Cękalski, the mentor for the team of young filmmakers involved in this production, was before the Second World War a member of START and the main creator of *The Ghosts*, widely regarded as the best Polish film of the interbellum (discussed in chapter 2). However, after the Second World War he was primarily involved in pedagogic work and administration of the Polish film industry. The handful of films he made after 1945 are documentaries and *Two Teams* is his only foray into fiction filmmaking during this period. *Two Teams* can thus be seen as a work about passing the baton from the old to the young and the need to do it in a friendly manner.

In an article written for the occasion of the film's premiere for the popular weekly *Film*, Cękalski himself draws attention to the parallels between the subject of the film and its production. He begins with a pronouncement that the shooting was finished twenty-five days before the deadline (Cękalski 1950: 8). In this way he accepts that film and any work of art should be assessed according to the same criteria as material products. That said, Cękalski admits that hurrying might be counterproductive to quality, although most likely this was not the case on this occasion; this was an opinion shared by the reviewers, including the eminent writer, Tadeusz Konwicki (Konwicki 1950) and leading critic and fellow START member, Jerzy Toeplitz (Toeplitz 1950). Practically all of them admitted that *Two*

Teams is not a perfect film, but it was not meant to be, being an experiment in work and art, a kind of work of progress – as was socialism in Poland.

Cękalski mentions that collective discussions, including some with the metal workers from Strzelczyk Mechanical Workshop in Łódź, strongly affected the film's production (ibid.: 9; see also Mruklik 1974: 231; Sobotka 1985: 43). The antagonism between the young and the old workers, which *Two Teams* shows, was a common problem in Poland at the time. Błażej Brzostek in his study of Warsaw workers in the years 1950–1954, drawing on research by Halina Najduchowska, mentions that the older workers who remembered the interbellum period, complained that the quality of work had gone down: quantity thwarted quality (Brzostek 2002: 69–71). Their attachment to the interwar work ethic made them suspicious in the eyes of the socialist ideologues and managers. At the same time they were still needed as specialists (ibid.: 71). In this sense their position mirrored that of the many Polish filmmakers active in the postwar period, especially the 'professionals': their ideological credentials were dubious, but their expert knowledge rendered them very useful in the new reality. *Two Teams* is perhaps the closest to the idea of socialist work due to its focus on practice (or praxis, to use the Marxist term) and collective work endeavour as a means of changing material reality and human consciousness. However, from this perspective it does not go far enough. It would have been more progressive or revolutionary if its characters had moved beyond observing each others' working practices and actually started to work together or exchange places, with the actors performing in the factory rather than in a theatre which is a bourgeois institution.[3]

Although the main subject of *Two Teams* is work, it touches on the subject of leisure. In the 1950s, leisure was seen as an appendage to work in at least two senses. Firstly, the workers had to work extra hard to create space and time for leisure. Secondly, the time and space of leisure were not meant to be used for pure relaxation, for doing nothing, but for self-improvement. As David Crowley argues, under socialism

> *Even the extent of privacy was to be parsed. The meagre proportions and limited facilities of the single-family apartments – the main unit of all new housing provision – were sometimes explained in terms of the new society being constructed in Poland. Leisure was no longer to be appropriated from the commonweal for private enjoyment, but was to be appointed outside the home for the collective good. Olgierd Szlekys, a prominent furniture designer, explained*

in 1955: '[In socialist Poland] we have changed the forms of our life. We have moved private life to the houses of culture, to clubs and cafes which are places replacing, we say, the old salons'. (Crowley 2002: 188)

In line with this description, leisure in *Two Teams* is fully integrated into socialist work. In their free time workers go to the theatre to watch the rehearsals and, finally, the finished play. And conversely, the artists staging the play use the workers' free time (or perhaps the time of work which was freed so that they can participate in culture) to improve on their performance. It thus feels like no minute of the workers' lives is 'wasted' for autonomous pursuits. Such an approach to leisure is not exclusive to Poland or state socialism. Theodor Adorno, in his essay 'Free Time', claims that leisure under capitalism is also merely an appendage to work and its ultimate purpose is increasing workers' productivity (Adorno 1991: 164–165). However, under capitalism, as Adorno argues, leisure is filled with shallow entertainment, so that it allows the employees to temporarily forget about alienated work and return to work rested. Under socialism in this particular period, as *Two Teams* shows, leisure helps society to realize why socialist work eludes alienation and how to work better. As I will demonstrate in due course, with the passage of time, leisure in Poland gained in autonomy, became privatized and filled with escapist pleasures, and started to resemble leisure as described by the critics of capitalism, such as Adorno, Herbert Marcuse or Guy Debord.

The scheme of *Bildungsroman*, with the older people maturing thanks to the influence of the young, is also used in *Przygoda na Mariensztacie* (*An Adventure at Marienstadt*, 1954), directed by Leonard Buczkowski, a romantic comedy with music, which commercially was the most successful Polish socialist realist film, still very popular with Polish audiences (Lubelski 2009a: 149). In comparison with *Two Teams*, the film introduces a new element: gender equality. Piotr Zwierzchowski begins a discussion of *An Adventure at Marienstadt* with such words:

> He – strong hands, holding a hammer and a trowel, proudly gazing into the future. She – a girl from the countryside. Her hand holding a sickle; song on her lips. Where we know this image from? The first association is with the sign of Mosfilm. But there are also associations closer to home. This can be Janek Szarliński and Hanka Ruczajówna – the characters in *An Adventure at Marienstadt*. (Zwierzchowski 2000: 125)

Indeed, the story presented in Buczkowski's film has much in common with a formula tested previously in Soviet art, especially the musical comedies of the 1930s, as it concerns social advancement and personal fulfilment. Although unusually successful for a socialist realistic film, it is typical in its concern with women's emancipation. Such films were very common both in Poland and across the whole socialist bloc (Ostrowska 2006a; Hanáková 2011). According to Hanáková, the heroines of such films, the bricklayers, tractor drivers, engineers, etc., acted as embodiments of the revolutionary change:

> *The exemplary figure [in those films] is the young single woman who, like the proverbial jackfish, forces the potbellied and slow-swimming carps in the pond to move. She understands the greatness of the new tasks and undertakes them with joy, as they form part of a broader project of the socialist future. ... Socialist realist films picture women successfully entering the workplace, becoming politically active and winning the heart of a man who shares their modern attitude to life, thus also revolutionizing their domestic division of roles.* (Hanáková 2011: 151)

In *An Adventure at Marienstadt* the revolution in gender roles is combined with the motif of the advancement of the peasantry by moving to the city. The film begins with a folk group from the province visiting Warsaw to take part in a music festival. Such folk festivals are common in socialist realist films and they point to the previously mentioned fact that leisure under socialism was expected to be consumed communally, in public spaces. They were also meant to give the impression of socialist authorities embracing national and regional variations of the dominant (socialist) culture (Toeplitz 1964: 8). However, they can also be read as pointing to the process of the 'museumisation' of such 'minor cultures' (Näripea 2008: 199), in this case the reification of the Polish countryside, as opposed to treating it as a space of living culture. Indeed, this message that the Polish country is stuck in the past while the rest of the country moves forward fast is also conveyed in the trajectory of its main protagonist.

The members of the folk band use their trip to Warsaw as an opportunity for a touristic exploration of the capital, which at the time was still in the process of rebuilding, including the titular Marienstadt (Polish Mariensztat), a district in the centre of Warsaw which was razed to the ground during the Warsaw Uprising in 1944. The district, like the whole centre of Warsaw, was meant to be populated by the members of the working class, according to the important statement of the policy, 'Six-Year Plan for the Reconstruction of Warsaw' (*Sześcioletni plan odbudowy Warszawy*), credited to the authorship of the Party leader himself, Bolesław Bierut. David Crowley maintains that

> Bierut expressed the ideological significance of the new housing in terms of its potential to redress historic wrongs. No longer was the centre of the city to be the domain of the bourgeoisie: the 'workers' capital' was to be reclaimed in a great programme of social engineering. As if in opposition to the pattern of suburban drift found in the West, Stalinist planning claimed to encourage the return of the workers to the centre of the city to enjoy cultural lives. (Crowley 2002: 183)

As if to illustrate the point that under communist authorities the centre of Warsaw belongs to the working class, Hanka wanders to Marienstadt and there

Illustration 3.1: Hanka and Janek building Warsaw in *An Adventure at Marienstadt*, directed by Leonard Buczkowski

encounters Janek Szarliński, a worker with whom she falls in love practically on the spot. After that we see her briefly back in her home village, working in the field. Work there, with no machines and involving mainly womenfolk, comes across as unrewarding and backward. Not surprisingly, the next shot shows Hanka on the train to Warsaw. Her migration is thus a solution to three problems: the overpopulation of the Polish countryside, the need to rebuild Warsaw, and women's emancipation. The rest of the film follows her budding romance with Janek and recognition of Hanka as a valuable worker, which requires changing the mindset of older male workers. All of this is achieved in the end, although not without struggle. Indeed, struggle, physical and mental, is needed to create a 'new personality'. The film shows that nobody is born a communist; one becomes one through praxis.

The success of this film consists of 'selling' the dominant ideology as if it was common sense, a fact appreciated by the reviewers who emphasized it being a 'light comedy', not unlike many Polish comedies produced in the interwar years (Merz 1954; Morawski 1954). The film promotes the idea that women should not only work but should perform similar jobs to men, achieve similar results and aim at positions of power previously reserved for men. Such an ideological project was a reflection of Marx and Engels' views on the lack of equality between men and women under the capitalist system, which communism was meant to reverse, and also a practical means to boost employment. However, gender equality in the spirit of Marx does not mean mechanically attributing the same tasks to women and men, but rather maximizing the chances of the fulfilment of women and equal recognition for their input to the communal welfare. For many feminists and socialists gender equality Stalinist style comes across as a travesty of Marxist ideas. *An Adventure at Marienstadt* refers to the concept of equality understood in such a mechanical, Stalinist way. What is thus at stake is women's ability to match men's achievements in bricklaying, the profession which Hanka chooses upon her arrival in Warsaw. This is both Hanka's ambition and that of Janek, with whom she initially works in the same team. Janek is a shock worker and at the beginning of the film is fulfilling 322 per cent of the bricklaying quota. When this drops below 300 per cent, it is viewed by his foreman Ciepielewski as a failure, caused by Janek's collaboration with Hanka. Ciepielewski, according to the socialist realist rule that older people possess outmoded views, is an old-school patriarch, who does not allow his wife to work outside the home and does not accept that women in Poland work in professions which were previously considered masculine, such as driving buses and trams. As a result of Ciepielewski's hostile attitude to women, Hanka joins an all-female team led by Rębaczowa. We thus see that although men and women work on the same building site, they do not really work together. Such a ghettoization of women encapsulates the state socialist approach to female employment: they were allowed into the masculine world of work, but were not fully integrated into it, which meant, for example, that they were paid less than men even if they worked in the same profession. However, *An Adventure at Marienstadt* shows not the real, but the ideal world, in which women outperform men and are rewarded according to their achievements. During Ciepielewski's peregrination through Warsaw, he encounters women working in traditionally male professions and ends his journey meeting a female director of the enterprise responsible for all construction work in Warsaw. Ironically, he tried to contact her (thinking the director was male) to complain about female power.

Rębaczowa's team achieves extraordinary results, applauded in the main Party paper, *Trybuna Ludu*, which greatly annoys Ciepielewski. Nevertheless, there are limits to women's opportunities, and they are to do with what can be described as 'horizontal progression', namely reaching positions of power in political structures. In such structures we see only men. The person addressed as 'comrade', who is most likely the first secretary of the Party organization in the building firm, is male, as are the political dignitaries, including the minister who is invited to the opening of the 'Bricklayer's House'. This pattern can be observed in other Polish socialist realist films, as well as in workplaces shown in later Polish films. In *An Adventure at Marienstadt* this comrade acts as an adjudicator and mentor, extinguishing conflicts between the workers and advising them on their private lives. It is he who states that 'love is a private initiative which we can accommodate in our industrial plans' and 'let them (Hanka and Janek) love each other – this way it is better for them and for us'. Such statements point to the totalizing character of the communist state which takes care of all aspects of citizen's lives. In due course the system of such total care would be accused not only of limiting the agency of those who were subjected to it, but also of producing the despised 'homo sovieticus'. In *An Adventure at Marienstadt*, however, this is given a positive spin – proof that after many years of misery and homelessness (of which the ruins of Warsaw are still a potent sign), Poles eventually found their home or safe haven in the socialist state. Although love between the workers is permitted, families with children are practically absent from Polish socialist realist films, as is the case with other Eastern European cinemas of the time (on Czech cinema, see Hanáková

2011). One guesses that the presence of children might undermine the idea that work is the most important thing in the lives of both men and women (Marszałek 2006: 46–48). Indeed, this was the case; the socialist countries with the highest proportion of working women suffered also from an underpopulation crisis (Scott 1976: 138–163).

Both Hanka and Janek are physically attractive, but they are represented differently. Hanka always wears modest clothes, which hide her physical allure. Janek, on the other hand, played by an athletic actor Tadeusz Szmidt, clad in a tight working vest, comes across as a Greek hero. When looking at and listening to them (Janek is rather shy and inarticulate), one gets the impression that under state socialism it was not so much gender equality that was achieved as a reversal of roles, with women being relocated from nature to culture and men representing wild nature. However, while Tarzan-like male heroes are the norm in socialist realist cinema, in Polish cinema they are a rarity, perhaps due to the fact that Polish filmmakers never truly warmed towards socialist realism and were unwilling to show nudity, even when ideology permitted.

Poland of state socialism was not only meant to ensure gender equality, but also achieve a classless society, based on the alliance between the workers and the peasants (*sojusz robotniczo-chłopski*). The situation of the intelligentsia in this scheme of things was somewhat ambiguous. On the one hand, renaming it the 'working intelligentsia' suggested that its position was similar to that of the workers. On the other hand, putting the utility of productive work higher than that of unproductive work rendered it less important and subservient to the needs of industrial workers. In *An Adventure at Marienstadt* this line of thinking is conveyed during the ceremony of awarding citizens the keys to their new apartments. Amongst the lucky ones are mostly manual workers who exceeded their quota, and forewomen in charge of exceptional teams. Still, one gets a sense that all of them are ordinary workers, with the same education and mental abilities. Among those awarded there is also one described as a 'man of letters' (*literat*). Such distribution of the awards points to the principle of tokenism, leaving some margin of recognition for less 'deserving' people. In both situations of working and getting an apartment people give and receive, rather than sell and buy, as is the case under capitalism.[4] Those who receive are, broadly speaking, the deserving ones, because of their hard work or their needs. *An Adventure at Marienstadt* plays up the first reason; in films made in the subsequent decades the second will be brought to the fore, usually as a way of showing how homo sovieticus types try to jump the queue for the deficit goods.

For Marx there are two principal reasons why work under capitalism is alienated. One is its sheer unpleasantness: the pain which is inflicted on the worker in a factory, leading to the fatigue of his muscles, not mentioning the pain and disability resulting from industrial accidents. The second is the lack of ownership; the worker under capitalism owns neither the means of production nor the fruit of her labour and is paid less than the product of her work is worth. By contrast, in *An Adventure at Marienstadt* the work appears to be pleasant. We never see the workers exhausted, as testified by their striving to exceed their quota. Although no specific artistic production takes place at the construction site, the site itself comes across as a stage, with builders laying bricks to the rhythm of music, as if overcoming the opposition between work and art. If we regard the construction site as a metaphor of the country, which at the time was undergoing material and ideological reconstruction, then we can conjecture that this process was easy and quasi-artistic.

In *An Adventure at Marienstadt* the workers claim that they own the fruit of their work. During her first meeting with Janek, Hanka hears that it is 'his Warsaw', because he is building it. Later we hear that 'this apartment block is mine', and this perception is confirmed by the builders leaving personal mementoes in the walls they are erecting. One cannot imagine a similar statement uttered by builders in Manchester or London. Buczkowski makes sure that such statements are supported by the (filmic) facts, most importantly by rewarding the builders with the keys to their own apartments.

The peak of the builders' success is erecting the Bricklayer's House, which is meant to include a library and a nursery for the workers' children, and to be the centre of the cultural life of the construction workers. The builders built it in their spare time, using 'saved' material. How this material was saved is not explained in the film, but a cynic might wonder whether it was not at the expense of the standard of the apartment blocks, in reality notorious for their low quality (as shown in many films of the 1970s and 1980s). The opening of the Bricklayer's House provides the grand finale of Buczkowski's film. This building has high ceilings, large chandeliers and is decorated with pseudo-Greek sculptures of working people. It can be described as a synthesis of what was supposedly the best in earlier periods, pointing to the fact that socialist realism did not need to reject bourgeois art to prove its originality, as Groys notes. There is a parallel between this hybrid building and *An Adventure at Marienstadt*, which is 'erected' by a veteran and merges the old, prewar style with the new content, as if to announce that to rebuild the country one has to be practical rather than dogmatic.

If we regard *An Adventure at Marienstadt* as the first Polish postwar musical, as it is often presented, then it is worth asking the question of whether it fits a certain pattern of Polish musicals, which is different from the American model. According to Robert Altman, American musicals are based on a duality of work and entertainment because work in American culture is the highest value. This is epitomized by self-referential musicals about preparing and staging shows, where artists-workers are sweating from exertion and suffer from accidents. A magical spectacle is in such case a reward for hard work, albeit that of only few particularly gifted artists, rather than the whole range of people, including technicians and manual workers (Altman 1987: 208–209). In Polish musicals, by contrast, as Piotr Fortuna maintains, we rarely see hard work and we barely see the viewers' enjoying the show, as the audience tends to yawn or talk during the performance. Fortuna explains the eschewing of both work and spectacle by a low work ethics under state socialism, including that of filmmakers who did not need to struggle to attract the audience (Fortuna 2015: 123). This might be the case, but another explanation might be the porous boundary between work and leisure, as previously mentioned. Whatever the reason, Fortuna's diagnosis fits later Polish musicals better. In *An Adventure at Marienstadt* we see more hard work and more enjoyment from looking at spectacles than in musicals produced in the 1960s, 1970s and 1980s.

The Problems of Polish Socialism and How to Overcome Them

While in *Two Teams* and *An Adventure at Marienstadt* everybody works well and is fully committed to the project of building socialist Poland, even if slightly hampered by old-style thinking, *Sprawa do załatwienia* (*Matter to Be Settled*, 1953), directed by Jan Fethke and Jan Rybkowski, focuses on those who are not integrated into the socialist project. Such a topic is facilitated by the film's genre – comedy. Comedy by its nature shows the world in a distorting mirror, exaggerating reality's negative traits. It is up to the viewer to decide to what extent it reflects the status quo.

In a similar way to *Two Teams*, *Matter to Be Settled* brings together representatives of two professional groups, who under capitalism would belong to two different classes: industrial and cultural workers. Zofia Lipińska works in a shoe factory somewhere in the provinces; Stefan Wiśniewski is a radio and television journalist. They meet for the first time when he visits her factory to prepare a report on a typical, hence excellent socialist enterprise, because under socialist realism everything has to be typical, yet very positive. This trait is revealed in the choice of the main protagonist – Zofia is the prettiest and most articulate of all the female workers. Yet, despite her assets, she is still tutored by the young journalist, who tells her what to say. By the same token, his method of work epitomizes the socialist realist method, in which nothing can be shown as it is, everything has to be staged. In one episode Stefan asks Zofia how she spends her free time and tells her to say that her free time is integrated into her working time. True to this statement, the rest of the film is filled with Zofia's trip to Warsaw, which can be classified as both work and leisure: fulfilling an assignment and engaging in tourism. She goes to Warsaw to get a piano for her workers' club, which would allow its members to take part in a competition for amateur groups. As in *An Adventure at Marienstadt*, the workers' leisure is thus communal, active and highly cultural.

Illustration 3.2: Adolf Dymsza in *Matter to Be Settled*, directed by Jan Fethke and Jan Rybkowski

Zofia's assignment turns out to be difficult to fulfil, because of obstacles created by various enemies of socialism whom she encounters on her way: lazy bureaucrats, chatterboxes, people buying deficit goods to sell them at a profit (*spekulanci*), taxi drivers taking only those passengers who go where it suits the drivers, and rude waiters who favour their acquaintances at the expense of ordinary customers. However, we do not find here any 'hardcore' enemies of socialism, such as foreign spies or rich peasants opposing collectivization of the land (*kułacy*), most likely because their activities were not seen as a laughing matter (Płażewski 1953: 8). All these 'minor enemies' of socialism are played by the same actor, Adolf Dymsza, one of the most popular actors of the interwar period.

Back then Dymsza frequently played a 'Warsaw fixer', who tried to make his living by outsmarting his opponents. In *Matter to Be Settled* he revisits this role, but unlike in the interwar films, when he was treated with sympathy because he stood alone against the might of foreign bureaucracies, in Fethke and Rybkowski's film he is put in a negative light, because now his ethos collides with that of state socialism. As Fethke and Rybkowski show, 'Dymsza' is not alone. There are many people prone to the same vices: laziness, excessive bureaucracy, avoiding responsibility and privatization of the public space. This might be a matter of personal attitudes, but is also a consequence of the system's shortcomings. For example, the shortage of consumer goods leads to the temptation to make an extra profit (Mazurek 2013). The film also shows that the shortage of labour force and the policy of full employment leads to a blasé attitude to one's work. Downgrading money as the main measure of goods results in excessive bureaucracy, which in theory is meant to ensure equality in distribution of goods, but in practice makes the lives of customers troublesome, fails to use people's skills appropriately, and provides fertile ground for corruption.

Matter to Be Settled is one of the earliest films made in socialist Poland to refer to the second economy. Some aspects of this economy are ridiculed in the film by showing that the supposedly western products sold illegally are of inferior type to the socialist commodities. Nevertheless, Fethke and Rybkowski point to the fact that after the war the West functioned in the minds of the Easterners as a consumer's paradise, a notion which the ideologues of state socialism were unable to quash. The film does not provide any answer as to how to eradicate the workers' vices, apart from appealing to their morality, which was the main strategy of the socialist authorities at the time, along with punishing the 'sinners' by confiscating their products, fines and jail sentences, as opposed to introducing elements of a market economy, making money more 'real'.

In the world created by Fethke and Rybkowski, positions of power are occupied by men, while women, like ordinary bees or ants, engage in mundane and lower paid work; this is the case with Zofia, who is an ordinary shopfloor worker. While some men also have similar humble occupations, others work as directors in large state institutions, foremen and radio reporters. Judging by the data concerning female occupation under socialism, *Matter to Be Settled* offers a more reliable picture than *An Adventure at Marienstadt*. By the early 1950s the idea of women replacing men in male occupations and positions of power was quietly abandoned and many women who before worked in male professions were demoted from their jobs, often on the grounds of health and safety, which meant lowering their salary and standard of living (Fidelis 2010: 1–5 and 130–169). At the same time, the question of gender equality was removed from the political agenda on the grounds that under socialism it had been resolved.

While in the provinces work, leisure and art are integrated, in metropolitan Warsaw we observe their separation. This is presented in an episode when Zofia, during her journey through the radio and television studio, encounters the filming of various programmes[5] and we get an insight into Stefan's work. We see the shooting of a traditional ballet and Stefan reporting from a holiday camp for children, as if he was there, although in reality he is elsewhere and only invents what the children are doing. Such a manner of reporting might be seen as a commentary on the overall character of socialist realist art as an art of projecting a desired world by those who themselves are removed from the proletariat.

Nationalizing the Countryside

In those films set in cities, nationalization of the means of production does not constitute a problem; it is taken for granted because it was widely accepted as a pragmatic measure. The situation is different in those films set in the countryside, where for many years after the war a fierce struggle concerning the character and scale of collectivization took place.

The struggle was ultimately won by the Polish peasants, who, after suffering serfdom and poverty for centuries, did not want to give up their plots of land. The authorities allowed private ownership of land initially as an intermediary measure, assuming that soon the peasants would give up their properties, as happened in the Soviet Union and other Eastern European countries, according to the Stalin's idea that under communism 'agrarian-industrial associations will gradually emerge, ... agriculture will combine organically with the industrial processing of its produce' and 'the kolkhoz villages will grow into amalgamated urban communities', leading to the 'elimination of socio-economic and cultural distinctions between town and country' (Stalin 1961: 438–439). Later, however, privately-owned farms were treated as a more or less permanent fixture of the Polish economy and the best way to ensure Poland's self-sufficiency of food. This does not mean that Polish farmers were against all forms of collaboration or self-help in the countryside. Poland enjoyed a long tradition, reaching as far back as the 1860s, of so called 'farmers' circles' (kółka rolnicze), self-help organizations which owned expensive machinery and offered individual farmers advice concerning methods of farming, financial assistance and general education. After the war the authorities wanted to use them as vehicles for full-scale collectivization, but without success and in 1956 the farmers' circles were reactivated in more or less their original form.[6]

Collectivization is the subject of a number of films from the 1950s, such as *Gromada* (*The Village Mill*, 1952), directed by Jerzy Kawalerowicz, *Jasne łany* (*Fair Cornfields*, 1947), directed by Eugeniusz Cękalski, *Trudna miłość* (*Difficult Love*, 1954), directed by Stanisław Różewicz, and *Pożegnanie z diabłem* (*Farewell to Devil*, 1957), directed by Wanda Jakubowska. The number of films about the countryside seems to be significant, given the low number of Polish socialist realist films overall. However, it is low in the light of the fact that at this time the majority of Poles belonged to the rural population. As with other socialist realistic works, the characters in these films are divided into neat categories: *kułacy*, the middle peasants and small holders. Those belonging to the last category are too poor to be self-sufficient and have to borrow from the rich and repay them with interest, which exacerbates the economic and social contrasts in the countryside. This situation could only be reversed by the intervention of an experienced communist, usually coming from outside the peasant community (Pełczyński 2002: 26–29). *The Village Mill* fits this pattern well. The conflict revolves around building a second cooperative mill in a village, as a means of fulfilling the farmers' needs and ensuring that they get flour at a reasonable price. This project acts as a symbol of collective welfare or even of communism itself, according to the rule that the workplace in Polish cinema acts as a metaphor of the country. The first mill belongs to the *kułak* Zieliński, who overcharges his neighbours, taking advantage of his monopoly position. He is modelled on a feudal lord, who tries to bring the poorer peasants into debt to such an extent that they stop being able to work for themselves and have to transfer all the fruits of their work to their 'master'. We see it already happening – one of the peasants owes Zieliński so much that he has to pass all his harvest to the rich peasant and still has to repay him with extra work in order to get even. However, unlike the Polish feudal lords, who had their beautiful mansions and good manners, Zieliński personifies naked greed. He is like a capitalist operating in the countryside. This reflects the fact that the main ideological enemies of the socialist systems at the time were no longer (prewar) gentry, as this class had been wiped out, but small capitalists, whose birth was facilitated by the shortcomings of the socialist economy.

Zieliński uses bribery, blackmail and sabotage to prevent the peasants' initiative, of which the most spectacular example is the destruction of a road to the new mill on the grounds that he bought the land with the road. The fight over the mill is also an ideological struggle over the souls of middle peasants, who hesitate between supporting the *kułak* and forging alliances with those in favour of collectivization. The background to these larger narratives is a melodrama centred on Maryśka, the daughter of a middle peasant, who against the will of her father chooses a boy from the 'progressive side'. According to the socialist scenario, the villain is defeated despite his extensive plotting, and the mill is built. Although a substantial part of the film is filled with meetings of the collective, styled on party meetings in the factories, we also see farmers working in the fields and in the mill. Women are as busy in the fields as men, and according to the patriarchal tradition, they are also allocated the bulk of the housework. Predictably, at the meetings men do all the (ideological) work and make all the important decisions.

The plot of *The Village Mill* is formulaic, with too much evil accumulated in a single character, yet the film was retrospectively praised by critics due to its realism in representing the Polish countryside, achieved by shooting it on location in Podhale region and casting real farmers in the secondary parts (Mruklik 1974: 236). In addition, true to its original title, which means 'collective' or 'crowd', the film frequently shows large groups of people working in harmony with nature and each other. Apart from Zieliński, *The Village Mill* does not have an individual character; the peasants come across as a musical band, which is united but in which each member has a chance to act as an individual. Other Polish films belonging to socialism realism attempted to achieve this communal effect, but in

Kawalerowicz's film it comes across as most natural, perhaps reflecting the ethos of working in the fields, which is indeed communal, or rather used to be before it was mechanized.

The Speechless Workers

Documentary films gained in importance in Poland after the Second World War. This was to do with their perceived educational and propagandistic value. In this period Poland had a large film studio devoted to the production of documentary films, Wytwórnia Filmów Dokumentalnych, set up in 1949. It was known as Chełmska Studio, from the street in Warsaw where it was based. There hundreds of documentary films were made, as well as thousands of hours of Polish newsreels (Polska Kronika Filmow). Their production increased from 1958, when film theatres in Poland were required to screen short films (animated, documentary or educational) before all features – a policy which resulted in a boom in short film production (Haltof 2002: 77).

Documentaries from the period of socialist realism were expected to adhere to the same ideological and aesthetic tenets as fiction films, even more so. Contemporary subjects and films concerning large groups of people had priority over historical subjects and personal issues (Bocheńska 1974: 260), which also reflects on the specificity of documentary film at large. The most common subject, especially of the films presented in the weekly newsreels (*Polska Kronika Filmowa*), is the Six-Year Plan. Many films are concerned with construction work and work in coalmines, such as *Wesoła II* (1952), directed by Witold Lesiewicz, and building the flagship of Polish industry of this period, the steelworks and city of Nowa Huta, as in *Kierunek Nowa Huta* (*Direction Nowa Huta*, 1951). There are also films about the first Polish factory producing cars, *Żerań – fabryka jutra* (*Żerań – Factory of the Future*, 1951), directed by Witld Lesiewicz, and *Brygada zaczyna szturm* (*A Team Starts an Offensive*, 1953), directed by Joanna Broniewska-Kozicka about the building of a power station (ibid.: 263–266). Socialist realist documentaries look like fiction films, except that the vast majority of them have off-screen commentaries, to reinforce (or correct) the messages conveyed through images. This treatment of the workers renders them as both heroes and victims of ideology: they embody socialist values, but at the same time are literally and metaphorically devoid of voice, agency and individuality. It can be added that in this respect socialist realist documentaries adhere to the dominant style of the western documentary films before the advent of direct cinema (Nichols 2001). However, in the Polish context this is usually seen as a symptom of the special ideologization of this genre.

Although socialist realist documentary films concern different enterprises, they follow the same pattern. In all of them the subject is building (understood as building the factory), the team of people coming from different parts of Poland and, finally, socialism. The narrator usually underlines the difficulty of the task, which renders it similar to a military struggle. We hear about teams working in difficult weather conditions, in snow and frost, and about the army helping the workers to accomplish their tasks. There is also the pressure of time: time has to be accelerated for the factory and socialism to be realized. This aspect is conveyed by the titles of the films, as in *A Team Starts an Offensive* or *Żerań – Factory of the Future*. This neverending fight with time, which appears to be more important than the fight with natural obstacles, brings to mind the observation of Stephen Hanson that 'If the ideal of "bourgeois" economists is a system in which each unit of time is utilized in as productive a manner as possible given scarce resources, the goal of Soviet socialism was to organize production in such a manner as to master time itself' (Hanson 1997: viii). The films also try to convince us that people are the crucial factor in achieving progress: more important than machines or natural circumstances, according to the Stalinist slogan 'Nothing is impossible for a Bolshevik' (Groys 1992: 60).

Another common denominator of these films is acknowledging the role of the Soviet Union in assisting Poles in their efforts. In *A Team Starts an Offensive* we learn that the building of an electric plant followed a Soviet design and in *Żerań – Factory of the Future* the machines used to build the first Polish cars were sent from the Soviet Union, together with experienced engineers who passed their knowledge onto their Polish counterparts. One gets the impression that Soviet assistance is given for free – it is just an expression of friendship and a desire to help one's younger 'brothers and sisters'. Visually the construction overshadows the constructors; the building sites are huge and they are monumentalized by camera angles, to reflect the Six-Year tenet that the more grandiose the investment, the better. The workers lack any individuality, being shown from the distance, and are presented only as workers; other aspects of their lives are occluded. The role of the young workers and the women is accentuated to reflect the special role these categories of workers were allocated by the socialist regime.

Some of the most memorable films from this period broke with this scheme, such as *Pamiętniki chłopów* (*Peasants' Memoirs*, 1952), *Kolejarskie słowo* (*A Railwayman's Word*, 1953) and *Gwiazdy muszą płonąć* (*The Stars Must Burn*, 1954), all directed by Andrzej Munk, known for creating the most iconic film about the Holocaust, *Pasażerka* (*Passenger*, 1963). *Peasants' Memoirs* could fill a gap in the first part of my book, because it concerns the situation in the countryside in the interwar period, based on memoirs published in 1935. The image which emerges from these accounts is compared with the lives of the same peasants in the early 1950s. This demonstrates, as one might expect, great improvements in the lives of these men (as these are all men) and an even more prosperous future awaiting their children. We learn that the past was marred by three interconnected problems: unemployment, poverty, and a lack of prospects due to the semi-feudal system, which dominated in the Polish countryside. In the recurrent stories we hear that sugar was such a luxury before the war that the peasants could afford it only for Easter, there was not enough oil for oil lamps, and children suffered horrible diseases due to malnutrition. Moreover, peasants' children were expected to finish their education after only three years of elementary school. The author of one memoir also recollects an incident when the local aristocrat did not allow children to glean the potatoes left in the fields after the harvest; he preferred the potatoes to rot than be used productively by his 'serfs'. Nothwithstanding the socialist propaganda, these are heartbreaking stories, which strongly affect the viewer even now. But Munk's aim is not only to show how bad life was in the 1930s, but how it had improved thanks to the communist policies. There is no longer hunger, but prosperity, thanks to the division of the aristocratic estates between the poor peasants, the introduction of the new machinery and, finally, collectivization. There is no longer unemployment but the opposite – not enough people to fulfil the (over)-ambitious Six-Year Plan, which attempts to make up for all the arrears of the interbellum. Finally, peasants' children have practically unlimited opportunities. We hear about a farmer's son who became a military pilot, another working as an advisor to the farmers' collective, acting as a bridge between the city and the country, somebody else's daughter whose ambition is to become a doctor, and a little girl who likes to dance, hence might become an actress.

If we look at this film with a sceptical eye, we might wonder how much in it is twisted to create the rosy picture of the 'socialist countryside', demanded by the Stalinist authorities. One such issue is collectivization. The narrator informs us that the peasants formed some kind of collective, but its precise nature is not clear. As mentioned earlier, Polish farmers were unwilling to give up private ownership of the land, although they were happy to share machines and other resources. There is also a question about the real standards of living in the country post-1945. It is true that poverty in the countryside was eradicated, but rural areas continued to lag behind urban areas till the end of state socialism, to a large extent because of the state policy of fixing prices for farmers' products. Furthermore, although there were doctors and pilots from farming families (as well as film historians), their representation was lower than those from the city.[7]

Ewelina Nurczyńska-Fidelska observes that *Peasants' Memoirs* both adheres to the socialist realistic aesthetics and enriches it by including truly realistic elements (Nurczyńska-Fidelska 1982: 18). The film's allegiance to socialist realism is conveyed by the (male) voice-over, reflecting the position of the filmmaker and the voice of the authorities, as in the previously mentioned films. The commentary praises the state which changed the lives of the peasants for the better. The realistic elements come in the form of the quotations from the *Peasants' Memoirs* published before the war, which are written in a colloquial and simple language. The overall impression is that, paradoxically, under capitalism, when the peasants were deprived of almost everything, they still kept their voice. After the war, under state socialism, they have everything except their speech – they cannot represent themselves; somebody has to do it for them.

A Railwayman's Word and *The Stars Must Burn* deal less with improvement in the lives of the Poles brought about by state socialism, and more with the challenges of the Six-Year Plan and its influence on the working practices of specific professions, respectively railway workers and miners. The first film asks why the railwaymen work so hard and bravely and answers: 'because they gave their word'. Such a claim can be read as a reference to the specific ethos of railway workers (a job which requires a high degree of responsibility, given that a mistake by a railwayman might cost many lives) or to the socialist ethos, with its emphasis on working for the common good, rather than for money. It appears that Munk purposefully conflates these two ideas, trying to show that the railwayman's ethos and the socialist ethos are in perfect harmony. As I will later show, in his subsequent film, *Człowiek na torze* (*Man on the Tracks*, 1956), this will be no longer the case.

A Railwayman's Word belongs to a subgenre of documentary cinema known as a story documentary. The employment of such a genre is meant to add drama to what might otherwise be seen as a mundane topic. The story is about coke coal being carried from Silesia in the south of Poland to a steelworks plant in Szczecin in the north: the plant needs it urgently because the Polish industry is short of steel. The film focuses on the obstacles in the way of fulfilling this goal, such as a broken railway line, which was eventually overcome thanks to the joint effort of different people working on the railway, so that the train reaches its destination on time. The film was compared to the Grierson School of documentary from the 1930s (ibid.: 20). The closest comparator is *Night Mail* (1936), directed by Harry Watt and Basil Wright, which also concerns the work of railwaymen and a requirement to fulfil a certain task in a specific amount of time. Also, on both occasions work is explained in terms of service to people, rather than creating profit. However, there is also a difference. In the Polish film the service is not directly to the consumers, but to other workers. Speaking metaphorically, the consumers in this film disappear below the horizon, as they disappeared behind the horizon of the Six-Year planners. As in *Peasants' Memoirs*, the information is transmitted by voice-over. However, on occasion we also hear the railway workers speaking, although typically just about simple things, like asking about the position of the train. Nevertheless, their voice gives some insight into the ethos of the work on the railways, marked by peace and precision, which is somewhat at odds with the pressure to speed up, to break working records, to overcome time, advocated by the socialist authorities at the time.

The Stars Must Burn, which Munk co-directed with Witold Lesiewicz, is a hybrid between a documentary and a fiction film, what we would describe today as docudrama. It is based on true events, set in authentic locations and has a cast of real miners, who more or less play themselves. However, its narrative is more developed than in *A Railwayman's Word*, which follows a script written by the two directors and, metaphorically, the Party ideologues. Set in 1953, hence roughly in the middle of the Six-Year Plan, it intermingles two stories. One concerns the rediscovery of long-abandoned but still potentially productive shafts in a Silesian coalmine, which is a condition of leaving the mine open and, as it is implied, preserving the local community, because without work the local miners and their families would be forced to seek employment elsewhere. The second story concerns an aged miner Górecki, who looks after the pit ponies but is faced with redundancy when the mine undergoes modernization and the horses are replaced by machines. The title of the film refers to the practice of erecting illuminated stars, signifying that the miners have achieved their production quotas. At the beginning, however, the star does not burn and the film admits that this is not an

Illustration 3.3: Work in the mine in *The Stars Must Burn*, directed by Andrzej Munk

unusual situation; there were many factories in Poland which by this point had not fulfilled their plans.

The entire film successfully navigates between two points: that the plan is unfulfilled (which is a historical fact), and that all will be well in the end. To some extent it also attempts to address the reasons why this unfortunate situation developed, such as the lack of realism of the planners who did not account for obsolete machinery, the lack of resources and poor coordination between different parts of the industry (the failure of coalmines, as the film says, affects production elsewhere), and the lack of entrepreneurial skills on the part of the leaders of industry. Overall, the film testifies to the problems resulting from the speed of modernization on which Poland embarked after the war. Yet, the film attempts to convince us that ultimately these problems will be overcome thanks to the workers, who are prepared to risk their lives for the benefit of the community. This is most likely because of their attachment to the miner's ethos, but one can also explain their commitment by referring to the Stalinist slogan that 'Nothing is impossible for a Bolshevik'.

Although working in a mine is one of the hardest and most dangerous occupations, the filmmakers are at pains to present it as attractive. They show that searching for seams of coal is an adventure, not unlike searching for gold, as it requires courage and strength, except that mining is communal and allows the building of lasting friendships between people and, as the example of Górecki shows, animals. Working in a mine is so addictive that the miners do not want to stop. Due to its communality, adventuressness and importance for the whole country, work in a mine can thus serve as a paradigm of socialist work. Indeed, it was portrayed as a privileged occupation during the whole postwar period.[8] That said, *The Stars Must Burn* has much in common with western representations of work in the mine, such as the classic documentary by Alberto Cavalcanti, *Coal Face* (1935), which argues that work in the pit is not merely a way of earning money, but a service to society. Both films also skilfully use montage and music (created by the leading composers of the time, Benjamin Britten in the British film, Jan Krenz in the Polish film) to create a mood of danger and foreboding of miner's work.

As in the two previous films by Munk, the narrator is the main transmitter of meaning. However, the characters have more to say in comparison with the two earlier films, and from their utterances we learn about their values and mindset. One can argue that even without the voice-over we can understand the film, which would be impossible in *Peasants' Memoirs* and *A Railwayman's Word*. Paradoxically, the further the director moves from documentary to fiction cinema, the more his characters are furnished with a voice. It thus appears as if the truly documentary protagonists could not be trusted in Polish socialist realist documentary films; only the fictional characters were trustworthy. Or to put it differently, irrespective of whether the characters were fictional or documentary, their narration had to come from above (the Party) rather than from below.

The same impression can be derived from another documentary from the 1950s, *Kobiety naszych dni* (*Women of Our Days*, 1951), directed by Jan Zelnik, whose production was inspired by the congress of the Polish Women's League. The whole film is devoted to the progress achieved by women under state socialism in Poland and the whole Eastern Bloc. One criterion of assessing this progress is women doing masculine jobs, such as a metal worker, driver, bricklayer and architect. The second is their education. These achievements are contrasted with the prewar period, when women were confined to the home and suffered from illiteracy. By the same token, the film implies that under socialism women achieved power, rather than merely plugging the gaps in their countries' economy. It is true that work outside the home allowed women to earn their own money and achieve independence, but in most cases it did not translate into having great spending power or occupying a high position in factories or even less in the Party structures. This fact is indirectly confirmed in Zelnik's documentary, which highlights the crucial role that men play in improving their situation (Ostrowska 2006a: 57–58; Toniak 2008: 103–104). We hear that one woman became a metal worker thanks to her son who explained to her the basics of this skill. Another woman receives an apprenticeship after writing to the male Party secretary. In the long list of case studies we find only two women who moved beyond manual work, which is obviously very hard. One is the previously mentioned architect; the other a woman who became the manager in a factory producing haberdashery items, which employs exclusively women. The subservient position of women under state socialism is also betrayed by the fact that the voice of the commentary again belongs to the man – the famous actor, Andrzej Łapicki, the voice of the Polish newsreels in the 1950s. His seductive voice represents the dominant ideology of the state and the Party. Moreover, as Elżbieta Ostrowska notes, two huge portraits of Josef Stalin and the Polish President, Bolesław Bierut, hang above the tribune, demonstrating that the ostensibly 'feminine public space is symbolically controlled by male power' (Ostrowska 2006a: 58).

Voices of Doubt and Criticism

During the period of the Six-Year-Plan it was difficult for filmmakers to criticize either the ideology behind this plan or its implementation. The situation changed after the end of Stalinism, when the new leaders in the Soviet Union, Poland and elsewhere began their rule by criticizing their predecessors. One such film which reflects on this new freedom to criticize is Czesław Petelski's *The Depot of the Dead*. It was made in 1958, when socialist realism was already an outmoded paradigm and the Polish School flourished, and premiered the following year. Predictably, it is an impure socialist realist film, both on account of its genre – a Western – and its lack of optimism. It is based on the work of Marek Hłasko, whose connections with socialist realism were tenuous and who later became a symbol

Illustration 3.4: Life at the end of the world in *The Depot of the Dead*, directed by Czesław Petelski

of the rebellion against socialist realist literature and ideology (Kurz 2005: 24–73; Detka 2006).

Yet, on the other hand, much connects *The Depot of the Dead* with other socialist realist films. The cinema of Czesław Petelski and his wife,[9] as Krzysztof Kornacki argues, was always tuned to the official vision of Polish history and validated socialism (Kornacki 2007: 43). This is reflected in the fact that Hłasko withdrew his name from the film's credits on the grounds that the film turned out too optimistic. The film portrays work as the highest duty of every Pole and an adventure, a new religion, ensuring transcendence, which characterized the official approach to work during the Six-Year Plan, even though the film itself is most likely set in an earlier period.[10] However, rather than taking these ideas for granted, Petelski sets out to confront them with the harsh reality of work. From this perspective, *The Depot of the Dead* can be classified as a meta-socialist realist films, in common with such later works as *Człowiek z marmuru* (*Man of Marble*, 1977) and some 1970s documents by Wojciech Wiszniewski (see chapter 5).

The film is set shortly after the Second World War in the remote part of the Bieszczady mountains, near the border with Ukraine. During the war, and for some years after, the Ukrainian Independent Army fought with the Polish forces there, trying to establish an independent Ukraine. The film's main character, Zabawa, who is an experienced lorry driver and a mechanic, as well as a Party member, is given a gun on his way there. This suggests that he will encounter enemies there, not unlike a sheriff sent to a new settlement in the Wild West. Zabawa's ultimate destination is the titular depot of dead people, a remote workers' hostel cum workshop, where a group of men are employed to transport wood from the Bieszczady forest. Their base is named this way not so much on account of the danger of the Ukrainian fighters, but due to the old and faulty trucks which the men have to drive, risking death at every corner, especially in winter when bad weather conspires with treacherous roads. The situation of the drivers brings to mind the stories about the gold rush in America, where many prospectors died before a few found the precious metal.[11] Zabawa's mission is to persuade the drivers, who are keen to leave the base and return to normal life, to stay there longer. He himself is persuaded by his boss that the country desperately needs wood – the factories and houses need this precious material and if Zabawa refuses to go, his boss will have to take his place. Zabawa might allow this to happen, if not for the fact that his boss is lacking a hand. Their discussion shows the basic difference between the type of motivation for work under capitalism and state socialism; in the former it is monetary reward; in the latter, the appeal to the worker's sense of responsibility to the community. Capitalist work is undertaken under conditions of surplus of product, socialist work under conditions of scarcity. While Zabawa himself is receptive to psychological blackmail of this kind, most likely on account of his Party membership, his co-workers are less so. To make them conform to his plan, Zabawa warns them that if they leave the depot, they will not find employment elsewhere. They do stay, but one by one die due to the harsh conditions of this 'Wild East' and in the end only two truck drivers remain in the depot: Zabawa and Warszawiak, who initially appeared to be Zabawa's chief foe. His decision to remain in Bieszczady is presented as an optimistic conclusion to the story, because it suggests that the ideological work undertaken by Zabawa paid off. As a reward, they receive new trucks and the struggle to fulfil the plan continues.

In its concern with the dangerous and alienating character of work, of 'the wear and tear of the worker', as Comolli put it (quoted in O'Shaugnessy 2012: 157), *The*

Depot of the Dead is a unique film in the whole postwar period. The extreme depletion of the workers shown there, bringing to mind Engels and Marx's description of working conditions in nineteenth-century England, throws into relief the question of the value of work at large and under socialism in particular. Can work, for whatever purpose, be rendered more important than physical survival? It is worth mentioning that a similar question was asked in the Polish School films made in this period, most importantly *Popiół i diament* (*Ashes and Diamonds*, 1957) by Andrzej Wajda; however, on this occasion the choice faced by the protagonist was not between working or living, but between fighting or living. Petelski, who must have been familiar with these films, leaves open the question of balancing life with other values, not unlike Wajda (who started his career as Petelski's assistant).

The work of both Hłasko and Petelski is marked by misogyny and *The Depot of the Dead* is no different in this respect. It includes only one female character, Zabawa's wife, Wanda, and her representation is sexist in a socialist realist way. Even before she enters the scene, so to speak, she is described by one of the truck drivers as a promiscuous and mercenary woman, who had an affair with somebody more prominent than her husband, inevitably in order to get some advantage from this liaison. This likens Wanda to women often portrayed in Westerns, but such women tended to help the men to survive in the challenging environment, while Wanda has a corrupting influence on the lorry drivers. Not surprisingly, she is made to look like a woman from the interwar films, who gladly sheds her independence in exchange of material advantages. Not only does she fail to compete with men at work, but she tends to her feminine needs such as bathing in warm water and wearing silk stockings, which are seen as frivolous.

Shot in winter, on location in the mountains, *The Depot of the Dead* gives a vivid sense of work as a struggle with nature and a means of building community and achieving personal transformation. The fact that the characters come across as very believable can be attributed to Petelski's own experience of working in the woods. Not surprisingly, Petelski's film was singled out by Dušan Makavejev as his favourite Polish film[12] and it is likely that it inspired the renowned Yugoslav director to make *Čovek nije tica* (*Man Is Not a Bird*, 1965). In both cases we witness a highly skilled worker who goes to the periphery in order to help the ailing enterprise to fulfil its plan. In Makavejev's film, Jan, a technician, comes to the copper foundry to install new machines. Zabawa and Jan both encounter demoralized workers, who stay there merely due to a lack of better prospects. Both men are also associated with women who prove to be promiscuous. Jan's girlfriend has an affair with a truck driver when he receives an award for his service to the socialist industry. However, Makavejev treats women's emotional and material needs with more sympathy and respect than Petelski, suggesting that private happiness should not be sacrificed for socialist production plans.

Doubts about some of the policies and practices of state socialism were also conveyed in a number of documentary films made in the second half of the 1950s, known as the 'dark series' (*czarna seria*). Unlike other Polish films of the 1950s, these films attracted comparison with western films, most importantly British Free Cinema (Kosińska 2011; Sørenssen 2012). Bjørn Sørenssen praises them for their unprecedented courage in venturing where western filmmakers would be reluctant to go. In relation to one of them, *Paragraf Zero* (*Article Zero*, 1957) by Włodzimierz Borowik, concerning prostitution in Poland, he writes: 'It takes on a subject matter that at the time was a taboo, not even behind the iron curtain, but in Western Europe and North America as well... Even more remarkable is the appearance of a film treating this social issue head on in the Eastern bloc countries' (Sørenssen 2012: 190).

However, together with some Polish historians (Jazdon 2000), I see the 'dark series' as at best consisting of liminal films, offering criticism of the status quo which validates the authoritarian attitude to ordinary people perpetuated by the Polish state during the Six-Year Plan. As their very name suggests, they concern negative phenomena in the Polish postwar reality, such as the low morale of Polish youth in *Ludzie z pustego obszaru* (*People from an Empty Zone*, 1957), directed by Kazimierz Karabasz and Władysław Ślesicki, the dying of small towns in *Miasteczko* (*Little Town*, 1956), directed by Jerzy Ziarnik, and prostitution in the previously mentioned *Article Zero*. Their style is similar to that of the 'classical' socialist realist films, as they also consist of images accompanied by the voice of the narrator, except that instead of praising the achievements of the Six-Year Plan, the narrator points to the problems of living in Poland at the time. These films focus on the group protagonist (hooligans, prostitutes, inhabitants of a small town), whom they reduce to a stereotype.

People from an Empty Zone concerns the apparent empty zone in the lives of young people. The testimony to this emptiness, almost horror vacui, is the fact that the youngsters are hanging out in cafes or at the town square or at parties in private apartments (*prywatki*). At another times or place such activities could be seen as proof that Poles are able to have fun even in times of shortage,[13] but the narrator informs us that these young people should not be left alone by the authorities. In the words of the narrator the reason for their misery is their loneliness, which can be interpreted as a lack of ideological grounding, but we might conjecture that a more important factor is their low salary. For example, we learn that a young woman earns 800 zloties per month and then see a shop window displaying a pair of shoes costing 900 zloties. The narrator also makes reference (even if only obliquely) to the alienating character of the jobs these young people perform and their lack of professional prospects. Finally, we learn that the 'people from an empty zone' usually live in poor accommodation, often with parents and siblings in one-bedroom apartments with minimal facilities. The film thus, even if reluctantly, compares the ideal of socialist Poland as a country of great opportunities and non-alienated work with the grim reality of working-class life in the first decade after the war.

Article Zero draws attention to prostitution in Warsaw as a paradoxical phenomenon: as widespread, but officially unacknowledged, due to the fact that under socialism women received the same rights as men, including sexual rights. This meant that they officially could engage in sex with whoever they wanted. However, such an approach by the authorities is criticized in the film on pragmatic grounds and on principle. The film argues that legalizing prostitution or treating it as non-existent leads to venereal diseases, high rates of crime, and poverty of prostitutes in their older age. It also implies that prostitution is degrading to women. This idea is transmitted by the quasi-religious language used by the narrator, dominated by words such as 'saving' and 'curing', referring to the diseased souls and bodies of the fallen women. The voice-over pronounces that 'in order to save and treat, legislation is necessary. There is no article in our law that would regulate the issue of prostitution'. The lack of a proper law (most likely a harsh law) leads to the police being 'soft' on prostitutes, intervening in their activities only when a crime is committed. Again, not unlike in *People from an Empty Zone*, the focus is on legislation and regulation, as opposed to enabling the disadvantaged to take care of their own affairs through improving their living conditions. At the same time the camera points to more important reasons – not just the lack of a specific article in the penal code – why so many Polish women choose this way of earning money, such as poverty, also an issue in the countryside leading many women to emigrate to the city in search of employment, and housing problems. A large proportion of prostitutes in Warsaw are effectively homeless and unemployed or at least unable to earn enough money to survive economically.

Selling sexual services allows them to buy food and shelter for the night, although it also sentences them to dwelling in sub-standard housing, even in cellars.

Although the narrator admits that sexual services are also offered in high-class private apartments, he focuses on those offered by poor and uneducated women. This might be seen as a sign of caring for the wellbeing of the disadvantaged, but also of a lack of respect for them. For example, the narrator admits with pride that the whole film was shot with a hidden camera and shows 'real women', except in the scenes in the restaurants where professional actors were used. In many scenes, such as during the interviews with women, the questions are asked in such a way that the women have to defend themselves against the accusation that they do not work, which means that they do not perform regular, Fordist labour. It is likely that such disrespect would be shown to the protagonists if they were of a higher social class. The narrator announces that the film was made for sociologists and legislators, not for the working-class audience or for the prostitutes. *Article Zero*, to a greater extent than the films about 'heroic' workers breaking production records, instrumentalizes the images of the workers to suit the purposes of the state. The fact that on this occasion the voice of the narrator is male while the subjects are female adds to the sense that the state is patriarchal. *Article Zero* is unique among the films belonging to the 'dark series' in that it allows its characters to speak. However, given the sensitive subject of the film and the fact that the prostitutes were filmed using a hidden camera, this should not be seen as a sign of its progressiveness but, on the contrary, its ideological conservatism and dubious moral standards.

Little Town offers a different recipe for the social malaise than the two films discussed so far. The problem here consists of the slow death of small towns in Poland due to the zealousness with which the authorities eradicate all non-socialist enterprises, including private trade and craft. The town we observe in this film used to be known for its leather workshops. Under Bierut's rule, private trade in leather became a serious offence and the town transformed from a centre of shoemaking to one of criminals. Not wanting to risk a jail sentence for buying leather illegally, many inhabitants left the town, leaving it in a state of mortal decline. Unlike the directors of the two previously discussed films belonging to the 'dark series', Ziarnik suggests that the state should intervene less rather than more in the lives of citizens, allowing them to engage in artisanal production and trade, which is not only politically innocuous, but also economically useful, unlike the production of bureaucratic paperwork, which is economically useless and politically dangerous. As far as I am aware, *Little Town* was the first Polish documentary film to draw attention to the perils of socialist style bureaucracy. However, it was not the last; in due course it would become a common subject of Polish documentaries, such as Krzysztof Kieślowski's *Urząd* (*The Office*, 1966) (see chapter 4), as well as fiction films, such as *Zezowate szczęście* (*Bad Luck*, 1960) by Andrzej Munk, and the comedies of Stanisław Bareja.

The last film I want to discuss in this section is *Man on the Tracks* by Andrzej Munk, regarded as the most critical film about Stalinism produced in the 1950s (Lubelski 2009a: 166). Its subject is the quest to find out why the train driver named Orzechowski (in the film addressed as a 'mechanic Orzechowski') threw himself on the tracks and was killed by the train. An informal investigation conducted by his superiors and members of the local nomenklatura is meant to establish the reasons for his suicide. The initial assumption is that he was a saboteur, bitter about being demoted from his job. However, a discussion of his work with three different people who give their insight into his life prove otherwise – Orzechowski sacrificed himself to save a train full of passengers which otherwise would have been derailed.

The investigation exposes the contrast between the working ethos advocated by the Six-Year Plan on the one hand and that pertaining to the interwar period – which can also be equated with the timeless ethos of the railway workers – on the other. In the earlier film, *A Railwayman's Word*, Munk implied that there is no contradiction between these two styles of work. In *Man on the Tracks* this is no longer the case. The logic of the Six-Year Plan is the logic of quantity: its requirement is to 'process' the maximum number of goods in a minimum amount of time using a minimum of resources. The logic of working on the railway is the logic of quality, ensuring the safe and punctual delivering of goods, and requiring great care for the machines, especially the locomotive. To such care, which he learnt before the war from an older mechanic, Orzechowski dedicated his life. The symbol of that is how he ostentatiously checks the state of the locomotive in white gloves. The old train driver objects to the new rules, introduced by the communist 'Young Turks', such as using low-quality coal and neglecting maintenance issues.. This leads to conflict with his superiors and initially also with his young assistant Zapora who was sent to his engine to spy on him. Yet, in due course Orzechowski gains the respect of Zapora, who appreciates the craftsmanship of his superior. Munk's film does not simply try to convince the viewers that old style work is better than the new ethos. Orzechowski's devotion to his workplace and the people he serves is commendable, but his attitude to the younger workers is unacceptable (at least according to today's standards), as he demands total obedience from them. One even gains the impression that Poland needed state socialism to allow for the faster promotion of younger workers.

Even if we agree that the content of *Man on the Tracks* likens it to socialist realist films, its form diverts from it. The structure of investigation, with different people presenting different versions of events, best known from *Citizen Kane* (1941) by Orson Welles and in the Polish context from Wajda's *Man of Marble*, introduces uncertainty into the narrative, implying that history can be manipulated. Lubelski also notices that unlike the majority of films made during the hegemony of socialist realism in Poland, which ostensibly were about work but disregarded the particularities of specific occupations, *Man on the Tracks* demonstrates an affectionate attitude to railway work (Lubelski 2009a: 167). This is true, but in part it can be explained by a special relationship between cinema and the railways. Few things are more photogenic than trains, a fact that was taken advantage of by western and eastern filmmakers. One can also notice parallels between train machinery and cinematic machinery, with their complicated systems of wheels.[14] If we read *Man on the Tracks* metaphorically, as a film not only about trains and railway people, but also about films and people working in the film industry, then Orzechowski's special care for his engine and his refusal to 'feed' low-quality coal into his machine can be interpreted as advocating 'quality' cinema, produced slowly, and with high-quality tools.

Notes

1. This argument is corroborated by Constantin Parvulescu's discussion of East German film, *Roman einer jungen Ehe* (*Story of a Young Couple*) by Kurt Maetzig (Parvulescu 2015: 44–70).
2. The play had its Polish premiere in 1949. It marked the opening of a new theatre, Teatr Nowy in Lodz. Like the film, it was directed by a team of directors, led by Jerzy Merunowicz.
3. This happens in *Story of a Young Couple* (Parvulescu 2015: 59–65).
4. However, this refers to 'pure capitalism'. In the capitalist welfare state people also receive many things from the state not because they earned it, but because they are disadvantaged.
5. In its representation of the working of the television studio *Matter to Be Settled* was futuristic rather than realistic, as at the time Polish television had only just begun to operate and its total broadcast amounted to one hour per week (Talarczyk-Gubała 2007: 38–39).
6. My father was a member of a farmers' circle and other volunatary collectives of farmers. I remember that my first trip to the Polish mountains and other trips in Poland in the 1970s

were organized by the local 'farmers' circle' in my native Kowal, as part of their cultural and educational programme.
7. The underrepresentation of children from this background was tackled in the 1970s, when the authorities decided to add special 'points for social background' to the results of the entrance exams to the university, which were meant to help candidates from working-class and peasant backgrounds to achieve university education.
8. Its elevation culminated in the 1970s when ex-miner Edward Gierek became the First Secretary of the Party.
9. *The Depot of the Dead* is signed only by Czesław Petelski, but his wife claimed that her input into its production was significant and this opinion is corroborated by the actors playing in the film (Kornacki 2007: 49).
10. It is not spelt out when it is set, therefore such information can be only deduced from its script, which locates it shortly after the war.
11. Such comparisons, implicit or explicit, between the (American) gold and Polish and socialist treasures, were common in Polish cinema. For example, Wojciech Has's *Gold* is about Polish gold – coal (see chapter 4).
12. Makavejev confessed to his enchantment with Petelski's film during an interview conducted with him in 2011.
13. Such a conclusion, however, can be derived from Roman Polanski's film made about the same time, *Rozbijemy zabawę* (*Let's Break the Ball*, 1957).
14. The similarity between trains and cinema was visible in the symbolism of Polish cinema. One of the film units was called 'Tor' (The Tracks) and another, 'Kadr' (Frame), had a logo which bears a resemblance to tracks.

CHAPTER 4
The 1960s
Industrial Expansion and Small Stabilization

In a political and economic sense the 1960s started in Poland earlier than elsewhere in Europe: in June 1956, with a series of workers' strikes and demonstrations, particularly in Poznań. The workers protested against the high prices of food, the decline of wages, and bad management of factories and the country as a whole. The workers also set up workers' councils, in protest against being subordinated to the Party and the trade unions, which they saw as representing the interests of the nomenklatura, rather than the workers. These events led to the reinstatement of Władysław Gomułka as the First Secretary of the Party in October of the same year, and the beginning of a period known as October's thaw, Gomułka's thaw or Polish thaw. This shift in power at the top was made possible only by a series of changes which took place in Moscow, beginning with Stalin's death in 1953, the denouncement of his methods by his successor, Nikita Khruschchev, the rehabilitation of the (prewar) Communist Party of Poland (KPP), of which Gomułka was a member, and finally the sudden death of Bolesław Bierut in 1956.

Gomułka, who was previously imprisoned for his alleged 'nationalistic deviation', started his term in office with great personal authority, as a true leader of the nation, able to stand up to the power of the Kremlin. He brought with him a hope that from 1956 state socialism would work more for the people and less for the state. Indeed, in a speech he delivered in October 1956 he promised that Polish-Soviet relations would be based on solidarity and equality, and the Party would guide, rather than govern. The national economy would be based on material incentives for the workers, peasants and craftsmen, and economic activity would no longer be based on compulsion. Gomułka also promised that workers' councils formed during 1956 in factories should become the foundation of industrial self-government (Dalecki 1971: 87). Queues for apartments were meant to be shortened, albeit at the price of building small apartments with 'blind', windowless kitchens (Crowley 2002: 182). Following his speech there was also an expectation of cultural liberalization. Then and throughout Gomułka's rule an emphasis was also put on the connection between socialism and patriotism, as demonstrated by the changes in history schoolbooks (Machalica 2010: 95-101). This trend of polonizing socialism would intensify in the subsequent decades.

Gomułka is typically seen as a 'pragmatist communist' who attempted to modernize the Polish economy for the welfare of the country, yet without risking any serious conflict with its eastern neighbour or jeopardizing the political hegemony of the Party. One of Gomułka's ideas was to postpone (in practice forever) collectivization of the land. Another was to grant greater autonomy to individual enterprises, which, like the establishment of workers' councils, was meant to liken the Polish economy to the Yugoslav model. However, the new leader was against the workers' self-government, seeing in it (and perhaps rightly so, as the situation in the early 1980s would prove) a danger to state socialism. He was also in favour of reforming wages and prices, paying more to those workers who produce more, increasing the prices of food and lowering those of other commodities. Furthermore, he was of the opinion that Poland should develop its industries selectively. Unlike his predecessor and the bulk of Eastern European leaders of this and the earlier period, he did not prioritize heavy industry. Instead, he wanted Poland to develop 'new industries', such as chemical production. During his rule the oil refinery in Płock and the chemical plant in Puławy were built. Yet he opposed the development of aviation in Poland, seeing it as too ambitious a project for a country of Poland's size and might (Morawski 2007: 329-332). Unlike capitalist economists, Gomułka saw investment and increase in consumption as contradictory tendencies. For him, consuming equalled the 'eating up of one's future', therefore industrial expansion was his priority, as it had been Bierut's. For this reason, he was also against Poland developing a car industry on a large scale (ibid.: 329).

Even though historians of the Polish economy see many of Gomułka's ideas as healthy, they claim that they backfired because of the circumstances he inherited or the lack of fit between his programme and social expectations. For example, paying workers for what they actually produced, as opposed to the number of hours spent in front of the machine, would have made sense if their productivity had depended only on their labour. However, this was not the case because of the frequent stoppages caused by the lack of materials and tools. Changing the structure of prices would have made sense if not for the fact that the standard of living depended more on the price of food and especially on meat (a kind of fetish-food in Poland of state socialism) than on anything else. Reducing consumption for the sake of future prosperity was accepted straight after the war, but less so twenty years after its end. Ultimately, Gomułka's reforms in this area were also a cause of his downfall (ibid.: 331–332).

The length of the thaw is the subject of debate. Some authors claim that it lasted as little as one year and finished with the closing down of the liberal journal *Po Prostu* in October 1957. Others see its ending only in the second half of the 1960s. Following authors such as Janusz Zielinski and Piotr Koryś, I suggest that the thaw lasted between 1956 and 1958 (Zielinski 1973: 14–16; Koryś 2007: 446). During this period it was decided that the economy should be decentralized and based on the 'guided market model', with relatively autonomous socialist enterprises, led by the managers and workers, exercising power through their councils. The private producers of consumer goods were meant to have an easier life than in the previous decade because the Party allowed for the setting up of small cooperatives producing goods which large factories could not cope with. This period also witnessed cultural liberalization.

The period following the thaw, up to 1968, is known as that of the 'small stabilization'. During this period the standard of living improved, but the speed of reform slowed and the problems haunting the first wave of changes accumulated. Finally, the years 1968–1970 saw a marked departure from both the spirit and the letter of the reform (Zielinski 1973: 15 and 17–21). This period can be described as an attempt at the re-Stalinization of the Polish economy. It was coupled with the re-Stalinization of Polish cultural life, following the Israeli-Palestinian (Six-Day) War in 1967, which was used as a pretext to get rid of some prominent Poles of Jewish descent from positions of power, including within the Party.

The famous year 1968 in Poland was marked by students' protests, triggered by the banning of the Romantic play by Adam Mickiewicz, *Dziady (Forefathers' Eve)*, directed by Kazimierz Dejmek, on the grounds of its containing anti-Soviet references. These events made Gomułka unpopular, but he managed to survive the crisis. A different situation occurred in the 1970s, when his regime was confronted with disgruntled workers protesting against the threat of price rises. This time the centre of the protest was northern Poland, especially the Baltic coast. The First Secretary ordered tanks onto the streets, leading to over forty casualties. This decision cost him his job and earned him the reputation of a hardliner and an enforcer of orders from Moscow. From a modern perspective he should rather be seen as somebody standing in-between these two extremes, trying to navigate between the pressure from Moscow, where he was always treated with distrust, from his own Party, where he had many powerful rivals, and from society as a whole, which expected a marked improvement in living standards. Dissatisfaction with the quality of life affected the politics of Gomułka's successor, Edward Gierek, whose priority became to meet Poles' consumerist expectations.

Some of the changes introduced by Gomułka, although not inscribed into the economic plan or the law, outlived his regime. One concerned the role of the Party. After 1956 it remodelled itself from a Church-like institution, which asked citizens to believe in it blindly and follow its demands, into a technocratic influence on Polish life. 'Progress', the main term in the vocabulary of socialist ideologues, changed its meaning, from signifying a road towards communism, where new people would live in a new way, to 'modernization', understood in technological terms, such as working in state of the art factories. The composition of the leadership of the Party also changed. As Wiesław Władyka observes, under Gomułka the place previously occupied by 'comrades with four classes of primary school, short-term courses for political leaders and experiences with introducing the new political order after the Second World War started to be filled by younger people, who began their political careers in the youth organizations and at the universities' (Władyka 2009: 116). With these shifts came a downgrading of the status of the working class as the force which was meant to deliver communism, and an upgrading of that of the intelligentsia, expected to ensure technological progress. The figure of the shock worker went out of fashion, as much in reality as in art. The status of the workplace also changed. It stopped being seen as a battlefield, where the future of the nation was decided, where people undertook super-human tasks and where 'we' fought with 'them' (saboteurs and people with outdated mindset). Instead, it started to be regarded as just a place of work, of mundane activities, often performed as slowly and reluctantly as possible, so that one could preserve one's vital forces for more pleasant activities after work. It should be added that this status of work and workplace reflected well the low productivity of the Polish worker during this period. A French journalist, Danielle Hunbelle, who in the early 1960s travelled to Poland, noticed that Poles earned little, but equally worked little. To produce a Polish Warszawa car, 450 working hours were needed, while the production of a Renault in Billancourt required only sixty hours. In the office half of the day was taken up with drinking tea and reading the newspaper. Polish industry was also marred by absenteeism, often used by the workers to earn extra income on the side, as well as theft of state property (Brzostek 2006: 23–24; see also Firlit and Chłopecki 1992).

The term 'small stabilization', capturing Poland in the 1960s, is borrowed from Tadeusz Różewicz's play *Świadkowie albo nasza mała stabilizacja* (*Witnesses or Our Small Stabilisation*), published in 1962. Its protagonists, He and She, define the crucial term as the diminishing of requirements and responsibilities. During a period of small stabilization morality takes a back seat, because people are preoccupied with material pursuits. However, they do not complain because they are anxious not to lose what they achieved (Różewicz 1986). The personality type described by Różewicz can be equated with 'homo sovieticus', also marked by a lack of ambition and by passivity. Although the playwright is critical about such an attitude to life, it can be condoned in the light of the experiences of the war and Stalinism, when the political situation was volatile, the difference between what was allegedly true and false was amplified, and people could be doomed for being preoccupied with material prosperity or not showing the right type of idealism.

The end of austerity in Poland and the country's adoption of a gentler, more 'user-friendly' version of socialism was nowhere better seen than in cinema. A sign of this was the reinstatement of film units in May 1955. They were conceived as groups of 'creative workers able to initiate and bring to fruition fiction films' (Zajiček 1992: 141). Between June 1955 and October 1957 eight units were set up, headed by leading directors such as Jerzy Kawalerowicz, Jan Rybkowski, Aleksander Ford and Wanda Jakubowska. The units followed in the footsteps of the interwar SAT (the Cooperative of Film Authors). They were collectives with significant artistic and financial autonomy (ibid.: 143–144). In many ways, the post-1955 system was an artists' paradise, in which filmmakers could shoot what they wanted, yet were able to use state money (Adamczak 2010: 229–239; Ostrowska 2012). Less bureaucratic intervention meant a faster route from writing a script to making a film and more films passed to production. In 1962 as many as twenty-two new films were produced (Werner 1985: 63), which was four to five times as many as during the first half of the 1950s.

In 1968 the Polish film industry underwent further changes in response to the political protests of that year and the authorities' anti-intelligentsia and anti-Semitic stance. They mostly affected the composition of film units and film education. Many filmmakers of Jewish origin left Poland. Among them was Aleksander Ford, one of the most prominent Polish filmmakers up to this point, who emigrated to Israel, and cinematographers Kurt Weber and Jerzy Lipman (Zajiček 1992: 196–207). Some film units, such as Kadr and Kamera, were dismantled and new ones set up. Inevitably, the new ones were headed by those whom the authorities regarded as trustworthy. They were usually people from outside the existing film establishment, such as Stanisław Kuszewski, who was to lead the Nike unit and Jerzy Jesionowski, put in charge of Wektor. Jerzy Toeplitz, who was the vice-chancellor of the Łódź Film School lost his post and there was no recruitment to some programmes for the academic year 1968/1969 (Lemann-Zajiček 2008: 47–58). The purges and institutional changes created space for newcomers and the cinema of the 1970s would be dominated by them.

I mentioned in the previous chapter that during the hegemony of socialist realism the role of the director-auteur was played down and cinema addressed the whole society. A split of cinema into popular and auteurist strands occurred with the advent of the Polish School in the second half of the 1950s, whose creators were seen as auteurs, conveying their own vision rather than one coming from above (Michałek and Turaj 1988: xi–xii). In 1960 a distinction between 'engaged cinema' and 'popular cinema' addressed to 'mass audience' was officially made by the state at the resolution of the Central Committee of the Party (Uchwała 1994: 33). Both types of films were meant to be socialist in spirit, but in due course it was assumed by the critics that popular cinema, being the natural heir of socialist realist cinema, was conformist, while auteurist cinema was oppositional (hence the focus on auteurist cinema in the scholarship of Eastern European cinema). Such a reading of Polish cinema is simplistic, as in both types of films and often even in one film we find examples of conformism and opposition to the dominant ideology. Moreover, it is often not obvious when filmmakers praise and when they criticize the socialist status quo. The 1960s films demonstrate this very well.

A Suffering Intelligent among the Industrial Sublime

The paradigm of arthouse cinema in the 1960s was the Polish New Wave, epitomized by the films of Roman Polanski and Jerzy Skolimowski. Many of these films foreground industrial expansion, as in *Walkower* (*Walkover*, 1965) by Jerzy Skolimowski, *Molo* (*The Pier*, 1969) by Wojciech Solarz, and *Złoto* (*Gold*, 1962) by Wojciech Has (even though Has is not considered as a New Wave director, but rather a 'wave in itself'). By the very fact of taking up such a subject they encourage comparison with socialist realist films. Some authors notice the connection between 1960s films and the socialist realist *produkcyjniaki*, but they typically point to the ironic approach adopted by the 1960s filmmakers to the old themes (Maron 2011). In contrast, I argue that in the films discussed the old themes and conventions, even if reworked, are treated with seriousness. At the same time, looking at them through the prism of socialist realism allows one to notice some ideological shifts which occurred in the 1960s. Unlike the films of the previous decade, which showed Poland under construction, they present Poland in its industrial might. This is partly because fifteen or twenty years after the war ended Poland had more to show off than in 1950 or 1955. Moreover, some of the flagship achievements of the 1960s, such as the oil refinery complex in Płock where Skolimowski's film is set, or the Gdynia shipyard which is the setting of *The Pier*, particularly lent themselves to the camera. They appeared to be ahead of their times, unlike the coal mines, favoured in the 1950s, which were either built in the pre-socialist period or on the surface did not look very different from the mines built a hundred year previously.

The European New Waves tended to privilege spatial discourse over narrative (Thompson and Bordwell 1976: 42; Heath 1976: 73). Such an approach suited young Polish directors, put off by the socialist realist idea of film as merely a screened script. In contrast to the films of the 1950s, which follow the protagonists overcoming obstacles till they reach their goal, *Walkover* and *The Pier*, and to some extent *Gold*, offer a new type of character: a traveller, a drifter, an outsider, who does not have a specific goal. Such a narrative reflects on the 1960s in Poland, when people did not lack the bare necessities and, thanks to an easing in the pressure to break production records, could drift, even if only for a short time. The figure of a drifter might additionally be seen as a metaphor of this decade, which lacked a grand ideological project, as the term 'small stabilization' indicates.

In the films discussed in this section, the manual workers, who were central to the socialist realist narratives, are relegated to secondary roles. Their lives are represented as dependent on the actions of the men belonging to the technical intelligentsia, who are devoted to their work and help working-class men in trouble. This shift reflects the loss of status of manual workers at work and in the sphere of politics, as mentioned earlier. It can also be seen, as Nebojša Jovanović argues in relation to a similar phenomenon in Yugoslavia, as an 'attempt to soften the class barrier between the working and middle class' (Jovanović 2015: 170), which was erected in the previous decade. The second difference pertains to the representation of women. Unlike socialist realist films, which illuminate the plight of women, who through industrial work break out of the shackles of patriarchy, the films of the 1960s offer male-centred stories, with women relegated to supporting roles. Women in these films are portrayed either as obstacles to finding the right solution to the middle-class men's problems or as their supporters. In this decade the typical role of a woman is thus that of a housewife or a barwoman. These women are interested in consumption and a comfortable life, rather than in production, and for that they are often lambasted in the films. In this respect the Polish New Wave is not different from Yugoslav cinema, where the trend of undermining the autonomy of women had already started in the late 1950s (Jovanović 2015: 170–175), and the Czechoslovak cinema of the 1960s (Hanáková 2011).

Gold and *Walkover* represent the abovementioned tendencies well. Each film is set in a combine (*kombinat*). This term, used in a number of Eastern European languages, refers to big industrial enterprises that link several factories, such as a mine and a power station, under one administration. A typical combine was accompanied by a housing estate built for its workforce. Combines signified modernity, because constructing and operating them required more advanced technical and administrative skills than managing a single factory, and situating several factories in one place was meant to make production more effective. Whether this happened is difficult to say. What is certain, however, was that in the 1960s the combines were hungry for people, because this was still a time of industrial expansion. However, the films suggest that at this period the shortage of specialists exceeded that of unskilled workforce.

Gold is set in Turoszów in Lower Silesia, where seams of brown coal were discovered in the nineteenth century, leading to the establishment of several small mines there. Under Gomułka they were integrated under a huge power plant, constituting one of the largest combines in Eastern Europe. Has's film is set during the period of this construction: its adventurous, 'heroic' moment. This is underlined by the title of the film, which brings to mind Western films, set during the gold rush in the nineteenth and early twentieth centuries, as in the famous classic by Charles Chaplin, *The Gold Rush* (1925). Turoszów is not far from the Polish border with Germany, a fact which is of significance for the film's narrative. In Has's film the combine appears to be a self-contained universe, not unlike the depot in *The Depot of the Dead*, discussed in the previous chapter, except that it is a huge place, in terms of its area, the number of inhabitants, and the complexity of the machinery. Predictably, the modernity of the equipment is not matched by the modernity of the housing and living conditions. The workers live in a cramped workers' hostel, where privacy is impossible, again recollecting the living conditions in Petelski's film. Many people who live there are drop-outs and outsiders. Such a choice of characters can be seen as a sign of the influence of the Western genre on Has's film and a reflection of the demography of the industrial centres situated far from large cities. Somebody needs to civilize this human menagerie. In the cinematic Wild West, it would be a good sheriff or a good woman; in *Gold* this task is attributed to Piotr, an engineer with managerial duties. Has idealizes this character by showing him to be utterly devoted to his work. Piotr waxes lyrical about the beauty of the minerals he found in Poland, which have almost no monetary value, but which matter for the geologists who discover them. The engineer also assumes the role of a mentor to Kazik, a young working-class character who found himself in the combine after escaping an accident when he was driving a truck. He fell asleep and thought that he had killed a man, although in reality he had only killed a dog. Kazik is restless and plans his escape to the other side of the Polish border. Piotr takes upon himself the challenge of stopping him by showing him that the factory offers a meaningful life. For his devotion to this working-class protégé, Piotr pays with his own life, as he catches cold and dies when trying to prevent his young friend from escaping to the West. To account for the ideological role played by Piotr, it is worth quoting Yugoslav author, Branislav Dimitrijević, who discussed the role of the technical intelligentsia in the works of Boris Arvatov, the Russian theorist of productivism:

> *The romanticisation of the 'technical intelligentsia' was a response to the romanticisation of the proletariat, and was founded upon the premise that unlike the bourgeoisie, the technical intelligentsia works closely with the proletariat, understands the conditions of their work and does not rule over the means of production. Hence, it can act in solidarity with the labourers and serve them as role models. (Dimitrijević, quoted in Jovanović 2015: 173–174)*

The character of Piotr can be seen as a means of justifying and smoothing over the growing gap in the salaries, living standards and status between Polish blue-collar and white-collar workers which took place in the 1960s. He is so talented and heroic that it is only natural that he stands above people like Kazik in the social hierarchy. At the same time, he cannot be compared to the managers in the capitalist factories, because he works for the good of his people, rather than for

Illustration 4.1: Kazik among the industrial sublime in *Gold*, directed by Wojciech Has

the capitalists. If we take into account that in the 1960s the Party tried to reposition itself as a technocratic force, then we can conjecture that Piotr also stands for the nomenklatura. His lionization can be seen as a way to idealize the class. This is achieved despite the lack of any obvious references to Piotr's political involvement (words such as 'the Party', 'socialism', 'progress', 'sacrifice' are not uttered in *Gold*) or even because of this lack, because ideology works better if it is transmitted in a subtle way. The fact that Piotr shows many traits of an existential hero or at least of a 'café existentialist' (Mazierska 2013), such as wearing dark jumpers and using sophisticated, irony-imbued language, does not undermine his link to the Party, but only adds to the attractiveness of this organization, rendering it 'cool'.

Unlike the eager workers in *The Adventure at Marienstadt*, their counterparts in *Gold* come across as lacking in enthusiasm. Neither of them is a shock worker or aspires to be one. Surviving rather than exceeding the daily quotas is everybody's objective. For one labourer, factory work is only a means of earning enough money to invest in his farm, reflecting on Gomułka's decision to stop collectivization of the land. He says that only then he will feel as if he is working for himself. Nobody encourages the workers to break their passivity and take responsibility for the organization of the plant; this is left to the management. The workers' lack of involvement in the running of the plant can be seen in the context of Gomułka's broken promise to give workers more power post-1956.

The centre of communal life in a combine is not the special 'house of the workers', but a restaurant with a friendly barwoman, in the vein of a Western film or Polish prewar melodrama. Here workers, managers and various shadowy local businessmen and drop-outs spend their free time chatting up the few available women and drinking alcohol, which is presented as an important way to survive the harsh reality of manual work and isolation from home.[1] This is a very different place than the 'Bricklayer's House', built in *An Adventure at Marienstadt*, because it is a site of unstructured leisure, divorced from work, not an extension of the workplace nor a means of creating a 'socialist man'. One can conjecture that such a place will be difficult to spot in socialist realist films because, as Nick Hodgin observes in relation to East German films about workers' lives, 'evidence of camaraderie and unity outside the control of the Party implied strength and power that might potentially be deployed against the Party – even if the films were not intended as subversive' (Hodgin 2015: 56). That we find it in Has's film suggests that the climate has changed: the Party now allows ordinary people to lead private lives in their free time.

Women in *Gold* have neither professional nor narrative autonomy. Their representation harks back to interwar melodrama. The most obvious 'transplant' is Piotr's wife, who wants him to return to Warsaw, not unlike Wanda in *The Depot of the Dead* who offered workmen sex in exchange for taking her to a big city. Piotr's wife also brings to mind the characters played by Maria Gorczyńska, as discussed in chapter 2. Her harsh treatment within the narrative can be linked to the emphasis placed by the socialist ideology on production at the expense of consumption. Nevertheless, allowing her to voice her desire for a better life points to the unfulfilled consumer needs of Polish women. By contrast, the barwoman is treated with sympathy, but this is because she has no plans to leave, but instead helps others to stay in the plant, giving ear to their stories. She is thus complicit with the patriarchy; her very job as a barwoman serving an almost exclusively male clientele confirms that. Finally, Has includes three young and pretty women who come to the plant, sporting high heels, seductive dresses and foreign-sounding nicknames. Unlike Hanka Ruczajówna, they do not come to the combine to lay bricks or operate heavy machinery, but like women in Westerns, are keen to take advantage of the shortage of women, offering the sex-hungry men their services as prostitutes. However, this is not spelt out openly, according to the official dogma that women in Poland do not need to earn their living in such a demeaning way.

Walkover is based on a similar premise as *Gold*: a young man named Leszczyc is lured to a chemical complex by its friendly director and a female colleague named Teresa, who came there to become, as she puts it, 'somebody important'. In common with Has, Skolimowski underscores the technocratic character of the industrial and political elite. The director's Party credentials are not even mentioned; instead his personal secretary gloats over his technical proficiency, which made him the youngest *kombinat* director in the whole country. The director is played by Krzysztof Chamiec, the same actor who was cast as engineer Piotr in *Gold*. This casting strategy shows that the technical intelligentsia of the 1960s consisted of urbane men, who gained their qualifications at the university, rather than on short courses for workers. In Skolimowski's film the director's technocratic approach is underscored by his lack of interest in individual workers as human beings, only in their usefulness for the factory. He is even deaf, which can be interpreted metaphorically as the deafness of the economic leadership to the needs of the workers, and does not sport an 'existential' costume, but a technocratic outfit consisting of a jacket and white shirt.

Teresa does not suit the type of woman whose role is limited to supporting a man, which prevailed in the 1960s, but comes across as an independent woman – a representative of the technical intelligentsia or at least somebody on the way to joining this exclusive club. However, she is not presented as a role model for the female audience, but denounced as an ex-activist of the student organization responsible for Leszczyc's expulsion from the university. Teresa's story might also signal the fact that, despite the rhetoric of equality, under state socialism it was more difficult for women than for men to climb the social ladder. This point is reinforced in an episode when she has to defend her project against a group of more experienced male engineers who regard it as too risky, and a female colleague who cannot stand the success of another woman.

At their first meeting, the director asks Teresa and Leszczyc to 'send wires to their acquaintances and friends to come, bringing their families with them'. Remarkably, he lures the potential workers not by appealing to the socialist cause, but by highlighting the advantages of working in the combine, essentially to their consumerist instincts. However, not all potential workers are welcomed with the same enthusiasm. For engineers there are apartments in the newly erected blocks, while the ordinary labourers must content themselves with places in the workers' hostel. Skolimowski thus implies that society in People's Poland was stratified and housing was an important vehicle to create and reinforce class divisions.

Leszczyc, who does not have a university degree, is packed in the workers' hostel. However, he is not an ordinary blue-collar worker, on account of having some university experience and earning his living not on the shop floor but through sport. He is a boxer, taking part in competitions for amateur boxers ('first steps') and making his living from selling trophies won this way. His position reflects the ambiguous status of sport in postwar Poland and the whole socialist bloc. Officially all sport was amateur; sportsmen were supposed to compete in their free time, after they finished working in the offices and factories. At the same time, sport was important in socialist propaganda for internal and external consumption. This demanded that the best sportsmen were given enough time and material resources to compete with the best from the West, which led to the typical 'socialist' situation when reality had to be squared with ideology. Many sportsmen were nominally employed in factories (often mines in the case of footballers), but in reality had nothing to do with production; they were just on the pay-books of these factories, negatively affecting the wages of ordinary workers. Upon his arrival Leszczyc hesitates between taking employment in the plant and continuing his life as a boxer. Work in the plant offers stability and the possibility of promotion. As a boxer Leszczyc has the chance to lead a more adventurous life. However, being almost thirty he cannot take part in many more fights for non-professionals and is probably too mediocre to embark on a truly professional career. He drifts, meeting people whose stories reveal various possibilities in Poland of small stabilization. In the end Leszczyc decides to stay, claiming that he does not want to give away his life in a 'walkover'. Given the enthusiasm of the director about sport, one can conjecture that such a decision might even widen Leszczyc's opportunities, allowing him to continue his sporting career, while receiving regular wages as a factory employee.

While in *Gold* and *Walkover* centre stage is still nominally taken by a (real or potential) manual worker or shared by him with a representative of the intelligentsia, *The Pier* offers privileges to a manager, relegating the working class to the background. The central character, named Andrzej, designs ships, supervises their construction and is responsible for preparing a ship-launching ceremony. He is thus a super-hero: a Batman for the technocratic state socialism. His talent and importance for the country's economy renders him a celebrity, as is testified by the crowd of journalists following him at the shipyard. Andrzej also enjoys an above-average standard of living, having a car and a 'trophy' wife who devotes herself to tending to his needs. Yet, he has so much to do that he does not even return home for the night, but sleeps in the factory and feels so exhausted that he hallucinates at work.

His gruelling schedule is a result of the 'dictatorship of plans', which Gomułka's regime did not give up, despite preaching sound economic knowledge. The pressure to finish a project on time is behind Andrzej's desire to escape from work. Another factor is its decadence and corruption, alluded to during a banquet prepared to celebrate the shipyard's success. We hear the words of a man who gives a speech praising the Polish ship industry, but the camera focuses on what happens under the tables. Someone is putting money in somebody else's pocket, a woman receives a key to use for a clandestine meeting, another person opens a bottle of wine and drinks it secretly. The dissociation of sounds and images creates a contrast between the façade of a successful and united Polish industry and its reality as ridden by corruption and clandestine hedonism. In this sense *The Pier* foretells the Cinema of Moral Concern of the 1970s.

When the celebration is over and Andrzej leaves for the countryside, he meets the same corrupted, selfish and snobbish people. Their final dance, reminiscent of the last dance from *Wesele* (*The Wedding*, 1901) by Stanisław Wyspiański, a critical play about Polish society of the nineteenth century, suggests that there is no escape from the situation. Significantly, among the people celebrating the shipyard's success there are no ordinary workers, only representatives of the nomenklatura and the media. This film thus symbolizes the demise of the ordinary worker which would not be reversed till the ascent to power of Solidarity. For Bolesław Michałek, *The Pier* offers a condensed vision of Polish society of the 1960s, of 'small people on the road' (Michałek 1970: 89) (a term evoking Różewicz's 'small stabilization'), as a society which did not fulfil its ambitions and ended up disappointed and exhausted. The narrative of *The Pier* finishes at dawn, with the image of a ship hitting water. As Michałek argues, this image calls for a return to work, duty, activity and normality, which in the opinion of the critic suggests an embracing of 'Prussian barracks morality', which states that a soldier should never be left idle, because idleness is a hotbed of dangerous thoughts. However, this conclusion sounds hollow (ibid.: 91); ultimately the film argues for a different approach to work and life, which allows one to be a human being, not a cog in a technocratic machine.

Although the three films focus on industrial expansion, they also refer to the role of agriculture and the countryside in the country's prosperity. In *Gold* and *Walkover* agriculture is represented as a poor relation of industry and a provider of cheap labour. In *Gold* the majority of the inhabitants of a workers' hostel come from the countryside, drawn there because of the low incomes and overpopulation of the countryside. Migration from the country to the city was meant to equalize the two parts of Poland, also in terms of their culture, and by the 1960s much progress had been made towards this goal. However, in these films this progress is either not acknowledged or assessed negatively as something which the peasants do not deserve. Has, in particular, follows a stereotypical representation of the Polish peasants as stubborn and not seeing anything beyond their own narrowly defined self-interest. As Zygmunt Kałużyński, the chief jester of Polish film criticism noticed, 'in Polish cinema one immediately sees a person from the countryside thanks to underscoring this person's exceptional stupidity' (Kałużyński 1976: 159). Polish postwar cinema was the most extreme among Eastern European cinemas in its derision of the peasantry. This might be explained by a combination of two factors: a perception that the Polish countryside was backward and hence a place to escape from; and the fact that the Polish intelligentsia, including filmmakers, had its origin there, but tried to disavow it by applying the perspective of the patronizing outsider.

The secondary importance of rural Poland is also indicated in the aforementioned films by the poor state of agricultural infrastructure, such as the dilapidated building on which one can decipher the words 'grain warehouse' (*magazyn zbożowy*) shown in *Walkover*, and the fact that most people who find the lowest type of employment in the combines come from the countryside. One example is a man feeding a goat near the plant who works as the factory night watchman. He belongs to a large group of Polish 'peasant-workers' (*chłoporobotnicy*): small farmers who in order to make ends meet took employment in the factories, but did not give up entirely their small plots of land. In Poland of state socialism they were at the bottom of the unspoken hierarchy of workers. Skolimowski also shows a huge cross, located at the crossroads, being pulled out of the ground to make way for a new road. This action indicates that Polish industrialization goes hand in hand with the eradication of religion. Indeed, in the newly created industrial centres people used to go to church less often than in the country, not least because there were fewer churches there. Yet in *Walkover* removing the cross proves difficult, suggesting that Poles were very attached to their Catholic faith, as they were attached to their scraps of land. In *The Pier* there is no sign of farming at all; an exotic sounding 'rancho' is a place where tired 'townies' can rest, as if rural Poland were reduced to an object of tourist pursuits.

The authors of these films also refer to the role of art under socialism. Piotr in *Gold* equates artistic creation with industrial work, claiming that work is able to transform worthless stones into beautiful jewels. What the earth gives us, after the workers' intervention, becomes so exquisite that there is no need to decorate one's apartment with pictures; industry is the highest art. Such a view, however, is undermined from the bottom, by the workers who read American adventure prose and cite French poetry. The director of the combine in *Walkover* does not consider industrial production either a work of art or a worthwhile topic for it. When two young women, possibly from art college, bring to his office some sketches of his plant, he dismisses them, saying that he has enough factory in the factory – he wants something different on the wall. His words can be taken as an expression of the need for autonomous art under socialism (which was achieved in the late 1950s and the 1960s) and as an ironic comment about the limited potential of attracting an audience to films about the achievements of socialist industry. In *The Pier*, the factory is clearly separated from artistic production. Andrzej visits the artist's studio when his job is finished and revels in what he sees there. He enters this place only as a 'tourist', to admire, but not participate. Ironically, with his nonchalant disregard for social recognition, and his idiosyncratic, 'surrealistic' way of looking at the world, Andrzej appears closer to the stereotype of an artist than his artist friend.

Although the choice of the settings in the three films can be classified as socialist realist, their representations are not; they are close to surrealism. There is something strange, even uncanny about the plants. The mise-en-scène in *Gold* was compared to cosmic and underwater landscapes from the paintings by Yves

Tanguy (Grodź 2009: 79–80) and this surrealist painter could be evoked in relation to the remaining films. In all of them machines and other human creations, such as the ship in *The Pier*, look like gigantic dragons and sea monsters, with lives of their own, rather than being obedient to their creators. Their sheer size brings to mind Marx's view of machines as a means to thwart and enslave the factory worker, hence can be regarded as a warning against the danger of alienation caused by the technocratic turn Poland took in the 1960s, but is also a way to show the industrial might of Poland of the 1960s in its dark glory. These contradictory associations bring to mind the concept of the industrial sublime (Jensen and Bland 2013), which can be also evoked in relation to western cinema of this period, most importantly the films of Michelangelo Antonioni.

Why *combine* working-class heroes, spaces and stories with surrealist motifs? For Wojciech Has, who annoyed the authorities with his earlier films, *Pętla* (*Noose*, 1957) and *Wspólny pokój* (*A Shared Room*, 1960), deemed as unacceptably bleak and detached from the Polish reality, making a *produkcyjniak* was a way of redeeming himself in their eyes, while remaining faithful to his favourite style. The move to surrealism, rather than simply constituting an attempt to purify socialist realism of its propagandist excess, might also signal that the filmmakers reject neither socialism nor realism, but want to offer their alternative versions. It is worth mentioning here that the advocates of surrealism argued that it is not anti-realism, but a superior type of realism, able to capture the deeper aspects of reality for which 'ordinary' realism is unable to account (Zusi 2004). Surrealism, not unlike socialist realism, was also a political project, close to Marxism, but distancing itself from 'the official vulgate of the Comintern' (Löwy 2009: 22). Michael Löwy labels surrealism of this kind as 'Gothic Marxism' and 'Romantic Marxism'. Henri Lefebvre, on the other hand, argues that 'by abandoning the everyday in order to find the marvellous and the surprising (at one and the same time immanent in the real and transcending it), Surrealism rendered triviality unbearable' (Lefebrre 2002: 226).

The Polish filmmakers' use of surrealism could be seen as an attempt to return to true Marxism, which was twisted by Stalinism and played down under the 'small stabilization' regime, or a subtle way of distancing themselves from state socialism by focusing on art rather than life. The importance of art is augmented by self-reflexive moments in these films, such as discussions about the character of artistic representations, and reference to earlier films about industrial production and iconic socialist realistic images. Another common denominator of the styles of these films is the extensive use of long shots and long takes, with *Walkover* setting a Polish record in this respect. Time in these films drags on, as if working and living in the 1960s became much slower than in the previous decade.

These New Wave films attracted much praise from the critics, as much in Poland as abroad, but did not fill cinema theatres, reflecting the official policy of this decade to divide Polish cinema into two strands: high-brow (auteurist) and low-brow (popular or populist).

Autonomous Leisure

In the previous part I mentioned that in *Gold* the leisure of working-class people is given more autonomy than in films of the 1950s. Still, its main subject is work: a young working-class man finding employment and settling in a new place thanks to his older and better educated mentor. By contrast, in one of the most celebrated Polish films of the 1960s, *Nóż w wodzie* (*Knife in the Water*, 1962) by Roman Polanski, leisure takes centre stage and is presented as leisure for pleasure. It is not the first film by Polanski on this topic; in 1957 he shot *Let's Break the Ball*, but this was only a short film: a rehearsal for his opus magnum.

Knife in the Water shows a married couple, Andrzej and Krystyna, driving a western car towards the Polish lake district of Mazury, where they are to go on an excursion in their privately owned yacht, on the way picking up a hitchhiker (described as the Student in subsequent reviews). Andrzej is a sports journalist and Krystyna a 'trophy wife', whose main occupation is making her husband's life pleasurable. In the 1960s such representation was suspect because it did not reflect the real status of journalists or other cultural workers, who were unlikely to have a western car, still less a sailing boat. Polanski was not just being unrealistic in this respect; more dangerously, the figure of Andrzej offered a veiled image of the nomenklatura, whose above-average standard of living could not be represented realistically due to censorship. Unlike the sympathetic managers in the films discussed in the previous sections, Andrzej is presented as selfish, arrogant, yet ultimately naive. Unlike Piotr in *Gold*, he does not want to help the younger man, but rather to use him to boost his ego and reaffirm his class position. If Andrzej's image could thus be projected on the 'Party class', then this class comes across as parasitic, incompetent and hypocritical. Krystyna, on the other hand, is treated more sympathetically than Piotr's wife, being intelligent and less consumption-oriented than her husband.

When the three travellers reach the marina, the Student, looking at the boat, asks, 'Club-owned?', to which Andrzej replies, 'No, our own'. Such exchange highlights the growing (private) prosperity during the period of small stabilization, but also the fact that at this time the norm was communal property and a modest standard of living. Once on the boat we observe two types of behaviour, both contrary to what was prescribed as correct conduct under socialist realism. One consists of playing with things. This is especially the prerogative of Andrzej, who likes to show off his expensive kitchen equipment, transistor radio and even a blow-up shark with which he plays with Krystyna in the water. If we regard Andrzej as representative of the decade, then the 1960s in this film come across as a period of the new social stratification based on the possession of consumer goods (Pobłocki 2012: 70–74). While Andrzej plays with things, the Student, whose rucksack is almost empty, spends his time on the boat doing nothing or rather allowing his senses to work. He squints and looks at the clouds passing and is able to tell the time without looking at a clock. While watching the film, we are forced to pay attention to what would normally be excluded in a fiction film, such as the movements of the characters' hands, or whether the characters walk with energy, grace or clumsiness. As there is little dialogue and conversations tend to be mundane, we manage to hear other sounds: seagulls calling, the splashing of water, bare feet walking on the deck, which go unnoticed in mainstream films.

The novelty of Polanski's film was noted by reviewers (Michałek 1962; Bryll 1962), but critics highlighted its focus on things, rather than its haptic dimension. Andrzej Werner, writing about *Knife in the Water* from a distance of two decades, claims that objects in this film are fetishized; their value to their owners exceeds their exchange or use value (Werner 1985: 99–100). Werner also suggests that such fascination with things pertains not only to the characters, but also to the director of the film, who in this way praises consumerism.

In my opinion, Polanski's approach to life as being reduced to consumption and a play provides the subversive potential of this film, hence its New-Wave-ness, because *Knife in the Water* invites viewers to experience the world in a new way: sensually. At the same time, Polanski shows that in order to sense the world, we have to enjoy comfort, measured by spare time and a certain amount of material possessions. Most importantly, our mind has to be occupied by the 'here and now', as opposed to thinking about the future, which was the prerogative of socialist realist heroes or the past, as was the case with the Polish School films.[2]

However, the focus on affluence and unstructured leisure and the suggestion that Polish society is a class society, in which consumption is a marker of one's class position, with the selfish nomenklatura consuming excessively while ordinary people are asked to work and be humble, were enough reasons for *Knife in the Water* to incur the personal dislike of the ascetic leader of the Party, Władysław Gomułka, who accused the film of being contrived, vacuous and alien to the Polish national character (Stachówna 1987: 24). That said, the film can also be interpreted as a subtle paean to the period of stabilization, which allowed (at least some) Poles to experience the world in a new way, enjoying themselves rather than suffering for past and future generations.

Beyond Bourgeois Life

The 1960s also gave birth to Polish popular cinema,[3] with the Party taking the role of the 'midwife'. The privileged genre was comedy, for which Polish audiences always had an immense thirst, which was rarely quenched.[4] It became the preserve of directors who only started their career around 1960, such as Tadeusz Chmielewski, Sylwester Chęciński, Jerzy Ziarnik and, most importantly, Stanisław Bareja. Not unlike Polish interwar cinema, which suffered a bad press, this cinema was met with reluctant acceptance as a necessary component of any national cinema, but which is not worthy of serious examination. The prominent Polish critic, Konrad Eberhardt, writing in 1967, claimed that Polish popular films lacked professionalism and originality (Eberhardt 1967: 13). In the same vein, Andrzej Werner, echoing Adorno's criticism of comedies and the culture industry at large (see part 1), accused them of being, paradoxically, not a young cinema, but a 'cinema du papa', devoid of experimental ambition. Werner also suggested that those who specialized in popular cinema were politically conformist, not through promoting the dominant ideology, but by avoiding any ideology, limiting themselves to telling a banal story and accepting subjects allocated to them by the authorities (Werner 1985: 98). If we use the vocabulary of Alexander Zinoviev, we can describe them as homini sovietici, because 'convictions are something Western man has, not Soviet man. Instead of having convictions the latter has a "stereotype of behaviour". This doesn't presuppose any convictions, and so it's compatible with every sort of conviction' (Zinoviev 1985: 11).

Only recently has the cycle of 1960s popular films attracted less caustic remarks, reflecting a wider trend of critics turning to popular cinema at the expense of arthouse cinema. Tadeusz Lubelski in his *History of Polish Cinema*, published in 2009, writes that the popular films which Eberhardt treated with contempt survived the passage of time (presumably better than some alleged masterpieces) and have been released on DVD, making a handsome profit. Lubelski suggests that this is because of their ethnographic value of allowing us to see how Poles looked, lived, worked and enjoyed free time, how the grand scheme of things was mapped onto ordinary lives (Lubelski 2009a: 269).

Monika Talarczyk-Gubała observes that comedies of this period broke with socialist realism by introducing a different type of character, who can be described as 'petit bourgeois': clerks working in state offices and banks, waiters, porters, shop assistants, customers in cafés, etc. (Talarczyk-Gubała 2007: 45). Previously such people would have been depicted as parasites, due to engaging in unproductive work or consumption. The fact that in the 1960s they became the main object of attention and were treated with sympathy points to their rehabilitation and, by the same token, the downgrading of those who used to be cherished by Polish filmmakers in the 1950s: workers and people who came to the large cities from the countryside. This is also reflected in the mise-en-scène of popular films of the 1960s, from which the sites of production are almost absent. By contrast, we see apartments and places of private consumption, such as restaurants and cafés, replacing 'houses and culture' and the Party headquarters, where citizens worked on their self-improvement. By the same token, these films are not as empty of ideology as their critics suggest.

Although popular films were made by different directors, including some, like Janusz Morgenstern, who navigated between the auteurist and popular pole of Polish cinema, this (mega)genre was dominated by Stanisław Bareja. In the 1960s he directed one criminal film and several comedies, which were met with popular acclaim, rendering him king of Polish comedy and popular cinema at large. As I will return to Bareja in subsequent chapters, it is worth mentioning that his career can be divided into two parts. In the first part, coinciding with the 1960s, the director showcased Polish achievements. In the second half, in the 1970s and 1980s, he became a relentless critic of what he regarded as the absurdities of socialist Poland. His earlier films were greatly influenced by the interwar comedies (Wiśniewski 1973: 15; Replewicz 2009: 53); in the later ones the director developed his own idiom. I will consider here Bareja's three films, *Mąż swojej żony (A Husband* of His Wife; 1960), Żona dla Australijczyka (Wife for an Australian, 1964) and Małżeństwo z rozsądku (Marriage of Convenience, 1966).

A Husband of His Wife is based on the play written by Jerzy Jurandot, a popular author of the interwar period.[5] Knowing that, we can identify what Bareja had to change in the original to make his film appeal to the audiences of the 1960s. The film is about a classical musician, Michał Karcz, whose achievements are overshadowed by the successes of his famous sportswoman wife. One can imagine that this problem (if one sees it as a problem) would be resolved differently in different periods. In the interwar cinema, the wife would probably be 'domesticated' by having a baby after winning an Olympic medal. In the 1950s, during the hegemony of socialist realism, the narrative would expose the patriarchal mindset of the husband who does not accept his wife's equality. In the end he would recognize her right to self-fulfilment through professional advancement and the couple would agree to share their domestic duties. A Husband of His Wife offers us a 'third way'. From the beginning Fołtasiówna has a sincere desire to be a traditional wife, who fries pork chops for her husband. Yet, she cannot succeed due to her lack of time and the opposition of her trainer who demands that she follows a strict low fat diet. This situation is not resolved by her husband taking on the domestic duties, but by the couple employing a maid. It is unlikely that such a figure would have appeared in the previous decade, when ideology fought with the remnants of bourgeois mindset. Now bourgeoisie is back in its privileged position (in film at least), even though it is not an old, but a new middle class.

The husband does not really mind his wife being a successful 'superwoman', but only resents the fact that his achievements are not appreciated. When he eventually receives a prestigious award and is allowed to travel to Edinburgh, they are both happy. The film thus points to the official recognition of popular culture as a distinct type of culture, which took place in the 1960s and which was accepted by the majority of the population. We see this poignantly in scenes showing the special treatment of sportsmen: they have no problems in acquiring passports, they are addressed politely by (otherwise rude) hotel receptionists, and their successes fill pages of national newspapers. However, although Fołtasiówna is a star, she is still officially only an amateur sportswoman, and works in an office. In contrast, Karcz's official job is that of a classical musician, but he gets no special treatment when applying for a passport and his international achievements are practically ignored by the media. This is because, as a sports journalist explains, everybody is interested in competitive sport, while symphonic music is enjoyed only by the few.[6] We should not, however, take such pronouncements about high art at face value. Artists creating 'serious art', be it musicians, painters or writers, received special protection from the state, on account of the educational role their work was expected to fulfil and simply because the state was the only purchaser of their work. These two factors led to a special sense of importance and entitlement, of which Karcz's attitude is paradigmatic.

A Husband of His Wife also points towards the 1960s shift to consumption, particularly in the episodes showing Karcz's old tutor and his daughter visiting Warsaw. The daughter, although she comes from the provincial Włocławek, looks like a Parisian lady and spends her time in Warsaw visiting elegant clothes shops, accompanied by a popular boxer, who shows her the beauty of the capital, like Phoenix rising from ashes.[7] A potent symbol of consumption and the shift from high to popular culture is a television set, which in the Fołtasiówna-Karcz household shows sports events. Bareja here spotted perfectly the new trend in Polish society. In 1955 there were only 1,700 television sets in Poland; in 1960 this number went up to 202,500 (Brodziński 1971: 120). Bareja also shows that improvement in living standards can be achieved through access to foreign travel. The experienced sportsmen, who frequently travel abroad, advise the naive Karcz what to buy and sell in each country: a photo camera here, alcohol there, caviar elsewhere, etc., to be able to buy presents to bring back home. In Bareja's later films, as I will demonstrate in due course, informal foreign trade will take more screen time, reflecting its increased importance in plugging the gaps in the country's economy.

Another of Bareja's films about a wife is *Wife for an Australian*. 'Marriage' in the titles of many films of this decade suggests that private life had gained in importance. *Wife for an Australian* concerns marriage as a pragmatic arrangement, with women being put on the market as commodities. On this occasion an Australian farmer of Polish origin visits Poland to find a wife with the intention of taking her back to Australia. The premise of the film is realistic, pointing on the one hand to the desire of Polish women to emigrate to the West and, on the other hand, to that of western men of low human capital (in this case resulting from having an unattractive job) to seek spouses in places where these shortcomings are balanced by their western-ness, seen as a great asset. Bareja uses this premise as a pretext to show Polish superiority over the West. The eponymous Australian finds the perfect candidate for a wife in a performer in the famous folk ensemble

Mazowsze and, enchanted by her appearance, the richness of Polish folk culture and the overall prosperity of Poland, decides not to 'traffic' her to Australia, but to stay with her in Poland. As Aleksander Jackiewicz notes, Bareja's film does not claim to show us the real Poland, in the same way that Mazowsze does not claim to show us the real Polish countryside (Jackiewicz 1964: 12) and the critic praises Bareja for being consistent in this approach. However, he mentions that he would be interested to see a film about Poles and their relatives who settled in the West, knowing that the former often amplify their poverty to extract something from the latter (ibid.: 12). For such a film, however, Jackiewicz would have to wait till the next decade, when Ewa and Czesław Petelscy made *Bilet powrotny (Return Ticket*, 1979), discussed in the next chapter.

The lack of realism in *Wife for an Australian* can be explained by it being a musical. Piotr Fortuna goes as far as to say that the strategy used by Bareja in this film is that of rejection: the (true) reality is rejected to give way to its idyllic image. Fortuna argues that *Wife for an Australian* and other Polish musicals of the 1960s compensated for the shortages of consumer goods in this period (Fortuna 2015: 127).[8]

The main part of the positive message of Bareja's films is that Poland is becoming prosperous and its citizens never had it so good. Not everything is perfect, but this is due to human not systemic failures. From this perspective, however, *Marriage of Convenience*, despite being a musical, comes across as a transitory piece, as on this occasion the director points as much to 1960s prosperity as to the absurdities of the socialist economy. The film brings to mind *Matter to Be Settled*, discussed in the previous chapter, in its focus on the second economy as a means of plugging the gaps in the first economy and a vehicle of social stratification. Yet Bareja presents this milieu from within, and by this very fact in a quite sympathetic way, which would be unacceptable under socialist realism. The film begins with a song sung by a band of street musicians, with the singer of satirical songs, Tadeusz Chyła, as its leader. The band would reappear later, like a chorus in a Greek play, commenting on the events unfolding in front of our eyes. The song, with lyrics by Agnieszka Osiecka, *Mr. Kwiatkowski, Mr. Kowalski*, includes the well-known motifs of socialist realism, such as rebuilding Warsaw, which is now full of schools and kindergartens and announcing that these are for the benefit of ordinary people, who are well cared for. The song also says that it does not matter whether one lives in a villa with a garden or a small, cramped place, because statistically it is getting better in Poland and everything Poles possess is a common good. It is worth recollecting here that the socialist project consisted of the nationalization of the country, namely taking away what belonged to private citizens to put into communal use. But the characters presented by Bareja base their actions on the opposite premise: if under socialism everything is common, appropriating it for private use is acceptable, because in this way the citizens take only what belongs to them anyway. This approach is exemplified most conspicuously by fake engineer Kwilecki, who with the assistance of a worker employed in a textile factory steals thread to weave cloth in his apartment. The thread comes directly from the factory to Kwilecki's flat which is located opposite the factory, via the windows in the factory and the apartment of the private entrepreneur.[9] If we are to believe the song performed by Chyła, such a practice does not constitute a crime because people engaged in this form of 'public-private partnership' ultimately work for the common good. Indeed, to some extent, they worked for the common good, by ameliorating acute shortages of consumer goods, by using sparse resources more efficiently. At the same time, they diminished the property of the state and those who worked for it and consumed its products, because stealing state property lowered the quantity and quality of state products and made them more expensive.

The main plot of *Marriage of Convenience* revolves around the relationship of Joanna, the pretty daughter of semi-legal traders from Różycki bazaar, trading in *ciuchy*, privately produced or imported clothes, and her two suitors: a slacker aristocrat Edzio and Andrzej, an artist. Although they are apparently both poor, Edzio and Andrzej rent a trendy loft in the Old City. Edzio, who makes Joanna's acquaintance first, asks for her hand in marriage, which her parents reject, claiming that their union would be disastrous for all concerned. In order to survive in the environment of state socialism, they have to look for partners favoured by the new ideology, such as artists who hardly earn anything but are allowed to possess everything, unlike Joanna's parents who earn a lot but cannot disclose their income, because they would risk losing it. Thanks to their daughter marrying Andrzej, Joanna's parents can launder their illegal earnings by buying an aristocratic mansion as a studio for their son-in-law while ensuring prosperity for their daughter and themselves. Bareja's representation of Joanna's parents conforms to the image of small capitalists (*prywaciarze*), as circulated not only in the official propaganda, but also unofficially. They lack education and wider horizons, as well as any communal instinct; making profit is their ultimate objective. They are also insensitive towards their daughter's desires, treating her as a tool to amass more money. However, their work ethic is commendable and it lays bare the shortcomings of work in state enterprises. They work hard, respond swiftly to the needs of their customers and do not exploit anybody, except the state industry, and that not because they are natural 'thieves', but because there is no other way to acquire the tools and materials they need. Moreover, if it were not for the fact that they cannot put their income into the bank, they would not need to invent tricks to hide it. Although in the light of the official socialist ideology and the law they are criminals, the novelty of Bareja's approach, in comparison with that offered by socialist realist films, is that they do not come across as criminals. Rather their criminal status renders the law and ideology absurd.

Money does not afford Joanna's parents prestige. On the contrary, they are treated like social pariahs by Polish society and they internalize this perception. Their status reflects on the convergence of two ideologies: prewar worshipping of gentry and ridiculing of those who attempted to join this class without possessing the right cultural capital; and postwar condemnation of people who sought money rather than more idealistic values such as knowledge. In both ideologies money was downgraded; one was expected to have it, but not strive for it and talk about it. The apogee of this attitude to money is a motif of dollars, buried by Joanna's

Illustration 4.2: Andrzej admiring Joanna's picture in *Marriage of Convenience*, directed by Stanisław Bareja

parents, which after being recovered by them literally stink. Ultimately, Joanna's parents cannot achieve social recognition because money is their only asset. Joanna herself understands this approach and hides her true background from Andrzej, pretending that her parents are ambassadors who rarely visit Poland. She also attempts to pass an art college entrance exam and works part-time posing for adverts. Her upper-class ways make Andrzej fall in love with her, therefore their marriage is ultimately not a marriage of convenience but of love. Joanna's union with Andrzej seals her departure from the social milieu of *prywaciarze*, entering the exclusive circle of the artists, intelligentsia and those working in the media. It could be suggested that in this way she stands for Bareja himself who was the son of a private producer (Replewicz 2009: 108), yet managed to transcend his class by becoming a filmmaker.[10]

Because *Marriage of Convenience* casts as main characters artists, aristocrats and traders, inevitably it shows the spaces they appropriate. The aristocratic house where Edzio's aunt lives is almost a ruin; whatever one touches there crumbles to dust. This material decline stands for the metaphorical decline of this stratum of Polish society, which appears to be deserved, as Edzio and his aunt are snobbish, selfish and ultimately useless. The flat of Joanna's parents also signifies the interwar past, due to its old-fashioned furniture, ornaments and a large wedding photograph of the couple. Only the loft inhabited by Andrzej and Edzio looks stylish and contemporary. Although Bareja's choice of characters leaves him little scope to explore the lifestyles and zones pertaining to the socialist mainstream (the bulk of the working classes, who settled in Warsaw), on several occasions they appear in the background. For example, at a certain stage Joanna and Andrzej visit the furniture shop 'Emilia', the best known furniture shop in Warsaw, to choose furniture for their new house. Although they are meant to live in an aristocratic mansion, they find themselves among the functional items designed for a miniature, one-bedroom or studio apartment. In his subsequent films Bareja would mock this socialist functionality by showing that it does not function properly, but on this occasion the socialist furniture exudes charm. To cover his illegal activities, 'engineer' Kwilecki makes his flat look like a *skansen* of folk art, complete with wooden cradle where he sits as if it was an armchair. In Bareja's later film, *Miś* (*Teddy Bear*, 1980), a pseudo-folk straw sculpture of a bear is used as a container for smuggling alcohol to London (see chapter 8). This emphasis on folk art, which acts as an empty signifier, reflects the neglect of the countryside by the socialist authorities, in comparison with the city and its culture.

Another romantic comedy, *Dwa żebra Adama* (*Adam's Two Ribs*, 1963), directed by Janusz Morgenstern, also provides insight into the changes which occurred in the 1960s in the dominant ideology concerning class and gender, as well as the operation of the political elite in the Polish provinces: the fictitious small town of Gody. According to one reviewer, it was the only Polish film by this point to show how political power operates outside the capital (*w terenie*) (Klaczyński 1964: 14). The film begins when the chairman of a local council, who is also a devoted historian of his town, announces that he would like to name a new street after his friend, engineer Wiktus. Wiktus is about to return to his birthplace after some years spent in Africa, where he was helping the local population to construct factories and housing estates. The discussions about bestowing such an honour on Wiktus points to the symbolic shift in the ideology of state socialism, consisting of the silent stripping from the working class of its distinction as the main creators of prosperous Poland, and transferring this honour to the technical intelligentsia, as was also demonstrated in *Walkover*, *Gold* and *The Pier*. In the same way, it highlights the Party's desire to present itself not as driven by abstract principles, but pragmatic considerations. The composition of the power elite in Gody reflects the political consensus post-October 1956, with the Party agreeing to accommodate some other viewpoints and groups, such as Catholics and 'free thinkers', to avoid conflict. Everybody who matters in Gody belongs to the intelligentsia[11] and these people owe their power not to their dedication to the communist cause, but to the fact that they belong to a local clique. Examples are the priest and the owner of a pharmacy, whose lineage points to the way in which political power was distributed in interwar Poland. Women in this group are marginalized, as they were in the Polish parliament, and represent provincial conservatism, as demonstrated by the stern demeanour and unfashionable clothes of the chairwoman of the League of Women. All of these people are middle-aged, suggesting that the period of fast progress, characteristic of the first postwar decade, is over. Those in the council who oppose their leader's idea of honouring Wiktus do not suggest naming the street after Lenin, Dzierżyński or any local Party activist, but Adam Mickiewicz, the Romantic poet-prophet, whose works provided the staple diet for Polish school children of every age. The turn to Mickiewicz reflects both the nationalistic bias of Gomułka's regime and a desire for stabilization, which means, among other things, returning to a 'safe', depoliticized tradition. Although ordinary workers build the housing estate in

Gody, they are not visible in the film, again pointing to their virtual disappearance from the socialist 'grand plan'.

The title of the film refers to Wiktus being a bigamist. He has a Polish wife and an Italian one whom he married during his stay in Africa and who follows him to his hometown.[12] One can imagine that under socialist realism such a premise would have led to a scenario of the 'original' wife's self-fulfilment through professional advancement, which would prove to her philandering husband that he made a mistake by betraying her. In *Adam's Two Ribs*, the wife who is essentially a housewife (she looks after a cow and some hens, but this is not presented as a source of any significant income) puts up with her husband's bigamy and even befriends his second wife, who is also a housewife with no professional aspirations. At some point we see the three of them going together to the church. In Gody there appears to be a surplus of women, with almost each man being served by a wife and a lover. Young women, in common with working-class men, have no authority of their own; they are just appendages to the older men.

Wiktus' is chastised for his bigamy, but because it undermines traditional Christian morality, not socialist principles. The communist apparatchiks behave as if they have lost any totalitarian ambitions; they are just satisfied when the citizens do not break the law. At one point Wiktus attempts to present himself as a 'new man', leading the way towards a new morality, based on sexual freedom. Today we associate such an attitude with the 1960s, but it was also attributed to the early communists, overthrown by Stalin, who advocated a return to traditional sexual morality. Wiktus' ideas are swiftly dismissed by Gody's political elite as preposterous, reflecting the conservatism of 'small stabilization' and the provinciality of the setting. The grand socialist project by this point serves merely as a fig leaf to hide a mundane, bourgeois existence. This impression is underscored by the film's style, with the majority of scenes shot in a studio, the camera lingering on the ornaments decorating the houses, smooth and slightly artificial dialogue and elegant acting, which lacks energy. It is, as Werner observed, the Polish equivalent of the 'cinema du papa', with the elegant Wanda Kossobudzka in the role of Gody's archivist and the narrator of the film encapsulating this style.

Gangsterzy i filantropi (*The Gangsters and the Philanthropists*, 1963), directed by Jerzy Hoffman and Edward Skórzewski, also attempts to merge the Polish reality of the 1960s with a bygone era, but on this occasion it is interwar Poland reality and the 'timeless' reality of English criminal comedies. The film consists of two loosely connected parts, the first concerned with 'gangsters', the second with 'philanthropists'. The first part, modelled on Ealing comedies, casts as the main character a gangster nicknamed Professor, not unlike the main protagonist of *The Ladykillers* (1955) by Alexander Mackendrick. He comes across as a true intellectual with elegance and good manners, and is played by the chief intellectual of the Polish screen, Gustaw Holoubek. Examples of Professor's sharp mind are winning a chess game against a judge, and the precision with which he prepares a robbery on a van carrying money from a department store to a bank. His prewar pedigree is also revealed by his spacious apartment full of books, old furniture and tasteful ornaments. His collaborators, by contrast, have the style of the criminal underclass, complete with criminal jargon, again not unlike the gangsters led by Professor in *The Ladykillers*. Professor's plan alludes to the opinion that there is no honest way for the interwar intelligentsia to regain the social position which they thought they deserved. The gentleman criminal ultimately fails, because he does not take into account the fact that his intricate plan can be sabotaged by less subtle criminals, who steal the wheels from his car. Although the film shows that in socialist Poland crime does not pay, rather than enjoying the punishment of a gangster we feel sympathy for the hapless Professor, whose versatile talents and strong work ethic are left to waste in a country where shabbiness and botch rule. As a film underscoring the clash between the high and low work ethics of different sections of the Polish population, *The Gangsters and the Philanthropists* foreshadows Bareja's comedies of the 1970s (see chapter 5).

In the second part of the film we are introduced to a shy chemist, who after causing an accident at work loses his lab job and by chance is taken for an inspector checking the quality of service in restaurants and specifically whether they sell alcohol and food in the quantities stated on the menu. In Poland it was not uncommon for cooks and waiters to serve 'under-weight' dishes in order to resell the 'saved' food for extra profit or use it for their own consumption; this was a consequence of the economy of shortages or of universal welfare. As Małgorzata Mazurek notes, 'state socialism fought "speculation" as much as it reproduced it' (Mazurek 2013; see also Mazurek 2012). The film argues that it is only the threat of criminalization, as opposed to the risk that a disgruntled customer might choose a different restaurant, that makes the restaurant employees behave differently. To avert this threat, the managers of the restaurants offer the fake inspector a huge bribe in exchange for visiting their premises less often. His activities are cut short only when he meets a real inspector. As the 'chemist' never claimed to represent the state office, he is cleared by the court, although not by the tax office, which demands an explanation for the source of his extra income. Hoffman and Skórzewski not only present the work of a fake inspector, but also the utilization of its fruits by his family. The relationship between the two is simple: the more the 'chemist' earns, the more consumer goods his wife and daughter acquire. They purchase fashionable shoes, clothes, a refrigerator and eventually pay instalments towards a detached house, which in socialist Poland was a great luxury. The simple translation of work into consumption and the extravagant scale of the latter testify to the film's post-Stalinist setting, when restrictions on private work and the second economy were eased, and there was less emphasis on accumulation. Still, it would look more realistic in the 1970s, which was the 'decade of consumption' than in the rather ascetic 1960s. But, of course, this discrepancy demonstrates that films not only reflect on the political and economic status quo, but on people's dreams and aspirations and this is especially the case with musicals and comedies, which have a licence to exaggerate. Linking men with hard work (even if this work is criminal) and women with consumption likens this film to other movies of the 1960s, as previously discussed. However, on this occasion women do not act as obstacles to male professional success, but as its facilitators. Consumption on this occasion does not preclude production (even if production here only means making profit), but is its engine, as is the case in the capitalist economy. Objects of consumption (especially dresses and shoes) are fetishized through close-ups, thus acknowledging the immense appetite for material goods, which in the 1960s was fulfilled only in small measure.

The Gangsters and the Philanthropists, not unlike Bareja's *Marriage of Convenience*, implies inconsistencies in the official approach to the second economy. After 1956 it was easier to earn money on the side, but accounting for the extra income remained difficult. By the same token the system transformed a large proportion of society into criminals. They were rarely penalized, but the fact that almost nobody could claim to have a clear conscience helped to retain control over the population.

Worker Above Work

Documentary films of the 1960s continued to feature many of the subjects that dominated Polish cinema during the previous decade, such as building mines, steelworks and chemical combines. However, documentary filmmakers now tried to observe people rather than illustrate with images a particular general thesis about them (Drozdowski 1985: 123–124). Many privileged the experience of an individual, as opposed to a group. Although the most common subject of documentaries in this decade is still work, it is presented in less heroic fashion as being marked by tiredness, boredom, even pain. Workers in these films tend to be more important than work.

A filmmaker who played a crucial role in introducing these changes is Kazimierz Karabasz. His *Muzykanci* (*The Musicians*, 1958) in a sense begins the 1960s documentary cinema by moving away from two aspects of documentaries of the 1950s: the voice of the narrator; and the portrayal of the workers as subservient to the grand project of building socialist Poland. In *The Musicians* the only sign of the narrator's intervention are the titles at the beginning which introduce the film's protagonists: older men, working in a tram depot, who play in a brass band. It is announced that these people have to give up their free time in order to play together. They are described as 'The Last Mohicans' and one wonders whether this is because younger men prefer more private pastimes or because this type of music went out of fashion in the 1960s, being replaced by jazz and later rock or big-beat, as it was called in Poland. Before we read these titles, we see the musicians engaged in welding, which gives way to different sounds: shoes tapping and instrument tuning. We get the impression that the musicians practice away from the controlling eyes of Party officials, even though, as we later learn, they do not do this in their own space, but in a factory, next to the place of industrial production. One can argue that such leisure is useful for work as it helps team building, or conversely that such camaraderie outside the control of the Party implies power than might be deployed against the Party. Both the representation of autonomous leisure and the lack of voice-over points to the workers gaining more independence from the state in this period and filmmakers seeing them more as autonomous subjects.

The 'worker above work'[13] approach is also applied by Karabasz in his *Rok Franka W.* (*The Year of Franek W.*, 1967), made almost ten years after *The Musicians*. The film follows a year in the life of Franek Wróbel, a young man from a village in the Kieleckie region, who joins the Voluntary Labour Corps (Ochotnicze Hufce Pracy, OHP), as presented in his diary, which Karabasz asked Franek to write for the purpose of making his film. The Voluntary Labour Corps was a semi-military youth organization set up in 1958, offering its members a chance to gain work experience and professional qualifications, as well as general and civic education.

It was a channel for social promotion for those living in the country, where such opportunities were scarcer.¹⁴ But this was at great personal cost for its members, as it involved working from early morning till afternoon, followed by studying till the late evening. The volunteers often worked in places where ordinary workers were reluctant to go (not unlike *gastarbeiters* in the West), such as road and railway constructions and building mines, and were poorly paid, because they were not treated as fully-fledged workers, but apprentices. All the advantages and problems pertaining to working in the OHP also concern Franek, who arrives in Silesia to initially work on the construction site, in the cold and mud. The work is so hard for him that he is first criticized for its low quality and then, when it is agreed that his health does not allow him to work in such severe conditions, moved to lighter work, on the conservation of the telephone lines. Studying also proves difficult for Franek; frequently he is too tired to concentrate in the classroom and cannot understand technical problems. Being shy, he feels lonely, a situation exacerbated by the fact that he is put in a room with some men who have known each other for longer. Nevertheless, he perseveres, as much for the sake of his own future, as out of shame to return home as a loser. As time goes by, his contacts with fellow

Illustration 4.3: Franek in *The Year of Franek W.*, directed by Kazimierz Karabasz

volunteers improve and he gets much pride from bringing presents to his large family on his visit home for Christmas.

The message of the film is optimistic, by pointing to the positive role played by the OHP in ensuring the social promotion of thousands of disadvantaged youngsters. Yet, it is different from the films discussed in the earlier chapter in its choice as protagonist somebody who merely survives in the harsh conditions and for whom work is a means, not a goal. In common with *The Musicians*, the intervention from the film's director is minimal. There is nobody to 'translate' the statements from Franek's diary into Party jargon. Karabasz appears to be interested in Franek alone, not in his place in the larger picture of modernizing Poland. For this reason, however, the film comes across as believable, both as a document about this young man's life and thousands like him, who left an overcrowded and poor countryside to seek a better life in large industrial centres. According to Mikołaj Jazdon, Franek is a typical Karabasz character in that he is an ordinary man, one in a crowd. This, however, does not make him mediocre, because he is represented as being heroic in his everyday struggle, as well as able to reflect on his life and wider reality (Jazdon 2009: 194–198). These aspects of the film were recognized and praised by critics, assuring *The Year of Franek W.* the status of one of the greatest documentary films in Polish history. Zygmunt Kałużyński claims that the film captured a kind of 'silent revolution' which took place in postwar Poland, consisting of 'the whole country changing its place' (Kałużyński 1976: 151), moving as much out as up. Kałużyński adds that this revolution was slow and painful and was undertaken not by heroes but by young people full of complexes, shy, clumsy, passive and uncertain about themselves. The fact that it remained largely unrepresented in the cinema of the previous decade had much to do with the ideology and aesthetics of socialist realism, which discouraged the presentation of ordinary people and work as an effort and pain, as opposed to triumph and pleasure. Kałużyński also points to the success of Karabasz's crew in becoming part of Franek's life. In order to achieve such a result Karabasz had to go beyond his role as a director and encompass that of pedagogue and sociologist, thus becoming one with his subject, able to say 'Franek is me', in the same way that Flaubert said that 'Madame Bovary is me' (ibid.: 153).

Against the background of the documentary films of the 1960s, which deal with heavy industry, Krzysztof Kieślowski's *Urząd* (*The Office*, 1966) is an oddity as it depicts unproductive work: the activities of the office of social security in Warsaw. By the same token, it touches on the link between the civil servants and those whom they served under state socialism. This was a touchy subject in postwar Poland and in all people's democracies. The general perception was that the socialist state was over-bureaucratic, reflecting a distrust of the state towards its citizens and its need to control them by collecting information. This aspect of state socialism is illuminated by Alexander Zinoviev in *Homo Sovieticus*:

> *Soviet people are trained to write Reports about everything. It is an indispensible element of the Communist organization of work. ... We usually write Reports not in order to do a summing-up or extract lessons, but by virtue of certain higher, mystical considerations. For the sake of ordered formality... But don't imagine that the Report is a superfluous bureaucratic operation. It is a powerful way of integrating people into the Communist system. The important thing is not the contents, just the fact that the Report exists. (Zinoviev 1985: 14–16)*[15]

The very act of collecting files was seen as a form of harassment of people by the communist authorities or at best as a useless activity. This aspect had already been pointed out in Jerzy Ziarnik's *Little Town*, as indicated in the previous chapter. The office clerks tended to be impolite and unhelpful, reflecting factors such as their low salaries, the lack of professional training, diluted responsibility so that a customer was constantly moved from one desk to another, the alienating character of their work, which was seen as pointless not only by their customers, but by the clerks themselves, combined with a high level of job security. Kieślowski's film confirms this perception: the office in his film is a Kafka-esque maze and an instrument of harassment (Coates 2015), reflecting his own experience of working as a clerk in a District National Council in Warsaw, in 1964 (Zawiśliński 2005: 74). Kieślowski shows the employees (all female) treating their customers in the same way, as if they existed merely as representations of the documents they bring. This fact is confirmed by the architecture of the office, where the employee and the customer are divided by a glass screen with two small windows, one to look through and one to pass documents through. Questions have to be shouted to be heard by the other side, which confirms the impression that the people who work there are rude towards their customers. Although the film is short, we have a sense of waiting, of time passing slowly due to standing in a queue, idly; this is highlighted by the repetition of the word 'wait' and the way in which the clerks are shown fulfilling their own needs, for example boiling water to make tea or coffee, while the customers are waiting. The role of the office as a vehicle of harassment is foregrounded in the last fragment of Kieślowski's film, when the clerks ask the customers to describe their whole lives, a request which cannot be fulfilled (Mazierska 2014b: 36). This demand brings to mind Zinoviev's story of an old Bolshevik who wrote a report about his entire life since the revolution, and brought it to the office in two battered old shopping bags, which were subsequently thrown into the rubbish dump (Zinoviev 1985: 14–15). In Kieślowski's film the worker is above the work, but not in a positive sense, as in the films previously discussed, but because her work make the recipients of her work suffer.

Kieślowski, who later in his career would be recognized for his penchant for metaphors, already shows this talent in *The Office*. He plays down the specificity of the office; it takes repeated viewing to realize that this is an office of social security. This approach is also shown in his choice of film title: *The Office*, as opposed to *The Office of Social Security* or *The Office of Social Security in Warsaw* (Mazierska 2014b: 38). We can conjecture that Kieślowski's office stands for a wider reality: the whole of Poland as a bureaucratic nightmare, where people work without commitment or pleasure and the same people wait for hours to be served by other alienated employees. An office can also be seen as an instrument of stabilization, of introducing order, so it is no surprise that this film was made during the decade of 'small stabilization'. Kieślowski's stabilization is, however, a stabilization of stagnation and petty inconvenience, not enjoyment and security as it was presented in Polanski's film from the beginning of the decade.

Notes

1. Alcohol was always a serious problem in postwar Poland (Marszałek 2006: 113–134).
2. In this respect *Knife in the Water* can be compared to another Eastern European example of the New Wave, *Sedmikrásky* (*Daisies*, 1966) by Věra Chytilová. Not unlike Polanski's characters, Chytilová's heroines engage in consumption and play, in an even more conspicuous way. Petra Hanáková draws a parallel between the excessive consumption of the female characters with that of the filmmaker, 'consuming' all the techniques she has at her disposal, and in this way rejecting the rigidity of socialist cinema, and, finally, of the viewer, overjoyed if not overwhelmed by this excess (Hanáková 2005: 71).
3. In this respect Polish cinema was similar to other Eastern European and Soviet cinema and art during the Thaw period, where lighter genres were used as a counterweight to the high Stalinist style.
4. This is testified by reviews of the 1950s comedies, which typically lambast the films, while simultaneously demanding for more comedies to be produced (for example Sokołowski 1953).

5. He wrote cabaret pieces, as well as dialogue for film comedies, such as *Manewry miłosne* (*Love Manoeuvres*, 1935), directed by Jan Nowina-Przybylski and Konrad Tom, and *Ada! To nie wypada!* (*Ada, Don't Do That!*, 1936), directed by Konrad Tom (Replewicz 2009: 53).
6. The importance attached to sport from the 1960s onwards was also due to the fact that in this decade the East lost the economic war with the West. Not being able to beat the West in the sphere of material production, it tried to win in specific fields of great symbolic importance. Sport was one of them; another was space exploration.
7. Konrad Klejsa observes that the changing representation of Warsaw is a perfect litmus test, measuring the changes in the ideology of Bareja's films. In his early films Warsaw looks very attractive; in the later ones it tends to be a scene of bad work and drunkenness (Klejsa 2007: 90–93; on the representation of Warsaw in Bareja's films, see also Mazierska 2008: 231–240).
8. Fortuna argues convincingly that in the first half of the 1970s, during Gierek's prosperity, Poland did not produce musicals, because then there was no need to compensate for material shortages (Fortuna 2015: 125).
9. This episode was based on a true event which took place in Lodz at the beginning of the 1960s and was described by a journalist from *Prawo i życie* (Replewicz 2009: 101).
10. That said, Bareja's cinema can be seen as reflecting his background and artistic trajectory because, on the one hand, he shows more inside knowledge about the ways of the lower classes than the bulk of Polish directors and, on the other, he has the boldness to make fun of them.
11. Władysław Władyka, in a dialogue with Andrzej Brzeziecki, draws attention to the fact that after October 1956 representatives of Catholic organizations were allocated a certain quota in parliament, but the leader of the worker's council, Lechosław Goździk, was refused a parliamentary post and sidelined in post-1956 politics (Władyka 2009: 108).
12. It would be more logical for him to have a black wife, as it is more likely that a Polish engineer would have met such a woman during his working time in Africa. The fact that she is replaced by an Italian, points, in my view, to the latent racism of Polish society, which Morgenstern was unable or unwilling to challenge.
13. One can observe a similar approach in East German films by Jürgen Böttcher (Hodgin 2015).
14. The Corps was set up in many socialist countries and everywhere helped young people to make the transition from the country to the city and climb the social ladder (on their representation in Yugoslav cinema, see Atanasovski and Petrov 2015).
15. This view on the function of the reports or indeed any data collected by the communist offices was confirmed when the the Stasi files were opened in 1990.

CHAPTER 5

The 1970s
Bad Work and Good Life

The 1970s symbolically began in Poland on 20 December 1970, when Moscow agreed to the dismissal of Władysław Gomułka and replaced him with Edward Gierek as the new First Secretary of the PZPR. This change at the top of the Party followed a bloody response by the Polish authorities to the strikes on the coast, caused by the threat of price rises, leading to a workers' revolt across much of northern Poland, as discussed in the previous chapter. Appointing Gierek was meant to prevent destabilization of the entire country. During this period of upheaval, somewhat conveniently, Gomułka suffered a stroke. Gierek averted the danger of a general strike by directly appealing to the workers of Szczecin and Gdańsk, promising them economic reform and improvements in living standards (Lukowski and Zawadzki 2001: 267). Gierek's ascent to power was thus similar to Gomułka's – he was a beneficiary of the workers' unrest which crushed his predecessor. His background was also no different from Gomulka – he came from a working-class family from the South of Poland and was involved in the communist movement for many decades, although not only in Poland, but also in France and Belgium, where he worked as a miner before returning to Poland in 1948. Gierek would also lose his power in the same way as Gomułka, by entering into open conflict with the disgruntled workers, again caused by the worsening of living conditions. However, on each occasion the situation was different. When Gierek was ousted from office in 1980, the anti-communist opposition in Poland was stronger and better organized than in 1956 and the Soviet Union, weakened by the bloody conflict in Afghanistan, was less likely to intervene in Poland than in 1970.

As Adam Bromke observes, 'Gierek adopted a new political style which emphasized greater respect on the part of the communist authorities for the citizens' rights and a readiness to enter into dialogue with the Polish people' (Bromke 1981: 6); this was in part a consequence of the Helsinki accord, signed in

1975, which required the countries of state socialism to respect human rights (Berend 1996: 233–236). Unlike his predecessor, he was prepared to go to the factories and talk to disgruntled workers (Zaremba 2009: 184). Gierek was also media-friendly and especially recognized the power of television in creating a positive image of the rulers (Cieśliński 2006: 115–136). To avert associations with the Eastern European leaders, accused of indulging in a 'personality cult', he did not allow his portraits to be displayed in schools and offices. The new First Secretary also had a more western outlook than his predecessors, no doubt resulting from living in the West and knowing foreign languages: French and Flemish. During his time in office he paid official visits to several western countries, and in return played host to the French president Giscard d'Estaing and the American presidents Nixon and Ford in Warsaw (Lukowski and Zawadzki 2001: 267). His government also eased foreign currency restrictions, giving many Poles access to otherwise rare western consumer goods. In the 1970s a network of shops, named Pewex, was opened, where Poles could buy shortage goods with western currency. This was a sign of recognizing the high value of western money on the black market, but also a means of dividing Poles into those with access to these deficit goods (or just wealthier) and the rest. Restriction of travel was eased in the 1970s, with the tacit hope that Poles (not unlike Yugoslavs in the 1960s) would work abroad and bring home their hard-earned savings, plugging gaps in the national economy.

In Gierek's economic policy emphasis was put on improving the standard of living. One of the priorities consisted of reversing the chronic housing shortage and expanding car production of the Fiat 125 and 126, the latter designed as a car for everybody (Koryś 2007: 452; Zaremba 2009: 189). To address the problem of Poland's technological backwardness, the government bought many licenses from the West, including for car production and components for building apartments in multi-storey blocks. The apartments built in the 1970s tended to be larger than 'Gomułka's apartments'. During Gierek's decade there was also significant growth in private entrepreneurship, epitomized by private shops (*sklepy ajencyjne*) (Koryś 2007: 452). In the first half of the decade, individual consumption increased by 50 per cent and individual income by 59 per cent (Mazurek 2012: 299). The new regime also introduced Saturdays free of work, beginning in 1972 with two Saturdays per year and finishing with three per month. The countryside was helped by the abolishment of compulsory deliveries in 1972 and an increase in the prices of agricultural products. Gierek's government also introduced pension plans for farmers. However, for those who were not able to pass their farms onto their children, the price for receiving a pension was giving the farm to the state. This was accompanied by the setting up of more state farms – a move which most likely resulted from pressure by Brezhnev, which was seen as a gentle form of re-Stalinization of agriculture (Zaremba 2009: 189). These improvements were possible because Gierek took advantage of the relatively cheap foreign credit available in the early 1970s. For Poland (and some other Eastern European countries, such as Hungary) this flood of dollars, which poured from multi-billionaire OPEC states, distributed by the international banking system, seemed a providential way of simultaneously paying for investment and raising their people's standard of living' (Hobsbawm 1995: 474). The negative result was debt to the West, which in 1978 reached almost 15 billion USD in long-term and about 2 billion USD in short-term credits (Bromke 1981: 6).[1] However, it was not so much debt per se which was the problem as the fact that during the 1970s Poland, in common with the socialist East at large, increased its economic and technological distance towards the West, which at the time was experiencing a new wave of modernization, re-directing its economy to new industries, most importantly electronics (Berend 1996: 238–239). Poland also attempted to move in this direction, as testified by the purchase of licenses to produce sophisticated commodities, but the speed of modernization was too slow, the 'technological revolution' was poorly coordinated and the drive to move towards information technology and post-industrial society clashed with the drive to do things 'the old way'. This rendered the products of Polish industry unattractive to western buyers, making the servicing of debt a heavy burden for the country. An example of the backward industrial policy was the building of Katowice Steelworks (Huta Katowice) in 1972, most likely on 'advice' from the Soviet Union. This project, not unlike the grand projects of the 1950s and the 1960s, strengthened the connection between Poland and the Soviet Union, as iron ore to be used there was transported from Poland's eastern neighbour. 1970s Polish westernization was thus limited to emulating western lifestyles without imitating its economic structure. To signal that the new political regime was modern and pragmatic, the word 'socialism' was frequently preceded by 'real' or 'actually existing'. Politicians paid lip service to ideology by recycling slogans.[2] In the state propaganda, the focus was on success – hence the description of the decade as that of the 'propaganda of success'. Such a term implied that there were no real successes in the 1970s – the image was divorced from reality – although there were real achievements behind the beautified façade, most importantly material improvement.

Although Gierek attempted to lift all Polish people to a higher standard of living, some benefited from his policies more than others. The most privileged was the metropolitan intelligentsia, who moved to larger apartments in new housing estates and took advantage of the liberal atmosphere prevailing during this decade. The nomenklatura was the most privileged. As Stanislaw Starski claims,

> *The new ruling class became over-zealous in the seventies – not only in a visible way (the amount of luxury cars, house furniture, housing itself, country clubs, etc.), but in a legal sense as well.*
>
> *In autumn of 1973 a bill was passed through the Polish parliament and quietly went into effect... The act is called 'On pensions granted to individuals who render particularly important services to the state' ... A rigid hierarchy was introduced which measured services rendered in terms of the post achieved and the length of time it was held – very elaborate criteria were used to divide all state, party and special (science, army, police) posts into separate groups, and in each of the groups the amount paid, the amount added and the amount of goods to be acquired while in office and then kept for the family and successors were meticulously determined. (Starski 1982: 23)*

In the same decade, mobility from the country to the city slowed (Koryś 2007: 452), to the detriment of the rural population for whom moving to the city was a principal method of social advancement.

Gierek's economic programme worked well in the first half of the 1970s. In the second half the situation worsened, in part due to world-wide stagnation, which led to the drying up of cheap credit and the quashing of Poland's hopes to export their products and repay the costs of licenses. This negative situation was compounded by several years of poor harvest, caused by unfavourable weather conditions. The second half of the 1970s also showed that Gierek's social reforms failed to establish an efficient administration and create a more transparent and egalitarian public sphere. There was a widespread perception that life in the 1970s became more bureaucratic and that professional advancement was linked to nepotism and corruption. When challenged with the difficulty of 'balancing the books', Gierek's government reacted in a similar way to that of Gomułka: by increasing food prices. The reaction of people was also similar: a wave of strikes, this time mainly in Ursus and Radom. In the second half of the 1970s investment was reduced and the government spent this decade in dealing with immediate economic problems. This eroded Gierek's personal authority and encouraged political opposition inside and outside the Party, as marked by the establishment of such organizations as the Committee for Social Self-Defense (KSS-KOR) and the Movement for the Defence of Human and Civil Rights (ROPCIO), and the flourishing of samizdat publications (Bromke 1981: 6–17; Berend 1996: 241–245). In due course they would play a significant role in setting up the independent trade union Solidarity, a crucial factor in dismantling state socialism in Poland and the whole Eastern bloc at the end of the 1980s.

Yet, in the 1970s only a minority in society engaged in the anti-government movement. To capture the specificity of Polish reality in the 1970s it is worth applying the concepts of 'post-totalitarian society', introduced by Václav Havel to describe Czech society post-1968. Post-totalitarian society is different from totalitarian society in that its regime is based not so much on naked power and the zealousness of its ideologically-driven supporters (as was the case under Stalinism), but on certain consumer rewards which citizens receive for putting up with the system (Havel 1985). Post-totalitarian people are those who are allowed and are even encouraged to withdraw from frontline politics into the private sphere. One can notice a similarity between the members of post-totalitarian society and homini sovietici as defined earlier. Although the concept of homo sovieticus was introduced earlier, the 1970s were very conducive to the proliferation of that type, as the regime allowed people and especially the middle classes to develop their 'small individualism', and to fight for a larger share of consumer goods and social privileges. 'Post-totalitarianization' and anti-state conspiracy can be seen as two sides of the same coin, as the lack of transparency in rewarding the privileged bred both conformity and a sense of unfairness, often in the same people. However, it was the declining living standards which led to full-scale protest and the overthrowing not only of Gierek's regime, but of socialism at large.

The change in the political regime in 1970 brought hope for changes in Polish cinema. Among film professionals there was an expectation of a significant increase in film production and investment in film infrastructure, fuelled by the promise of introducing a 'technological revolution' through using audio-visual means in other spheres of social life such as education. Indeed, more films were produced in the early 1970s, but this was mainly limited to television production and shorter films. Under Gierek the second television channel was set up and it began to broadcast in colour. The changes in the production of full-length fiction films for theatrical release were slow to come. This decade also saw a decrease in the number of cinemas and in cinema audiences (Zajiček 1992: 208). In this respect Poland was not unique; practically everywhere in Europe the 1970s belonged to television. Television also affected the style of cine-films made then: many of them looked like television productions, most importantly the Cinema of Moral Concern, the only distinct movement in Polish cinema, after the films of the Polish School. At the same time, in order to carve a space for cinema as a distinctive medium, Poland invested in producing a number of lavish super-productions, such as Jerzy Hoffman's *Potop* (*The Deluge*, 1974), *Ziemia obiecana* (*The Promised Land*, 1974) by Andrzej Wajda, and the unfinished *On the Silver Globe*, directed by Andrzej Żuławski.

In the 1970s film audiences not only shrank, but also became more specialized. This was facilitated by the creation of spaces for more sophisticated, often student audiences, thanks to a flourishing of film festivals, most importantly in Łagów, and a special type of cinemas (*kina studyjne*), which exhibited films unavailable in ordinary cinemas. In these spaces criticism of the state could be conveyed almost openly (Dabert 2003: 43). This milder censorship reflected the conciliatory position of Gierek's regime, which preferred to woo society with concessions and allow them to vent their frustration in special 'spaces of freedom', rather than confront it with naked force.

The most distinct feature of Polish cinema of the 1970s is its critical tone. Watching films produced in this period one gets the impression that their authors did not like anything about the reality in which they operated. At the same time, the criticism is focused on small, human vices, rather than on the system. The cinema of this period can be thus described as a 'cinema of grumpiness'. This grumpiness can be explained by censorship which did not allow filmmakers to make a frontal attack on the authorities, and the conciliatory position taken by the government, which emboldened filmmakers to express their dissatisfaction.

I mentioned in the previous chapter that after the end of socialist realism Polish cinema broke into two strands: auteurist (art) and popular. Not only was the latter consciously manufactured to fulfil specific social needs, but a special discourse was created around it, predicated on the assumption that there was a huge gap between popular and auteur films in terms of their style and artistic quality. However, this discourse in relation to the 1970s cinema cannot be sustained, because many popular films of this decade overtook auteur films in their stylistic boldness: they became the new avant-garde. This is particularly visible if we compare the films made by directors such as Marek Piwowski, Janusz Kondratiuk and Stanisław Bareja from the first half of the 1970s, with films belonging to the Cinema of Moral Concern, produced in the second half. These popular films could also compete with auteurist productions in their criticism of the socialist regime. Hence, they also deserve the label 'Cinema of Moral Concern', even more so than the films of Kieślowski, Holland and Falk.

Consuming Free Time

In this section I will focus on three examples of such 'experimental popular films': *Rejs* (*Cruise* aka *A Trip down the River*, 1970), directed by Marek Piwowski, *Dziewczyny do wzięcia* (*Girls to Pick Up*, 1972), directed by Janusz Kondratiuk, and *Brunet wieczorową porą* (*Brunet Will Call*, 1976), directed by Stanisław Bareja. All mix the conventions of fiction film with documentary, and cine-film with television productions, which is reflected in the first two having a non-standard length, of sixty-five and forty-five minutes respectively. They also eschew a tightly constructed narrative in favour of a whole made up of episodes. In the case of Piwowski and Kondratiuk's films, such a structure is inspired by Czech New Wave films. As I argued earlier, style is not ideologically neutral. In this case it conveys living in and for the present, which means without a great design, as opposed to some future goal, which was the case in the films of the 1950s and, albeit to a lesser extent, the 1960s. Moreover, episodic structure, as John Hill argued in relation to the *Carry On* series, is more egalitarian because it does not allow us to focus on the main protagonist, but disperses our attention to many characters (Hill 1986: 140–143). These films bear witness to the state's attempts at improving everybody's life by creating spaces where leisure can be consumed by everybody, not only the privileged elite, as in Polanski's *Knife in the Water*. They focus on free time, which, however, is presented as an awkward gift. *Cruise*, being made in 1970, is a borderline film, connecting Gomułka's 1960s, to which it bids farewell, with Gierek's 1970s, which it anticipates. It is set on a boat, like Polanski's film, but leisure in Piwowski's film is not individual but communal and organized according to specific rules, using people whose designated role is to entertain others. It is not just a film about leisure, but also about the leisure industry.

Cruise does not have a straightforward narrative but is built up of short scenes, some of which are scripted, while others are improvised by their cast consisting of professional and amateur actors. It has a main character, but his role is somewhat smaller in comparison with mainstream cinema, while the secondary characters have more narrative autonomy than one would expect in an ordinary fiction film. These secondary characters often embark on a common task, creating a group protagonist, which is emphasized by the cinematography and editing.[3] The film begins with the sign 'You work on the land, you rest on the water', advertising a cruise down the Vistula river in a pleasure boat. Yet, the sign is accompanied by the hand-written information 'No tickets', subtly pointing to the reality of shortages behind the façade of plenty. The cruise is populated by people on medium to low income, showing that it is a relatively cheap form of relaxation which does not allow its participants to enjoy much privacy. This also explains why the group is so heterogeneous in terms of education, with some people sounding like working-class men and women, while others use the language of Hegel. What is characteristic of the way in which people talk is their desire to sound more refined than they really are. This is reflected in one of them adopting the (most likely fake) title of 'engineer'. The film thus shows that even if officially the working class was still the leading class, in reality the ambitions of everybody was to move up to the educated 'middle class', exemplified by the technical intelligentsia and the academics; a fact which New Wave films already implied (see chapter 4). By the 1970s the gap between the working and the middle class increased and being a manual worker became a source of shame. Not by chance do the main characters in the most popular television series of the 1970s, *Czterdziestolatek* (*Forty Years Old*, 1974–1977), Mr and Mrs Karwowski, both have university degrees.

The main character in *Cruise* is a chancer, who cons his way on board the boat and is taken for an entertainment officer (Polish *kaowiec*, from K&O, culture and education), a role which he accepts without protesting. Such a character would not be out of place in western cinema; think of Steven Spielberg's *Catch Me If You Can* (2002). However, con men in western films are highly skilled in their profession of cheating. Piwowski, by contrast, shows that in Poland one can become a successful con man without having any special skills. This motif is presented in an early scene when the captain interviews the chancer to get him to fill in a job questionnaire. It is obvious that the passenger without a ticket does not try to present himself as suitable for any profession and the captain is not interested in getting the best man for the job. For example, he does not mind that the candidate does not know any foreign languages or does not have a university education; its absence is even seen as an asset. The captain's approach can be seen as a metonymy of the attitude to professionalism in People's Poland. The actor playing the *kaowiec*, Stanisław Tym, who also contributed to the script, complained off-screen that Poland of state socialism was a paradise for losers and ignoramuses (Tym 2000: 14).[4] It should be added, however, that such opinions are always made from a specific vantage point – that of intellectual superiority. *Cruise*, despite its documentary feel, reveals the looking down/talking down attitude to those who try to look better than they are that pertains to a large chunk of Polish cinema of the 1970s. Its quasi-documentary character acts as a fig leaf to cover and condone such a patronizing attitude.

What follows in the film confirms Tym's diagnosis by showing that in Poland 'bad work' could bring distinct social advantages. But also, most likely against the filmmakers' intentions, this 'bad work' comes across as fun. One way to show this is by obliterating the division between work and leisure. In *Cruise* we are rarely sure who is a member of the crew and who is a passenger, who is working and who is not.[5] There are several silent episodes, shot in the style of slapstick comedy, showing a man carrying a long pole, who passes it to somebody else, who then passes it to another person, as in a game of musical chairs. This situation can be seen as symbolic of the Polish habit of avoiding work by passing it to others. We also see some people practicing gymnastics and it is not clear whether they are doing it for pleasure or whether they are professional acrobats. The passengers are expected to put their effort into preparing a celebration event for the captain. Everybody has to do what he supposedly does best: to write a poem, sing a song, etc. The role of the entertainment officer is not to entertain others but to make sure that they entertain each other and please the ship's hierarchy. On board the roles of the producer and consumer of leisure are thus reversed: the consumer is supposed to behave like a worker. Leisure is meant to be organized and enjoyed in public spaces, but because of the general ineptitude, people are still able to live their private lives. This can be seen as reflecting Gomułka's regime, and foretelling that of Gierek, where the political authorities no longer encroached on people's private lives, but rather private affairs colonized public time and space.

There are two contradictory tendencies in the behaviour of the passengers. On the one hand, they are conformist, as testified by their agreement to do what they are asked to do. On the other hand, they cannot be harnessed to any project, because every idea proposed to them is circumvented either by their incompetence or their inability to reach a consensus. Consequently, they are suspended between conformity and free play. This peculiar position is reflected in the language they use, which is a mixture of different linguistic regimes: the language of a party meeting, television information, philosophical discourse and vernacular speech. Iwona Kurz describes the official language as 'the language of public discourse which penetrates, like a cancerous growth, the vernacular and everyday linguistic practices as the universal language of collected truth' (Kurz 2008b: 97). However, this official language never conquers other types of speech; they always coexist with each other, creating an effect of incongruity. This is an important reason why the language of *Cruise* is so funny, as is the whole life on the boat. Although the people shown on the boat come across as incompetent, this does not prevent them from chastising others for their ineptitude. The most quoted example is the monologue of engineer Mamoń, played by iconic actor, Zdzisław Maklakiewicz, about the low quality of Polish cinema. Mamoń complains that nothing dramatic happens in Polish films. He also asks rhetorically why Polish films cannot look more like foreign films, by which he means American films. Mamoń's tirade remains unanswered, but *Cruise*'s position as the ultimate Polish cult film is an answer of sorts to this question, by demonstrating that a film can be made according to the opposite standards than those followed by the American 'culture industry', yet achieve success on its own terms.

Throughout most of its afterlife *Cruise* was perceived as a satire on life in socialist Poland, marked by excessive bureaucracy, an acceptance of mediocrity, and state interference in the private affairs of citizens. In this respect the opinion of a distinguished film historian, Małgorzata Hendrykowska, is symptomatic. She argues that *Cruise* provides a metaphor of Poland as a 'cage', hence a totalitarian state (Hendrykowska 2007b: 156).[6] However, somewhat different opinions emerge from answers to a questionnaire circulated among Polish film and media historians in connection with a sequel to *Cruise*, planned by Piwowski. While some suggested that the film captures the totalitarian character of life in Poland of state socialism, others argued that it offers an 'eternal' portrait of Polish society or even that this portrait might awaken nostalgia (Tumiłowicz 2010).[7]

Girls to Pick Up presents three working-class girls from the province, travelling on Saturday to Warsaw in search for fun and partners. There they meet two young men, who have a similar desire: to meet girls. The film follows their attempts to fill their spare time and make each other look interesting. At the same time, it reveals (as well as adds to) many hidden assumption about the class system in Poland and Polish aspirations in the 1970s. As all the characters are young, we receive a fair dose of puppy awkwardness, especially in situations which are meant to lead to erotic encounters, as was the case in the early films of Miloš Forman, especially *Lásky jedné plavovlásky* (*A Blonde in Love*, 1965), where men play various roles to attract women. However, in the Czech film men did not lie about their jobs, education and titles, only about their marital status, and women did not search for men with 'titles'. By contrast, in Kondratiuk's film one girl confesses that in Warsaw she would like to meet a 'doctor' or 'somebody like that'. As if in response to this expectation, the men whom they meet introduce themselves as 'Engineer' and 'Magister' (a man with a master's degree), bringing to mind the title-mania from *Cruise*. One of them even repeats several times that he has 'a quiet white-collar job'. They talk about their plans to buy a colour TV and a larger apartment than their friend's studio or one-bedroom flat, which they use as a place to spend their time with the girls. From their talks, however, it transpires that neither of them is a university graduate and they most likely perform manual jobs, as suggested by the fact that they live in the workers' hostel. The men's waiter friend betrays his desire to be seen as somebody better by having at home a row of bottles of foreign alcohol which in reality contain no alcohol, only diluted juice. As Justyna Jaworska argues, the 'culture of ersatz' permeates consumption in this film, encapsulated by the posh-sounding 'sultan cream' offered in the restaurant, which in reality is whipped cream with some raisins (Jaworska 2014). However, as we only see in the films the consumption of working-class people, we get a sense that it pertains only to this class; people of higher class have access to more genuine things. We are thus far removed from the times when Hanka Ruczajówna arrived in Warsaw and found there a proud and dashing shock worker. The message of Kondratiuk's film is that nobody is proud to be a manual worker anymore; it has become a shameful condition. Kondratiuk makes it even more shameful by rendering his young characters embarrassing in their ambition to appear more educated and worldly than they are. The only attractive girl, played in this group by a professional actress, Ewa Szykulska, has golden crowns on her teeth, although such 'body ornaments', then regarded as extremely tasteless, would be a rarity in the 1970s even among people from the province.

While Forman's Andula, despite being provincial, comes across as a dignified individual whose anguish we share, Kondratiuk creates caricatures, from whom we feel inevitably distanced. This reflects the patronizing attitude Polish filmmakers adopted towards working-class provincials in the 1970s. The seeds of such an attitude can be identified in socialist realist films, where the working-class characters were in need of tutelage by the mature Party members. But these films suggested that after learning their (political) lessons, they would go on to climb the social ladder. Watching *Girls to Pick Up* one gets the impression that these girls and boys will stay forever in the place where they started their journey: in the province, understood as both a physical and cultural place. I see *Girls to Pick Up* as being made from the perspective of somebody who achieved social promotion and guards his position against possible attack by outsiders. The fact that Kondratiuk's film, in common with *Cruise*, achieved the status of a cult film has much to do with the secret communication between the filmmakers and the metropolitan intelligentsia (the target audience of this film), united in their sense of superiority over characters trying to invade their territory.

Brunet Will Call is set during a free Saturday, which from the perspective of ordinary people was perhaps the greatest gift of Gierek's regime. However, Bareja suggests that a free Saturday is an unnecessary or even a harmful present, because Polish workers (which here mean manual workers and lower-class clerks) have too much time on their hands anyway; an extra free day only decreases their already poor work ethic. This point is conveyed through a thin narrative about a journalist or writer, Michał Roman, who wants to use his free Saturday to correct a

Illustration 5.1: Michał Roman in *Brunet Will Call*, directed by Stanisław Bareja

manuscript. This proves impossible, less because of a murder committed in his house, and more because of petty inconveniences he suffers on the way to capturing the murderer.

A shop manager closes the shop during its working hours to have sex with a man bringing supplies. City council workers employed to get rid of snow from the streets of Warsaw unload their cargo not into the Vistula river but in the middle of the city, because as one of them puts it, 'it will melt anyway'. A museum employee meets attractive women (perhaps prostitutes) during his working hours. The show in a cinema is called off on the grounds that a heater was broken, although the true reason is that the cashier sold tickets for the same seats twice. Waiters cheat on their clients by selling sub-standard food. Construction workers drink during their working hours. People working in the state sector steal or keep aside something from their work to exchange it for other deficit goods. A number of people, such as a taxi driver and a car mechanic, refuse, delay or charge extra for a service because it is a free Saturday. In Bareja's Poland the unofficial economy takes precedence over the official one.[8] The film also suggests that in Poland good work makes no sense because one person's good work is undermined by another person's sloppy work, as pointed out by a janitor who says that there is no point in correcting a manuscript because somebody else will make mistakes in it. Yet, bad work is represented from the vantage point of a disadvantaged middle-class consumer and cultural worker, whose working time is not regulated and who cannot make a profit from putting something aside. The idea of the middle class as disadvantaged workers and consumers was common in Poland in the 1970s and 1980s, even leading to a concept of Poland as a 'republic of lousy workers' (*republika roboli*). Such a term suggested that manual and service workers effectively governed Poland at the expense of the more committed and professional intelligentsia.[9] However, Bareja shows that despite bad work, the country is functioning, even enjoying a degree of prosperity. Paradoxically, the most affluent is Roman, who owns a car and a spacious house in the Warsaw suburbs, and for whom money is never an issue. This reflects well on the status of the metropolitan intelligentsia in Gierek's Poland, even Bareja himself, which films like *Brunet Will Call* tried to disavow.

A shared motif of these three films is sex work. In *Girls to Pick Up* and *Brunet Will Call* we see striptease workers performing in a high-class restaurant, most likely Hala Kongresowa in the Palace of Culture. In *Girls to Pick Up* the striptease is presented through the gaze of the girls from the province who are mesmerized by the performance. In *Cruise* such references are more subtle: Engineer Mamoń looks through binoculars at some scantily dressed young women stepping on board of the ship. Although there is no suggestion that they do it for money, this scene refers to the Polish appetite for sex both on screen and in real life, which Gierek's regime quenched in some measure by easing film censorship. In the 1970s prostitution was more tolerated than in previous decades, not least because the earnings of Polish prostitutes, some of whom operated in higher class hotels frequented by foreign guests, was a source of hard currency badly needed by a country indebted to the West. It might not be an accident that although prostitution is rarely shown in contemporary films produced in this decade, it is frequently relocated to historical films, such as *Dzieje grzechu* (*The Story of Sin*, 1975), directed by Walerian Borowczyk, an ex-patriate who returned to Poland in this decade to take advantage of its new liberal climate, and *The Promised Land* by Andrzej Wajda.

Moral Concern in the Workplace

Stylistically the films discussed so far were forerunners to the Cinema of Moral Concern, which was created in the second half of the 1970s and lasted till the imposition of martial law in 1981. This movement also drew on the techniques of documentary cinema and television, but the construction of the Moral Concern films is more classical and their tone is consistently darker, reflecting the worsening economic situation, and Gierek's loss of trust of Polish citizens, even though the criticism of the socialist reality in the films of Bareja is more consistent.

Films belonging to this paradigm attempted to tell the truth about Polish society, in contrast to the perceived lies and omissions of the propaganda emitted from state-owned television and the Party press. Such a programme was in tune with the approach favoured by some Polish writers and poets active in this period, most importantly those belonging to the movement of Młoda Kultura (Young Culture). Their aim was to show what existed and demanded unbiased representation, but remained unrepresented in the official media, 'the unrepresented world', as conveyed by the title of the manifesto of two Kraków poets, Julian Kornhauser and Adam Zagajewski, *Świat nie przedstawiony* (*The Unrepresented World*, 1974) (Jankun-Dopartowa 1996: 92–101; Lubelski 1999: 56). Inevitably, 'telling the truth' required using opposite techniques from those employed in the official 'propaganda of success'. If the official representations favoured ornamental expressions and glamorous images, the creators of the Cinema of Moral Concern opted for simple, colloquial language and unattractive images, and drew heavily on documentary techniques, in the conviction that documentary image and sound is less prone to manipulation. The character was often more important than the action and much information was conveyed through dialogue. Many films were set in provincial towns, which tended to be neglected by the authorities, and featured less well known and less glamorous actors and even amateurs (Stanisław Latałło, Tadeusz Huk, Teresa Sawicka, Maria Chwalibóg) whose unfamiliar and ordinary faces represented the unglamorous peripheries of Poland. In their ambition to reveal the ugly truth about the society, these filmmakers were not unique. Such a tendency can be found in many national cinemas of different periods, for example in the British Free Cinema, Brazilian Cinema Novo or Russian 'dark film' (*chernukha*). From the distance of time, the 'truth' of these movements looks like another convention which became obsolete when new styles were developed, and the Cinema of Moral Concern is no different in this respect.

The bulk of films of Moral Concern depict conflict at work, sometimes reflected in and exacerbated by the characters' situation at home. Privileging work links this movement to the cinema of socialist realism. The directors also borrowed some of the narrative schemes from this paradigm, such as that of a young person starting his/her working life, as in *Personel* (*Personnel*, 1976) by Krzysztof Kieślowski; of an over-ambitious worker, as in *Człowiek z marmuru* (*Man of Marble*, 1977); and the tendency to reduce characters to types (Kornatowska 1990: 184; Dabert 2003: 166–167). However, while socialist realistic films tended to reduce characters to their function as cogs in the central plan (hence the tendency of assessing their family life and leisure against their usefulness to fulfil the great design), the films from the 1970s reject such reductionism. The characters are presented as individuals among other individuals. The overarching ideological project – the great design – is nowhere to be seen, reflecting the fact that Gierek's government lacked such a project. While socialist realist films were usually set in factories or on construction sites, the directors of Moral Concern films preferred sites of immaterial production, such as offices, theatres and television studios. The focus on cultural production, as exemplified by *Aktorzy prowincjonalni* (*Provincial Actors*, 1978) by Agnieszka Holland, Wajda's *Man of Marble* and *Dyrygent* (*Conductor*, 1979), Krzysztof Kieślowski's *Amator* (*Camera Buff*, 1979) and Feliks Falk's *Wodzirej*

(*Dance Leader*, 1977), can be seen as a reflection of Poland's neverending drive for modernization, in this case marked by the ambition to become a post-industrial society. Another possible reason to move to sites of immaterial production was the filmmakers' desire to comment on their own situation as cultural workers, mediating between the power elites and ordinary people.

Although the Cinema of Moral Concern was critical of Gierek's rule, it refrained from advocating an overthrow of the system. On some occasions it is difficult to establish exactly what the films advocate. This can be viewed as a form of self-censorship; it would be impossible to take money from the state for a film which openly pronounces that the state should be overthrown. The ideological ambiguities of the Moral Concern productions might also testify to their makers' difficulty in describing the situation, attributing responsibility and offering convincing strategies to improve it. Hence the emphasis on 'morality' rather than on 'politics', where 'morality' designates the sphere of individual actions, affecting only a small number of people, as opposed to communal struggles with wide-ranging implications (on the meanings of 'moral' in the Cinema of Moral Concern, see Dabert 2003: 30–33) and the focus on the workplace rather than the spaces of political action. That said, some of the work-centred films can be read as metaphors of much larger realities than a specific workplace, as in many films discussed in the previous chapters.

One such film is *Personnel*, which is also one of the earliest manifestations of the Cinema of Moral Concern (Dabert 2003: 13). I shall begin with this film, both due to its chronology and the way in which it sets the tone for many later examples of the movement. The film draws on Kieślowski's experience of working as a junior dresser at the Teatr Współczesny in Warsaw, after studying at the Warsaw College for Theatre Technicians in 1962. Romek Januchta in *Personnel*, fresh from the college for theatre technicians, like Kieślowski in his youth, joins a group of dressers making costumes for actors (in the opera house in this case). He is full of enthusiasm, not unlike the young characters in the films of the 1950s. The opera house is a Fordist institution, employing a large group of artists and technical staff on a permanent basis. In Poland this was possible because of the state protection of institutions of high culture. Kieślowski suggests that such a policy leads to artists feeling excessively self-important and neglecting the needs of the audience. Some of the singers even regard their status as an excuse to insult the 'personnel'. We are thus clearly not in the times of the 'dictatorship of the proletariat', but rather that of the dictatorship over manual workers by cultural and white-collar workers, broadly reflecting Gierek's policies which favoured the middle classes. We can appreciate how times have changed by comparing Kieślowski's film with *Two Teams* (discussed in chapter 3), where actors learnt from the workers how to behave on stage. The positions of professional power in *Personnel* are imbricated with political power, as was the case in the films of the 1950s and the 1960s. However, in the earlier films, the mature, selfless and unbiased Party secretary used to be the arbiter in conflicts between workers. Now he behaves as a recruiter to some secret organization, like the Masonic Lodge. Promotion in the theatre depends on political loyalty, rather than talent and hard work. The existence of vertical and horizontal hierarchy ultimately renders the theatre class ridden, with ordinary workers being at the bottom of the hierarchy, suffering insults and enjoying little job security. Romek gets an offer of informal promotion when he proves vocal at a meeting and proposes that the technical staff set up their own theatre or rather a cabaret. The Party boss's positive attitude to Romek's initiative might be explained by the specific strategies of dealing with social discontentment

Illustration 5.2: Romek Januchta and his work pals in *Personnel*, directed by Krzysztof Kieślowski

pertaining to Gierek's regime. They consisted of diffusing, bribing and integrating potential dissidents into the official political project, rather than openly fighting them. This strategy inevitably led to a blurring of the division between friends and enemies, 'them' and 'us'. In *Personnel* the difficulty of making the right choice is reflected in the last scene of the film when Romek is faced with a dilemma: to sign a paper denouncing a colleague and be promoted or to reject signing it and foreclose such an opportunity. From observing his earlier behaviour, we expect him not to sign, but Kieślowski leaves his film open-ended, to show the dilemmas many Poles, including himself, experienced at the time.

In the opinion of Tadeusz Lubelski the opera and cabaret are two models of Polish culture in the 1970s. The opera stands for official culture which, due to its inability to describe the world adequately, has lost its power to communicate with the nation. However, nobody in the film suggests closing it down; all talk is about improving it. If the opera stands for socialist Poland, then the conclusion is that it should continue to exist, only be reformed. The proposed cabaret is a model of the Youth Culture which Zagajewski and Kornhauser had proposed in *The Unrepresented World*: its role is to describe the world adequately (Lubelski 1999: 61). By the same token, we can argue that in *Personnel* Kieślowski captures a moment when an alternative layer of social life in Poland came into existence and which one can identify with the future Solidarity movement. The director shows the advantages and disadvantages of such an alternative society. The advantages consist of its being more open and democratic (in Romek's cabaret everybody can play, irrespective of his/her education) and enjoying more autonomy than the opera, which is constrained by its archaic form and dependence on state sponsorship. The disadvantages are its limited visibility and some dependence on the official sphere, because its actors still need the opera house as a meeting place and possible performance venue (at least at no point do they discuss the possibility of creating the cabaret outside the walls of the opera), and a stable income to allow them to devote some of their time to creating such an alternative culture. Kieślowski also alludes to the danger of parallel, unofficial culture being incorporated into the official culture, in the same way that the Cinema of Moral Concern was part of the official, state-sponsored Polish film culture, with leading filmmakers, including Kieślowski, being showcased at national and international festivals as proof of the sympathy of the state towards dissents. It is impossible to establish whether creating such an alternative culture ultimately led to establishing a second society, which in the 1980s dismantled state socialism in Poland, or whether, on the contrary, as Elemer Hankiss argues in relation to Hungary, it prolonged the life of state socialism and even strengthened the existing power structures by compensating for the malfunctioning of the first society (Hankiss 1990: 108).

Dance Leader invites comparison with *Personnel* because it is also set in a place where culture is produced, only this time popular culture: Estrada. In the French tradition *estrada* means 'small stage'. David MacFadyen, a historian of Soviet culture, defines it as 'a wide ranging term that includes pop music as well as modern dance, comedy, circus arts, and any other performance not on the "big", classical stage' (quoted in Ventsel 2016). In Poland 'Estrada' referred to popular music which was not pop-rock and various types of entertainment as listed by MacFadyen and the institution promoting it. Understood this way, Estrada has a particular 1970s flavour, because professional entertainers proliferated in this

Illustration 5.3: Lutek Danielak as Estrada employee in *Dance Leader*, directed by Feliks Falk

decade, as then Poles had more free time and television was more entertainment-oriented than was previously the case. Unlike theatre and cinema, which were freed from economic constraints by generous state subsidies, Estrada did not enjoy such privileges. It had to be financially self-sufficient and competitive, giving its patrons what they wanted, rather than trying to shape their taste. In a sense Estrada employees had to work harder than artists in state-protected institutions, but this was not reflected in their status, which was lower than that of opera singers, theatre actors or film directors. In Falk's film their underprivileged status is highlighted through the motif of money. We frequently see the film's protagonist, Lutek Danielak, the titular 'dance leader', queuing at the cashier or negotiating his salary. 'Dance leaders' of this period, as shown by Falk, are at the service of two types of propaganda: socialism and consumerism. One day Lutek performs at strictly political events, encouraging the audience to sing political songs in socialist realist style, another day he works at balls where the message is 'eat, drink and enjoy yourself'. However, no matter whether he entertains kindergarten children or wedding guests, he sings the same cheerful, kitschy song.

The lack of a stable place of work, in contrast with the theatre where the vast majority of Polish actors worked at the time, renders Lutek very mobile. This condition is exacerbated by his lack of a home; he is doubly uprooted, as he has moved to the city from the country, and following his divorce he rents a room from a workmate. He cannot dissociate himself from work, and neither does he want to, as demonstrated by his attempts to introduce his girlfriend into the arcane show business. In this respect he comes across as a model post-Fordist worker, for whom toil has no end. That said, in his real occupation as a professional entertainer Lutek behaves like a worker on a conveyer belt. He does not care about the overall quality of the show but about 'ticking off' his working day, and rushes out from his shows like a labourer leaving a factory. His dismissive attitude to his proper job contrasts with his work 'behind the scenes' (literally and figuratively) to progress his career, which becomes his all-consuming obsession. This homo sovieticus style 'small individualism' is represented as the most deplorable trait of Lutek's character. Although almost everybody around him bends the rules, he is prepared to go further: there is no meanness too mean or dirty trick too dirty for him, if it helps him to eliminate his competitors. His greatest ambition is to lead a ball in a newly opened hotel 'Lux'. Ultimately he fails and ends up disgraced and lonely. Yet it is doubtful that his downfall will lead to a restoration of the moral order. More likely, somebody else will take Lutek's place, as suggested by the fact that the film ends with the same kitschy song, which we heard at the beginning. For Falk, like Kieślowski, the 1970s, metaphorically speaking, have no end or at least these directors were not able to imagine a conclusion to them.

Lutek's on-screen and off-screen work points to two types of economy flourishing in Poland at the time: official and unofficial. Officially one could purchase only second-class goods, such as unfashionable clothes and cheese spread, which Lutek encourages the audience to consume at one of his gigs. Behind the scenes, he trades in such shortage goods as car vouchers and tickets for events at which one could meet people with political power. In both spheres Lutek is incessantly performing. Yet ultimately, Falk is not concerned with the idea of the 'efficacy of performing' (Auslander 1992), namely he does not believe in the power of transforming people and their environment through performance. For Falk, people remain who they originally are; in the case of Lutek he remains a simple peasant despite his 'culture industry' garb. This essentialist construction of human identity, which Falk shares with many Polish directors, such as Andrzej Wajda, can be seen as a backlash against the socialist realist concept of human personality as malleable through education and work. In a narrower sense, Falk's depiction of Lutek shows that despite being nominally socialist, Polish cinema of the 1970s was anti-working class and even more anti-peasant and anti-province. Falk represents boys and girls from the country trying to make good in the city as a highly dangerous category, by exacerbating the 1970s stereotype of rich and greedy peasants who exploit the city. We see that the main private patrons of professional entertainment are rich farmers, who do not spare any money when organizing weddings, and Lutek's brother, who visits him, asks for money to build a new pigsty. Money, Falk suggests, moves from the city to the country. In reality, as was mentioned earlier in this book, in Poland, as elsewhere in the socialist bloc, the provinces lagged behind the centre, agriculture behind industry. Rather than seeing in Lutek's ruthlessness the incurable flaw of his character, we can regard his immoral behaviour as the heavy price Polish provincials had to pay to reach positions that their metropolitan counterparts took for granted.

Lutek is juxtaposed with Romek, his friend who also works in Estrada. Unlike Lutek, Romek is not 'pushy', as he himself admits, which might have something to do with him being a native of Warsaw. From the current perspective Romek will be regarded as a mediocre 'Fordist' worker and a typical product of the socialist system, which ensured that everybody had secure employment without having to push themselves or others. Falk represents him as a good worker and man, unlike Lutek, who is too competitive. The film advocates a certain work ethic, according to which 'less is more'. In this respect the Cinema of Moral Concern was at odds with the popular films of this period, especially those by Stanisław Bareja which tended to mock mediocrity in the workplace, particularly in the 'protected zone' of high culture, as exemplified by the museum or film industry. The difference in the filmmakers' attitude can be explained by the contrasting positions occupied by popular and arthouse directors. The popular ones saw themselves much more as entrepreneurs than auteurs[10] and suggested that 'Estrada' and 'opera' should be treated equally in terms of state sponsorship. Falk, on the other hand, who was a beneficiary of the division of Polish culture institutionally into 'high' and 'low art', made a film which advocated upholding this division.

The dilemma of how to be a good and honest worker under state socialism is also at the centre of Krzysztof Kieślowski's *Amator*. The title is translated into English as *Camera Buff*, which does not reflect its Polish meaning of 'amateur'. Giving the film such a title and repeating it many times in the film suggests that the concept of amateurism was very important to the director. The word 'amateur' brings to mind the Marxist discourse of amateurism, as presented in the introduction. It is worth repeating that Marx contrasted working as a specialist under the capitalist regime, which leads to alienation, with working as or being an amateur under communism. Transforming alienated workers into amateurs was meant to create and sustain an egalitarian society, in which there is no fight for power, and everybody has a chance to develop his/her talents. Under classical capitalism, however, amateurism is not welcome; specialization of labour is seen as the best way of optimizing the creation of surplus value.

As state socialism was introduced in Poland under conditions of backwardness and scarcity, amateurism was not something in which society was allowed to indulge; large-scale production and division of labour were seen as the best way to catch up with better developed countries. However, the first decade or so of the existence of socialist Poland had something amateurish about it thanks to the ease with which uneducated people could move to various professions and positions of power (see chapter 3). Gradually these channels of promotions were closed down. The authorities erected high barriers between professionals and amateurs by demanding that candidates for specific jobs have the right education and at the same time introducing very competitive entrance exams to universities. Nowhere was this more the case than among filmmakers. For a long time the only institution in Poland educating film professionals, the Łódź Film School, produced only three to four graduates in film directing per year, to ensure that they would find suitable employment, and breaking into professional filmmaking by a different route became very difficult.

Given that the amateur in *Cinema Buff* is a film amateur, it is also worth looking at the concept of amateurism in the context of the divisions within the film industry. The history of cinema, as with the history of all capitalist production, is a history of increased specialization of labour, with large Hollywood studios, the 'dream factories', representing the culmination of this process. Documentary filmmaking was an enclave in which amateurism was allowed to prevail. This is because documentaries are typically made away from the studio by small crews on low budgets, and their narrative language is less constrained than in fiction films. The pioneering documentarist Joris Ivens described documentary as a 'creative no-man's land, an interloper in the genre system' (quoted in Chanan 2009: 17). In Poland after the Second World War there existed a well-developed movement of amateur filmmaking, consisting of over 5,000 filmmakers, fostered by state enterprises, trade unions, various societies (of tourists, collectors, etc.) and supported by television ('Film amatorski' 1962: 113–118), to which the film makes reference. It is possible to see this movement either as a means of becoming professional filmmakers through a different route than obtaining formal training in the film school or, conversely, as a way to maintain a rigid division between film professionals and amateurs. Or one can suggest that thanks to state-sponsored fostering of film amateurs, Poland developed a special third category: 'professional film amateurs' (not unlike the category of 'professional sport amateurs', discussed in the previous chapter).

Camera Buff shows the gradual professionalization of a film amateur. The titular character, Filip Mosz, a man employed in the purchasing department of a socialist enterprise somewhere in the provinces, buys a cine-camera to capture the life of his new-born daughter. Initially Filip wants to be a pure amateur, working with the camera for the happiness of his family. Soon, however, other purposes, such as documenting the events on his housing estate and the life of his firm, become more important to him. His film about the anniversary of his plant, commissioned by the factory's manager, receives one of the main awards at an amateur film festival. In this way Filip begins his career as a 'professional amateur filmmaker'. Moving to this role means that his main job has to take a back seat; his principal occupation becomes filmmaking. We can imagine that this could have been the trajectory of Romek Januchta, had his cabaret become an official success. This was also the trajectory of Kieślowski, who first trained as a theatre technician, as already stated. Filip gets a special office-workshop in the basement, an assistant and a semi-official role as the chronicler of his factory and his town. He also gains some recognition in the national media, as one of his films is shown on a national television channel. His identity changes in step with the expansion of time devoted to filmmaking and his external recognition – he starts to see himself more as an artist than a factory worker or a family man, a transition sealed with the split from his wife.

This shift, however, brings with it problems which reflect on working in Poland of the 1970s, being a documentary filmmaker and an artist, all issues reflecting Kieślowski's own position at the time. With increasing external recognition Filip loses his autonomy as a filmmaker, because the manager regards Filip's work as the factory's property rather than the filmmaker's and he intends to use Filip's work to showcase the factory's achievements. The manager does not want the amateur to include anything in his film which would undermine the rosy picture of the plant. Filip, by contrast, does not want to show merely the façade, but rather document the negative aspects of his environs. The television editor has a similar attitude to Filip as that of his boss – he wants him to fulfil a specific task, for which he will be paid with high-quality materials and tools, allowing him to make more films. The television editor mentions that Filip can shoot whatever he wants, but the editor retains the right to edit it. As in *Personnel*, the situation at a specific workplace can be seen as a metonym of a larger reality: that of filmmaking or even producing art in socialist Poland, where artists enjoyed a secure existence and official recognition, but at the price of their freedom being circumvented and the recognition that ultimately their work belongs to the state. Such a situation parallels that of the directors working in a Hollywood studio, who are limited by the requirement to make profitable films. Filip's dissatisfaction with other people meddling with his films reflects the fact that socialist filmmakers yearned for a double freedom – from financial constraints and ideological pressures. One can even argue that in the 1970s, when censorship was mild, they succeeded – an opinion which was rarely voiced then, but which is not uncommon now, many years after state socialism collapsed.[11]

By showing the reception of Filip's films by different types of audiences, Kieślowski refers to the multiple roles documentary film can play in society, such as preserving the past of individuals and communities, and political intervention.

All these functions are derivatives of the main function of the documentary: that of documenting reality. That said, Kieślowski demonstrates that what the film presents never exists by itself, but in multiple contexts. By showing something, the filmmaker foregrounds one context but suppresses another. This is illustrated by one of the films Filip made against the will of his superiors, about the brickworks in his city which stopped producing bricks. The filmmaker believes that this film will help his community by disclosing how wastefully the city authority uses its resources. When the film is made, however, he learns that the truth about the idle brickworks obscures a more complex truth concerning hidden unemployment in the region and the transfer of financial resources allocated centrally in a way which helps the local community. By making his 'truthful' film about the brickworks, Filip risks these resources being withdrawn. Moreover, Filip's disobedience to his superior leads to the punishment not of the filmmaker, but of his older colleague and a trade union official, who allowed Filip to develop this 'second' career. Filip's last exchange with the factory's manager points to a difference between the manager of a socialist enterprise and his capitalist counterpart and, by extension, state socialism and capitalism. The ultimate goal of the former is ensuring full employment in his community and its cohesiveness, rather than maximizing profit (although profit is also a goal of socialist firms). A negative by-product of this attitude is a high degree of waste (keeping the brickworks officially open, while in reality it had stopped producing bricks), a perceived low standard of living, and a pervasive sense of irrationality on the level of individual firms, town, region and country at large. The capitalist manager, by contrast, would close the brickworks without troubling him/herself about the fate of sacked workers and such a scenario took place everywhere in Eastern Europe after 1989, leading to mass unemployment, social pathology and the devastation of a large proportion of Eastern Europe. By focusing on the shortcomings of the state socialist system, films like those produced by Filip Mosz, Kieślowski and the whole group of Moral Concern directors facilitated the shift towards capitalism, even if their intention was to improve state socialism rather than dismantling it.

I argued in the previous chapters that in 1950s films women were engaged in the production and rebuilding of the country and were even more eager and successful producers than their male counterparts. In 1960s films their role as producers diminished and they started to occupy the sphere of consumption. This is also broadly the case in films of the 1970s, but there are differences. Firstly, on this occasion consumption is conflated with domesticity. Women typically occupy the domestic sphere and their main goal is to keep their husbands away from politics. Filip's wife is a typical example here. Second, the gender question in these films is subdued. The films discussed here seem to be blind to gender; they do not ask whether it is easier for a woman or a man to make a career. Such a position – the official position of the socialist state – was ultimately disadvantageous to women.

The Past Is a Different Country

In the 1970s the period of Stalinism started to feel like the distant past. This sense, combined with a relaxation of censorship, encouraged Polish filmmakers to revisit this period, as in *Opowieść o człowieku, który wykonał 552% normy* (*A Story of a Man Who Filled 552% of the Quota*, 1973), directed by Wojciech Wiszniewski, *Murarz* (*The Bricklayer*, 1973), directed by Krzysztof Kieślowski, and *Man of Marble*, directed by Andrzej Wajda. Their aim was not simply to recreate this part of Polish history, but also to use it as a lens to look at the present, as well as to use the present to revaluate Polish Stalinism.

Wojciech Wiszniewski, the author of *A Story of a Man Who Filled 552% of the Quota*, was one of the leading documentary filmmakers of the 1970s, representing a style described as 'creative documentary' (Przylipiak 1984: 16). This term suggests that he wanted to do something more with the past than simply revisit it. As the title suggests, this is the past of a shock worker, Bernard Bugdol, who in the years 1948–1949 broke records in extracting coal when working in a team with his brother. Wiszniewski assesses Bugdol's successes from a 1970s perspective, as indicated by an introduction and a coda, which is set in a television studio where a programme about Bugdol is being made. This frame points to the fact that Wiszniewski is interested not so much in Bugdol's real life, as the play between his life and its media image. This might be seen as a reflection on the 1970s, when state propaganda became more staged than in the earlier periods.

The early shot shows an ordinary block where the majority of working-class people lived in Poland of state socialism and where presumably Bugdol dwelt during a large chunk of his life, although later we see him in his own house or his summer dacha. For a moment Wiszniewski shoots Bugdol from the back and then edits it with the image of the back of a statue, one of a number of statues adorning the Palace of Culture in Warsaw, which represents Bugdol, or rather a generic shock worker based on his image. This editing announces that the film will confront the real man with his monument. For the remainder of the film Wiszniewski offers us numerous official and unofficial representations of Bugdol, as if he wanted to account for different perspectives from which he can be approached, bringing to mind the structure of Citizen Kane or Munk's Man on the Tracks.

We hear verses and songs devoted to shock workers such as Wincenty Pstrowski, Bugdol's better known predecessor, who introduced competition into Polish factories after the Second World War. Wiszniewski also shows fragments of old newsreels and a kind of comic strip or family album devoted to Bugdol's achievements, which is set into motion thanks to fast editing. These official representations are juxtaposed with the memories of members of Bugdol's family and his work mates. While in official representations Bugdol's attitude to work is presented as an example to be followed by everybody, in the memories of others we get a less flattering portrayal. Some people claim that his successes had a negative effect on other workers because they undermined their achievements and led to an increase in their quotas. The shock worker thus made everybody else look mediocre. The second criticism comes from his wife who says that her husband's preoccupation with work made him neglect his family and treat his wife with a sense of superiority. To the first criticism Bugdol responds that work quotas would have increased anyway due to gains in productivity resulting from technological and managerial advancement. Shock working was a temporary measure and his pioneering work was meant to make people ultimately work less rather than more. Bugdol adds that the improvements in working methods were necessary in the context of the postwar destruction and backwardness of the Polish industry in the late 1940s. Without the work he pioneered Poland would have lagged behind forever. Instead, thanks to the efforts of Bugdol and others like him, modernization and universal welfare were achieved, as demonstrated by his own prosperous life. Bugdol also achieved success in other spheres of public life. He was a director of two mines, an MP and chairman of one of the most successful Polish football clubs, Górnik Zabrze. While working, he received a university education, becoming an engineer. These successes are not mentioned in the film, implying that Wiszniewski did not want to praise the state socialist system too much, as a regime under which hard work and enthusiasm are enough to achieve extraordinary successes. Still, Bugdol's professional successes and his affluence that are shown in the film are confirmation that socialist competition led to the

Illustration 5.4: Bugdol tending to his medals in *A Story of a Man Who Filled 552% of the Quota*, directed by Wojciech Wiszniewski

enrichment of the worker. One cannot find a better advertisement for state socialism as a system which rewards hard work than Bugdol's career.

Bugdol's prosperity might also be seen as a partial response to his wife's criticism that the shock worker became obsessed with his work and arrogant. If this was indeed the case, his attitude was typical of people who are very successful. We see Bugdol's family together, signalling that any differences the couple might have had in the past were put aside. Ultimately it remained at least a functioning family. Watching the film now I cannot help but think about the family of another Polish exceptional worker as portrayed on screen: the family of Lech Wałęsa in the film by Andrzej Wajda, *Wałęsa: Człowiek z nadziei* (*Wałęsa: Man of Hope*, 2013). In this family, we also encounter a wife who resents her husband for putting his work first (although in Wałęsa's case it is political work) and for being big-headed, but this is not a reason to leave him. If anything, such a situation reflects on the patriarchal system affecting how many families function both in the East and in the West, under the conditions of state socialism and capitalism. Despite all his successes Bugdol's face expresses discomfort or sadness, as if he felt obliged to defend his position rather than being able to bask in its glory. This sadness does not mean either that Wiszniewski depicts Bugdol's life as wasted or that he presents him, as Jadwiga Głowa puts it, as 'fossilized': locked in the past and immune to new ideas (Głowa 1996: 207). On the contrary, Bugdol strikes me as possessing an acute sense of his place in history. His sadness results from realizing that his successes were so spectacular that he would not be able to match them in the future; he can only re-live them by polishing his trophies, looking at old pictures or giving interviews to people like Wiszniewski. But who at an advanced age would not like to be in such a position? Watching the film now, when opportunities for social promotion have diminished due to fierce competition for scarce jobs, Bugdol's story comes across almost as a fairy tale.

The Bricklayer is also a documentary about a manual worker from the Stalinist period who turned political activist, but with a somewhat different outcome. The style of the film is simpler, bringing to mind the films of Kazimierz Karabasz, Kieślowski's mentor, most importantly *The Year of Franek W.*, discussed in the previous chapter. The film shows May Day of 1971, which seen through Kieślowski's lens comes across as a staged and media driven event. The off-screen reminiscences of the protagonist, Malesa, are juxtaposed with the voice of the speaker who talks about the large number of participants representing political organizations and leading enterprises taking part in the May Day festivities, and the sound of a brass band. In the past such bands signified working-class culture, especially the mining tradition, but in the 1970s they stand for old, stuffy culture. At the same time, the festivities have a picnic atmosphere, with children with balloons enjoying themselves. For Malesa and his old colleagues May Day is an opportunity to meet and chat. There is plenty of red everywhere. Red is the colour of the banners, of the flowers and of the balloons carried by the children. The red of the May Day decorations contrasts with the greyness of the blocks of flats and Malesa's own apartment, perhaps suggesting a gap between the colourful surface and the grey reality of Gierek's Poland.

For Malesa, May Day provides an opportunity to compare the Stalinist past with the present of Gierek's rule. We learn that after the Second World War the eponymous character, not unlike Bugdol in Wiszniewski's film, became one of the leaders of socialist work competition and his professional achievements facilitated his political career in the early 1950s. Malesa started to play an important role first in the socialist youth organization and then in the Party structures. Such a trajectory was natural for him, as he came from a family with a communist tradition. Yet, Malesa comes across as somewhat bitter about his political career.

He points to numerous mistakes the Party made during the Stalinist years, which led to the political crisis of 1956, de-Stalinization and, as we know with the benefit of hindsight, to subsequent political crises. In the opinion of Malesa, a huge mistake made by the political establishment consisted of creating political enemies of innocuous people who could have been productively incorporated into the communist project, such as those who had family in the West, or youngsters who embraced western values. Malesa also refers to the precedence of the political sphere over the economy, mentioning that some young people worked badly but could not be dismissed from the factories because they were members of communist organizations. He also complains that instead of giving him more power, working as a politician actually disempowered him. In his role as a political activist he felt like a clerk, merely transmitting orders from above.

The year 1956 had shaken Malesa's confidence in the project of state socialism. Since then he had become suspicious of politics. By this point he yearned to do a 'real' job, and asked for transfer back to the building site. This decision cost him much in terms of prestige and material standing, as testified by his mentioning that his old colleagues and protégés ended up holding ministerial positions (with many perks attached, such as larger apartments and government cars), while we see Malesa in a cramped apartment and catching a tram, thus leading, in economic terms, a typical working-class life. However, the film finishes with a eulogy of bricklaying as 'real work'. The bricklayer says that building houses is similar to art because bricks can be assembled in different ways, leaving space for one's creativity. Its other advantage is that it is done in the fresh air, which can be interpreted, both literally and metaphorically, as work allowing a degree of freedom which is not permitted in political work. To use Marxist language, Malesa categorizes bricklaying as non-alienated work. His verbal praise is accompanied by a bird's eye view of Warsaw Old City. The Old City, despite its Renaissance style, is in fact new because it was re-built from scratch after the Second World War. This perfect simulacra contrasts with the staged and kitschy May festivities, convincing us that Malesa made the right decision. Yet, despite his disillusionment with state socialism Malesa still takes part in the May parade. We see him among his old mates, most likely other 'apparatchiks'. The question arises why he still supports the 'real socialist' May Day. Kieślowski suggests that this might be due to his nostalgia or belief that, even in its crude form, socialism in Poland is still better than the system which Malesa remembers from his youth.

By exalting Malesa's bricklaying achievements Kieślowski suggests that a certain type of work is valuable irrespective of its wider political and economic context. The idea that work can be intrinsically valuable is not Marxist, because according to Marx work which serves capitalism (or for that matter any system which does not serve the workers), even or especially if it leads to producing the most attractive commodities, is alienated. Kieślowski's extolling such work probably reflected his need to find justification for millions like Malesa, who might have lost faith in state socialism, but who carried on working and even participating in state ceremonies. In this sense Malesa can be seen as somebody who helped Kieślowski's own transformation from politically-minded filmmaker to one who avoids politics altogether and just tries to produce work of high quality.

Andrzej Wajda's *Man of Marble* could be also renamed *A Story of a Man Who Filled 552% of the Quota* or *Bricklayer*, because it deals with a bricklayer and shock worker who started his career in Stalinist times, and assesses his achievements and afterlife from a 1970s perspective. The film begins with a fragment of what looks like a 1950s newsreel, showing a man energetically laying bricks to the accompaniment of a cheerful song from the period. After that, the film introduces Agnieszka, who is a final-year film college student. She is making a diploma film, financed by state television, to be entitled *Gwiazdy jednego sezonu* (*Falling Stars*), about bricklayer Mateusz Birkut, the same man who appeared in the opening sequence. He took part in building the city of Nowa Huta, regarded as the greatest enterprise of the Six-Year Plan. Birkut enjoyed a short career in the 1950s as a champion of socialist work, with his team laying over 30,000 bricks in one shift. He served as an example to be followed by ordinary workers, was captured on camera, and immortalized in huge portraits and marble sculptures. After that he disappeared virtually without trace from Polish politics and culture. It is the mystery of his downfall that prompts Agnieszka to make a film based on his life.

Before Agnieszka begins her investigation, we see her looking at the television studio building that she had just left, disappointed by the hostility of the executive towards her plan. In this sequence the camera is placed near the ground, which renders her monumental, evoking visual codes of socialist realism, whose purpose was to aggrandize socialist heroes. In all seriousness Wajda portrays Agnieszka as a towering figure, able to stand up to everybody and conquer everything. Such an idea is confirmed in the subsequent scene, when she reaches the cellars of the National Museum in Warsaw, finding there a marble statue of Birkut, locked in a dark room amongst dozens of other socialist realist statues. When Agnieszka enters the cellars of the museum, we hear a familiar, joyful, socialist realist song and the mobile camera gives the impression that the statues are moving. It thus feels as if Agnieszka's presence has brought the marble statues back to life. She decides to shoot in these poorly lit interiors, but not as her aged cameraman suggests, by putting the camera on a tripod, but holding the camera with her hand, to breathe life into the 'sleeping knights' of Polish socialism. To do so, she sits astride a statue of Birkut, which is lying on the floor. In this position Agnieszka looks as if she is having sex with the huge but passive Birkut. Subsequently Agnieszka looks for her elusive 'lover' in the film archive, which allows us to see how work was represented in the 1950s. The newsreels employ a male narrator who draws on military jargon, for example talking about 'workers *fighting* for a better future'. This militarism is underscored by the use of dynamic, march-like songs in the soundtrack. The work is spectacular; Birkut's act of breaking the bricklaying record is admired by hundreds of onlookers and captured on camera. The off-screen narrator talks not about the simple task of bricklaying, but about the art of bricklaying and about Birkut being a virtuoso of his art. As if to confirm this statement, in the following fragment the builder is transformed into an object of art, not unlike in Wiszniewski's film about Bugdol. The camera shows him from below, rendering him as super-human and points to his multiplication in huge socialist realist portraits and sculptures, adorning halls used to celebrate the successes of socialist industries. The voice-over offers a familiar, Stalinist trajectory of progress, marked by a transition from the country to the city and conquering the virginal space (Mroz 2007; see also chapter 3). Birkut leaves behind a family farm and moves to a place where the steelworks and the city of Nowa Huta is to be built and the whole country progresses because the fields and meadows give way to industrial complexes and new housing estates. Economic advancement is accompanied by progress in education and changes in personal life. Birkut attends evening classes to overcome his illiteracy and in Nowa Huta meets a nice girl named Hanka Tomczyk, whom he subsequently marries (or at least this is what the socialist propaganda tells us).

By accessing the rejected footage and meeting people who knew Birkut first hand, Agnieszka learns that his life and the country's trajectory did not adhere to the official version. The builders of Nowa Huta were not as joyful as the newsreels show, because they had to work in appalling conditions and were not even given enough food. The stakhanovite successes of Birkut and others like him were also paid for by workers' disunity, as the ordinary workers were hostile towards the record-breakers who drove the standards up, which is an issue raised in Wiszniewski's film. Birkut was punished for his extra effort by a fellow worker who passed him a hot brick, which permanently damaged his hands. In due course he distanced himself from Stalinism and became an activist, engaged in the struggle to improve workers' conditions. For this, he was again punished, but this time by the authorities, who deprived him of a public voice (literalized by switching off the microphone when he tries to address a union meeting) and knocked his figure off the pedestal. By the time Agnieszka starts researching Birkut's life, he is no longer alive – he died in 1970 during an anti-state protest. What Agnieszka unearths is not a simple reversal of a socialist realist narrative, which would lead to a wholesome condemnation of state socialism and extolling the opposite system – capitalism. The memories of people who knew Birkut show that although his work was extremely hard, it was not alienated, as he laboured with enthusiasm, like a sportsman trying to achieve something nobody had done before him, and he felt that he was working for himself and for a greater cause: to build a better, prosperous Poland. Birkut's story thus supports the idea conveyed in the popular 1970s slogan 'Socialism – yes, distortions – no',[12] which might also be one reason why the film's script was accepted by the censors. This slogan conveyed the idea that Gierek's regime should not be held responsible for the mistakes of its predecessor (in common with Gomułka not being responsible for the mistakes of Bierut). The material about Birkut that Agnieszka collected during her peregrinations leads to the rejection of her project by the television producer, here representing the voice of the Party. Rather than do what he (and by extension the authorities) want her to do, she decides to quit the media altogether, go to the north of Poland, the cradle of Polish anti-communist opposition, and join the Polish workers' struggle to overthrow the oppressive system, as shown in *Man of Marble*'s sequel, *Man of Iron* (discussed in chapter 6). Agnieszka does so because, paradoxically, she is a socialist – the workers' lot matters to her more than her career. Her ideal is a country in which everybody can live in peace and prosperity, and workers have political power, rather than being subjected to the decisions of the nomenklatura. While making her film, Agnieszka learns that the previous failures in the workers' struggle for a 'better socialism' resulted from disunity, especially between the workers and the intelligentsia. When one class rebelled, the other kept quiet and vice versa. She decides to cross the class barriers and work with and for the workers. Agnieszka's act is an important step towards creating Solidarity: a heterogeneous, yet ultimately united force, which can be compared to Michael Hardt and Antonio Negri's 'multitude' (Hardt and Negri 2006). Hardt and Negri use this term to describe the situation under capitalism but, as state socialism bears many similarities to capitalism, it can be mapped onto the class relations in Eastern Europe, while 'Empire' can be compared to the nomenklatura in Poland and the entire Eastern bloc. Indeed, several years later Solidarity declared war against such an Empire and won (although this victory paved the way to introducing neoliberalism, a system more hostile to the working class than state socialism).

Although Agnieszka never completed her film, in a sense we see it – this is Wajda's *Man of Marble*. In it, in place of the old, socialist realist language of work, Wajda offers a new language. The old language was static and patriarchal, the new is dynamic and female; the old gave answers, the new asks questions; the old created spectacles, the new excavates truth; the old offered a coherent and smooth narrative, the new focuses on gaps and privileges outtakes; the old hides the creator to give the impression of objectivity, the new places the author at the centre of the story. In the process of replacing old language with the new, Wajda also furnishes the film director with a dignity which creators of the Cinema of Moral Concern stripped representatives of the media. *Man of Marble* succeeds in returning the diminished socialist culture industry to the level of art. Another consequence of this approach, less positive from the perspective of the workers, is rendering them passive, as mere material to be shaped by talented and committed filmmakers. As I argued elsewhere, despite the film's title, which pronounces the importance of Birkut and material production, *Man of Marble* is more about Agnieszka and cultural production (Mazierska 2002b). The sense of workers' passivity will be overcome in *Man of Iron*, but each of these films also alludes to the postcommunist future, when workers would lose their privileged position in the country's history and disappear from the 'big picture' altogether.

Comparing the films by Wiszniewski and Kieślowski with that of Wajda reveals an interesting paradox – the fiction film is more critical about the Stalinist past and Gierek's present than the documentary films. This might suggest that for many manual workers work and life in Poland was better than the creators of the Cinema of Moral Concern wanted us to believe. If we accept this hypothesis, then the critical tone of the fiction films should rather be attributed to a special prestige a critical tone afforded filmmakers. To put it simply, in the 1970s one was considered a great director or auteur not by being stylistically innovative or intellectually profound (as the bulk of the films belonging to this paradigm are not), but by being (usually vaguely) critical about the state and extolling the predicament of a creative worker.

Propaganda of Success in Polish Documentaries

The term 'propaganda of success' is associated largely with Polish television of the 1970s, especially television news. However, among the 1970s documentaries we also find some films making the point that Poland is a successful country. One such film is *Krystyna M.* (1973) by Kazimierz Karabasz. In common with the films discussed in the previous section, it also harks back to the past, but on this occasion by referencing Karabasz's own film from the previous decade, *The Year of Franek W.* (discussed in chapter 4). The film's protagonist is a young woman who moved to Warsaw from a village in the economically underdeveloped East of Poland, so called 'Poland B' or 'Eastern Wall', to work in the Ursus tractor factory. In common with *The Year of Franek W.*, the filmmaker allows the character to speak with her own voice. Krystyna, who is in her early twenties, comes across as intelligent, articulate and mature for her age. She is able to locate herself in history,

Illustration 5.5: Krystyna in *Krystyna M.*, directed by Kazimierz Karabasz

confirming Mikołaj Jazdon's opinion that Karabasz's characters have a deeper insight into reality (Jazdon 2009: 195). She mentions that due to her modest background, young age and gender, she experienced various prejudices in the workplace and had to prove herself. She did so by being a very good worker and enrolling in a technical college to learn more and ensure her promotion to a better job. She also mentions that in due course she would like to live in her own apartment, as the one she currently dwells in is rented (possibly thanks to a subsidy from her firm). For that reason she would have to stay in Ursus for at least five more years, to qualify for a loan she would not need to pay back. We thus receive an image of a socialist welfare state which tries to help working people, rewarding them for good work and their loyalty to the firm.

The picture of the workplace Krystyna paints is that of a world when men are privileged, but not excessively so. Women can make in-roads there, not at the expense of devoting all their life to work, but just by being good at their job. Krystyna has time to meet friends in Warsaw and visit her relatives in her village. Although the film is not explicit about when it is set, it conveys the affluence and optimism pertaining to the 'early Gierek' period. For example, at some stage we see bottles of Coca Cola in a cafe where Krystyna meets her friend. Her girlfriends from Warsaw all talk about fashion. The spirit of the early 1970s is also implied by the lack of reference to the communist ideology. Krystyna herself talks about her life as her private affair: her best girlfriend, the boys whom she met, her desire to marry a man who will understand her. She shows no interest in socialism or any other large communal project and she is probably not a member of the Party or any youth organization. An illustration of this is the fact that in order to improve her job situation she did not go to the Party secretary, but to an engineer with a managerial position. To a greater extent than in the 1960s, Poland of the 1970s is portrayed in this film as a technocratic country, where specialists, not politicians, dictate what happens on the shop floor. *Krystyna M.* can be seen as a corrective to films such as *Girls to Pick Up* which make fun of provincials or *Dance Leader* which depict them as sponging on the 'urbanites'. Karabasz's film shows Krystyna as being ahead of her peers from the city and suggests that the industrialization of Poland could take place only thanks to a transfer of the population from the country to the city. Such a transfer, as I will demonstrate in subsequent chapters, is still taking place, but its main cause is the pauperization of the countryside post-1989 rather than an increase in opportunities awaiting those who left it.

Another documentary which suggests that the 1970s was a decade of prosperity is *Sztygar na zagrodzie...* (*Foreman on a Farm...*, 1978) by Wojciech Wiszniewski. Its main character, Stanisław Mazur, is a successful miner who embarks on the task of helping an ailing farming community he left a long time ago, most likely to pursue a more attractive career in coalmining. The story has a distinct beginning and an end, 7 May 1976 to 11 November 1977, the dates when the protagonist and his family came and then left Rydułty Nowe, a village in the South of Poland. It is suggested that the miner did not come of his own accord, but in response to a request from the political authorities. On his arrival he found his own house in ruins and embarked on the task of bringing prosperity back to 'his' people by producing sausages. Yet as with Bugdol, Mazur's efforts are not appreciated by the whole community. Some of his countrymen treat the newcomers with hostility, of which the most obvious sign is torching Mazur's car. The countrymen begrudge him his success because it shows them up as failing and makes them work hard. If the film is critical of the socialist way of work, this is not because the exceptional workers failed, but rather because the rest of society did not live up to the socialist ideals, behaving like a disruptive and reactionary lumpenproletariat, as described by Marx in 'The Eighteenth Brumaire of Louis Bonaparte' (Marx 1978).

Mirosław Przylipiak argues that the story of the foreman can be interpreted as an allegory of Edward Gierek's career (Przylipiak 2008a). Gierek worked in his youth as an ordinary miner in France and Belgium, where he was also active in the communist movement, before he returned to Poland, where he was promoted up the Party ranks. He became the new Secretary in response to the invitation of the Party's executive, which needed a new man able to modernize the country. After the fall of state socialism, the prevailing opinion is that Gierek's modernization was a failure. However, a significant proportion of Poles look with nostalgia at his decade, believing that Gierek's was the last attempt to improve socialism from within. If not for unfavourable external circumstances (such as the oil crisis in the mid-1970s) and his countrymen's refusal to collaborate with Gierek, he would have succeeded and achieved universal prosperity. If we accept such an allegorical reading of *Foreman on a Farm...*, then the conclusion is that Wiszniewski anticipated Gierek's demise and suggested that this would not be due to the Secretary's incompetence, but rather the failure of ordinary people to give him a helping hand.

Although Wiszniewski's film appears to be based on true events, its style is unrealistic. The connections between episodes are unclear and the gestures of the characters are monumentalized, as if they were not real people but actors playing them, such as in a stylized shot showing a miner and his family wreathed in rings of sausage in a pose which was compared to a Laokoon group. This style prompted some critics to claim that the film is a kind of satire on Gierek and Gierek's socialism (Śliwińska 2006) rather than testimony to Wiszniewski's admiration for his protagonist. In my opinion, the film is purposefully ambiguous in this respect. It can be seen both as the apology of an unlucky economic and political leader or a subtle mockery of his efforts.

Into the West

The West was always present in postwar Polish cinema, although till the 1960s it functioned more as a meaningful absence than presence (Beinek 2011). In the 1970s this situation has changed, as during this decade more films about the West were made and it was actually shown on screen. It is no longer demonized as enemy territory, but depicted more realistically as a place where Poles travelled to improve their lot. In the 1970s unofficial trade with the Eastern and Western countries became an important part of the second economy. This was facilitated by Gierek's easing of restrictions on travelling and the private production of consumer goods. As a result, in the 1970s Poles became the 'new Phoenicians of Eastern Europe', often making profitable exchanges in a number of countries before finally returning to Poland. The authorities had a somewhat schizophrenic attitude to this phenomenon. On the one hand, from 1972 the country was covered by a network of shops first called Pekao (from the name of the state bank) and then Pewex, selling goods in western currency. On the other hand, buying western currency officially from a bank was impossible and buying it privately was illegal, as was bringing foreign money and goods from abroad to resell them. The assumption was that people would circumvent the law, but at the same time feel guilty about it, which would help to keep them in check. Illegal foreign trade was easiest for those who travelled officially, on business trips or 'friendly' exchanges with other countries, in a nutshell, the nomenklatura. The scornful attitude to the foreign traders was reflected in the terminology used to describe people engaging in unofficial foreign trade, such as *cinkciarz*, referring to a person facilitating the exchange of foreign currency on the black market. The term juxtaposes a butchered version of the English word *change* and Polish *cienki* (thin), alluding to the fact that those involved in such trade usually did not speak good English and often operated on a small scale.

A number of films from the 1970s allude to illegal foreign trade. Stanislaw Bareja's *Co mi zrobisz, jak mnie złapiesz* (*What Will You Do When You Catch Me?*, 1978) begins with its protagonist, Krzakoski, director of a large enterprise, arriving in Paris. There, with the help of some Polish men living locally, he buys fifty computers to sell at a profit back in Poland. However, this is only a small element of Krzakoski's misdemeanours, which also include adultery, bad management of his firm and using state money for private purposes. The foreign dealings only add to the impression that he has no morals. *Rewizja osobista* (*Strip Search*, 1973) by Andrzej Kostenko and Witold Leszczyński is devoted to foreign travel as a means of acquiring extra income and status. The film is set on the Polish border which a middle-class woman with her two children tries to cross in their 'bahama yellow' coloured Polish Fiat, the favourite car of the Polish nouveaux riches of the 1970s, whose boot is full of western goods. The travellers are stopped by a zealous custom officer, who orders a personal search. The film picks up on the consumerism of Gierek's Poland: striving to have a flashy car, a packet of foreign cigarettes and playing cards. It also reveals the contradictory approach of the authorities to consumerist ambitions of Poles: on the one hand awakening them by facilitating foreign travel, on the other hand not allowing them to develop and bring it into the open. The film itself has an anti-consumerist and anti-western bias, revelling in the sadistic pleasure the custom officer gets in tormenting the petty smugglers and the scornful gaze the teenage son directs towards his materialist mother and sister. It focuses on the garishness of items brought from abroad by travellers; their display brings to mind things in Jean-Luc Godard's *Deux ou trois choses que je sais d'elle* (1966). However, in common with Godard's films, whose original meaning was changed in the process of interpretation (his critical way of displaying things was used as a blueprint for presenting them favourably by producers of television adverts), it is possible that instead of awakening anti-consumerism in the viewers, *Strip Search* actually made them jealous of their better-off countrymen.

In the previous chapter I discussed *Wife for an Australian*, which touched on Polish economic migration to the West. Although the film was unrealistic and used the motif of an ex-patriate looking for a Polish wife largely as a means of showcasing the performance of the Polish folk band Mazowsze, it nevertheless pointed to a specific type of human capital that the foreigners sought among the

Polish candidates for emigration: physical attractiveness, combined with an ability to work in the fields. This is because after the Second World War in many western countries there was a shortage of workforce in the countryside. Young women in particular did not want to stay there, but preferred to move to the city, hence they needed to be replaced by migrants from poorer countries. *Bilet powrotny* (*Return Ticket*, 1979) by Ewa and Czesław Petelscy addresses this phenomenon, albeit in a more realistic fashion than Bareja, not least because *Return Ticket* is based on a true story. Its scriptwriter, Jerzy Stefan Stawiński, based it on his encounter with a woman who travelled from rural Poland to rural Canada and back. Her cinematic equivalent, Antonina, is a widow at the beginning of the film who lives on a farm somewhere in Poland. She is looking after the farm herself as her only son is training to become a car mechanic, and she wants them to relocate to the city and live there in a box-like two-storey house, fashionable at the time. The opportunity to fulfil this dream appears when Antonina is invited by her uncle to Canada, to a remote and sparsely populated region of Ontario, where many of the early Polish emigrants settled before the Second World War. These Polish pioneers made their living by transforming the forests into fields. While they were happy just to make their living in a foreign country, many of their children moved to the city, put off by the harshness of country life; this led to family feuds. This is the case of Antonina's uncle, whose children moved away to Vancouver and are on bad terms with him. He lives on the farm with Antonina's sister, Zośka. Because she limps, Zośka is seen by her uncle as a defective worker and woman, and hence merely as a servant. In contrast, he finds Antonina, who is able-bodied and has a feminine, curvaceous figure, attractive and tries to seduce her. Antonina, however, resists him and makes it clear that she is only interested in earning money to send to her son so he can start building a house for them. Soon she meets her uncle's French neighbour, Pierre, who is also a farmer. After some deliberation Antonina agrees to marry him, persuaded by her son who regards it as a way to save more money for their dream house. However, the marriage finishes tragically, when Antonina sends some of Pierre's money to Poland, taking advantage of his absence, only to find out that there is no dream house waiting for her. The son used her money for consumption.

Return Ticket testifies to the times it was made by highlighting the lack of finality of Antonina's travels, and reflecting on Gierek's good relations with the West. Until her marriage to Pierre, Antonina keeps her options open: she wants to stay in Canada for longer to earn money for the house for her son, but ultimately she intends to return to Poland to live there. There are also references to Gierek's policies affecting the countryside, such as facilitating trading in land or giving land to the state in exchange for a pension. Ultimately, however, Antonina's story has a distinct anti-western bias, as was to be expected from the Petelskis, who belonged to the most loyal supporters of the socialist regime (see chapter 3). Life in the West, as rendered in *Return Ticket*, is lonely and spiritually impoverished. In such an environment the only distraction is provided by consumption. The places of consumption, such as supermarkets and a drive-in cinema, where Pierre takes Antonina to watch a porn film together, come across as kitschy and alienating. The Petelskis also draw parallels between trading in cattle and trading in women in the West; Pierre talks about Antonina as if she was the best woman he could buy for his money and shortly after marrying her he sells his cattle, as if to balance his possessions. But the novelty of Petelskis' approach consists of demonstrating that Polish people in the 1970s do not behave differently from Westerners, assessing people according to their monetary capital rather than spiritual values. The ambition of living in the East in western luxury pertains most to the young generation, exemplified by Antonina's lazy and greedy son. Even before his mother moves to Canada, he complains that he has no car and when Antonina tells him about a letter she received from her uncle, he immediately asks if he sent anything extra. When Antonina takes money from Pierre, it is to buy goods which even Pierre, the Westerner, does not have, such as a colour television set. This can be seen as a reference to the Polish ambition to outdo the West in this decade. This ambition ultimately fails: the western money disappears, 'eaten up' by excessive and unwise consumption, leading to Poland being 'crippled' for the remainder of state socialism.

Notes

1. This debt seems enormous in comparison with the practically debt-free rule of Gomułka, but is very low in comparison with the debt Poland amassed after the transition to neoliberalism, which in 2009 reached 275 billion USD (Ciborowski and Konat 2010: 46).
2. This is one reason why in the 1970s political slogans and language in general became an important source of comedy (Kurz 2008b).
3. Due to the film's unusual style and even production, Piwowski met with significant resistance when preparing his project, including by Antoni Bohdziewicz who was an artistic mentor of Piwowski in the film studio Tor, which produced *Cruise* (Stachówna and Zmudziński 2007: 66).

4. Such a description captures an important characteristic of communism. In this system prosperity and self-fulfilment is granted not only to exceptional individuals, but also to those who have lower abilities. This implies, as Tym makes explicit, that the talents of the 'natural winners' are less appreciated and rewarded, but for me, being a socialist, it is a price worth paying for building an inclusive and prosperous society.
5. This can also be seen as a reference to the difficulty of establishing who in Poland (and Eastern Europe at large) was employed to work and who was employed to spy on others. There are other instances in the film which can be regarded as an allusion to spying and its consequences; for example, at the beginning we see a man approaching a boat but he is not among the passengers. This might be due to his being captured by secret services.
6. It will be more productive to use here a metaphor of 'heterotopia', which I applied to another ship, presented in Polish film: the spaceship in *Test Pilota Pirxa* (*The Test of Pilot Pirx*, 1979), directed by Marek Piestrak (Mazierska 2012c).
7. Piwowski himself today sees his film not so much as a critique of socialist Poland, but as a document about better times. He confessed to me that his life in the 1970s was too easy, too comfortable, which led him to miss many opportunities to make films. He appreciates this easiness especially against the background of the new rules, introduced in the last decade, when the process became more market-oriented yet also more bureaucratic, with many specialists assessing the quality of the project. This, in his opinion, paradoxically does not lead to films which are either especially original or which attract many viewers, but rather to the production of films following the same formula.
8. It makes sense to watch Bareja's film in conjunction with reading the book *The Unplanned Society* (Wedel 1992), as it appears to be an adaptation of sorts of this book.
9. In the cinema of the 1980s the main representative of such an approach was Marek Koterski, the main follower of Stanislaw Bareja who died in 1987.
10. Maciej Replewicz in his biography of Bareja emphasizes his entrepreneurial, 'capitalist' attitude to filmmaking, his wish to take as little from the state as possible, epitomized by him buying a second-hand western car rather than waiting for the coupon for a car which was given by the authorities to film directors.
11. Such an opinion was presented to me by Marek Piwowski, when I interviewed him in 2013.
12. It became a rule in postwar Poland, as in other Eastern European countries, that each new regime criticized its predecessor for not living up to the ideals of Marxism.

CHAPTER 6

The 1980s
Between Refusal to Work and Alienation of Labour

The 1980s in Poland began in a similar way to the 1970s: with a wave of strikes and protests, which was a reaction to the rapidly worsening economic conditions, marked by shortages of basic goods, as well as transport and fuel problems. The authorities tried to extinguish them by offering pay rises to the striking workers, in particular in Lublin. However, when the strike broke in August 1980 in the Gdańsk shipyard, this approach did not work, because the strikers also made openly political demands, such as the reinstatement at work of previously fired political activist Anna Walentynowicz, the right to set up free trade unions, and the right to build a monument to the shipyard workers killed in 1970.

In the past such demands would have been met with military intervention. On this occasion the government decided to negotiate and bowed to the workers' demands, which paved the way to the setting up of Solidarity (Solidarność), an independent trade union, in August 1980. The conciliatory position of the authorities resulted from the unprecedented strength of the protests on the one hand (often explained by the moral support given to the anti-communist opposition by the Polish Pope, John Paul II) and the weakness of the Party on the other. Inevitably, the result was, as in 1970, a change of regime, with Gierek being overthrown in September 1980 and later removed from the Party on the grounds of financial misdemeanours; this being clearly a sign that in moments of crisis the Party was always looking for a scapegoat. Stanisław Kania briefly became the new Secretary. The changes at the top of the Party were not sufficient to appease the discontented population, because for the first time the Party had a powerful opponent in Solidarity, which from the beginning was something more than a trade union or even a political party: it was a mass movement against state socialism. This was demonstrated by its numerical strength and its objectives. Already in its first summit in September 1980 it had 3 million members and the number soon grew to 10 million. By contrast, the Party had at the time 2.5 million members and its ranks were emptying with unprecedented speed (Toporek 1999: 91). Solidarity had a young and charismatic leader in Lech Wałęsa, who in 1980 was thirty-seven years old; the Party, being effectively a gerontocracy, lacked such young leaders. Solidarity was united, the Party was divided; Solidarity had a clear programme and was not carrying the heavy baggage of past mistakes, the Party was tainted by its inglorious past. The bulk of society saw it as the root of Polish social and economic problems and gave it no opportunity to reform itself. For the next year and a half Poland had effectively two centres of power, the Party and Solidarity, both claiming to represent the whole society and the working masses especially. Inevitably, they were in conflict which manifested itself in continuous strikes and demands by Solidarity, which led to further reshuffles at the top of the Party and the function of the First Secretary and prime minister being given to General Wojciech Jaruzelski in February 1981.

In 1980 and 1981 the authorities worked on two fronts: seeking consensus with Solidarity; and preparing for military confrontation, favoured by Moscow. The last attempt to reach a compromise took place on 4 November 1981, during a meeting between Lech Wałęsa, Cardinal Glemp, the leader of the Catholic Church in Poland, and General Jaruzelski. Following the announcement of martial law over 100,000 troops were deployed, Solidarity was suspended, strikes and demonstrations were forbidden, a curfew was introduced, freedom of movement was restricted, and most newspapers and magazines ceased publication. In the first week of martial law over 5,000 people were interned in special camps, primarily prominent Solidarity members, including Wałęsa. Many branches of industry, including public transport and the production of energy, were militarized. The powers of government were transferred to the military body, the Military Council of National Salvation (Wojskowa Rada Ocalenia Narodowego), headed by Jaruzelski.

Force was used to crush some spontaneous strikes which erupted in the country, including in the 'Wujek' coalmine in Katowice, but large-scale bloodshed was avoided. In total, there were approximately ninety fatalities during the whole period of martial law. As Norman Davies observes: 'The conduct of policy in Poland lacked many of the characteristic ingredients not only of military takeovers elsewhere in the world but also of the usual Soviet-style programmes of "normalization". The repression was highly selective and strangely half-hearted' (Davies 2005: 494). Despite the widespread containment of political opposition, underground political and cultural life flourished. Its main centre became the

Catholic Church, which distributed food and clothing sent to Poland from the West, helped interned politicians, and organized charity cultural events and discussions about the future of Solidarity and the Polish state.

From March 1982, the authorities started to remove restrictions and release the interned politicians. In December 1982 martial law was suspended. An important factor in this decision was the death of the leader of the Soviet communist party, Leonid Brezhnev in November 1982, whose hardline stance was an obstacle to any earlier attempts to find a compromise between Solidarity and the Party. In July 1983, martial law was abolished. The six years that followed can be described as a period of the nomenklatura gradually losing their grip on power to Solidarity and the Church, who emerged from the period of martial law as the moral victors. It culminated in the Round-table Negotiations between February and April 1989, in which the state authorities, the Church and Solidarity, including Lech Wałęsa and Adam Michnik, agreed to the conditions of political and economic transformation of Poland. In August 1989, Tadeusz Mazowiecki, a high-profile member of Solidarity and editor of its magazine, *Tygodnik Solidarność*, became the first, democratically elected prime minister of postwar Poland. This event can be seen as the symbolic end of state socialism in Poland and elsewhere, giving way to a new system: that of neoliberal capitalism.

In the 1980s state socialism was in a state of mortal decline. While every leader of the Party in postwar Poland, from Bierut to Gierek, had embarked on a programme of modernizing Polish economy, the 1980s lacked any such programmes. The nomenklatura merely fought for political and eventually economic survival. The only attempt at reform took place at the end of the decade in the form of the so-called 'Wilczek Parliamemtary Act' (Ustawa Wilczka) or 'Rakowski Reform' (from the names of the minister of industry and prime minister respectively), which allowed each citizen to set up a private firm. However, this liberalization of the economy is seen less as reforming the socialist economy, and more as marking its end and introducing capitalism (Koryś 2007: 454).

The early 1980s allowed the working class to gain the position of a dominant historical agent. In this respect this period can be seen as a return to the 1950s, when industrial workers were rendered the leading force in society. Back then, however, the role was given to this class by the ruling elites rather than won in class struggle. In the early 1980s the workers took it themselves, as should happen during a proletariat revolution, according to Marx. Solidarity leader, Lech Wałęsa, himself belonged to this class, being an electrician, who had already once lost his job due to his political activities. This made him unusual, as the role of prominent dissidents in Eastern Europe was normally taken by members of the intelligentsia. However, as the decade drew to an end, and Solidarity gave rise to numerous parties, of which the most powerful subscribed to a neoliberal programme, the role of the workers diminished. Ultimately, the Solidarity revolution not only failed to achieve its main objective of creating an egalitarian and prosperous society, but exacerbated existing class divisions. Wałęsa's loss of power in the mid-1990s and his growing irrelevance in Polish politics illustrates this shift very well (see part 3).

The difficult situation which the Polish economy as a whole experienced at the beginning of the 1980s severely affected Polish cinema. Despite the showing of films which had previously been shelved and the spectacular success of several new Polish films, including *Robotnicy '80* (*Workers 1980*, 1980), directed by Andrzej Chodakowski et al., and Andrzej Wajda's *Człowiek z żelaza* (*Man of Iron*, 1981), the film industry was in a difficult situation. There were insufficient funds to produce new films or even to complete the production of those already started, and to cover the cost of prints and cinema equipment. Furthermore, the income of people employed in the film industry declined, in 1981 being less than 70 per cent of the average income. This influenced the condition of such respected institutions as film societies and art cinemas; after 1980 they fought for survival. There was also little money to buy new films from abroad. While in 1980 thirty-three western films were distributed in Poland, in the first half of 1981 the number was reduced to two.

To offset the downturn in the Polish cinema, the Society of Polish Filmmakers, together with Solidarity activists in the media industry, convened the Committee for Rescuing Polish Cinema, led by two distinguished directors: Jerzy Kawalerowicz and Andrzej Wajda. In its manifesto it criticized the current structures of the film industry, as well as the political authorities for cutting investment and subsidies to films, heavy censorship and the use of Polish films merely as propaganda. The main task of the Committee was to establish a new model for Polish cinema, able to produce and distribute more and better films than in previous years. The resulting project assumed that film production in Poland would not only be politically independent from the state, but also financially self-sufficient. Thus, in a nutshell, the Committee advocated the neoliberalization of the Polish film industry. Imposition of martial law slowed the widely awaited film reform and alienated many leading figures from participating in the reform and even working in the film industry altogether. Filmmakers such as Andrzej Wajda, Agnieszka Holland and Krzysztof Zanussi temporarily relocated abroad.

The most spectacular manifestation of the conflict between the authorities and film professionals was the metropolitan actors' boycott of television and cinema, described as the longest strike in the history of Polish cinema (Zbieg 2012). Rather than play for a mass television audience, actors who supported Solidarity decided to perform for small groups of people in informal gatherings, such as churches and private houses. As a result, television in this period employed actors from provincial theatres, many of whom regarded it as once in a life opportunity to show their talent to a large audience. Gaps in cinema and television programmes were also filled by imports of western genre films, such as those featuring martial artist Bruce Lee, which turned out to be very popular. Tadeusz Lubelski laments that as a result of this policy Polish cinema audiences changed: mature (in age and intellectual development) cinemagoers, looking for food for thought, disappeared from cinema theatres, giving way to teenagers seeking pure entertainment (Lubelski 2009a: 444). While martial law might have played some part in the transformation of film taste of Poles and the structure of cinema audiences, the more important factor was a wider process of neoliberalization which at the time brought Polish cinema closer to the western model. Martial law was also a period of 'verifications', when political authorities (often pretending to be motivated solely by economic criteria) decided which people working in various cultural industries (journalists, filmmakers) were fit to perform their statutory obligations, and whether particular cultural institutions deserved continuing state support. As a result of such assessments, by the end of April 1983 the leaders of some film units were sacked, including Rondo, led by Wojciech Has and Studio X, whose director was Andrzej Wajda. Wajda was particularly criticized for not toeing the Party line (Zajiček 1992: 247–248).

The end of martial law was marked by a return to social and political normality, however unsatisfactory this normality was for filmmakers. The Society of Polish Filmmakers was re-invigorated and it held a special congress in December 1983. In September 1984 Gdańsk Film Festival took place after a three-year break. At the same time the attitude to the film industry of both political authorities and the audience changed – both expected films to make a profit. Film critics started to publish the first box office results and analysed which types of film and which directors were able to fill the theatres. The year 1984 should be regarded as a success: Polish films were watched by 56.6 million people, which was a Polish record, even when the interwar period was taken into account. However, only a handful of Polish films recouped their costs. In subsequent years the gap between the cost of production and distribution of Polish films on the one hand, and the income, generated from selling cinema tickets, on the other, widened even further, caused by the low price of tickets. In 1985, only one Polish film, *Och, Karol!* (1985), a comedy, directed by Roman Załuski, recouped its costs out of forty films distributed that year.

In 1987, after five years of discussing various options for reform, a new act of parliament was passed, regulating the Polish film industry. One of its main points was to demonopolize and decentralize the production, distribution and exhibition of films, which up to this point were solely the preserve of the state. The act guaranteed film studios greater financial and artistic independence. Polish films and masterpieces of world cinema were given preference in promotion and distribution. The act also introduced the Committee of Cinema (Komitet Kinematografii), which was meant to be in charge of all aspects of the film industry. The power in the new Committee of Cinema rested mainly with the filmmakers themselves, especially those of significant artistic achievement, such as Andrzej Wajda and Krzysztof Zanussi (by this point labelled 'barons' or 'dinosaurs' of the Polish cinema). Since then a criticism has arisen that the new body was used as a vehicle to promote their interests at the expense of younger directors and other film institutions. This criticism intensified in the 1990s when large sums of public money were spent on historical super-productions of Wajda and Kawalerowicz. The 1987 bill guaranteed the state the right to censor films and decide the level of the subsidy, but in practice political censorship was rarely used in the second half of the 1980s. The 1980s are also marked by an important technological change in recording and viewing films: the video. According to estimates there were 3,000 video sets in Poland in 1981 and over a million by 1990. The proliferation of this medium had major implications for the cinema industry. As in the whole of Europe in the 1980s, it deepened the crisis of cinema theatres and undermined the censoring power of the state, as many films which were shelved in the early 1980s, such as *Interrogation* and *Workers 1980*, were widely available on video. The 1980s can be described as a period particularly conducive to the documentary genre. This is because in this decade much happened between the people and the rulers which called for documenting, and documentary film was more suitable as a response to this call (Hučková 2015).

The 1980s was the decade of the working class; it became the main political agent, a class for itself, to use the Marxist term. This is reflected in films of this period, especially those devoted to strikes. Their number is not very high, but two of them, Wajda's *Man of Iron* and *Workers 1980*, constitute the most iconic films of this period. Another important subject in this decade is the everyday hardship of the workers. Finally, in this period we observe the production of films which predict a neoliberal future.

Workers Go on Strike

Andrzej Wajda's *Man of Iron*, a sequel to his *Man of Marble*, is no doubt the best known film about Solidarity ever made. It concerns the creation of Solidarity, the movement in which Polish society was united against the authorities and which, through strikes and negotiations with the government, succeeded in breaking the communist monopoly on power first in the workplace and then in the whole country. It is also a film about solidarity, a principle which needs to be followed by the workers to improve their lot, as opposed to competition, which is promoted by their employers, even under more egalitarian state socialism. This movement and the idea is encapsulated by the figure of Maciek Tomczyk, the son of Mateusz Birkut, the 'man of marble' of Wajda's previous film and Agnieszka's husband. The film is built of retrospectives, which demonstrate Maciek's maturation from a young student, concerned with what were regarded as 'student issues', such as freedom of speech, to a worker in the shipyard. As Kristi Long observes, Maciek exemplifies the union of the working class and the intelligentsia in his person as well as in his personal relations:

> He is a university student who becomes a worker and marries an intelligentsia filmmaker (and KOR-style activist). The turning points in Tomczyk's life are moments of crisis in which there is a refusal of solidarity ... Early in the film, we see Tomczyk demonstrating as a student in 1968 and his worker father refusing to support the student demonstration. Two years later, Tomczyk and his fellow students stand by as shipyard workers' strikes on the Baltic coast turn violent. Tomczyk's father is among the victims. His father's death provokes a crisis in Tomczyk's life, and he abandons the life of the intelligentsia to work in the Gdansk shipyard. Fragmented, Tomczyk is first an intellectual, and then a worker. As a worker, though, he becomes unified with the liberal intellectual opposition (i.e. KOR, ROPCIO) in his marriage to an opposition filmmaker...

Transformed into an icon of the unified Poland, Tomczyk becomes the centre of the Solidarity movement. (Long 1996: 164-165)

The fact that Maciek is not an ordinary worker but also a member of the intelligentsia, unlike Lech Wałęsa, who was a worker through and through, reflects Wajda's identification with the intelligentsia rather than the working class (Mazierska 2002a) and his desire to acknowledge the role of the intellectuals in toppling the communist regime.

The main character is not Maciek, but Winkel, a radio journalist, who in the summer of 1980 is sent to Gdańsk to collect discrediting material on Maciek. Not unlike Maciek, Winkel was a political dissident, involved in the anti-government protests of 1968, which led to his imprisonment. He was freed, but at the expense of being loyal to the authorities. One guesses that he was chosen for the 'Gdańsk mission' because of his debt towards those who helped him out of prison. Instead of exonerating himself in the eyes of his superiors, he moves to the Solidarity side without their knowledge. As a political convert, he encapsulates a large section of Polish society that was previously loyal to the regime but joined Solidarity in the 1980s. The most prominent member of this group was Leszek Balcerowicz, the later author of the 'Balcerowicz Plan' (see part 3). In the film, Winkel's 'double game' is exposed and he loses the trust of Solidarity, but as we can gather from the career of people like Balcerowicz, in reality many 'Winkels' not only joined the Solidarity movement, but changed its agenda from pro-worker to pro-capitalist.

Man of Iron is in a large part devoted to the injustice of the nominally socialist state towards the workers. Wajda makes his point using archival footage from the 1970s strikes and demonstrations and interviews with the workers from 1980. Because we tend to believe documentaries more than fiction films, the power of this testimony is immense and no doubt Wajda uses it for this very reason.[1] Yet it might be surprising in the light of the profound distrust in the documentary form that this director revealed in *Man of Marble*. This shift, from scepticism towards an almost naive embracing of documentary, has to do with the specific moment when *Man of Iron* was made, when Poland went through 'historical times', calling for their preservation in celluloid (Wyżyński 2008: 220; Hučková 2015). The documentary footage Wajda includes in his film demonstrates that when workers took to the streets, the state made them toe the line by naked force, as shown in the scenes when the police beat protesters with truncheons. Such brutality is not atypical under capitalism, but there the state does not present itself as a defender of workers' rights. Under state socialism, this goes against the official pro-worker ideology. The interviewed workers, mostly women, also complain about their everyday hardship, caused by low wages and high prices, and the trade unions and the Party, which, instead of representing them, oppress them. Ultimately, they point to the gap between state socialism and 'true communism' as envisaged by Marx. They also talk about what should be done to transform Poland from a fake workers' state to a true workers' state: instead of being ruled by the nomenklatura, they should rule themselves through their democratically elected representatives. They also demand that their living standard is improved. This is also the request which Maciek presents when interviewed by a foreign journalist.

When Dzidek, a radio technician and anti-government conspirator, shows Winkel footage presenting police brutality towards workers in 1970, he comments that the workers should watch this footage over and over again so they will lose faith in the socialist system, implying that capitalism is superior. He also suggests that the meaning of this material cannot be modified by its context: it will always say 'the truth' about how bad state socialism was. In my opinion history proved Dzidek wrong. For example, in 2014, when global media were dominated by the images of police brutality towards black people in the United States, the Polish footage would most likely fail to convince the viewer that the police in the socialist Poland was particularly violent. It only demonstrates that whenever there are large-scale protests, the police arrive with their tools of repression. The footage, kept by Dzidek, also shows that there were once times when strikes and street demonstrations really mattered in Poland, unlike under neoliberalism, when they attract relatively little attention from the media. This footage, shown by Dzidek, might thus awaken not only pity for the mistreated workers, but also envy of their power, which was a consequence of the socialist mode of production and to some extent the power of the official ideology, which gave the workers a sense of importance. Wajda's film has a happy ending, marked by the victory of the striking workers, who force the authorities to accept their conditions. By the same token, it is a victory for Maciek and Agnieszka, but not for Winkel, who gets lost in the no man's land between 'us' and 'them': the rulers and the ruled.

As many authors argued, *Man of Iron*, in contrast to *Man of Marble*, offers us a masculine world, in which women are reduced to helping male fighters (for example Roszkowska 1992; Mazierska 2002b). Although Maciek mentions that the shipyard strike is a response to the sacking of Anna Walentynowicz, her role in the anti-government struggle or the role of other prominent Solidarity women, such as Anna Pienkowska, is not acknowledged. Neither is this lack made up by any fictional female Solidarity activists. The role of Agnieszka in *Man of Iron* is reduced in comparison with *Man of Marble*. At the time of the strikes in Gdańsk she is imprisoned and cannot participate in the opposition activities or become a media celebrity. In this way Wajda foretells the situation after the fall of state socialism when the position of women significantly worsened due to the reduction of the welfare state, the collapse of 'female' branches of industry, such as the production of textile and cooperative farms, and the introduction of a restrictive abortion law. The message of the film is that at times of great political upheaval the grievances and demands of specific categories of people should be put aside to achieve a greater political objective, such as the right to set up an independent trade union. This approach would be acceptable if in such times the whole collective was represented by the most disadvantaged, in this case women who tend to earn less than men, as this will ensure that their specific needs are not forgotten when the shared objectives are achieved. When the strongest section represent the whole collective, the danger is that the weak gain less than the strong, which was indeed the case during and after the 'Solidarity revolution'.

Workers 1980 by Andrzej Chodakowski and Andrzej Zajączkowski is seen as a companion piece to *Man of Iron*, because it refers to the same events as *Man of Iron* and proposes a similar assessment to that offered by Wajda. At the same time, it is a unique document in Polish history due to its showing the insubordination of the workers towards the Polish state. Before *Workers 1980* practically the only documents on this subject were made by Polish Newsreel (Polska Kronika Filmowa, PKF), which were carefully edited and furnished with a commentary, expounding the Party line (Wyżyński 2008: 219). When the crews of PKF documentarists were sent to film 'risky' events, they had no sound-recording equipment, to avoid recording the voices of protesting workers. To distance themselves from this practice and emphasize that *Workers 1980* is an 'authentic documentary', the makers of *Workers 1980* recorded the sound and vision on the spot, in synchrony. When this was impossible, they decided to include only the sound without vision. The 'black images' add to the feeling of authenticity of the film (ibid.: 221–222).

Workers 1980 documents the negotiations between the striking workers and the representatives of the ruling elite, most importantly Mieczysław Jagielski, then the vice-prime minister and member of the Party's politburo, and Tadeusz Fiszbach, the regional leader of the PZPR in the Coastal region. Like *Man of Iron*, *Workers 1980* conveys the 'August fever' with a sense that something momentous is about to happen and offers a similar take on the class composition of the Polish society. There is a sense that it is divided into two classes: the rulers ('they') and the ruled ('us'). Among the ruled, the most important is the industrial working class. The ordinary workers and their leaders talk about their significance to the country's economy and complain that this is not reflected in their economic and political position: they earn little and are excluded from decisions concerning their workplace and country. In a situation of such blatant injustice strike action is their only weapon. While in Wajda's film the union between the workers and the intelligentsia is represented by the figure of Maciek, who is an educated worker, in *Workers 1980*, somewhat more realistically, the union is encapsulated by two groups working together: the mainly proletarian leaders of the strike and their advisors ('experts'). Among the former the most prominent is Lech Wałęsa. The latter come from the milieu of metropolitan intellectuals, such as historian Bronisław Geremek and Tadeusz Mazowiecki, the future prime minister of Poland. The 'experts' come across as modest, underscoring their merely advisory role. Watching this film now, in the knowledge of the subsequent conflict between Mazowiecki and Wałęsa and practically all the main 'actors' of this film, such as Andrzej Gwiazda and Bogdan Lis, one wonders whether already at this stage they harboured distinct political ambitions, yet strategically concealed them, or whether such ambitions appeared later, after the Solidarity 'revolution'.

Another important characteristic of the negotiations is the universal agreement that the workers do not strike against socialism but for its improvement, to make it represent the workers' interests rather than the nomenklatura's. In the early part of the film, in what can be seen as a Freudian slip attesting to the deep-seated assumption that state socialism will stay in Poland forever, one worker says: 'Nobody wants the change of the government; sorry, the change of the system'. This is also something which Lech Wałęsa says: socialism in Poland should stay. Agreement on this point is the basis of the negotiations between the Solidarity camp and the Party camp. The only area of disagreement is how to make state socialism work better. The ruling elite is lambasted by Solidarity for being greedy, arrogant, hypocritical and incompetent, bringing the country to the brink of economic catastrophe. One man talks about the 'official' trade unions, which act as an additional means of extraction of surplus value from the workers, used to finance the lavish lifestyles of the union 'barons'. The workers argue that free unions and the right to strike are key to the improvement of their situation and in the whole country. This is eventually accepted and the agreement is signed in an almost euphoric mood. One gets a sense that as soon as the workers are democratically represented in government, the economic crisis will be reversed. Such an opinion is voiced by Wałęsa, who says (perhaps for the first time) that if the workers are allowed to govern themselves, Poland will overtake Japan, because Polish workers are able to work better than their Japanese counterparts. These words were subsequently mocked, rendering Wałęsa a false prophet. A similar view is expressed by Anna Walentynowicz, who talks about the extraordinary conviction and patriotism of Polish workers which, however, bears little fruit because workers are excluded from polity.

A Solidarity expert, Professor Jerzy Stembrowicz, compares the coastal strikes to the Paris Commune. Such comparison is as ennobling as it is ominous. This is because the Paris Commune is seen as the first communist revolution and an important influence on the ideas of Marx, most importantly *The Civil War in France* (Marx 2009). On the other hand, the Commune did not lead to a permanent leadership of the proletariat, but to a reactionary government. In a nutshell, it helped the bourgeoisie to consolidate its power. The same scenario, as I will argue in the next part, also took place in Poland, despite the fact that in 1990, the leader of the coastal strike, Lech Wałęsa, became the first democratically elected President of Poland. As with *Man of Iron*, one is struck by the lack of women among those debating Poland's future. On both sides of the negotiation table we see mostly men. Men also prevail among ordinary workers, voicing their complaints to the filmmakers. The only woman who has a prominent position is Anna Walentynowicz, but she is presented as a trigger of the strike rather than its leader. During the negotiations she sits in the second row and is less vocal than the main Solidarity men, such as Wałęsa and Andrzej Gwiazda. From a contemporary perspective the lack of women looks like a premonition of the rolling back of the welfare state and abolition of the privileges women enjoyed under state socialism.

Man of Iron and *Workers 1980* tried to convince the viewers about the necessity to go on strike as the only means to prevent the economic downfall of Poland. During martial law the official line was that the difficult economic situation was caused by strikes, therefore strikes were forbidden, at the sanction of a violent suppression. The authorities also used ideological arguments to support their stance and Roman Wionczek took upon himself the role of the main government spokesman for the community of filmmakers. His two films, *Godność* (*Dignity*, 1984) and *Czas nadziei* (*Time of Hope*, 1986), deal specifically with this topic. Wionczek's principal method is 'part pro toto': the depiction of a small fragment is meant to illuminate the whole, not unlike in *Man of Iron*, where Maciek's trajectory encapsulates the route taken by the whole country. In *Dignity* this method is applied in two stages. First, the story of one working-class family is meant to illustrate the situation of the whole Polish nation during martial law. Secondly, problems suffered by Poles during this period are deployed as a metonym of the entire Polish postwar history, even Polish fate. The main character in *Dignity*, which is set shortly before the military takeover, is Karol Szostak, a worker in the 'Metalpol' metal plant. Szostak is chosen as the new leader of the 'old' trade union (dominated by the nomenklatura) in his factory, now known as the 'branch' trade union. During the period of martial law the government sponsored its expansion as a counterbalance to the banned Solidarity (Lukowski and Zawadzki 2001: 277). It is in this context that we should view the actions of the characters. In 'Metalpol' Solidarity activists demand that all the workers go on strike, and following Szostak's refusal to toe the Solidarity line, eject him from the factory in a wheelbarrow. Such an undignified disposal of communist supporters was a common practice in 1980–1981, but the targets were factory managers and Party officials rather than ordinary

Illustration 6.1: Karol Szostak in *Dignity*, directed by Roman Wionczek

workers. *Time of Hope* depicts Szostak's attempts to reinstate himself in the factory, following the imposition of martial law. Although all the people in positions of power in 'Metalpol' sympathize with his plight, the task proves difficult, as the new manager is wary that bringing Szostak back to the factory will anger fellow workers. Only after the intervention of the local representative of WRON does Szostak find his way back to his old position.

To defend the socialist authorities, Wionczek employs socialist realistic aesthetics, albeit trying to adjust it to the new set of circumstances (Sobolewski 1987a). The characters are divided into honest workers, impeccable communist leaders, 'naïve people' and enemies of the state. The epitome of an honest worker is Karol Szostak, who worked in the same factory for forty-six years, before being stripped of his job and dignity by Solidarity activists. In common with characters from socialist realist films, Szostak adheres to communist ideals, rejecting materialism and consumerism, which were poisoning Polish society in the 1980s. He admits that he used to go to May Day demonstrations when they were forbidden and gets very angry when his wife brings home some gifts from the West, distributed in the local church, claiming that they do not need any western help. Despite these occasional differences of opinion, Szostak and his wife are a model couple, thanks to sharing the same working-class experiences. Yet the Szostaks and his old comrades, veterans of the prewar anti-capitalist movement, are being replaced by less noble generations of people who have a more pragmatic attitude to state socialism. Szostak's son in-law, Rzewiński, is in the pro-government camp, but he is a womanizer and opportunist, which can be seen as a reference to the downward trajectory of the PZPR, from being a party of idealists to careerists. Rzewiński's wife is very religious, unlike her parents who stay away from the church. Their son Marcin is involved in an anti-communist conspiracy and at some point is captured by the police. Marcin fits the image of a socialist realistic 'naïve person', who joins the wrong camp and must be guided by a mature communist to avoid serious mistakes, but nobody manages to put Marcin on the right path. Through this character Wionczek shows that communism in Poland is the preserve of the old; the young embrace a different vision of Poland – the one offered by Solidarity (although Solidarity, as *Workers 80* shows, was in its spirit a Marxist organization).[2] Ideological differences pertain also to gender. Practically every man represented by Wionczek is a *homo politicus*, while women stay away from politics, again reminding us of the 'Solidarity' films, where women were also excluded from frontline politics.

Not surprisingly, taking into account the time of the film's production, the role of impeccable communist leader is given by Wionczek to a military commissioner. He arranges Szostak's return to the factory, when other members of the establishment lack the courage or authority to do so. He is a 'good master', who tries to avoid any harsh decisions, works for the welfare of the wider population and looks at every issue from a human perspective, rather than slavishly following the letter of the law. As in any such propagandist work, the arguments on the side of the conflict privileged in the film are not only spelt out, but repeated by positive characters. The opinion that martial law was introduced to free the country from looming political and economic disaster is presented first by General Jaruzelski, addressing the nation on TV, and then echoed by local Party dignitaries, the military commissioner, old Szostak, people from his circle and eventually even by people queuing for basic groceries. The view that thanks to the military takeover factories are working again and there is now hope of 'normalization', as the very title of Wionczek's film pronounces, trickles down from the communist hierarchy to ordinary people. It is worth mentioning that the demand that 'things return to normal', with each individual doing his or her particular job, is, according to Jacques Rancière and Slavoj Žižek, the main sign of anti-democratic politics, whose basic aim is the depoliticization of the population (Žižek 2006: 70). Predictably, in Wionczek's film normalization and depoliticization receive a positive spin, due to being associated with honesty, modesty, altruism and hard work. In contrast to the opinions of the authorities, the views of Solidarity are not spelt out; we only see interned Solidarity members squabbling among themselves about the best way to disrupt the government's attempts to bring order to Poland. The young supporters of Solidarity, one of whom is Marcin, are labelled *wyrostki* (as in official documents of the time): immature youngsters looking for adventure, who have no right to partake in the affairs of their elders.

In common with socialist realistic classics, Wionczek deploys his discourse mostly through dialogue. The film includes long discussions between the factory Party members, conducted in a solemn tone. Everyday conversations about trivial matters are generously peppered with discussions about workers' dignity. This aspect of the film was criticized even by those reviewers who wrote about his films from a pro-government position (Karbowiak 1984; Pawlukiewicz 1987; Sadowski 1987). One of the rare moments when Wionczek allows the 'image to speak' is at the end of the film, when a peaceful May Day demonstration is interrupted by the shouting and stone throwing of young Solidarity supporters. Their behaviour is eventually halted by the arrival of ZOMO, special anti-riot police, widely used during martial law, but even then the security forces come across as civilized while the youngsters escalate their brutality. The image of May Day demonstrators under attack is styled on socialist realist classics, such as *Mat* (*Mother*, 1926) by Vsevolod Pudovkin, and the Polish *Pod gwiazdą frygijską* (*Under the Phrygian Star*, 1954) by Jerzy Kawalerowicz, in its use of close-ups of faces and meaningful details, such as red flowers and hands. This part of the film works best, thanks to its dynamism, breaking the monotony of talking heads.

Wionczek's diptych is not a successful work even on its own terms, namely as a piece of pro-socialist propaganda. Its crucial shortcomings are its avoidance of any confrontation with Solidarity's position and its use of an outmoded aesthetic. Not surprisingly, the films were box office flops. Tadeusz Szyma, reviewer for the Catholic weekly *Tygodnik Powszechny*, confessed not without Schadenfreude that he was the only viewer of *Dignity* in the cinema in the essentially working-class town of Nowa Huta (Szyma 1985). In a similar vein, Tadeusz Sobolewski observed that the special showing of *Time of Hope* for workers, organized during a Festival of Polish Films in Gdańsk, was called off due to lack of interest (Sobolewski 1987b: 12). In order to assess Wionczek's work, we should realize how difficult his task actually was. Unlike filmmakers working under conditions of Stalinism, who only needed to please the political leaders, he attempted to address both the political establishment and 'ordinary people', who in their masses were against the government. Moreover, paradoxically, since the demise of socialist realism, propagandist pro-socialist films in Poland were rare and they were largely unsuccessful (Zwierzchowski 2000: 150–153); thus Wionczek had few models to follow.

The ardour with which Wionczek defended martial law was recognized by the political authorities at the time. From newspapers of the time of *Dignity*'s premiere we learn that General Jaruzelski and Deputy Prime Minister Rakowski watched the film and promised to support similar projects. The director, the scriptwriter, Jerzy Grzymkowski and the most important members of the cast were invited to meet political leaders ('Spotkanie z twórcami filmu *Godność*' 1984: 8). Such a cosy relationship with the political authorities, such as Wionczek enjoyed in the 1980s, did not bode well after the collapse of state socialism. Wionczek made his last film *Rzeczpospolitej dni pierwsze* (*First Days of the Republic*) in 1988. The actors playing the Szostaks ceased to work in the 1990s. This wiping out (bar the composer) of practically the entire crew of *Dignity* and *Time of Hope* from Polish cultural life post-1989 is highly symbolic, suggesting that a positive approach to martial law was tantamount to political and cultural suicide after the fall of the Berlin Wall.

The End of the Road

While 'Solidarity films' and even, to a certain extent, the 'martial law films', have an upbeat tone, suggesting that from now on things can only get better, films concerning the quotidian lives of manual workers, especially women, exude pessimism. The most famous in this group is *Kobieta samotna* (*A Woman Alone*, 1981) by Agnieszka Holland, one of the last films belonging to the Moral Concern wave. Made about the same time as Wajda's *Man of Iron*, *A Woman Alone* demotes the Solidarity movement to the background of events, and places in centre stage someone apolitical. This is because Holland's protagonist is, on the one hand, too downtrodden to find the time and energy to engage in politics and, on the other, is of little interest to the main centres of political power in Poland: Solidarity and the Party.

Irena, the eponymous 'woman alone', works as a postwoman. Postal workers, unlike coalminers or shipyard workers, did not belong to the privileged section of the working class, because they did not produce, only served and, being dispersed, hardly constituted a threat to the political authorities. For this reason they were paid little. Although a postal worker is by no means a new profession, by choosing a postwoman as her heroine, Holland pointed to the future of the working class in Poland as being dispersed, mobile and having little chance to communicate with each other. Irena is, indeed, depicted in this manner: as a woman alone (Ostrowska 2006b: 201). She is also a single mother, bringing up an eight-year-old son; the child's father is serving a jail sentence and does not provide for his offspring. Unlike the higher echelons of the working class, who by the 1970s had usually acquired cooperative apartments in newly built blocks, Irena lives in a room without running water or heating, in a house on the outskirts of town. Even in this modest place she does not feel at home, as another poor family hopes that she will move out, so they can take over her room. Clearly, in this world there is not enough room for poor people – survival is at the expense of one's neighbour. Neither the Party nor Solidarity are willing to solve Irena's housing problems. These organizations privilege the 'monopoly sector', as in previous decades. The rationale behind their reluctance is the assumption that once the big issues are resolved, there will be time to deal with the smaller ones. However, as I will argue in the next chapter, the situation of the weakest workers post-1989 worsened, with many moving from poorly paid work to unemployment.

Abandoned by everybody, Irena asks herself 'Who am I?' and replies 'I am nobody'. In a sense, she is right, as her circumstances have stripped her of all resources. Yet love offers her a chance to escape from her predicament. Irena becomes romantically involved with Jacek, a man who lives less than modestly on incapacity benefit, being disabled after an industrial accident. He is able to survive emotionally thanks to his belief that one day he will emigrate to the West. For him it is a utopian place, where, as he puts it, 'people are respected'. This utopia stands for what socialism failed to bring. Irena and Jacek unite in a 'solidarity of the weak'. Jacek infects Irena with his dream and to fulfil it, she steals money from work and embarks with her lover on a car journey that is cut short when they suffer an accident. In the hotel where they stop, Jacek strangles Irena and proceeds on his own to the American embassy. There he threatens an employee that he will detonate a bomb if he is not granted asylum in the United States. As one might guess, the people in the embassy have no desire to grant him his demands and thus Jacek's last source of hope is about to disappear. *A Woman Alone* thus offers us a sense of the end of the road for the poor, proving more prophetic than the grandiose *Man of Iron*, which foretells a future with workers as a leading class in a Poland which is self-governing, affluent and free.

One gets a similar impression to that offered by Holland from two documentary films by Irena Kamieńska, one from the beginning of the decade, *Robotnice* (*Workwomen*, 1981), and one from its end, *Dzień za dniem* (*Day after Day*, 1988). Not unlike the documentary part of *Man of Iron*, they adopt a tone of grievance, accusing those in power of not delivering on the promise to ensure the workers a decent life. The first film presents a group of women working in a textile factory in Krosno, intertwining shots from the shop floor with those made during the breaks. Although the labourers are probably answering questions asked by the director, these questions are cut out, giving the impression of them talking freely. The women complain about the inadequate air conditioning which makes breathing difficult, the wooden clogs and heavy aprons they are required to wear during working hours which renders their work unnecessarily hard. They also claim that working on the textile machines is the hardest work in the factory, yet it is allocated to women rather than men. This argument brings to mind the times of Stalinism, when allowing women to do the hardest work was presented as a testimony of the Party's faith in their strength and ambition.

Kamieńska's characters also compare unfavourably the conditions of blue-collar with white-collar workers, claiming that they have to work in an old-fashioned plant without proper sanitary facilities or enough space to eat, while the plant administrators enjoy a large office block. They do not have free Saturdays, supposedly because they did not fulfil their production quotas, although officially they reached their target. There is surprisingly little complaint about wages, although one woman mentions that what she earns is not enough to support her six children. She recounts that when she told this to the factory manager, he dismissed her grievance, asking her whether the father of her children contributes anything to the family budget. Such an answer is presented as outrageous, because it stands in contradiction to the state's promise to take care of workers' welfare. Other statements of the workers confirm that we are in an age of expectations of generous welfare provision. The women show no interest in the profitability of their production or their specific achievements and talk only about their needs which cannot be met because of the deficiencies of their workplace.

There is a particular mismatch between what was promised by the state to the blue-collar workers and the women and what was given. The mise-en-scène is used to justify the complaints. The plant looks like a nineteenth-century factory, calling to mind the textile mills in the acclaimed film by Andrzej Wajda from the previous decade, *Ziemia obiecana* (*The Promised Land*, 1974) (Jazdon 2008). The impression that the plant is archaic is underscored by the use of black and white print, which accentuates the clouds of dust filling the interior of the factory. Unlike *Krystyna T.*, described in the previous chapter, there is no interaction between the workers during their working time; the camera shows each woman separately, behind her machine, working in terrible noise. It frequently zeroes in on the workers' damaged hands and legs with varicose veins, the result of long hours of working in a standing position. One can draw two conclusions from the film: either the socialist system should be preserved, but reformed to make it more worker-friendly, offering higher wages and better welfare: better shoes, quieter machines and more time off. The second, more radical conclusion is that if the state were not able to ensure this minimal standard of work over thirty years since the communist takeover, it should be abolished. Kamieńska's characters appear to choose the former: they just want to have a better life within the existing political framework.

In *Day after Day* Kamieńska follows in the footsteps of films such as Kieślowski's *The Bricklayer* and Wiszniewski's *A Story of a Man Who Filled 552% of the Quota*, discussed in the previous chapter, by showing characters who started their working lives in the 1950s. On this occasion these are twin sisters, employed at Transbud in Katowice, a firm specializing in transporting building material. One of them is also the narrator of the film. Their induction into the world of labour followed a campaign of mobilizing women into masculine occupations, as demonstrated by the old newsreels inserted into the narrative, showing smiling female bricklayers. However, unlike the stories of Malesa and Bugdol, their lives show no progress. The two women have worked at Transbud for over thirty years and their hard work never brought them more than their daily bread. The narrator could not even afford a white dress for her wedding and she never travelled; her only trip to Warsaw ended in failure as the bus broke down. The woman also mentions that she was pregnant three times but never had a child, most likely because she miscarried, which could be explained by her hard work (although this is for the viewer to guess). As if this narrative was not depressing enough, the images compound the effect, showing two older women in masculine clothes performing labour consisting of loading and unloading bricks on a lorry, working in silence. We barely recognize their faces or the shapes of their bodies, as if they have lost their identities through labour and their whole existence were reduced to repetitive gestures.

Illustration 6.2: The hard work of a female worker in *Day after Day*, directed by Irena Kamieńska

The title of her film, capturing the monotony of manual work, suggests that Kamieńska's intention was not only to present the specific fate of the two women, but to illustrate a larger phenomenon – the lives of female manual workers in Poland. From this perspective the film raises a number of questions. For example, one wonders whether the lives of both sisters were equally hard, or whether the director chose this particular sister as a narrator because her life was tougher. The same question appears in regards to Kamieńska's choice of occupation of her protagonists. Someone unaware of the specificities of the wage structure might assume that her protagonists earned roughly the same as other manual workers performing masculine jobs. This is also suggested by juxtaposing the shots from their work with those of the old newsreels and posters showing female bricklayers. Yet, according to Błażej Brzostek, in 1950s Warsaw the wages of those working in 'transport supporting construction work', hence in such firms as Transbud, often constituted only 25 per cent of the wages of bricklayers (Brzostek 2002: 57). In due course the gap was reduced, but it was always much better to work on a building site than in 'transport supporting construction work'. Apart from higher wages, the construction workers had more autonomy and free time during their working hours (as Bareja often shows us in his films).

One also wonders about the impact of the changes of political regimes on the lives of the two women. At least the introduction of free Saturdays under Gierek must have influenced their lives through freeing up more time for leisure. Did Transbud not introduce free Saturdays because it did not hit its target, as with the textile factory shown in *Workwomen*, or did free Saturdays make little difference for the women? Perhaps Kamieńska deliberately omitted this topic in her conversations with the women, as it could undermine her thesis that their lives constituted a continuum of misery. One also wonders whether the ascent of Solidarity, even if it did not improve the material side of women's lives, at least affected their consciousness, sparking hope for a better future. By not referring to (grand) politics in a film made in the decade when politics was on the lips of almost everybody, Kamieńska, not unlike Agnieszka Holland in *A Woman Alone*, suggests that working-class women in Poland remained outside the political realm and practically outside history. This reflects the way in which a large section of Polish filmmakers and intelligentsia used to see the working class as helpless and passive. Such a representation would be reinforced after the fall of state socialism, including in Kamieńska's own work. In an interview about her film the director confessed that the women's passivity made her angry, suggesting (in the early neoliberal fashion) that people are to blame for their misery (Serafin 2000: 264). She also admitted that she never showed her film to its protagonists, because 'people do not understand the film in which they participate' (ibid.: 266), undermining the socialist (and humanist) belief that seeing ourselves on screen can revolutionize us. This view chimes with her other confessions, that she makes films purely for herself, to enrich her experience (ibid.: 260).

Being made in 1988, only one year before the fall of state socialism in Poland, *Day after Day* can be seen as a film summarizing this system as anti-working class, which, as I argued throughout this chapter, was the dominant theme of the cinema of this decade. As with Holland's film, one gets a sense that in place of a propaganda of success, the director offered us a propaganda of failure. The sense of the ending of state socialist Poland is also conveyed by a woman talking about retiring the following year. With the benefit of hindsight one can consider her (and most likely her sister) lucky, because if she did not retire, she would probably be made redundant, following her employer's privatization and bankruptcy.

Cinema of the Early Neoliberalization

While films such as *Man of Iron* and *Dignity* show the plight of workers fighting for their right to go on strike or return to work, other films of the 1980s look ahead, to the time when state socialism would be abolished and give way to a neoliberal version of capitalism. I will consider here four such films: *Miś* (*Teddy Bear*, 1981) by Stanisław Bareja, *Moonlighting* (1982) by Jerzy Skolimowski, *Bez miłości* (*Without Love*, 1980) by Barbara Sass, and *Bohater roku* (*Hero of the Year*, 1987) by Feliks Falk.

Teddy Bear belongs to the most critical films about state socialism ever made in Poland. Tadeusz Lubelski singles it out, together with *Cruise*, as the film which gave up on the conciliatory tone and optimism characteristic of earlier comedies (Lubelski 2009b: 292). Indeed, in *Teddy Bear* there are practically no positive characters; everybody is corrupted by the system and inevitably the workplace is presented as a place where this corruption is perpetuated. The two main sins of Bareja's ountrymen are using time and space of work for leisure and using state resources for private consumption. The former misdemeanour pertains to manual workers; the latter to managers. We see builders who drink alcohol and play cards during their working hours and cleaners who eat and gossip. However, the film focuses on the misdeeds of people who hold economic power, which they use to informally privatize state resources. Jan Hochwander, the film producer responsible for a historical super-production, uses part of his casting budget to help his friend, Ryszard Ochódzki, chairman of the sports' club 'Tęcza' to find him a double. He also steals sausage (always a deficit good in Poland, but especially in the 1980s when the authorities introduced coupons for meat) from the set to share it with Ochódzki. Ochódzki, on the other hand, advises his friend on how to boost their extra side income by paying maximal fees to their contractors for bogus services, from which they would receive high 'consultant fees'. A general rule is that the larger the waste of state property, the higher the profit of those responsible for the waste. Ochódzki also masterminds the smuggling of large quantities of alcohol abroad inside a huge straw bear, when he travels with the sportsmen to represent his club. Most likely the bear plays the role of a mascot or a gift to their foreign hosts. Polish sportsmen using their privileged access to foreign travel appeared in an earlier film of Bareja, *A Husband of His Wife*, as discussed in chapter 4. Back then, however, the informal foreign trade was done on a small scale, while in *Teddy Bear* it is a huge operation, as symbolized by the size of the bear, which at one point had to be carried by helicopter. For his extra income Ochódzki has a special account in a British bank. The main plot of the film concerns his attempts to prevent his ex-wife, currently married to a government minister, from cashing in their joint assets. The motif of a Polish member of the nomenklatura siphoning (state) money out of Poland to invest abroad (as in Skolimowski's *Moonlighting*) points to one reason why state socialism collapsed: the nomenklatura wanted to become 'legal capitalists' and the change of the system allowed them to achieve this goal.

Bareja presents the theft of state property as a unique malady of state socialism. However, the practices we see in the film also pertain to neoliberal capitalism. Some of the most successful neoliberal capitalists do not enrich themselves through investing their own money in risky operations, but through managing state-private hybrids. In such hybrids (in the UK described as private-public partnerships) profit is privatized, while risks and losses are socialized, in a similar way as is shown by Bareja. Such practices also became common in Poland after the fall of state socialism. It looks like Bareja's film provided a blueprint for making big money almost risk-free. He also showed that such practices are possible only in situations where there is a huge imbalance of political power, with some people having easy access to state property, and others having none. *Teddy Bear* also demonstrates that the nomenklatura is able to amass their economic and political power thanks to the rest of the population colluding in their plans. One example is Ochódzki involving his subordinates from 'Tęcza' into smuggling alcohol abroad, another when he uses his double to procure a passport. Such practices are possible when the people exploited are either cowardly or ignorant, and Bareja suggests the majority of Poles fit this description. Paradoxically, the filmmaker who more than any other Polish director is associated with pandering to the 'bad taste' of ordinary people shows these people and especially the working class in a much worse light than does Andrzej Wajda, the director strongly associated with the ethos of the Polish intelligentsia.

Unlike in Bareja's 1970s films, where bad work does not affect consumption negatively, a result of Gierek's 'miracle', in *Teddy Bear* the quality of work does influence consumption. The most famous example is an episode set in a milk bar, where people eat unappealing pulp from metal bowls using spoons chained to the table.[3] We witness a vicious circle of sub-standard service leading to consumers becoming anti-social, in turn causing those serving them to treat them with hostility. Another example of low-quality work which leads to a substandard product is shooting a historical super-production, entitled *The Last Sausage of Earl Barry Kent*. The very title of this film captures the problems of late socialism: the disappearance of idealism on the part of artists who were supposed to instil communist ideology in the masses and their lack of original things to say. The first problem is signalled by putting the phrase 'the last sausage', where one expects 'the last supper'; the second by using an English aristocratic title and name in what is supposed to be an epic story from the times when Poland had feudal lords.[4] The shooting is a scene of multiple substitutions: a cat replaces a hare in a hunting scene and the landlords and peasants wear inappropriate costumes. The film's director has little idea of what he wants to do with the resources at his disposal, except that it should fit the 'socialist precepts'. One thus expects that the final product will look shabby and lacking in any intellectual content, symbolizing the exhaustion of the state socialist project. Ironically, *Teddy Bear* itself falls short of the standard of a good cinematic work, at least as defined by the conventions of Hollywood cinema. It is very fragmented; many episodes do not move the action forward, as in 'experimental popular films', discussed in the previous chapter. The dialogue is crude and often the criticism of social reality is obvious or forced, somewhat mirroring the crude propaganda of the socialist state; in addition, its production values are low, giving the impression that it was made on the cheap, particularly the part set in London. It comes across as a product of state socialism as defined by Bareja (Łuczak 2007: 12; Klejsa 2007: 84–85). And yet, *Teddy Bear*, along with Piwowski's *Cruise*, is the most 'cult' Polish film. It probably reached this status not despite having all the markers of 'bad work' (from the capitalist perspective) but because of them. Hence the film raises an interesting question: if 'bad' cinematic work can be experienced as something valuable, can the same apply to other types of production and political systems?

Another film from the 1980s which shows ordinary Poles working for a member of the nomenklatura who has assets abroad is *Moonlighting* (1982) by Jerzy Skolimowski. At the time of shooting this film Skolimowski was an émigré director living in London. *Moonlighting* can be considered as a film about martial law and I already discussed it in this context (Mazierska 2011: 161–166). What interests me this time is Skolimowski's take on the work of Polish emigrants in the West. This subject had already been tackled in the previous decade, in *Return Ticket* by the Petelskis, but on this occasion the director applied an insider's perspective, thanks to living abroad and knowing about the life of Polish guest workers first hand. This is an important reason why the film avoids idealizing the West, characteristic of other Polish films produced in the 1980s. *Moonlighting* presents a group of Polish workers, led by Nowak, who at the end of November 1981 travel to London to renovate the house of Nowak's mysterious Polish 'Boss'. In order to fulfil their assignment, they have to live in appalling conditions, in the very house which they are meant to renovate, and work hard to save for their families, and they suffer from isolation, not knowing the local language. Being unable to manage the financial resources allocated to him by the Boss, Nowak is forced to drastically limit their needs and their contacts with the outside world. He changes the time on the workmen's watches so they think they have slept more than they actually have, steals food from a local supermarket, as well as clothes and cosmetics from department stores, so that they do not have to buy gifts for their families. He also hides from his co-workers the fact that during their stay martial law was imposed, concerned that they would demand to be sent back to Poland immediately. Thus the men not only have to work extra hard, but in ignorance, like slaves.

By showing the lives of Poles in London at a time when there is 'war' at home to be more miserable than if they were there during a time of peace, Skolimowski implies that capitalism offers no help to Poles oppressed by their system. The immigrant workers in the West might earn more than at home, but at the price of working in a 'neoliberal way': harder, refusing oneself almost everything, isolated, and losing one's working and civil rights. Although London in *Moonlighting* is full

Illustration 6.3: Polish guest workers in London in *Moonlighting*, directed by Jerzy Skolimowski

of posters proclaiming the solidarity of British people with Poles suffering due to the military coup, the real Brits in contact with the real Poles come across as bigoted. In the end the neighbours of the Boss call the illegal workers 'communists' and demand that they leave England immediately. The hostility towards uninvited guests foreshadows resentment towards the 'Polish plumber' (French *plombier polonais*), who became a symbol of Western Europe's resistance towards the cheap workforce coming from Eastern Europe and especially Poland after the country joined the European Union in 2005 (Skrodzka-Bates 2011: 76–77). Easy access to consumer goods, which in Poland and elsewhere in the Eastern bloc was regarded as one of the advantages of living in the West, here adds to the Poles' misery, because it underscores their status as pariahs in a land of plenty. This is presented most clearly in the scenes shot around Christmas when the jingles and decorations posit the greatest contrast to the impoverished and claustrophobic lives of Novak's brigade.

Skolimowski's film is also prophetic as it draws attention to the (in)visibility of manual work and the physical distance between the places it is performed and planned, controlled and taken advantage of. As Slavoj Žižek observes, after the fall of state socialism, manual work had become a 'site of obscene indecency to be concealed from the public eye' (Žižek 2001b: 133). This takes place in *Moonlighting* as Nowak's 'brigade' is working according to the rules: 'no strikes, limited freedom of movement for the work force, low wages' (ibid.: 134). Skolimowski also shows that the physical distance between the exploited worker and the exploiting capitalist works to the advantage of the latter, because it frees him from involvement in the production and any displeasure such involvement might bring. In *Moonlighting* it is only Nowak who suffers moral discomfort due to having to exploit his brigade; his Boss is too far away to know anything about it or take responsibility for the situation which he created. The figure of Nowak's Boss, who possesses a house in London and is most likely a Party official, can be regarded as a member of the Polish nomenklatura who shortly after the end of martial law agreed to exchange some of his political power for wealth. In a more fundamental way, the film argues against capitalism as an antidote to state socialism because neither system is interested in promoting workers' rights.

Another film which draws attention to the fact that in the 1980s Poland started to resemble the capitalist world is Barbara Sass's *Without Love*. The film is seen as one of the last examples of the Cinema of Moral Concern and a companion piece to two other Polish films belonging to this paradigm. However, unlike the characters of Moral Concern films, such as Wajda's Agnieszka, who worked in the nationalized film industry, Ewa, who is a photojournalist, is a neoliberal worker. Agnieszka used state equipment, state archives, state van and a crew consisting of two cameramen, also paid by the state, and had centrally allocated funds to produce her film. This rendered her financially comfortable; we never saw her struggling with money or having to do any side-jobs to earn her living,[5] and allowed her to concentrate on the most important tasks, delegating the remaining ones to her (male) crew. On the other hand, her dependence on the state frustrated her, as she did not want to accept any political compromises. Ewa works freelance and has to invest in her own equipment. As she is only paid for the photos and articles she sells to the press, as opposed to the hours spent in the office, she is always seeking work and is often in financial difficulties. Unlike Agnieszka, she assesses her subjects not according to what reflects best her specific interests or artistic sensibility, but according to their potential market value. This puts her in a different position vis-à-vis political subjects than Agnieszka. Agnieszka could afford idealism. In her film she planned to denounce the immorality of Stalinist working practices. Ewa decides to write about the poor management of state property, doctors taking bribes at state hospitals and the hopelessness of living in the workers' hostels because such subjects interest a wide public, therefore increase the sales of magazines to whom she offers her service. As a cultural worker trying to sell her work in the marketplace Ewa is similar to Danielak, who was prepared to offer his services to all possible buyers, be it organizers of political events, school parties or wedding receptions. Unlike Agnieszka, who focused only on the most important jobs, Ewa is multitasking; she takes photographs, processes them at home, tries to sell them to the press, and writes articles. To increase the value of her offer, she uses her erotic capital. She invests much in her clothing[6] and is prepared to sleep with men who can help her in her career. Ewa does not appreciate her freelance status. She yearns to have a permanent post, either in the magazine where she is freelancing or as a foreign correspondent in Rome, where her lover got promoted. Yet, getting such positions is difficult, as she did not finish her studies, but instead moved to Italy where she gained some journalistic experience (Talarczyk-Gubała 2013: 152). Another difficulty concerns the fact that in the Polish press of the 1980s men occupy the most important positions, with female journalists reduced to making coffee in the office.

Illustration 6.4: Ewa investing in her appearance in *Without Love*, directed by Barbara Sass

Ewa's attempts to make a career for herself in the media ultimately fail, following the suicide attempt of a young woman to whom the journalist devoted one of her reports. This punishment of an ambitious, yet immoral woman is in accordance both with the narrative schemes of the Cinema of Moral Concern, and the tradition of the films about career women, where women striving for a career tend to be represented as betraying their 'true self' (Kuhn and Radstone 1990: 64–65). Naming the main character 'Ewa' after the first woman who attempted to resist her fate foretells this unhappy ending. However, Ewa's defeat does not undermine her overall life strategy; it rather comes across as one of the mishaps a precarious female worker has to take into account when choosing her life path. Casting Dorota Stalińska in the role of Ewa, and thereby rendering her character very attractive and charismatic, adds to the sense that Ewa's trajectory is the right one.[7]

When Sass made *Without Love*, Ewa was seen as a pale imitation of Agnieszka and, like Danielak in *Dance Leader*, an epitome of the pathologies of the world in which she operated. From a current perspective, however, when neoliberal principles rule in the workplace, Agnieszka might come across as an anachronism, epitomizing the state socialist system, with its worship of formal education and high art. Ewa, by contrast, seemed to be a premonition of things to come; when permanent positions become scarce, people work in a precarious way, being paid for what they accomplished, and higher education become less important than work experience. In such circumstances workers tend to be humble and prepared to pay extra, to jump the queue to the diminishing pool of available jobs by offering sexual services to their employers.

While the two films discussed so far in this section were made before the martial law, *Hero of the Year* is set after this event. Falk portrays this period as a time of political and social stagnation, and an anthology of the worst traits of Polish postwar decades. Everything which is proposed in this film as a means of rejuvenating the Polish culture industry is in fact a recycling of old ideas, including the central one – changing an ordinary man into the 'hero of the year', to be consumed by a mass audience. Such an idea harks back to the 1950s, when shock workers acted as models to be emulated by ordinary people. Individual people also seem to be recycled; we have a sense that almost everybody whom we encounter in this film played a similar role earlier. The main character, Lucjan Danielak, is a case in point. We met him for the first time in the previous decade, when he was a protagonist of *Dance Leader*. Back then he was a man focused on his career in show business to such an extent that he devoted to it all his energy and sacrificed his family and friends to reach the top of his profession. This strategy did not pay; in the end his dishonesty was exposed, he lost his friends and professional allies, and his career was halted. *Hero of the Year* alludes to this situation, by mentioning that Danielak was put on trial in criminal or professional court and forbidden to practice his trade. To earn his living, he teamed up with his farmer brother, with whom he started a leatherware business. The film begins when Danielak attempts to return to show business. His hope that he will make it is fuelled by martial law, which eliminated (often by self-elimination) many people from show business who did not want to collaborate with the disgraced regime. Danielak, being a careerist, sees his chance in filling a gap. He is proved right; although people remember his shameful past, they agree that bygones are bygones. Danielak himself insists that he has repaid his moral debt which, ultimately, was small, proving that deep down he has not changed. His chance to rise again comes when he spots on television a man named Tataj who prevents a gas explosion in a multi-storey building. This gives Danielak the idea of organizing a series of live performances with Tataj as 'hero of the year', balanced with light entertainment. This kind of 'variety show' recollects socialist realism, which played down the division between high and low art.

Tataj agrees to become 'hero of the year' because he sees it as a chance to publicize the issue of safety in the gas industry. For the authorities Tataj is useful because as a simple, 'honest' man he gives credibility to the regime, which is suffering from a crisis in that regard. However, Falk shows that the strategy of using Tataj cannot work. This is because to be acceptable for the authorities, Tataj cannot go 'too far' in his criticism, therefore his communication with the audience has to be carefully staged and monitored by his superiors. Such communication can be seen as a metaphor of the way in which the regime acted in the 1980s: it appeared to strive for a dialogue with society, but in reality wanted this dialogue on its own terms (Preizner 2007: 103).[8] The 'honest man' is ultimately manipulated by the regime, in a similar way to how shock workers were used in the 1950s, as shown in *Man of Marble*. We might ask the question of why Tataj trusts the authorities, especially in the light of the rise of Solidarity and the imposition of martial law. Falk's answer, betraying his position as a member of the intelligentsia, is that simple people are always gullible.

In his dealings with Tataj and his business partners Danielak reveals the same flaws of character as in *Dance Leader*: he lies, blackmails, threatens fellow workers and still pretends to be a good man who commits misdemeanours only because he is forced by his superiors and the 'rules of the game'. Although it is suggested that martial law led to some reshuffles in the media, ultimately the old professional and class hierarchies remained intact. This impression is augmented by the casting. The actors who played journalists in the films of previous decades, such as Bogusław Sobczuk and Marian Opania, are again cast as journalists, virtually in the same roles. The style of the film is also very similar to that of *Dance Leader*, underscoring the continuity between the 1970s and 1980s. And yet, there are also differences. The people and the system are exhausted: apart from Danielak, nobody works with enthusiasm and even he seems to have less energy than during his *Dance Leader* period. For most people, making a career appears to be less important than in the 1970s and many 'opt out of the system', either by setting up private business or investing their energy outside the professional sphere. This, according to Tadeusz Sobolewski, rendered Poles 'better people' (Sobolewski 1987a: 11). Such a change can be seen in the context of the easing of restrictions on private businesses in the late 1980s and a different moral climate surrounding those working on their own account. According to Winicjusz Narojek, in the 1980s working privately was seen as a sign of nonconformity, therefore this path was increasingly chosen by the educated and younger Poles (Narojek 1991: 39), as opposed to the situation in the previous decades, when it tended to be a preserve of the prewar petit bourgeoisie. This point is made in an episode when Danielak goes to buy flowers and the owner of the florist shop turns out to be Romek, his old pal from Estrada. When Danielak asks Romek whether he is still attracted to show business, he answers 'yes', which points to Romek choosing to be a florist in order to work in an honest job and despite his love of the culture industry.

Danielak could also choose 'honest' work in the leather business with his brother, but for a man who came from a peasant family, permanently struggling to make ends meet, 'going private' does not mean progression, but regression. Yet, Falk shows that even people who still have state jobs invest their energies elsewhere. For example, Tataj waxes lyrical about his garden, which is full of flowers. In this way a contrast is established between 'honest people' who work manually, producing beautiful or useful objects, and the hyena-like journalists and professional entertainers who feed on the work and enthusiasm of others. This idealization of an apolitical man who loves nature and fresh air brings to mind the protagonist of Kieślowski's *The Bricklayer*, who also exchanged ugly ideological work for beautiful manual work (although in a state firm). I already criticized such exalting of non-political work, typical for the authors of the Cinema of Moral Concern, as being conducive to preserving the status quo, because by their withdrawal from politics the 'good people' leave political decisions to their enemies.

'Hero of the Year' not only harks back to the past, but also foreshadows the neoliberal period when reality shows featuring 'ordinary people' would constitute an important part of television programmes. If the show was produced in the 1990s, 2000s or 2010s, it would probably involve auditions of hundreds of prospective 'heroes of the year', eager to partake in the television programme as a means of reaching fame and gain extra income. The fact that in Falk's films the media people chase a prospective participant in a reality show, not the other way round, points to the fact that we are still in the 'age of scarcity' when producing a commodity, not selling it, is the main problem. But as I also argued in this chapter, this period is coming to an end.

Notes

1. Mirosław Przylipiak, in a perceptive article about Wajda, argues that the director saw documenting as the most important function of film and had significant ambitions in this direction (Przylipiak 2008b; on the documentary in Wajda's film, see also Falkowska 1996: 79–92).
2. The image of a 'divided house', in which the old members of the family show wisdom while the young are confused, also brings to mind earlier renderings of political conflict in postwar Poland, such as *Popiół i diament* (*Ashes and Diamonds*, 1958) by Andrzej Wajda, where Szczuka's son was an anti-communist conspirator, estranged from his father.
3. Much of what we see in the milk bar in fact consists of Bareja's reworking of an old Polish newsreel, mocking the unsocial behaviour of customers of bars and restaurants, such as stealing crockery, and calling for drastic measures to prevent it.
4. In this sense Bareja's film also foretells Polish postcommunist films, most importantly the works of Władysław Pasikowski, whose films are full of men with foreign names or pseudonyms, such as Franz Maurer and Jack Strong.
5. Andrzej Wajda's characters almost never struggle materially, which in my opinion reflects on his own privileged material status and lack of understanding of the impact of material deprivation on human life.
6. Ewa's exclusive wardrobe, different from what was worn at the time on the average Polish street, attracted much criticism (see, for example, Kłopotowski 1981).
7. In this case we can talk about 'resistance through charisma', as discussed by Richard Dyer in relation to *Gilda* (Dyer 1998), namely an actress changing the meaning of her role, as conceived in the script.
8. It is worth mentioning that various shows with 'ordinary people', presented in western television, such as game shows, are also scripted and staged. This, however, is tacitly accepted by the audience and performers as a specific convention of such programmes.

PART III
Postcommunist Cinema
From Triumphant Neoliberalism to Accumulation by Dispossession

In the late 1980s-early 1990s the system of state socialism collapsed in the whole of Eastern Europe, as symbolized by the fall of the Berlin Wall in 1989 and, in the Polish context, the first semi-democratic parliamentary elections. It is not my intention here to pinpoint the precise moment when one economic and political system ended and another began, not least because I believe that this process started earlier and was gradual (see chapter 6), but to describe the new one, known as neoliberal capitalism or simply neoliberalism (also known as monetarism, laissez-faire, global or cognitive capitalism).[1] In common with state socialism, which had a crucial influence on class structure, work and consumption in Poland in the years 1945–1989, neoliberalism has also exerted such an influence on the post-1989 period. Although the last quarter of a century saw numerous changes of governments and political leaders, in reality it is more homogeneous than the period of state socialism. Postcommunist political elites, be they from the centre-right or centre-left, led by anti-communist Lech Wałęsa or postcommunist Aleksander Kwaśniewski, follow the same political agenda: that of neoliberalization, which in the first decade or so was presented as 'economic reform' or simply 'reform'. The difference consists only in the speed with which they implemented neoliberal principles.

Rather than presenting the political situation in detail, I will focus here on describing the principles of neoliberalism and their applications in the Polish context. David Harvey, its leading analyst and critic, defines neoliberalism as a version of capitalism, in which accumulation of capital is achieved by ruthless dispossession consisting of 1) privatization and the commodification of public assets; 2) financialization, so that any commodity can become an instrument of economic speculation; 3) management and manipulation of crises; and 4) state redistribution, by which wealth and income is distributed upwards, from lower to upper classes and from poorer to wealthier countries and regions (Harvey 2005a: 160–162). These four features of neoliberalism reverse the principles on which Eastern European economies, including the Polish one, were built after the Second World War. Privatization is the reverse of nationalization of industries, which was meant to ensure that the whole of society, and especially the workers rather than the capitalists, own the means of production. Financialization is the reverse of non-monetary distribution of welfare, such as communal apartments, heavily subsidized culture and childcare, and the rationing of shortage goods to ensure that everybody receives some of them. Management and manipulation of crises is the reverse of the principle of planning, which was meant to prevent economic and social crises. State redistribution of income from the poor to the rich is the reverse of the policy of redistribution from the rich to the poor by land reform, nationalization of factories, capping salaries of the managers in state firms, and heavy tax on private producers. As already mentioned, the attempts at marketization did not start in Poland and Eastern Europe at large after the fall of the Berlin Wall, but began as early as the 1960s and gained momentum in the late 1980s. However, these attempts were patchy and slow in comparison with the torrent of changes which affected Eastern Europe from 1989 onwards.

Harvey's notion of accumulation by dispossession follows Karl Marx's concept of 'primitive' or 'original accumulation', introduced in the first volume of *Capital*. Marx maintains that 'primitive accumulation' is the historical process of divorcing the producer from the means of production, during which great masses of men are suddenly and forcibly torn from their means of subsistence, and hurled onto the labour-market as rightless proletarians. Harvey argues that the essentially violent primitive accumulation is still alive, remaining 'powerfully present within capitalism's historical geography up until now' (Harvey 2005b: 145). It is even more ruthless than in the times of classical capitalism because of the current concentration of capital and hence great problems of finding adequate outlets for surplus capital (Harvey 2010b: 216–217). Similarly, the notion of crisis as a structural feature of neoliberalism is Marxist. Marx devoted to it a substantial part of his *Capital* (see especially Marx 1974: 211–266) and of *The Communist Manifesto*, where he put it succinctly:

> The conditions of bourgeois society are too narrow to comprise the wealth created by them. And how does the bourgeoisie get over these crises? On the one hand by enforced destruction of a mass of productive forces; on the other, by the

conquest of new markets, and by the more thorough exploitation of the old ones. That is to say, by paving the way for more extensive and more destructive crises, and by diminishing the means whereby crises are prevented. (Marx and Engels 2008: 42)

For foreign and to a smaller extent domestic capital, the fall of state socialism provided an excellent opportunity to conquer new markets, because Eastern Europe was a 'land of scarcity' (of consumer goods). Since the 1990s Poland has been flooded by foreign products, for which it has paid largely by credit. Since 1989 Polish domestic and foreign debt has steadily grown, the latter reaching 275 billion USD in 2009 (Ciborowski and Konat 2010: 46). In comparison with this, 'Gierek's debt' comes across as rather small.

The political shift to neoliberalism has been supported by a specific system of working practices, known as post-Fordism. Its main feature is flexibility, especially in terms of working hours. Flexibility is frequently presented as benefiting the worker as it frees him or her from the shackles of rigid working hours and the confinement to a specific place, such as a factory or an office. Flexibility was even demanded by French workers who went on strike in 1968 as a means of alleviating alienation (Boltanski and Chiapello 2005). However, in most cases it disadvantages the worker, as s/he spends more hours at work, often at home and during a holiday, indeed devoting practically all of his or her life to work. By the same token, it allows employers to effectively lower the wages. Unlike under Fordism, where people are paid for the number of hours spent in an office or factory, under a post-Fordist system they are paid for fulfilling specific tasks. Accordingly, we observe a growing proportion of people whose work is precarious. Precarious workers have few employment rights and are permanently competing for disappearing work (on the precariat see Ross 2008; Berardi 2009; on its representation in film see Bardan 2013).

The situation of the precariat, as well as that of those in more stable, Fordist employment, is exacerbated by technological progress (hence the term 'cognitive capitalism') (Levy and Murnane 2004), which, as Marx observed, under capitalism is to the worker's disadvantage,[2] because it reduces the need for work and allows for less visible, yet more effective surveillance. Another factor is opening borders for foreign workers, which makes the workers in one country compete not only with their countrymen, but also with foreign workers, typically more disciplined, because more desperate. As a result of these changes, the reserve army of workers is growing, leading to fiercer competition for disappearing jobs, as captured by

Pierre Bourdieu: 'a Darwinian world emerges – it is the struggle of all against all at all levels of the hierarchy, which finds support through everyone clinging to their job and organization under conditions of insecurity, suffering, and stress. ...This reserve army exists at all levels of the hierarchy, even at the higher levels, especially among managers' (Bourdieu 1998).

To justify this situation, a new work and life ethics was introduced, consisting of promoting individual effort at gaining employment and wealth, and chastising those unable to achieve this value as incompetent and lazy (Bauman 2005). As Harvey observes:

> *As the state withdraws from welfare provision and diminishes its role in arenas such as health care, public education, and social services, which were once so fundamental to embedded liberalism, it leaves larger and larger segments of the population exposed to impoverishment. The social safety net is reduced to a bare minimum in favour of a system that emphasizes personal responsibility. Personal failure is generally attributed to personal failings, and the victim is too often blamed. (Harvey 2005a: 76)*

The ideologues of neoliberalism present crisis (as much on the large scale of a country, as on the small scale of family) and uncertainty not as a problem but an opportunity for, to use Joseph Schumpeter's term, 'creative destruction' or, to paraphrase the famous words of Norman Tebbit, a chance to get on one's bike and find success.

Critics of neoliberalism, such as Harvey and Bourdieu, although concerned with the situation in the West and in the case of Harvey South America and China, capture well the situation in Eastern Europe and Poland specifically. There the main tool of neoliberalization was the so called 'Balcerowicz Plan'. It took its name from Leszek Balcerowicz, vice-prime minister in Tadeusz Mazowiecki's government and a follower of Milton Friedman's economic theory. In 1989 Balcerowicz proposed a programme of economic reform, which was implemented in the early 1990s. Its explicit goal was the transformation of the Polish economy from state socialist to capitalist. One of its principles was the idea that low unemployment should be sacrificed for low inflation. Consequently, in the 1990s the unemployment rate in Poland was above 10 per cent and this rate also prevailed in subsequent decades. Another ideological pillar of Balcerowicz's reform was the conviction that to become a modern state Poland needs the 'middle class', understood as a large and politically strong group of entrepreneurs and managers. The principal vehicle of creating this new historical agent was through privatizing state assets, effectively in a way that privileged the few, usually those close to the new political establishment.

The upgrading of the middle class was accompanied by the downgrading of the working class. Privatization and bankruptcy of unprofitable firms left many workers and working communities in a more precarious position than they were under state socialism. The intensification of capitalism has a particularly devastating effect on blue-collar workers living in the provinces. This was because during the period of state socialism towns were built around a single industry, and if the industry collapsed, the entire town has lost its livelihood. Although unemployment has affected the entire population, women have suffered more because the industries in which they predominated, such as textile and the government sector, underwent the greatest downsizing. At the same time women were less likely to be compensated than men for their loss of livelihood. Many women previously employed in cooperative farms migrated to cities in search of employment and a significant proportion of them ended up as trafficked sex workers (Ray 2006: 925). The working class was downgraded not only literally, but also symbolically. Manual labour in Poland, as well as in other countries of the ex-Eastern bloc, as Slavoj Žižek observes, had become 'the site of obscene indecency to be concealed from the public eye' (Žižek 2001b: 133), as mentioned in the previous chapter. This can be observed in the media, which practically stopped showing manual workers and when they did, only as a background or to illustrate the obverse of the success stories of those who managed to escape this class: as a site of social pathology.

Given that neoliberalism is so anti-worker and non-egalitarian and that the main agent of political change in Eastern Europe was the industrial working class, epitomized by the Solidarity trade union and its leader, Lech Wałęsa, the question arises: why did this class choose to go the 'neoliberal way'? The answer is that the majority of the workers striking in the 1980s did not choose neoliberalism. They voted for a system which prevailed in Western Europe after the end of the Second World War, namely embedded liberalism: arguably a better hybrid between capitalism and socialism than that offered by state socialism. This opinion is supported by the answer given to the question 'Would you call the capitalists back?', printed in a Hungarian oppositional journal *Ter-kep*, published in 1989: 'Many Hungarians have been in the West and everybody can see the standard of living and social security there even if there is unemployment. I have read somewhere that the labour movement achieved real results precisely in the capitalist countries. And I don't think that the defence of workers' interests would only be demagogy on behalf of capitalists' (quoted in Bartha 2013: 1). Hungarians were not alone in their views; Poles thought along similar lines. However, when the words of the Hungarian worker were printed, the West was already fast transforming, leaving the socialist element behind and introducing neoliberalism.

There are two main theories explaining why neoliberalism prevailed in Poland and the whole Eastern bloc. One can be summarized as a 'betrayal of the masses by their leaders' (Ost 2005). These leaders colluded with the nomenklatura, as demonstrated by the fact that the principles of transition were established during the Round-table Negotiations between the leaders of Solidarity, the communist authorities and the Church. In this context it is worth mentioning that the chief architect of neoliberal reform in Poland, Leszek Balcerowicz, is a transitory figure in Polish politics: a bridge between the state socialist past and a neoliberal future. Until the announcement of martial law in 1981, he was a member of the PZPR; he worked in the Institute of Marxism-Leninism and advised the Prime Minister in the late 1970s. Balcerowicz's career confirms the opinion that the PZPR was a vehicle for the self-advancement of people of various ideological persuasions and the system of state socialism collapsed partly because its demise served the economic interests of the nomenklatura. The situation I just sketched out applies to most revolutions 'which devour their own children'. On this occasion, however, the 'children', namely the industrial working class, were not only devoured, but also mocked by their previous leaders. In his perceptive essay concerning the fate of this class after the fall of state socialism, Don Kalb refers to Adam Michnik, one of the symbols of the fight against the socialist state

> who in a speech commemorating the fall of the Wall contrasted his own post-Round Table experiences as a successful newspaper publisher and global civil society intellectual with the current misery of industrial workers in Poland. He explained the impoverishment of those rank and file participants in the social movement that made his own victory possible by arguing that they had only been trained to manufacture statues of V.I. Lenin, which nobody wanted to buy any more after 1989. A metaphor, of course, but an intensely humiliating metaphor, and one that retrospectively represses any alternative path out of the economic impasse of the late-socialist 1980s by radically disqualifying the

capacities of labour for the new capitalist economy and civil society. (Kalb 2002: 319-320)

According to the second theory as to why state socialism was replaced by neoliberalism, this was because the labour-friendly Eastern European political elites had no choice but to give in to powerful pressure from abroad to go the neoliberal way. As Valerie Bunce observes, 'We cannot understate the impact of this reigning ideology on the postsocialist world. With its weak states, shattered economies, and fragile regimes, this scared new world would seem to be unusually receptive to international guidance' (Bunce 1999a: 757), and the guidance was that 'there is no alternative' (to neoliberalism). Gay Seidman sketches an analogy between the situation in postcommunist Europe and countries such as Brazil and South Africa. There 'elected officials also came to power promising redistribution, and found themselves restructuring and privatizing instead' (Seidman 2007: 98).

Here it is worth returning to Immanuel Wallerstein's World-System theory and its application to Poland after the Second World War, as offered by Jakub Majmurek who argued that at the time Poland attempted to overcome its peripheral status by modernizing from the top (see part 2). Joining the neoliberal world by adopting its principles with even greater zeal than observed in the pioneer countries of neoliberalization, such as Great Britain, could be seen as another attempt at modernization. The jury is still out as to whether this project will be successful in Poland and Eastern Europe at large or whether it will, on the contrary, reinforce its marginal status (as is the case with, for example, Greece, for whom joining the Euro proved unfortunate). What is clear is that the price of this modernization was a change in the function of the state from 'provider' to 'enabler', which assists citizens in enjoying their freedoms, most importantly the economic freedom of seeking employment and creating wealth. This shift was symbolized by the requirement that citizens fill their own tax return, a sign of taking their affairs into their own hands.

Harvey observes that although neoliberalism is a hegemonic system, it comes in different national variations. The specificity of the Polish version is best captured by comparing it with other Eastern European states. According to Dorothee Bohle and Béla Greskovits, Poland, together with other Visegrad countries, is somewhere in the middle of the region, between the Baltic countries which embraced neoliberalism with greatest zeal, and Slovenia, which became the least market-radical state, choosing its own path of economic development (Bohle and

Greskovits 2007: 447). The fact that the respective authorities in Poland did not attempt to dismantle all structures of the state socialist's welfare system might also be explained by the relatively strong position of some sections of the industrial working class and peasantry, in comparison with their counterparts elsewhere in Eastern Europe. This also explains the uneven treatment of different sections of the workforce in Poland: on the one hand miners and shipyard workers, who received relatively generous benefits when their factories were closed down, and on the other employees of cooperative farms, who were virtually abandoned by the state. The different approach to different categories of workers also had a distinct gender bias, as previously indicated. Many of the negative effects of neoliberalism were experienced with some delay. First, there was almost universal joy at the toppling of the old and by this point deeply disliked system, and the opening of new opportunities, such as the chance to set up one's own firm with fewer administrative hurdles and acquire one's own apartment almost immediately, thanks to taking out a mortgage. Even unemployment was first presented not as a cause of poverty, homelessness and social exclusion, but as a way to make workers more ambitious and innovative. The stories of great fortunes made by postcommunist entrepreneurs circulating in the media made many believe that everybody could be a winner. In the course of time, however, many of these stories turned out to be financial and political scandals.

Neoliberalization in the Polish film industry began even before state socialism collapsed, in 1987, but this process was accelerated in the 1990s. By 1991 the old institutions, through which Polish cinema was financed, were dismantled and new ones created. Amongst them were Film Studios (Studia Filmowe), which replaced the old Film Units (Zespoły Filmowe). They continued to receive funds from the government, via the Committee of Cinema, albeit relatively smaller sums. At the same time, unlike the old Film Units which only managed the property of the state, the Film Studios became the owners of this property. The executive director of the Committee of Cinema, appointed by the Prime Minister, became the most powerful figure in the Polish film industry. In this way the industry also remained dependent on current politics.

The initial economic consequences of the neoliberalization of the film industry in Poland were the same as across the rest of Eastern Europe: reduced budgets, layoffs of workers, and a fall in the number of feature films produced, in combination with increased ticket prices, lower audience figures, and falling market shares for domestic productions which faced massive competition from popular Hollywood imports. However, in the first half of the 1990s the state of film production in Poland was relatively healthy. Between 1991 and 1994 on average thirty films were produced and distributed per year and in 1995 the number even rose to thirty-nine. The vast majority of them were made thanks to government subsidy, and about a quarter were co-productions with foreign firms. In the second half of the decade production dropped to below twenty films produced/distributed per year. For example, in 1999 only sixteen new Polish films were shown in cinemas. Although fewer films were produced, they were relatively more expensive than the films of the earlier periods. This partly reflects the rising costs of making films, including the rapidly growing fees of actors, especially stars such as Bogusław Linda, Michał Żebrowski, Cezary Pazura, Janusz Gajos or Marek Kondrat (on average the fees of male stars were higher than those of female stars). Another reason was the change in the type of films made at the end of the 1990s and at the beginning of the 2000s, especially the upsurge in the production of lavish heritage films, based on classics of Polish literature, such as *Ogniem i mieczem* (*With Fire and Sword*, 1999), directed by Jerzy Hoffman, and *Quo Vadis* (2001) by Jerzy Kawalerowicz, at the expense of a larger number of cheaper films.[3] The first decade after the fall of state socialism also saw gangster films flourishing, in part reflecting the pressure to produce profitable films and to comment on the then present. The need to respond to market demands was eased in the next decade and especially after 2005, following the setting up of the Polish Film Institute (Polski Instytut Sztuki Filmowej, the PISF), which is meant to support the production of films of a high artistic standard (on the effect of these changes on the film industry, see Adamczak 2010: 333–362). Since then we have observed a greater diversification of films, with the heritage and gangster wave on the wane, and more films adhering to the ideas of arthouse cinema, albeit while trying to be popular at the same time.

The change in attitude towards neoliberalism, from affirmative to critical, is reflected in the Polish films made after 1989. Consequently, I will divide them into two parts, with the first roughly coinciding with the 1990s, the second with the 2000s and later years. In the first part we find more films about the new middle classes; in the second the workers and the unemployed come to the fore.

Notes

1. Each of these terms has different connotations, but they refer to the same empirical phenomenon. Elucidating the differences between these terms is not essential to my discussion of neoliberalism. However, some of them will be explained in the course of my discussion.
2. In Marx's *The Poverty of Philosophy* we can read: 'In England, strikes have regularly given rise to the invention and application of new machines. Machines were, it may be said, the weapon employed by the capitalists to quell the revolt of specialized labour. The *self-acting mule*, the greatest invention of modern industry, put out of action the spinners who were in revolt. If combinations and strikes had no other effect than that of making the efforts of mechanical genius react against them, they would still exercise an immense influence on the development of industry' (Marx 1963: 167–168).
3. A detailed discussion of the Polish film industry in the postcommunist period can be found in my book on Polish postcommunist cinema (Mazierska 2007) and Marcin Adamczak's (2010). Both authors pay particular attention to the development of genre cinema post-1989 as a consequence of the marketization of the film industry.

CHAPTER 7
The 1990s
Heroic Neoliberalism or Everybody Can Be a Winner

Funny Capitalism

Since the early 1990s neoliberalism has been intensively promoted by Polish politicians and the media. 'X is a winner and you can be too' was also the message dominating television screens and glossy magazines. Polish cinema could not ignore this message and in the cinema of this decade we find many winners. They might be put in a negative light, bruised and punished within the course of the narrative. Still, it is success, not failure, which interests the filmmakers in this period and it is defined in narrow, monetary terms. The trials and tribulations of young (either in age or in experience) businessmen fill narratives of films belonging to two genres – comedies and gangster films – with the former prevailing in the first half of the decade, the latter in the second. As mentioned in this book on several occasions, the choice of genre is not neutral, as genres tend to convey specific worldviews. Comedy on this occasion allowed filmmakers to mock the amateurism with which people, used to a different political and economic regime, tried to achieve success under capitalist conditions. This reflects the fact that new phenomena are open to ridicule, in the same way as babies, clumsily doing things for the first time, are funny. Yet, babies grow and lose their clumsiness, often becoming fierce and frightening. The shift from comedy to gangster cinema reflects this trajectory.

The 'business comedies' of the 1990s often take the form of a mock manual, instructing the naïve viewer how to become rich, as in *Lepiej być piękną i bogatą* (*Better to Be Beautiful and Rich*, 1993), directed by Filip Bajon, and *Kapitał, czyli jak zrobić pieniądze w Polsce...* (*Capital, or How to Make Money in Poland*, 1990), directed by Feliks Falk, which I will discuss in detail, as well as the films by Juliusz Machulski from this decade, *Kiler* (1997) and *Kilerów dwóch* (*Two Kilers*, 1999).

Capital, shot in 1989 and premiered in 1990, was the first fiction film which tried to assess the impact of the new economic reality on the lives and minds of ordinary Poles. Its director, Feliks Falk, is renowned for two films about Lutek Danielak, *Dance Leader* and *The Hero of the Year* (discussed in chapters 5 and 6). These films suggested that success, as measured in wealth and social privileges, should be rejected in Poland of state socialism, because achieving success was tantamount to collaborating with the disgraced system. Implicitly, they advocated avoiding success and cultivating integrity and inner peace.

The protagonist of *Capital*, named Piotr Nowosad, is different from the people previously portrayed by Falk, being a sociologist with a PhD. In the 1970s cinema he would have epitomized the frustrated 'unmonied elite', but in 1989 he has 40,000 USD in his bank account thanks to working for three years in an American university. Before the fall of state socialism this would have seemed like a large sum, but after 1989 the value of foreign currency diminished, rendering work abroad less profitable, yet also more needed in the light of the problems in finding employment in Poland. On the way home from the airport, Nowosad learns from the taxi driver that he will faint when he discovers the current low value of the US dollar. Maybe for this reason, or because of the Zeitgeist which encourages everybody to 'play' with one's money as opposed to consuming it, the sociologist decides to invest his savings. This explains the title of the film – Falk suggests that money in postcommunist Poland started to be seen as 'capital': money used to create more money. The film, foreshadowing a similar scene in the famous German film, *Good Bye Lenin!* (2003), directed by Wolfgang Becker, begins with an image of a helicopter carrying a statue of Marx, most likely to dump it. The film, however, acts as a vindication of Marx's assessment of capitalism. Some of the dialogue from the film even sound like quotations from this thinker.

The narrative revolves around Nowosad's attempts to become a capitalist by engaging in a plethora of enterprises. As the title indicates, he tries to 'make' money, as opposed to earning it, which suggests that he wants to get it fast, and there are many signs suggesting that fortunes can be made quickly in the new Poland. Nowosad's friend, an actor who works as the sidekick of various shadowy businessmen, shows him a new housing estate in Warsaw, full of tasteless houses, this being in accordance with the conviction that being nouveau riche is vulgar. One such house belongs to Nowosad's colleague from the university, who is now the owner of a small factory which produces clothes. All subsequent businesses, offered to Nowosad, are small- to medium-size ventures in manufacturing or providing low-cost, unsophisticated services. They reflect the modest capital of the ex-academic and the stage of the Polish economy with its 'primitive accumulation', to use a Marxist term, also in the sense that the prevailing businesses do not require complicated technology and high cultural capital. Examples are a fast food bar, a matrimonial agency and a frog farm. However, none of the businesses proves a success. The fast food bar is marred by the low quality of its product, competition with a neighbouring shop, and failure to comply with the hygiene standards required by law. As co-owner of the matrimonial agency, Nowosad makes the mistake of offering the same woman to two men. The frog farm is an eyesore to local defenders of animal rights. Nowosad's choice of businesses and his behaviour as their owner also testify to the lowering of moral, intellectual and aesthetic standards, in comparison with the times he worked at the university, which can be viewed as a metonym of low moral, intellectual and aesthetic standards pertaining to neoliberalism or at least its 'teething' stage. For example, he tells his wife that he has the right to do what he wants with his money because he earned it. In an internal monologue he also confesses that as a businessman he should have a more attractive spouse, thus suggesting that personal relationships should reflect one's financial position. During his forays into the world of business Nowosad's autonomous activities shrink to nothing. Everything he does, be it going to parties or playing tennis, is geared towards making useful contacts, and ultimately making more money, according to the rule that under neoliberalism everything is financialized. And yet Nowosad fails. It is difficult to say whether this is because he is not fit for business or because the circumstances are not conducive to honest ventures; the film points to both explanations. From what we observe, we also get contrasting messages about the advantages of bringing capitalism to Poland. On the one hand, everybody tries to 'make money' and the standard of living of many Poles goes up, as is testified by new housing estates mushrooming where there was earlier fallow land, many foreign cars on the streets, and lavish parties, to which Nowosad is invited. On the other hand, the success of the new businesses depends not on their good long-term prospects, but on the ability of their owners to sell them to some dupes with spare money before their enterprises fail. These businesses are thus in the style of the infamous 'pyramid schemes'. Nowosad appears to be such a dupe who goes into a venture when it stops being profitable and he proves unable to change its course.

Illustration 7.1: An Intellectual turned into a businessmen in *Capital, or How to Make Money in Poland*, directed by Feliks Falk

While Nowosad is enthusiastic about the new opportunities brought about by the fall of state socialism, his wife, who works as an editor in a publishing house, is sceptical about the change, as reflected by her setting up a society protecting citizens from the consequences of economic reform. The group meet in the Nowosads' apartment, not unlike how ten or twenty years previously people would meet to conspire against the hated communist state. She provides a rationale for her action by saying 'let people be richer, but not at our expense'. These words, in a nutshell, convey the Marxist idea that the capitalists get rich at the expense of the (broadly understood) working class. However, we learn that the group opposing the reform eventually dispersed because, as she admits, everybody eventually wanted to make money rather than be protected against the power of the rich. This can be explained by the fact that at the inception of neoliberalism in Poland the opportunities of making money seemed infinite while the negative consequences were not obvious. Although Falk (in a manner typical of the creators of the Cinema of Moral Concern) is principally concerned with the wellbeing of the intelligentsia, rather than the working class, he also alludes to the worsening position of the latter by showing the new, privately-owned sweatshops, employing women. One such sweatshop is in the villa of Nowosad's old university colleague; another is a frog farm, where women pack the animals to be exported to the West. The women come across as a silent and anonymous crowd and receive no attention from the factory owners who see them merely as a vehicle in their own enrichment.

Capital has a happy, although rather unlikely ending. Nowosad learns that his old book (which he previously described as a commercial flop) was translated into English and received some prestigious award in Britain, worth £50,000,[1] in this way balancing his losses in business and convincing the ex-academic to stick to what he knows best: sociology. This is not bad advice in the light of the fact that thanks to the expansion of university education, including the opening of many private universities, being an academic became a profitable profession in the neoliberal sense of providing a good salary. In the final scene of *Capital* we see what was shown at the beginning: a helicopter carrying the statue of Marx, as if signalling that Marx cannot be defeated in Poland, if not as a prophet of communism, then at least as a profound analyst of capitalism.

Although Falk in his film criticizes the vulgarity and sloppiness of postcommunist work and culture, his own film betrays the same vices which he criticizes. The plot is crude, the characters are reduced to caricatures, the dialogue lacks subtlety and the transition from one episode to another is abrupt. This fit between content and style of the film calls to mind the late films by Stanisław Bareja, which revealed the same shortcomings as the late state socialist reality which they ridiculed (see chapter 6). Yet Falk's film lacks the charm of Bareja's production and fails on its own terms: as a satire on the new capitalist reality. At the same time as criticizing the new entrepreneurial spirit pertaining to early neoliberalism, Falk, albeit unwittingly, criticizes its cinema, suggesting that it needs a thorough reform by eliminating the weaker 'players'.

Bandit Capitalists

The new capitalism is also brought to the fore in a series of films described as 'bandit cinema' (*kino bandyckie*) (Przylipiak and Szyłak 1999: 178–187). This term might suggest films just presenting 'bandits' (who should be understood rather as 'gangsters' or the 'mafia') or endorsing gangster values, such as ruthlessness, selfishness, bad manners and vulgarity. It mainly means the former, although some films reveal enchantment with the lifestyle of gangsters. This category includes *Balanga* (*Party*, 1993), directed by Łukasz Wylężałek, *Miasto prywatne* (*Private City*, 1994) by Jacek Skalski, *Fuks* (*Stroke of Luck*, 1999) by Maciej Dutkiewicz, and *Pierwszy million* (*First Million*, 2000) by Waldemar Dziki. I will take a close look at two films which finish this cycle. This is because unlike earlier 'bandit films', which focus on the mayhem caused by gangsters and the sensationalist side of their lives, the later are more interested in the way in which they acquire capital, what can be described as the ordinary work of gangsters, including their involvement in legal businesses, and the changes in class structure post-1989. Both films, in a way that is typical of gangster films, include a love story, with *Stroke of Luck* being a hybrid of a gangster film and a romantic comedy.

The fact that in this period the stories of earning money in Poland are presented as stories of gangsterism chimes with David Harvey's discussion of neoliberal capitalism as 'feral'. Harvey argues that neoliberalism, because it made the richest capitalists more powerful than state institutions and society at large, hence almost invincible, became a fertile ground for 'feral', namely criminal behaviour on the part of both capitalists and those who should represent the people:

> *We live in a society where capitalism itself has become rampantly feral. Feral politicians cheat on their expenses, feral bankers plunder the public purse for all its worth, CEOs, hedge fund operators and private equity geniuses loot the world of wealth, telephone and credit card companies load mysterious charges on everyone's bills; corporations and the wealthy don't pay taxes while they feed at the trough of public finance; shopkeepers price-gouge; and, at the drop of a hat swindlers and scam artists get to practice three-card monte right up into the highest echelons of the corporate and political world.* (Harvey 2012: 156)

In postcommunist Poland the most famous example of feral capitalism was the so-called 'Oscylator' scheme, invented by two young businessmen, Bogusław Bagsik and Andrzej Gąsiorowski, in 1989. This scheme consisted of collecting interest from the same capital in numerous banks by taking a cheque in one bank and cashing it in a different bank. The story of these two businessmen is characteristic of neoliberalism for two reasons. First, it crossed the boundary between what is legal and illegal, as well as moral, as the profit made by Bagsik and

Gąsiorowski was made by capital which the businessmen did not possess, but which belonged to society. Second, it involved not only the businessmen but also politicians, while in democracies the spheres of business and politics are presumed to be separate. Stories like 'Oscylator' were foretold in the films by Stanisław Bareja, but in comparison with people like Bagsik and Gąsiorowski Bareja's characters were amateurs.

In the 'bandit films' feral capitalism is at the same time criticized and glorified, not unlike in American films about the 'wolves of Wall Street', including the mega-hit by Martin Scorsese from 2013. A case in point is *Stroke of Luck*. We meet its main character, eighteen-year-old Aleks, for the first time when he is spying from the roof of his apartment block on his attractive neighbour, Sonia, when she has a date with a well-off suitor who takes her to a restaurant in a foreign car. However, the date does not lead to sex, much to this man's dissatisfaction, who complains 'Do you know how much I paid?', to which she responds with irony 'How romantic!' This exchange illustrates the fact that the film is set in the period of neoliberalism, when everything has its price, including love. As in every transaction, the buyers bargain in the hope of getting as much as possible for the minimum price. Soon Aleks steals a car from rich businessman Bagiński. He tells Sonia that he did so to impress her. However, he has another motive: to expose Bagiński's machinations. It appears that both the media and the police know that Bagiński is a feral capitalist, but are unable or unwilling to prove it. Indeed, Bagiński organizes an illegal deal, acting as an intermediary between some Korean businessmen willing to pay a bribe to get permission to build a shopping centre in Warsaw and a civil servant willing to grant such permission for a bribe. Deals of this type impoverish ordinary citizens, yet they do not look like accumulation by dispossession, but rather a foreign investment which would benefit the whole population. The ultimate reason behind Aleks's resolve to expose Bagiński's criminal activities is revenge on Bagiński, who turns out to be his estranged father, suggesting that what this young man objects to is not 'feral capitalism', but his particular life situation. To use the distinction made in chapter 5, *Stroke of Luck* turns out to be at best a film of 'moral' (private) rather than 'political' (public) concern. It ends with Aleks proclaiming to Sonia: 'The world is ours, you only have to believe in it!' We see the couple in a red sports car approaching a city full of skyscrapers, perhaps standing for New York, the proverbial capital of capitalism. It is difficult to imagine a better way to promote neoliberalism. What ultimately matters to the characters is not social justice, but money and the luxuries one can buy with it. The film proclaims that 'everybody can be a winner' – s/he has just put effort into his/her project. Such a message is augmented by the soundtrack, dominated by songs about success, and even by the original title of the film: 'fuks' refers to doing something by circumventing the rules, not unlike 'embezzling', but in a 'cute, sexy way'. Ultimately, the film does not argue against doing immoral things, but against doing them in a charmless, brutal way, which is Bagiński senior's domain.

Stroke of Luck is full of violence and much of it takes place in the workplace. This reflects the new realities of work, where the employee has to submit her/himself (her/his time, mind and body) to the power of the employer, as exemplified by Bagiński's bodyguards, who live under the threat that if they do not do as they are told, they will be fired and harmed. What they are expected to do is often illegal and cruel, such as beating up Bagiński's enemies. Sonia is also expected to do more, entertaining Bagiński's guests, even offering them sexual services. Such mixing of professional and personal activities brings to mind the situations presented in Polish prewar films. We can recollect here, for example, Bronka in *Girls from Nowolipki* and Krystyna in *Krystyna's Lie*, who were objects of erotic attention from their middle-aged bosses. However, on each occasion the men were genuinely in love with the poor women and were able to pay much in terms of money and emotional investment to keep their beloved employees happy. Bagiński senior, by contrast, has no romantic interests and for him all women are disposable: they can be purchased and exchanged for money. Such an attitude also ultimately applies to the young Bagiński. Being romantically involved with Sonia does not stop him from using her sexual capital to extract money from his father. Like a pimp, Aleks first promises to share with Sonia the money they earned this way, but later decides to return it to Bagiński senior, so that Sonia ends up with no money and no job. In such a situation she has no choice but to cling to Aleks, who promises her a better future. Their trip to New York can be unmasked as the journey of a naïve girl from Eastern Europe, who, after proving herself as a valuable sex worker in her own country, is taken abroad to earn more money in the West, yet most likely again for her 'minder' rather than herself. One of the reviewers also noticed that *Stroke of Luck* bears witness to the relationship between age and class in postcommunist Poland. For the generation of Bagiński senior making money was easy, because the year 1989 brought them the chance of a lifetime to become millionaires. Those who, like Aleks, were born in 1981 or later, are aware that for them becoming rich would be more difficult (Pietrasik 1999: 46). Indeed, in the next decade the image of a young bankrupt will be more common in Polish cinema than that of a young millionaire.

First Million is also a story of people who became very rich in postcommunist Poland thanks to rapid neoliberalization. However, unlike Dutkiewicz, who reveals nothing about Bagiński's past, Dziki provides his three characters, Frik, Kurtz and Piki, with a history. We learn that these three friends started as businessmen or rather 'business boys' in the 1980s. This was a period of great shortages of basic commodities, of which the youngsters took advantage by collecting waste paper which they exchanged for toilet paper re-sold at a handsome profit. Then they recycled the recycled goods by stealing from the waste paper shop the paper which they already sold in order to sell it again, till they were caught. Under state socialism and especially in the 1980s, as argued in the previous chapters, theft of state property was not seen as theft. That said, the characters in Dziki's film went further in this respect than the average Pole.

The attitude of the young Frik, Kurtz and Piki renders them perfect material to become 'feral capitalists' when such opportunity arises. In the meantime, still in the period of state socialism, the friends devote themselves to more serious commerce, trading in Poland and abroad in cigarettes, alcohol, sausages and computers, till they realize that the best commodity of all is money itself. Such a conclusion chimes with Marx's claim that under advanced capitalism financial capital gets precedence over other types of capital. Countries rich in natural resources tend to be poor, while those whose natural resources are scarce, but which have a well developed banking and stock exchange system, tend to be rich, as exemplified by Switzerland or Liechtenstein. For the same reason, the renowned socialist economist Karl Polanyi argues that money should be a protected good: people should not be allowed to trade with it in the same way that they trade with groceries or clothes.[2] The defining moment for Frik, Kurtz and Piki comes with the opening of the stock market in Warsaw. Trading in the stock market was practically a guaranteed way of earning money because initially the prices of all shares went up; this was a consequence of the best Polish state firms being privatized first and sold cheaply. A proportion of the shares of such firms was awarded to their employees, with those in higher positions receiving more. Privatization in Poland, as elsewhere under neoliberalism, privileged the elites and disadvantaged the masses. However, even those who were given or were able to buy a couple of shares felt as if they were richer than under late state socialism, because back then they usually felt that their workplaces belonged to the amorphous, alienated 'state' rather than to them. Frik, Piki and Kurtz's situation changes, however, when their shares go down and suddenly they lose most of what they earned on the stock market. This might be because by this point they were dealing mostly with 'old' shares or due to the activities of more powerful 'wolves of Polish Wall Street' than they. The friends realize that they cannot make up for their losses in an honest way, but only by 'going feral' on a large scale by getting access to secret information, achieved through bribery and blackmail. They are helped by a local policeman and even a priest in exchange for financial advice. One would expect journalists to also be implicated in these dealings, but they are miraculously spared, most likely because they represent the same group as filmmakers.

The businessmen soon earn their first million (dollars) and their road to success appears to be clear, which they celebrate by travelling to Paris with their childhood friend, Dominika, who in the meantime has became an affluent career woman. Around that time their worldview is crystallized, as epitomized by their saying 'shares, the media, real estates – everything is up for grabs. Let's buy them before they buy us'. This form of social Darwinism is precipitated by their sense that they live as if at the beginning of times. On this point, however, they are mistaken. In Poland the year 1989 or 1990 might feel like 'year zero', but in the global history of capitalism or even neoliberalism, it was much further down the line. Even in Poland Frik, Kurtz and Piki are not the only ones who want to carve for themselves a large part of the market of shares and power. On their return home they are punished for trying to trespass on territory already claimed by their competitor. The rest of the film is taken by a turf war between two gangs, one led by Frik, Kurtz and Piki, the other by a more elusive 'syndicate' linked to Warsaw's power elite, yet most likely with its centre outside Poland. The conflict leads to the killing or seriously wounding of a number of people, including Dominika. *First Million* finishes with a scene showing the ending of the collaboration and one of them throwing away two 200,000 dollars, which might be seen as a sign that they have lost interest in money after earning so much, but also learning that their 'play' has its limits, established by more powerful feral capitalists.

Although these two films do not idealize the postcommunist entrepreneurs-gangsters – therefore labelling them as 'bandit cinema' is off the mark – they fail to offer any alternative to their lifestyles and mindsets. To use Bloch's terminology, evoked in the first part of my book, there are no moments of objective or subjective hope or a desire to give voice to different subjects. The moments which might open the viewer to an alternative reality are immediately closed off. For example, the working-class people, whom Frik, Kurtz and Piki use to buy more shares, are presented as a human herd, whom the businessmen do a favour by paying them a pittance for their service. There is no suggestion in the film that these poor people lose something when others become millionaires or billionaires. At one point we also learn that Dominika was sent abroad to have her face mended after being severely beaten up by the people working for her boss and that the three friends paid for the operation. This statement finishes Dominika's story, giving the impression that money can buy everything, including a new face, a literal and metaphorical marker of one's identity.

The limitation of Dziki's film as a morality tale is especially visible if we compare it with the films to which it makes reference. The most obvious example is *Ziemia obiecana* (*The Promised Land*, 1974) by Andrzej Wajda. Wajda's film presented the birth of industrial capitalism in Łódź at the end of the nineteenth century; Dziki's film attempts to depict the birth of neoliberal capitalism in Warsaw at the end of the twentieth century. Both films cast in the main roles three friends trying to get rich in difficult circumstances. However, *The Promised Land* pinpoints the connection between labour and capital; capital in this film is like a vampire sucking the blood of its proletarian victims, as conveyed by the images of bleeding, maimed and dead factory workers. *First Million* lacks any insight into the workings of the capital; in this respect it is as myopic as its characters who narrate the film. We even get the impression that the growth of capital is a question of squabbling by competing gangs rather than appropriating the product of the work of many by the few. Warsaw, where Dziki's film is set, seems to be unaffected by the shift to neoliberalism, unlike Wajda's Łódź, which is, in the words of Władysław Reymont on whose novel the film is based, 'disgusting, but at the same time horribly powerful and great' (quoted in Nurczyńska-Fidelska 2003: 147). Finally, Wajda's film points to the power of capitalism to render all differences between humans insignificant except for those pertaining to their wealth. In line with this idea, *The Promised Land* shows how the pursuit of income destroys national, ethnic and personal loyalties and forces Poles, Germans and Jews to collaborate with each other or destroy each other, if this proves more profitable. In Dziki's film nothing old is destroyed and nothing new created.

The second film to which *First Million* invites comparison is *The Treasure of the Sierra Madre* (1948) by John Huston. From this film, set in Mexico of the 1920s, Dziki borrows the idea of three men searching for treasure, which in the final scene is blown away by the wind and wasted, except that in Huston's film it is gold, while in Dziki's film it is paper money. However, in the two films the episode of the destruction of wealth has different meanings. In *Treasure of the Sierra Madre* it marks the characters' understanding of the way capitalism works and the rejection of its logic: their refusal to treat wealth as humans' ultimate goal. Dziki's characters do not reach this stage of indifference towards wealth. Nobody in this film represents an alternative to the capitalist set of values; for everybody the social world is reduced to monetary exchange. Their throwing money away comes across as an irrational gesture.

The building of Polish capitalism also became the subject of one chapter in Krzysztof Kieślowski's celebrated 'Three Colours' Trilogy – *White* (1993–1994). As Joseph Kickasola observes, in 'Three Colours' Kieślowski for the first time presents wealthy protagonists and this might reflect the emergence of capitalism in his homeland (Kickasola 1996: 269). The story concerns a Polish hairdresser Karol Karol, whose French wife, Dominique, divorces him and deprives him of his belongings. This is a punishment for him becoming impotent on foreign soil. Following his misfortune, Karol leaves Paris and returns to Poland, smuggled in a large suitcase,[3] helped by another Pole. There he quickly becomes rich, thanks to a number of tricks of which some are reminiscent of those shown in the films discussed so far. For example, thanks to a piece of information he acquires when penetrating the Warsaw underworld, he buys some land and sells it with an exorbitant profit when it becomes very valuable. Kieślowski thus suggests that in postcommunist Poland money comes easily for those who are smart. Karol's enrichment appears not to be at anybody's expense, except, perhaps, of some crooks. This situation contrasts with France, where we observe accumulation through dispossession in the most blatant form, when Dominique becomes wealthy by robbing Karol of everything he earned, which can be read as a metaphor of Polish-western relationships as a form of colonialism. Karol's ultimate motif is not gaining wealth but revenge on his ex-wife and regaining her affection. The hairdresser's wealth and feigned death are meant to lure her to Poland, where he frames her for murder. The plan works and Dominique finds herself in prison, waiting for Karol's forgiveness. Karol's revenge on Dominique can be read as the revenge exercised by a poor Poland on the rich West for the centuries of colonial exploitation, although this point would be clearer if Dominique came from Germany or Austria, rather than France, with whom Poland historically had better relations. Kieślowski also includes in the film a blasé Polish millionaire, Mikołaj, who despite his successful life wants to commit suicide. For Mikołaj money matters little, but it is only wealth which affords a horizon from which one can see its ultimate poverty.

Kieślowski's 'Trilogy' concerns the values propagated by the French Revolution – solidarity, equality and freedom – with 'white' standing for equality. This value pertains both to the capitalist and communist ideologies, as demonstrated by the fact that it was one of the aims of the French bourgeoisie, the main agent of the French revolution. However, Marx claimed that under capitalism equality is an empty letter, because those who have more money have more power and therefore they are 'more equal than others', as George Orwell later said. Economic equality is thus the most important of all equalities and without it there is no social justice. Economic inequalities can be exacerbated by other factors, like those pertaining to nationality, gender or age. Karol's story is first a tale about multi-layered inequalities suffered by an emigrant and later about making up for these inequalities by becoming smart and entrepreneurial. The fact that Karol could not achieve success in France but succeeds in Poland renders Polish capitalism more egalitarian or perhaps more Polish-friendly. As Kickasola noticed, the protagonist's name Karol Karol, which can be regarded as the Polish 'Charlie Charlie', together with certain elements of his outfit, such as his worn-out shoes in which he traverses the streets of Paris, renders him a Polish incarnation of Chaplin's Tramp (Kickasola 1996: 282–283). However, these similarities are ultimately superficial. Chaplin's Tramp (who does not have a real name) stands for the whole category of people struggling during economic depression. These people, despite being poor and dispossessed, do not lose their dignity, morality and manners. A Tramp remains the same, as if to remind us that there will always be poor people as long as the capitalist system persists. Kieślowski's Karol, by contrast, is an individual (throughout his career Kieślowski has been increasingly more interested in individuals than communities) who undergoes a profound transformation during the course of the narrative. These two characters overcome their predicament in different ways. In *City Lights* (1931) the Tramp, on the run from the police, jumps into the car of the millionaire on one side, to step out of it on the other. As Johan Siebers notices, that montage of rich and poor sets off the action in which a blind girl mistakes the Tramp for a millionaire. The Tramp's jump through the car is a leap of the imagination on the part of Chaplin (Siebers 2014: 53; chapter 1). Karol Karol traverses the boundary between the poor and the rich in reality, suggesting that anybody with some brains can emulate Kieślowski's character. By the same token, poverty in *White* is blamed on the poor and associated with laziness and lack of initiative, and its significance and impact on society is downplayed.

The Arrival of Homo Sacer and the New Face of the Shock Worker

As I argued earlier, documentary films tend to be produced faster and more cheaply than fiction films, hence they are better equipped to convey a sense of actuality. They also bring to centre stage the people marginalized in the dominant ideology and mainstream films, and give less mediated access to what ordinary people think. In line with these rules, Polish documentaries in the 1990s tackled less attractive facets of neoliberalism, such as the pauperization of a large chunk of Polish society, chiefly as a result of unemployment, which, once it came to Poland, oscillated between 10 and 15 per cent. This does not mean that Polish documentary filmmakers in this period rejected the dominant pro-neoliberal ideology *tout court*. In most cases, in the 1990s the opposite was the case, which reflected the fact that the main purchaser of the documentaries was Polish state television, which represented the views of the ruling elites. The relatively low number of documentary films concerned with unemployment in this decade points to it not being a subject favoured by the authorities. Even those which were made at the time tended to adopt a neoliberal position, rendering the unemployed responsible for their predicament.

One film about unemployment from this period is *Ta wspaniała praca* (*This Wonderful Work*, 1993) by Piotr Morawski. The very title harks back to the period of socialist realism, when work was officially proclaimed the most important good, also in an aesthetic sense, as something providing the worker with a valuable aesthetic experience and rendering him/her beautiful. The film tells the story of three female textile workers from Łódź, who lost their jobs when their factory was closed down in the early 1990s. The women describe their current situation, while comparing it with their past. The past was not rosy, because their work was hard, poorly paid and damaged their health. However, they also mention the stability of their lives and the sense of camaraderie and joy derived from a job well done. All this has gone and now one woman is unemployed, one gets temporary jobs as a seamstress and the third, the 'lucky one', is a pensioner. Their stories are juxtaposed with images of the textile factory, which looks like a ghost town, and those connoting consumption, such as display windows with mannequins and sex shops.

In one of them we see a woman performing a strip-tease. Eventually the sex worker tells her story and we learn that she was also a textile worker, laid off the same time as the other women. She was accepted into the sex club, which was not an option for the older and less attractive women. She presents herself as a winner, due to the fact that she can support herself and afford some luxuries, such as expensive clothes and cosmetics, although she mentions the moral turmoil she experienced when she had to retrain herself. The ultimate message of the film is that any work, including backbreaking physical work and sex work, is wonderful in comparison with unemployment. This would not be the case if unemployment benefit allowed a decent life and there was no stigma attached to those who do not work. It is worth adding that in 2006 the textile factory where Morawski's heroines worked gave way to a large shopping mall called Manufaktura (Manufacture). Such transformations became very common in postcommunist Europe, implying that production gave way to consumption. But, of course, consumption is only for those who can afford it; the lack of the opportunity to produce for many means exclusion from even the most basic consumption.

Another film concerned with unemployment, euphemistically termed in the 1990s 'restructuring', is Tomasz Dobrowolski's *Koniec epoki węgla kamiennego (The End of the Epoch of Coal*, 1993). In common with Morawski's film, its title is ironic, as it can be interpreted as either referring to an epoch in the geological history of Earth or the role of coal in human history. The conflation of the two meanings points to the archaic mindset of the Polish miners, who do not accept that their time is over. They use the past as a way to legitimize their demand for the preservation of their jobs and their ways of living, saying that 'Poland is based on coal. Our entire industry is based on coal'. Their supposed status as 'dinosaurs' is confirmed by their conviction that the plans to close down the mines are the consequence of some conspiracy, as opposed to a healthy economic calculation, which is an opinion espoused by the film's author. As Przylipak notes, the responsibility for finding a new job and adjusting to the new reality is ultimately placed on the miners, rather than the neoliberal state which inherited the supposedly unprofitable mines or their new, private owners (Przylipak 2015). From this perspective it is worth comparing *The End of the Epoch of Coal* with the British film *Brassed Off* (1996) by Mark Herman, which referred to a similar process, albeit taking place in Britain over twenty years before Dobrowolski's film is set. However, Herman questioned the view that British coalmines were unprofitable and that their laid-off employees should take care of their own future. The difference in the approach might reflect the context of these films: in Britain of 1996 neoliberalism, especially in the version practiced by Thatcher, brought largely negative memories; in Poland of 1993 it was seen as a source of hope.

Although the 1990s brought many fiction films set in the countryside, such as the acclaimed films by Jan Jakub Kolski, for example *Pograbek* (1992), *Cudowne miejsce* (*Miraculous Place*, 1994) and *Szabla od komendanta* (*Sabre from the Commander*, 1995), they do not offer a realistic depiction of making a living from farming post-1989. Perhaps this was because, as Paul Coates argues, after 1989 the countryside in Polish cinema was relegated (or upgraded) to the position of a metaphor of Poland as a backward, yet spiritual country, resisting joining 'Europe' or the 'West' on the West's terms (Coates 2008). The countryside as a place of daily struggle attracted more attention from the Polish documentarists, who addressed the fate of people working in state farms (the PGRs), which after the fall of state socialism were dismantled and sold off to private owners. The best known examples of this cycle are *Mgła* (*Fog*, 1993) by Irena Kamieńska and *Arizona* (1997) by Ewa Borzęcka. *Fog* is set in an unnamed place where there was previously a PGR. Shots of what was before a functioning microcosm and now looks like a ghost town are juxtaposed with the utterances of the inhabitants, who compare the present, which for them is a time of misery, resulting from unemployment, with the communist past. One man says: 'When I had work, I had everything. Now, with no work, I'm a common beggar'. Some try to pinpoint the reasons why they cannot get work. First, they were deprived of their means of production by being excluded from privatization of the common land. One man says that if he gets ten hectares, a horse and a cow, he will be fine now. Others express the view that a cooperative farm should be created on the ruins of the old PGR and the old workers should be its new owners and managers. This raises the question of why this did not happen, suggesting that privatization of state land in Poland was conducted according to the rule of accumulation through dispossession, as identified by Harvey. The characters also notice that as ex-farm workers, whose professional capital became obsolete, they have no chance of finding employment in agriculture elsewhere. Neither did they get a chance to upgrade their capital by attending courses to learn foreign languages and new professional skills. On top of that, they are not eligible to get credit to set up their own businesses. The only help they get from the postcommunist rulers is unemployment benefit (*kuroniówka*), which is so low that they live below the poverty line, lagging behind with rent and owing money to the local grocery shop. One woman mentions that she has no money to call a doctor or buy medicine for her sick child. Kamieńska's interlocutors are not blindly nostalgic for bygone times; they list their shortcomings, such as the waste of material and human energy and the undeserved privileges of those in positions of power. That said, they admit that even though the communist elites enjoyed disproportionate benefits, the crumbs from their table allowed the common people to survive. Under state socialism there was always enough work, which ensured both income and self-respect. The postcommunist regime took all of this away, bringing nothing valuable. We hear somebody saying 'I would never believe Wałęsa will do it to the people. If I knew it, I would not vote for him'.

In their discussion of *Fog*, Mikołaj Jazdon and Mirosław Przylipiak argue that the title refers to the state of mind of the inhabitants of the post-PGR village. Their minds are 'clouded' by their sense of helplessness, which prevents them from improving their lot (Jazdon 2008; Przylipiak 2015). According to these critics they are homini sovietici, locked in the past. In my opinion the titular fog might refer rather to an invisible calamity coming from outside, as suggested by the shots showing the village enveloped in this immaterial substance. I read the 'fog' as a barely visible, yet real means through which the village and its inhabitants are cut from the centre and condemned to civil and eventually material death. One example of this 'enfoggement strategy' is the discontinuing of the only train connecting the village with the city on the grounds that it is not profitable. The lack of transport creates an extra obstacle in finding work or selling the fruit of local labour in the city. They also mention the lack of interest of the authorities, who refuse to visit such a 'shithole'.

Unlike *Fog*, whose exact setting is not revealed, *Arizona* is set in the post-PGR village Zagórki in the Słupsk region in northern Poland. Its title is taken from a cheap wine, and drinking it is the main entertainment of its inhabitants. The film paints an image of the world which has reached its end and is going through a 'slow apocalypse'. The sign is the end of profitable production and the return of the inhabitants of Zagórki to some kind of natural state (which in *Fog* was only hinted at). We learn that they poach animals living in the nearby forest and that it is easier for them to survive in summer than in winter because in summer they collect berries and mushrooms which they sell in the city of Słupsk. One of Borzęcka's interviewees admits with pride that he has enough wood for five years; this is wood which he 'gleaned' rather than bought. Deprived of paid employment, money and any chance of decent entertainment, they amuse themselves with spying on each other and drinking Arizona. As with all socially excluded people, on the one hand alcohol allows them to forget their miserable existence and reach utopia (one character admits that 'Arizona saves our lives'), but on the other hand it reduces their chance to leave the vicious circle of unemployment, poverty and social exclusion.

The majority of the people presented in the film looked after the animals when they worked in the PGRs, with many milking cows. Their attachment to the animals crops up throughout the narrative. Some look after the few animals which survived the privatization of the PGR, such as a pig and a horse. The horse is now over thirty years old and the owner takes him for walks, as if he was a beloved pet. An old woman, who presents herself as an ex-prisoner of Ravensbrück, lives with numerous cats and dogs, which is her way of redeeming her shameful deed of eating a dog after she left the camp (possibly out of hunger). This draws attention to the danger that the unemployed farmhands will also be reduced to eating their pets. Borzęcka also points to the fact that they are treated like animals rather than human beings by the authorities and by each other. One of the characters even compares his wife to a horse who only moves 'from here to there'. The fact that these people were used to their narrow habitat is seen as a reason why they are unable to adapt to the neoliberal world of greater mobility. Being a homo sovieticus precludes becoming a neoliberal (wo)man.

The way Borzęcka shoots her characters through the gates augments the connection between their situation and that of caged animals. The reference to animals and life in a concentration camp brings to mind the concept of 'homo sacer', as elaborated by Georgio Agamben. According to Agamben, 'homo sacer' has only his physical existence (*zoo* as opposed to *bio*), therefore can be killed with impunity. This condition is epitomized by the inmates of Nazi concentration camps, who were devoid of any individuality, reduced to numbers and practically dead even when they were still alive (Agamben 1998: 181–188). However, as I argued elsewhere, the condition of an unemployed or precarious worker under neoliberalism has much in common with homo sacer (Mazierska 2015a: 155–191). This is also true of the villagers of Zagórki. One factor in their 'homosacerization' is the lack of social security, which leads to debt and their physical and social degeneration. The death in the film of two animals, the pig and the horse, who featured extensively in the film underscores the point that the people from Zagórki are sentenced to death.

Borzęcka focuses on the here and now of her characters, as opposed to asking the question of who is responsible for the status quo. The 'authorities' or the 'system' are not visible in this film. According to Tadeusz Sobolewski (a critic regularly working for the *Wyborcza* daily, which is the main voice of neoliberalism in Poland), Borzęcka departed from the rule governing the Polish documentary cinema of the 1970s, namely that 'people are good, the system is bad' (Sobolewski 1998: 70). This might reflect the fact that, paradoxically, under state socialism filmmakers had more freedom to criticize the state than under neoliberalism. The critic also suggests that the film is about a certain category of people, which is universal. He writes:

There always were, are and will be near us excluded people who failed, who were left behind, who sank, for whom the only refuge is a bottle [of alcohol] and empty laughter... I had such neighbours everywhere, where I lived: on Woronicza Street, on Wilcza, Chłodna, Hoża. There were plenty of them on Praga, where my father came from. After watching Borzęcka film, they paraded in front of my memory all these neighbours whom so easy – too easy – we describe as 'degenerates'. We, concerned about the fate of society. (Sobolewski 1998: 70)

Of course, it is possible to see *Arizona* in this way and it is especially tempting for those who try to merge a humanist concern for the excluded with the conviction that neoliberalism is the only viable political route for Poland. From such a perspective the title of the film can be interpreted as referring to the post-PGR village as a new 'wild West' which needs to be re-captured and re-civilized the 'neoliberal way'. However, on repeated viewing, one picks up signals that it is the neoliberal system which produces those whom Sobolowski describes as 'degenerates', even though he himself distances himself from such a label. For example, one of the characters, a wealthy incomer who apparently wanted to rejuvenate the bankrupt PGR, mentions that under state socialism the PGR had 300 cattle and 300 hectares of land which post-1989 went wild. One wonders who is responsible for this decline – surely not the workers who lament the disappearance of their livelihood. In common with the characters in Kamieńska's film, one ex-worker mentions that communist times were better than now because the communists stole from the workers but also allowed the workers to steal. Nowadays, on the other hand, the rulers still steal from the workers, but the workers are not allowed to steal any more. It is difficult to find a better summary of the neoliberal condition.

Arizona received some important awards, such as the Grand Prix at the 1998 Kraków Film Festival, and is widely regarded as one of the most important Polish films of the 1990s. But it also brought accusations that the filmmaker behaved in an immoral way by picking characters who best illustrated her point and buying them Arizona so that they could better play the role of degenerated lumpenproletariat. One critic compared the reality presented by Borzęcka to that created by Pieter Bruegel (Nowak 2011: 47). Without diminishing this comparison, I will evoke here the concepts of 'dark tourism' (Lennon and Foley 2010) and 'ruin porn' (Millington 2013), which refer to the phenomenon of special interest granted to sites of poverty and misery, and the attempts to make money out of them. No doubt Borzęcka uses the aesthetics of 'ruin porn' by exaggerating the negative aspects of life in Zagórki. That said, these attacks on the filmmaker themselves were ideological, as they allowed attention to be moved away from what the film shows, to the integrity of its author.

In contrast to films about the bankrupt PGRs, *Witajcie w życiu!* (*Welcome to Life!*, 1997) by Henryk Dederko takes as his characters those who bought into the rhetoric of capitalism, choosing, to use the well-known slogans from Danny Boyle's *Trainspotting* (1996), 'life, career and electric tin opener'. The film shows the operation of the American firm Amway which sells cleaning products and food supplements, juxtaposing fragments of the firm's own promotional material with interviews with its employees and recordings of interviews between more experienced workers and those who only recently joined the firm. Amway entered the Polish market in the early 1990s and by the time Dederko's film was made had over 80,000 employees. Amway is shortened from 'American way', suggesting that its methods epitomize an American approach to business and life. The film focuses on the recruitment and training of new employees, because these two processes ensure Amway's longevity and are an important source of its income, accounting for about 30 per cent of the firm's total revenue. The new recruits are asked to buy cassettes and books from which they can learn how to become successful businessmen. Rather than being taught how to sell washing powder and toilet cleaner, they are told how to recruit new people willing to sell Amway products. Ultimately, Dederko's film suggests that Amway is not selling commodities, but ideology – the ideology of capitalism (Piątek 2011). It declares that everybody can be a winner if only she puts her heart into it. We hear such statements as 'We have to think what we desire and money will come automatically'. Conversely, losers choose to be losers, because 'poverty is a state of mind' and 'if we surround ourselves with poor people, we become impoverished ourselves', as the Amway gurus teach us. Such views are peddled in the promotional sessions by the most successful people in the organization: the Americans who are high up in firm's hierarchy, as well as some Poles who have proved themselves as outstanding workers. The former address the newcomers from the Amway tapes and travel to Poland to preach Amway modus operandi in training courses which look like political rallies or religious gatherings. The latter recruit new agents, trying to convince them that by joining Amway all their dreams will come true.

The main idea promoted by these people is that it is not technology or material resources, but faith that makes a successful capitalist. This is demonstrated by images of new recruits who during the Amway rally sing the Polish national anthem or lie on the floor in their apartments with headphones, listening to the 'Amway gospel' emanating from the cassettes. These people use their family relations and friendships to sell Amway's products. Hence the title of the film: 'welcome to life' rather than 'welcome to Amway'. By the same token, Dederko's film announces a return of the shock worker or 'new Soviet man', known from Stalinist times. As Boris Groys observes,

> The slogan of the age became 'Nothing is impossible for a Bolshevik'. Any references to facts, technical realities, or objective limits was treated as 'cowardice' and 'unbelief' unworthy of a true Stalinist. It was thought that willpower alone could overcome anything that the bureaucratic, formalistic eye perceived as an insurmountable obstacle. ... Generations were raised on the examples of Pavka Korchagin and Mares'ev, invalids who overcame their physical infirmity through sheer willpower. (Groys 1992: 60; see also chapter 3)

The difference between now and then is that in the past the saying was that 'Nothing is impossible for a Bolshevik' and now 'Nothing is impossible for those embracing capitalism'. However, this claim is undermined by the statistical data presented at the end of the film. The closing titles state that 0.2 per cent of Amway employees earn 95 per cent of the income of the firm. Amway's structure is thus similar to a pyramid (even if this is not a pyramid scheme in the strict sense of the term), in which the few take the chunk of the surplus value created by the many. The many thus work for a pittance in the hope that one day they will join those at the top. This scheme can be seen as a metonym of neoliberal capitalism, with the employees of Amway fitting the type of 'homo neoliberalis', who replaced the old 'homo sovieticus', as suggested by Tomasz Piątek (Piątek 2011: 155).

Predictably, the film was not to the taste of Amway bosses and the firm tried to prevent the broadcast of *Welcome to Life!* on television by suing its producers; they won the court case. This fact attracted much attention in the Polish press as it undermined the widely held view that the media under capitalism are free, unlike under state socialism (for example Malatyńska 1998; Jałoszewski 2002). Unfortunately, the outrage caused by this crude act of censorship overshadowed discussions about the content of the film, namely the inegalitarian character of neoliberalism. The perceptive essay by Tomasz Piątek is the only article I found which attempts to engage with the film text, rather than its production and distribution history.

Notes

1. The unlikely film ending of this sort, referring to great successes of Eastern European intellectuals or artists in the West, can be seen as projections of Eastern filmmakers, hungry for international recognition. In this case this was merely a projection. *Capital* did not travel beyond the borders of Polish cinema.
2. Polanyi describes money as a 'fictitious commodity', together with land and labour, which should not be sold at the market, as much for moral as practical reasons (Polanyi 2001).
3. This can be seen as a nod to Dušan Makavejev's *Sweet Movie* (1974), whose protagonist also travelled in such a way, trying to escape the vicissitudes of capitalism.

CHAPTER 8
The 2000s and Beyond
Accumulation by Dispossession

The Dispossessing and Dispossessed Middle Classes

While in the first decade after the fall of state socialism makers of fiction films focused on 'feral capitalists' and their milder versions, lucky entrepreneurs, who gained as a result of the transition, in the following decade we observe an upsurge of films dealing with the losers in the neoliberal game and the mechanics of accumulation by dispossession. Such a shift can be explained by the evaporation of enthusiasm for neoliberalization, caused by the increased difficulty of making money in Poland and the effect (real and propaganded) of the world economic crisis at the end of the 1990s. Another possible factor was the establishment of the Polish Film Institute in 2005, with its generous system of film subsidies, especially for contemporary films, which allowed for the re-emergence of the auteurist paradigm in Polish cinema, traditionally marked by a pessimistic outlook, even if the new auteurist films employed some conventions of popular cinema.

However, as the first film belonging to this cycle I list *Psy* (*Dogs*, 1992) by Władysław Pasikowski, which was made shortly after the fall of state socialism. *Dogs* was met with enthusiasm by viewers and also achieved critical recognition, despite its surprisingly sympathetic portrayal of the environment of ex-Secret Servicemen (Służba Bezpieczeństwa, the SB), the titular 'dogs'. However, in my opinion its positive reception had less to do with its iconoclastic praising of the functionaries of the apparatus of oppression, and more with its recognition of the existence of the 'other Poland', whose members were attached to their (usually) meagre possessions from the past and frightened by the direction and speed of the changes brought about by the shift to neoliberalism. Setting the film in the environment of the SB showed this risk well because it was particularly affected by this shift. The old SB was dismantled and it was assumed that the institution to replace it would be staffed with a different type of people.

Pasikowski shows that employees of this institution (so called *ubecy* or *esbecy*), who under state socialism constituted the police elite and enjoyed an above-average standard of living, after 1989 are threatened by mass unemployment and the loss of privileges, including free housing. Their only chance of survival in the new world is to prove that they possess 'transferable skills', which could be used in the civil police. The mechanism to determine whether a former secret policeman is fit to make the transition to the civil police is 'verification': a cross between a job interview and a court trial. The film's protagonist, Franz Maurer, is subjected to such a process. We see him for the first time sitting alone in front of about twenty people hidden behind their desks and giving him hostile or curious glances. Outnumbered by his adversaries, Maurer has little chance to win this encounter, but he succeeds thanks to his charisma. From the statements read from Maurer's file by the chair of the Tribunal we learn that he was a professional of the highest standard (he was able to shoot a man from over 200 metres), acted independently and saved the lives of many innocent people. We gather that Maurer joined the secret service not for political reasons, but to prove himself as a man at a time when wars and uprisings were no longer on the agenda. In this sense he can be compared to fictional western secret agents such as James Bond. In his chief interrogator, Senator Wencel, Maurer recognizes a functionary who 'verified' him (professionally and politically) many times before and he comments sarcastically that the systems change, but his interrogator carries on with his job as before. Wencel stands for the old nomenklatura returning to power in the postcommunist world as a representative of the new order. This phenomenon has been discussed by, among other authors, Slavoj Žižek (1997), but Pasikowski refers to the nomenklatura's resurrection before it properly happened; in this sense his film was truly prophetic.

Maurer fights not only for his job, but also for his house. The house is eventually repossessed by his ex-wife, the daughter of an ex-communist dignitary, who currently lives abroad. Her enrichment at Maurer's expense is symbolic of dispossession caused by two agents, who gained economically as a result of the fall of communism: the old nomenklatura and foreigners. His old colleague from the SB also has to return his job-tied flat. This loss of privileges can be seen as a just punishment of oppressors of the people, but also as an example of reducing state property, which was previously in private use, in order to sell or give it to the

Illustration 8.1: Franz Maurer in *Dogs*, directed by Władysław Pasikowski

new elite. An important motif of the SB's dispossession is throwing away the files, on which they worked for many years, to a rubbish dump, pointing to the obsolescence of the professional capital of this particular group of employees or of a much larger group of people, who, as Michnik scornfully said, 'have been trained to manufacture statues of V.I. Lenin, which nobody wanted to buy any more after 1989'.

Pasikowski not only shows the dismantling of the SB, but also the after-life of its employees. Some, including Maurer, pass the 'verification' test and are accepted into the civil police; others, like Maurer's friend Olo, fail and join the mafia, working alongside their counterparts from the Stasi. Neither route comes across as satisfying. Maurer's new boss makes clear to those who passed the verification that while in the past they had little work, were well paid, enjoyed many privileges and their work was secure, under the new regime they will have to work hard for little money and have no additional perks, and if they prove useless, they will face summary dismissal. Although these conditions apply specifically to ex-*ubeks*, they sound like a metaphor of life under neoliberalism in the new Poland. Not surprisingly, the policemen appear shell-shocked. In his new employment in the mafia Olo has to turn against his old friends, who became policemen. A war is thus declared between those who previously were as united as a pack of dogs. During this conflict the majority of Maurer's old pals are killed or wounded. Unable to protect his subordinates and betrayed by those close to him, Maurer ends up in jail and cuts a solitary figure. We are led to believe that without people like Maurer, the new Poland will become a 'mafia republic', in which professionalism will not matter, profit will go to the most ruthless and corrupt few while the bulk of ordinary people will have no protection.

The postcommunist political and social order in *Dogs* mirrors that represented in the Cinema of Moral Concern, except that the postcommunist hierarchy comes across as less worthy than the old communist moghuls and the situation at the bottom is more desperate than in the films of Kieślowski or Holland. A marker of this turn for the worse is the widespread use of violence. Most visible is the physical violence: shootings, beatings, torture, in which members of both the mafia and the police engage. Violence is used against enemies, but also against one's own comrades. We also witness the use of vulgar language which is meant to intimidate opponents and subordinates. While condemning the changes occurring after 1989, Pasikowski suggests that they are inevitable; nobody, except for Maurer, attempts to counter them. Although *Dogs* is routinely described as an example of 'gangster cinema' (Haltof 2002: 248–254), stylistically it is very different from the gangster films discussed in the previous chapter. The film does not focus on action, but stasis, and its tone is melancholic, conveyed by de-saturated colours and sparse mise-en-scène, rendering postcommunist Poland like a desert. The melancholic mood is reinforced by the characters' preference for using the past tense and some unusual grammatical structures (Lisowski 1997: 238) and the jazzy music.

While in the early 1990s *Dogs*, with its focus on losers, was an exception, by the end of the decade and after 2000 we could observe an upsurge of films tackling dispossession. One such film was *Dług* (*Debt*, 1999) by Krzysztof Krauze. The title refers to what was a new phenomenon in Poland and Eastern Europe at large: personal debt. The socialist economy was based on the principle of postponing gratification, of sacrificing the present for the future through saving. By contrast, debt is at the core of the capitalist economy, because to develop their businesses, entrepreneurs have to take out credit. According to Maurizio Lazzarato, the author of *The Making of the Indebted Man*, the neoliberal economy is a debt economy in more senses than one. The majority of citizens living under this system begin and finish their lives having debt and debt affects their behaviour and identity to a greater extent that labour affected earlier generations. As he puts it, 'Debt acts as a "capture", "predation" and "extraction" machine on the whole society, as an instrument for macroeconomic prescription and management, and as a mechanism for income redistribution. It also functions as a mechanism for the production and "government" of collective and individual subjectivities' (Lazzarato 2012: 29).

Because debt is so common under neoliberalism, it is presented as something normal or even positive. 'Borrow now and do not worry about tomorrow' is the approach propagated by the media. Yet, by borrowing we often foreclose our future, becoming slaves to our debt; debt not only fails to multiply our income but extracts what we possessed. Krauze's film presents such an extreme case of dispossession, based on the true story of two budding businessmen who in the 1990s set up a wholesale firm selling cosmetics, but who lacked capital to import the first consignment. As a result, they contacted an acquaintance who promised to lend them the cash they lacked. He did not fulfil his promise, but demanded compensation for his effort and when they were unable to pay it, increased their debt and with his bodyguard began a campaign of intimidation. Brought to the end of their tether, the friends killed their oppressors, and cut off their heads so that the murder looked as if committed by the Russian mafia. They were caught and in 1997 received a severe sentence of twenty-five years in prison. Their story attracted the attention of some journalists, who argued that the punishment was too severe in proportion to the crime. Krauze shared this view and wanted his film to become a 'socially engaged film' (Lubelski 2007: 206–214). As a social intervention *Debt* achieved success – President Kwaśniewski pardoned one of the men in 2005 and his successor, President Kaczyński, pardoned the other man in 2006, largely as a result of the film's outcry.

The style of *Debt* is ascetic, beginning like a 'crime watch' programme, with police arriving at the scene of the crime, trying to find out who was killed and why. The main actors playing in *Debt* were still largely unknown, which helped audiences to see them as real people. As in *Dogs*, the mise-en-scène is limited; there is no attempt to charm us with images of excessive consumption of the 'young wolves' of Polish business. As noted by Krzysztof Ociepa, the diegetic world on this occasion comes across as an extension of the real world (Ociepa 2003: 64). The soundtrack conveys melancholia, as if pointing to a loss which cannot be redeemed, not unlike in *Dogs*.

The main characters are Adam and Stefan, two friends in their late twenties, whose main ambition is to set up a successful business. Their third partner is Tadeusz, nominally a student, but mostly a dealer in second-hand cars. In this respect they are no different from the characters in *First Million*, except that in comparison with them, Frik, Kurtz and Piki were by this point veterans, as they had started as entrepreneurs in childhood. Moreover, they played with their own capital and got more pleasure from the very activity of making money than from the lifestyle which their wealth afforded them. Adam and Stefan, by contrast, come across as amateurs, lured by the mirage of fast 'postcommunist' money. However, they are not into consumption for consumption's sake. For them money is chiefly a means of fulfilling an ideal of bourgeois life. They want to have families and ensure their prosperity; in addition, Adam wants to measure up to his father. Their ambitions render them easy prey for all sorts of unscrupulous people and institutions: they are ideal debtors. We meet them when a bank refuses them credit. Anxious that their plan may never materialize, they accept the offer of an acquaintance, Gerard, that they contact somebody who can guarantee their credit in exchange for paying him a bribe. The transaction is not finalized, but Gerard asks the friends to pay his expenses of several thousand dollars. The story of Adam and Stefan finishes like the real story I already described.

Debt points to the failure of state institutions to help ordinary citizens to realize their potential and protect them against the violence of fellow citizens. We see it during the friends' unsuccessful visit to the bank when an employee makes clear to them that in order to get credit one already has to have money. Another telling moment takes place when Adam and Stefan turn to the police, asking for protection against the extortionist, and the officer expresses his helplessness. However, the policemen prove very effective in finding Gerard's killers and the court punishes them harshly for what was ultimately a killing in self-defence. Krauze also acknowledges the misdemeanours of Adam, Stefan and Tadeusz, and of the extortionist, as the cause of the final tragedy. The fault of Gerard comes across as greater than that of his killers, but none are free of guilt. The principal sins of the three aspiring businessmen are greed and impatience. Off-screen the director described them as people who were anxious not to miss 'the train to Europe' (Chyb 1999: 105). Although the case depicted by Krauze is exceptional in its gruesome consequences, it represents well the logic of neoliberal capitalism, according to which those who do not use their credit (debt) wisely are reduced to slavery. This situation leads to violence, inflicted on those who cannot pay and, if they muster enough courage and strength, on their oppressors.

Krauze also shows that, paradoxically, although younger people have little knowledge of Poland of the period of state socialism, they are less well adjusted to the circumstances of the market economy than their parents. This is because the older generation, not unlike the older generation in the Cinema of Moral Concern, established itself during relatively stable times, owning apartments and cars, having steady jobs and good connections. Young people, on the other hand, must struggle to reach this level of prosperity and power. Those in their forties or older are accustomed to shortages of consumer goods (waiting twenty years for one's own flat and ten years for a car was a typical phenomenon in Poland of the 1970s and 1980s). Younger Poles have less patience; many of them believe that it is possible to become a millionaire overnight, as the careers of Bagsik and Gąsiorowski demonstrate. If Stefan and Adam had been prepared to wait longer to open their business, the father of one of them would have helped them by using his old connections.

Komornik (*Bailiff*, 2005) by Feliks Falk can be seen as a companion piece to *Debt*: a similarity revealed by the films' titles. But there are also differences. *Debt* deals with private debt, *Bailiff* refers to that collected by the representative of the state: the bailiff. This profession nominally existed under state socialism, but then there were fewer bailiffs than after 1989 and their actions were conspicuous due to the ideological dogma that every citizen in a socialist country has the right to a dignified existence free from economic worries. In Polish cinema, the figure of the bailiff was first tackled in the documentary *Urząd* (*Office*) by Maria Zmarz-Koczanowicz, made in 1986, when state socialism in Poland was crumbling. During the postcommunist period, bailiffs cropped up as secondary characters in many films. Falk's protagonist, Lucjan Boehme, is a man of humble background and great ambition. Falk used such a character, in his *Dance Leader* and *Hero of the Year*, as discussed in chapters 5 and 6. Lutek Danielak in these two films could be seen as a living incarnation of late state socialism: he took and gave bribes, acted as a pimp for his girlfriend and prostituted himself, and from time to time had pangs of conscience, but silenced them, regarding his misdemeanours as a condition of survival. He was also malleable and social. He tried to adjust to different circumstances and craved popularity – his very profession as a dance leader testified to this. The people who knew him despised him but were able to live with him. By naming his protagonist Lucjan Falk suggests that in Poland history repeats itself – a sickness pertaining to late state socialism is poisoning Polish society under the postcommunist order. Lutek (which is a shortened version of Lucjan), however, has matured and has to be treated with respect, which points to an opposite trajectory for history to that offered by Marx: not from tragedy to farce, but from farce to tragedy, where 'tragedy' stands for capitalism which came to Poland in 1989. Lucjan's German surname, Boehme, reflects the fact that *Bailiff* is set in Wałbrzych in Lower Silesia, a town which before the Second World War belonged to Germany, and makes its bearer appear more menacing. Wałbrzych was prosperous during the state socialist period thanks to its rich seams of coal, but after 1989 it declined, as did other coalmining regions of Eastern Europe (on the decline of coalmining in Eastern Europe, see Kideckel 2002).

The deadly character of the bailiff's actions is already highlighted in the first scene of Falk's film, when Lucjan repossesses life-saving machines in a hospital. Lucjan's subsequent decisions have comparable gravity. Determined to prove that the signature of an elderly woman who had taken out a bank credit was falsified, he digs up her corpse buried in a field belonging to her family. The discovery ruins the fraudulent family, including a promising footballer, who commits suicide. The very fact that the family uses the dead to get credit can be linked to the idea of self-exploitation, including the exploitation of the dead, as a means of surviving under neoliberalism. Lucjan also repossesses the accordion of a disabled child, which is tantamount to causing the girl's 'spiritual death'. Wherever the bailiff appears, he awakens fear and disgust, but nobody can resist his power. On each occasion we see individuals or small groups of people looking passively at him doing his job or protesting without effect. These images can be viewed as a reflection of the state of the working class after the fall of the Berlin Wall as fragmented, powerless and dispirited (Bunce 2000b; Kideckel 2002; Mazierska 2012d).

The difference between the late socialist past and early capitalist present is also reflected in the contrast between Lucjan and his aging mentor, Robert, who is now terminally ill. Robert claims that he was no angel and always worked to have a good life, but he also respected the need of others to survive and he would never have switched off a life-support machine. Robert stands for a world which was far from perfect, but bearable and comprehensible. Lucjan represents the new world, which is frightening and abstract, and not even fully understood from within, as demonstrated by the fact that Lucjan cannot explain what prompts him and whom he serves, except for his references to the abstract value of 'keeping his files

Illustration 8.2: Lucjan looking for a corpse in *Bailiff*, directed by Feliks Falk

in order'. Such an explanation brings association with capitalism as a system expressing universal rationality (although in reality it serves the capitalist class), as opposed to feudalism or socialism, which were explicitly governed by specific class interests.

The connection of Robert with the old system and Lucjan with the new is augmented by casting. Robert is played by Marian Opania, an actor whose popularity was at its peak in the 1970s and 1980s, while Lucjan is played by Andrzej Chyra, who played the role of a debt collector in *Debt*. While Opania stands for the old world of small people, who inhabited a grey zone between legality and criminality, conformity and dissidence, Lucjan represents a polarized world, in which one either wins or loses everything. As a man who works alone and is accountable only to himself, he also represents the ideal of an 'entrepreneurial individual', promoted in the official rhetoric after the collapse of state socialism in Poland. He is contrasted with other lawyers working in Wałbrzych, who act as a corporation, representing a united front and curbing the individualistic excesses of any one of them. Falk compares their modus operandi with that of the late state socialism, when those seeking power formed 'cliques' and, consequently, corruption and nepotism reigned in Poland. The film suggests that the very worst in Polish history has returned because postcommunist elites are partly made up of the old nomenklatura (on this hypothesis see Wasilewski 1995). Both the individualistic entrepreneurs and corporatist post-nomenklatura advance their positions at the expense of the poor.

Moved by the plight of the child of his ex-girlfriend whom he harmed, Lucjan tries to undo his actions by helping financially those to whom he has caused misery. Yet, nobody wants Lucjan's money; poor people avoid him as much in his new Robin Hood role as they avoided him in his 'punishing angel' guise. This refusal can be seen as proof of the honesty and dignity of the common Polish folk, perhaps motivated by Christian values. At the same time, those dispossessed Poles, as depicted by Falk, cannot move beyond this negative act. They are shown as completely passive and mute recipients of the decisions of those standing above them: the capitalists, politicians and judiciary, who form one 'postcommunist complex'. Falk's film offers no positive vision for postcommunist Poland, rejecting as unworkable and/or immoral three different political-economic systems: the individualistic, 'modern' capitalism, represented by Lucjan at the beginning of the film; the 'new socialism', encapsulated by the contrived and reformed bailiff; and the new, corporatist capitalism, represented by the members of the Wałbrzych establishment, who come across as a new incarnation of the old nomenklatura. In Falk's film, everybody is guilty and, therefore, nobody is really guilty and the status quo is unchallenged. This differentiates *Bailiff* from *Debt*, which avoids using generalizations and metaphors and attempts to identify with precision who is responsible for the final tragedy. Moreover, while *Debt* allows the viewer to understand the characters, *Bailiff* renders them distant by exaggerating their behaviour. There also some stylistic differences between these two films. While *Debt* is slow and melancholic, *Bailiff* is fast and hysterical. Its mise-en-scène exaggerates the kitsch of the new, capitalist Poland and its poverty and despair, adding a surrealist tone to the film. Vivid music also plays such a function. Falk, not unlike in his previous films, implies that both poverty and affluence are aesthetically and morally repulsive. Krauze, in a more realistic way, does not denigrate the attractions of affluence. On the contrary, in a way which sets him apart from the bulk of Polish production of the postcommunist period, he demonstrates that it brings not so much the pleasure of 'wild consumption' (epitomized by expensive cars, drugs and prostitutes), as of social respectability.

Dispossessing and Disciplining of the Proletariat

Dogs, *Debt* and *Bailiff* focus on the plight of middle-class, educated characters who either become dispossessed themselves or act as the dispossessors of others. The 2000s and 2010s also saw the production of films about the plight of manual workers under neoliberalism. I will focus here on two films about shop employees, whose inhumane conditions became famous. These are *Dzień kobiet* (*Women's Day*, 2012) by Maria Sadowska and *Supermarket* (2012) by Maciej Żak.

Women's Day, as its title suggests, concerns the plight of working-class women. Its title alludes to International Women's Day, which was originally called International Working Women's Day, and celebrated women's fight for their rights as workers. Under state socialism, this holiday, together with May Day celebrations, was used not to signify the need for continuous struggle to improve female workers' lot, but to celebrate the achievements of women under this system. Consequently, many Eastern European feminists boycotted it, seeing it as a smokescreen obscuring the real gender inequality which was not properly addressed by the authorities. However, while state socialism fell short of its promise to emancipate women, it offered them certain benefits, such as heavily subsidized childcare and access to termination of pregnancy. After its fall, many of these privileges were withdrawn, without giving women any compensation for their loss and this was often done under the banner of 'retraditionalization': a return to family life, and religion (Kligman 1994: 256). Instead of allowing women to work at a time convenient to them, flexible employment – a cornerstone of neoliberal working practices – forces them to work when it suits their employers, which usually means longer hours on lower wages at more inconvenient times. The retail sector, where more women than men find employment, is particularly disadvantageous, because shops under neoliberalism tend to be open much longer than under state socialism and in the quest for savings, fewer employees are asked to do more jobs. Stories about horrendous exploitation of labourers, perpetuated by supermarket managers, started to fill the pages of national newspapers in Poland in the 2000s. One of them concerned Bożena Łopacka, a shop assistant in the Biedronka supermarket chain, who took her employer to court on the grounds of particularly harsh and unfair working conditions, including having to do extra hours without pay and not being able to leave the cash register for many hours, even to go to the toilet. Łopacka's story was the main source of inspiration for Sadowska's movie, although she enriched it with other motifs, no doubt to increase the dramatic effect of the film.

Women's Day begins when Halina, an ordinary employee in the Motylek supermarket (Motylek means 'butterfly', a nod to the infamous Biedronka, which means 'ladybird'), is promoted to a managerial position. For Halina it means more money she badly needs, being a single mother with a teenage daughter. She also believes that her promotion will lead to better organization of work in the shop, hence improvement for her work mates. However, she soon learns that it means more duties than privileges. Halina is asked to work extra hours for free and to force others to work the same way, including a pregnant colleague who miscarries while on duty. She also has to fire another woman to ensure more savings for her company. All the work which the women have to do is back-breaking physical labour, such as unloading large quantities of commodities, because the firm, to create more profit, refuses to use trolleys: all the work has to be done manually. This calls to mind concentration camps, where the survival of one group of prisoners was always at the expense of another group and, despite the claim of the modernity of the Nazi state, the labourers used primitive tools so that their work looked like a road back to medieval times (on work in concentration camp see Piper 2002; on their representation in films see Mazierska 2013). As a reward for her loyalty to the firm, Halina is sent to a training camp for Motylek's managers, where she learns that the highest value for her firm is productivity and hence it should also be the goal for their employees. The employees are expected to internalize their employer's ethos by singing songs praising the firm. Again, this practice likens Sadowska's Motylek to the Nazi concentration camps where playing music and singing songs was added to the oppression of the prisoners, as shown, for example, in Wanda Jakubowska's *Ostatni etap* (*The Last Stage*, 1947) (Talarczyk-Gubała 2015: 212). Another 'perk' which Halina receives at work is sex with her boss. Initially she believes that he is seriously interested in her, only to learn later that he also has sex with other female employees. In Motylek private and public spheres intermingle; sex is used by men in positions of power to extract pleasure for themselves and extra commitment from the gullible women, as demonstrated by the fact that the type of sex prevailing in this environment is fellatio. As mentioned in the previous chapters, under state socialism the private and the public was also intermingled. One recalls an episode in *Brunet Will Call* when the female shop manager closed the shop to have sex with the man who brought her supplies.

However, in Bareja's film the public sphere was used for private advantage and the employer (the state) suffered, as well as the customers who could not buy the goods when the shop was closed. Under neoliberalism, by contrast, private resources are used to enrich the owner of the supermarket and the employee suffers. Ultimately Halina's promotion in *Motylek* not only fails to bring her any considerable improvement, but actually worsens her material situation and drives a wedge between her and her female co-workers. Brought to the brink of despair, she decides to fight back, and wins in the court, receiving compensation, moral satisfaction and a victory for other mistreated employees.

The director herself compared her film to a western (Sadowska 2013), but it has more in common with a melodrama, a genre which uses exaggeration to illuminate the plight of (often naive) women. In *Women's Day* men abuse women and women abuse other women for the sake of getting favours from men, who in this film represent not so much the 'voice of the father', as the 'voice of Capital'. *Women's Day* is, to use Robert Bechtold Heilman's terminology (see chapter 1), 'monopathic', painting a black and white world, where bad corporations feed on the bodies of good female workers, like male vampires feeding on the bodies of virgins. At one point Halina even compares herself to a virgin, before she has sex with her vampiric manager. To strengthen its emotional effect, the film is filled with (melo)dramatic events, such as the death of Halina's mother. There is also an obligatory episode with a bailiff trying to evict Halina from her apartment. This accumulation of misfortune does not render the film particularly subtle, yet registers the precarious position of Polish manual workers in the neoliberal reality, as well as, perhaps, pointing to the Polish audience's desensitization to ordinary misfortunes. While the shift from state socialism to postcommunism is associated with the eastern world gaining access to advanced technology, most importantly electronic equipment, Sadowska shows that for those at the receiving end the new system means returning to a more primitive technological stage, epitomized by Halina's fishing trip to get food for supper.[1] Although *Women's Day* criticizes neoliberalism, its political programme is modest, merely requiring that the employers obey the law and respect some minimal standards of employment. A return to any form of socialism is nowhere on the agenda.

Supermarket can be seen as a companion piece to *Women's Day*, as it also shows work in a supermarket, albeit from a distinctly male perspective: that of security, employing the conventions of a thriller, with the titular supermarket being like a prison, entrapping the customers and the employees. The most constrained are the security guards, as they cannot leave their workplace and are under immense pressure to produce results, capturing thieving customers or 'creating' them by any means available. Technology in the form of CCTV cameras is presented as an effective tool for the security guards to spy on the customers and each other. The supermarket thus comes across as a gigantic panopticon, confirming Harvey's observation that although neoliberalism preaches freedom, its true concern is security, most importantly protecting private property (Harvey 2005a: 183–206). As in other films discussed in this chapter, *Supermarket* also draws attention to debt as an effective means of creating 'docile bodies'. The guilt of being indebted is inculcated in the security guards, who are told by the supermarket's manager that a large amount of goods were stolen from under their noses (we find in due course that it is the manager himself who is stealing them). Although they are not asked to pay for them from their own pocket, they are threatened with the termination of their contract. This leads their head, Jaśmiński, to double his efforts to be vigilant, putting extra pressure on his team to find guilty customers and, when such a customer is found, tormenting him to confess that he is guilty of a serious theft, although in reality he only forgot to pay for a chocolate bar which he ate in the shop. As in Krauze's *Debt*, the violence escalates till it leads to the death of this innocent man, for which another innocent man is accused. As one of the reviewers noted, the film shows how little is needed to be killed under capitalism (Tambor 2013: 67).

Like *Women's Day*, *Supermarket* plays on the contrast between the facade of the supermarket as a 'temple of joy' and the violence perpetrated in its back rooms. The film is set during the last day of the year and the management wants to finish the year on an upbeat note by offering an artistic programme. The programme is meant to include the performance of a pop star and a lottery for customers. As is usually the case in capitalist firms, the supermarket 'markets itself' as a charitable institution by declaring that it supports the local orphans. It is worth mentioning in this context that when McDonalds' opened its first restaurant in Poland in 1992, it was also presented as a charitable organization entering the Polish market. During its opening the firm's boss presented to the then minister of work and social affairs, Jacek Kuroń, who was also a famous Polish dissident, a cheque for poor people (Szcześniak 2012). Nobody asked then where this money came from, although one can imagine that it was stolen from the underpaid employees. In Żak's film, the artistic programme for the customers comes at the expense of extra work put in by the staff and violence inflicted on them. At one point we see the manager humiliating a female employee for making a spelling mistake when preparing a slogan. This episode can be compared to a mistake committed by the team preparing a poster with Stalin's face in Jerzy Skolimowski's *Ręce do góry* (*Hands Up!*, 1967). It feels like the sanctions of making mistakes in a commercial environment are at least as serious as making them under Stalinism. However, as with *Women's Day*, Żak offers no 'way out' of this hell, no social or political alternative. The impression that there is no alternative is augmented by how the exteriors are presented in a similar way to the interiors. Both spaces come across as Marc Augé's 'non-places', devoid of culture and human warmth or even the severe beauty of factories in the 1960s films of Skolimowski or Has. People do not want to be there, but they end up there nevertheless (Augé 1995). Such a situation brings to mind Jean-Luc Godard's film, *Tout va bien* (1972), where the female protagonist says that outside the supermarket is only a supermarket. Still, in *Tout va bien* the characters envisaged a different future and were able to fight for it individually and collectively. In *Supermarket* this is no longer the case.

Into the West and Back

Among the freedoms achieved by Poles following the fall of state socialism was the freedom to seek employment abroad. This subject is tackled by several films, such as *Bar na Viktorii* (*A Bar at Victoria Station*, 2003), a documentary directed by Leszek Dawid about two unskilled young men from Kluczbork, a small town in southwestern Poland, seeking work in England. The film premiered only one year before Poland joined the European Union, of which a major benefit was the possibility of gaining legal employment in Britain. It depicts a time when it was still illegal for Poles to work in Britain and hence getting the work permit is an important factor in the two men's circumstances. By the same token, it is an opportunity for various feral entrepreneurs to make money, taking advantage of the naiveté and despair of poor foreigners. The film's protagonists, Piotr and Marek, are promised a job in a hotel if they pay 45, 120 or 150 GBP for a false work permit and then discover that they have paid to get jobs which in reality do not exist. As the days pass, they get more desperate to get any work, even a job paid as little as two pounds per hour, but it does not materialize, while their situation worsens. They spend the little money they brought to the UK, have to leave the room of their friend who allowed them to stay with them for free, and their shoes get worn out. In the end they ask the question: 'Why do Poles have to go abroad to earn their living?' The director leaves the characters at the time when one of them decides to return to Poland, although from the closing titles we learn that they both stayed in London where they eventually found employment. Even if *A Bar at Victoria Station* has an off-screen happy ending, we get the impression that it comes at a heavy price: misery, humiliation and home sickness. The title of the film refers to a dream one of the characters shares with the viewers: having a small bar at Victoria station, where he could sell Polish dishes, such as bigos and borsch with croquets. They also talk about their desire to get married, have a child and a house. Although the men are victims of the capitalist order, they identify with the ideal of a private entrepreneur and the bourgeois lifestyle, not unlike the protagonists of *Debt*. Having this film in mind, we realize that under neoliberalism trying to fulfil such a dream might lead to tragedy.

A Bar at Victoria Station was Dawid's student film and it was made under the supervision of Kazimierz Karabasz, whose films I discussed in the previous chapters. Karabasz's influence can be detected in the film's style, consisting of following a working-class character (or two in this case) who describe their situation in their own words. Although it would be easy to make fun of Piotr and Marek, whose coarse language might put off a sensitive ear, ultimately the film elicits compassion and conveys well some universal emotions pertaining to those seeking jobs: anxiety, low self-esteem and a sense of injustice. What the film is missing, however, is any attempt to explain why thousands of people like Piotr and Marek have to leave their towns and villages to earn their daily bread. As the director admits in the interview, he merely wanted to make a film about two young men who might choose a different path, for example fall in love during their journey, rather than one which analyses a social phenomenon (quoted in Pietrzak 2011: 107). In his analysis of *A Bar at Victoria Station* Jarosław Pietrzak, rightly, in my view, attributes such lack of political ambition on the part of the director to the dominant ideology, which discourages attacks on its (neoliberal) foundations (ibid.: 108).

By contrast, an explanation of why young Polish people leave Poland is offered in *Śląsk* (*Silesia*), directed by Anna Kazejak-Dawid, which constitutes one part of an omnibus film, *Oda do radości* (*Ode to Joy*, 2006), directed, apart from Kazejak-Dawid, also by Jan Komasa and Maciej Migas, and it might in fact please the neoliberal rulers. The film was made after Poland joined the European Union, which for Polish migrants removed the problem of getting a false work permit in order to work in Britain. Although the film tackles migration, it is largely set in Bytom, where before 1989 the working classes enjoyed an above-average standard of living. Bytom even acted as a magnet for young men from far away who sought employment there in the coalmines, and later proved a stronghold for the Solidarity movement because workers' organizations were most powerful in large industrial centres. Due to Bytom's previous prosperity and heroic past, the economic crisis it suffered after 1989 appeared especially acute, although Silesia is still considered the land of plenty, compared to the 'post-PGR Poland'. In the first scene of the film the main character, Aga, hears on the radio that there are strikes in several Silesian coalmines. This information reaches her in London, during a bus journey to her home town. The radio also mentions Polish victims of the London underground bombing of 7 July 2005. Thus we can deduce that for Aga there is no good place to live. In England, she is condemned to a lack of personal security, and in Poland to the harsh reality of factories closing down and the political conflict to which such closures lead. In subsequent parts, the film underscores this message by visually connecting London with Bytom, showing in both cities vast areas covered by apartment blocks, which come across as soulless machines for living. By pointing to the propinquity of London and Bytom, Kazejak-Dawid also connects the end of state socialism with the current state of the First World. As Charity Scribner notes, 'The [state socialist] system's collapse prompted comparisons to the exhausted welfare states of the West, particularly in Britain and France' (Scribner 2005: 64). This relationship provides a framework for Aga's story.

Unlike Piotr and Marek, Aga belongs to the 'lucky ones': those who found employment in London. However, following a year of hard work there, and the realization that in England she would be condemned to menial work, Aga is determined to find a place in her home town. Concerned with the mental health of her mother, who is an unemployed hairdresser, Aga decides to invest her savings in a hairdressing salon with up-to-date tanning facilities, where she can also work. The film suggests that her 'Calvinist trajectory' from a hard-working manual labourer to a capitalist would have been successful if not for the workers themselves, who prevent the more resourceful from improving their lot. This is demonstrated in a scene depicting a Solidarity demonstration against the mine's closure, which changes into hooligan attacks on local businesses, including the hairdressing salon which Aga and her mother were about to open. In this case we do not really witness accumulation by dispossession, but merely dispossession of the poor by the poor, with nothing being accumulated. The result is not only the loss of material possessions, and for Aga the need to return to London to recuperate her losses, but the loss of language, as conveyed by Aga's mother's silence.

Aga's father, who is one of the leaders of the strike, feels little remorse for causing such mayhem. When confronted by Aga, he tells her that organizing the demonstration was the right thing to do because it led the authorities to reverse their decision to close the mine and showed that Solidarity still mattered. For him, the destruction of small businesses was merely a hiccup in a successful action. Yet, Kazejak-Dawid makes us identify with the perspective of Aga, who disagrees. Solidarity in *Silesia* is a force of conservatism, preventing ex-workers from becoming small entrepreneurs and Poland moving from the Fordist to the post-Fordist stage of capitalism. Its reactionary character is underscored by the fact that the strikers are obsessively attached to symbols. Aga's father is offended when she sits on the Solidarity banner, which provides a poignant contrast to his indifference to the news about the vandalizing of the hairdressing salon. Kazejak-Dawid's criticism of Solidarity as the skansen of people with a 'homo sovieticus' mindset is made from a gender perspective. The director does not miss the opportunity to show that the custodians of the working-class traditions are all male and middle-aged, for whom the ambitions and plans of their wives and daughters are of little importance. The people who destroy Aga's business are also male, although younger. Such a situation encourages one to look back to the times of the 'first Solidarity', led by Lech Wałęsa. During this period, which ended with the victory of the Solidarity camp in the 1989 and 1990 elections, there appeared voices articulating the need to cater for the specific interests of female workers, as well as other disadvantaged groups. Yet, these voices were suppressed in order, as it was presented at the time, to prevent the fragmentation of the workers' movement. The assumption was that after the victory of Solidarity, these 'minor voices' would be heard and their needs addressed. This hope, however, was never fulfilled: subsequent governments, many of them dominated by Solidarity activists, proved anti-female. Kazejak-Dawid's film thus suggests that accepting unity in the 1980s led to disunity in the 2000s, and further discourages such unity along the lines of gender politics. This does not mean that identity politics has to oppose (pro-worker) class politics; but the challenge is to make them work for each other (Harvey 2010b: 227–260). For that, however, both similarities and differences between different types of interests should be acknowledged and respected, which poignantly does not happen in either Polish political reality[2] or in Kazejak-Dawid's film.

Warszawa do wzięcia (*Warsaw Available*, 2009) by Karolina Bielawska and Julia Ruszkiewicz does not tackle foreign migration, only migration from the country to the city, but I decided to discuss it in this section, as migrants portrayed in this film encounter similar problems to those in *Silesia* and *A Bar at Victoria Station*. The film can also be seen in the context of the 'post-PGR films', analysed in the previous chapter, because it concerns people who are determined to leave a post-PGR village. To an even larger extent than Dawid's film, *Warsaw Available* shows the strong influence of Kazimierz Karabasz's style, most importantly his film *Krystyna M.*, discussed in chapter 5. The film follows in the footsteps of an ordinary person, who is meant to represent a larger group of those who moved from the country to the city. However, there are also differences. Karabasz in *Krystyna M.* presented the story of only one young woman. Her character thus appeared, on the one hand, more individualized, but on the other hand paradigmatic for the whole generation of young people, who moved from the province to Warsaw. Bielawska and Ruszkiewicz follow three young women as if to reflect on the fact that there is no single or even dominant scenario of migration; much depends, for example, on the person's initial circumstances. The three women, Ania, Gosia and Ilona, move from the countryside to the city, taking advantage of a 'Bursa' (Boarding School) programme offered to young women from villages where there used to be PGRs to relocate to Warsaw. Each of the girls, who are between eighteen and twenty-one years old, comes from a modest, although not very poor or pathological background. They only finished secondary school and never had a job requiring advanced skills. There are also differences between them. Gosia has little to tie her to her native village and is most optimistic about her metropolitan future. Ania left a boyfriend in another village and Ilona, who is a single mother, left her little son with her own mother, to find employment in the capital. The film just points to two forces in the lives of Ania and Ilona: centripetal and centrifugal. Each force is very strong – the girls are under great pressure to succeed in Warsaw, but also they miss what they have left in the province. In this respect only Gosia can be seen as a contemporary version of Karabasz's Krystyna M. Life in Warsaw turns out to be hard. The manual work in service industries – such as restaurants, bars, shops and in security – which the girls eventually find requires working long hours and being available to their employers all the time. It is a 'zero-hour contract' type of work. As a result, even a monthly visit to see their family and friends becomes a luxury. Another reason why the young women find it difficult to achieve success in Warsaw is the harsh regime of surveillance, to which they are subjected both at work and at home. After work they have to attend courses where they learn new skills, mostly how to wear the right type of clothes when attending a job interview, talk to one's boss, and prepare food and eat in a 'middle class' way. In the dormitory, where they are allowed to live for several months free of charge, they have to leave the shelves and the floor perfectly clean and make their beds to the satisfaction of a stern, even mildly sadistic supervisor. The whole regime is geared towards producing Foucauldian 'docile bodies'. This is unlike Krystyna in Karabasz's film, for whom it was enough to fulfil her duty to be accepted and rewarded at work and who did what she pleased in her small apartment. *Warsaw Available* is the story of a contemporary precariat, with few employment rights and no security.

During the course of the narrative Ania and Ilona give up and return to the provinces, blaming it on their weakness, not being able to bear separation from their loved ones. Their attitude reflects on the neoliberal ethics, which makes the individual responsible for her failure. We assume that Gosia will stay in Warsaw but the final titles state that she also lost her job and had to leave Warsaw. From the closing titles we also learn that out of 892 girls who took part in the 'Bursa' programme, 479 finished it and found employment in Warsaw, but nobody knows how many of them remained there long-term. The film intimates that its overall success rate might be low; hence this is not the best way to address the problem of unemployment and poverty in the Polish countryside. A better way would be to change the provinces, to make them more prosperous, so that girls like Ania, Gosia and Ilona could stay there, where they all ultimately wanted to be. This message is reiterated by the girls' comments about Warsaw and the film's mise-en-scène. Ania and Ilona mention again and again that they dislike Warsaw, that they feel alien there and have acquired a sense of inferiority which they did not have in their home villages. Warsaw, previously known to them only from the media, on direct experience turns out to be greyer than the villages which they left behind. The space in which they move, such as the railway station ('Warszawa Centralna') and the nearby shopping mall, full of adverts encouraging consumption, underscore their transitory status and inferiority as consumers, as they cannot afford any of the things which are advertised; similarly, their work in bars and restaurants points to their status as servants with practically no rights.

Unlike under state socialism, when the state took upon itself the duty of facilitating the transition of the workers from the country to the city, now this task is relocated to a Catholic charity. Although this fact is merely mentioned in passing in the film, its importance cannot be overestimated. This is because charities are not accountable to the whole society but only to those who support them, they often act against the interests of the whole society, and they offer less sustainable help than that of state institutions. Furthermore, as the word 'charity' indicates, the recipients of their assistance have to accept it as an act of somebody's good will, thus without complaining, unlike a client of the state, who might demand better treatment. This is what we observe in the film – the girls are subjected to a tremendous pressure to succeed in a short period, because this might be their only chance.

In Lieu of Conclusions: Solidarity's Ghost Town

I decided to finish this chapter with *Solidarność, Solidarność* (*Solidarity, Solidarity...*, 2005), an omnibus film made by thirteen directors of different generations, asked to commemorate the twenty-fifth anniversary of the strikes of 1980, which led to the legalization of the Solidarity trade union in the same year. Through its very structure, the film acknowledges that there is no 'master narrative' about Solidarity; its history is open to multiple interpretations which compete with each other for the viewers' attention and sympathy. As Tadeusz Szyma admits, the subject is now too big and too complex to be tackled by one director (Szyma 2005: 54). Yet it should be added that the film was initiated by Andrzej Wajda, who suggested its production to Polish state television. By presenting himself as the 'father' of this project and making an episode which includes the stars of *Man of Iron*, Krystyna Janda and Jerzy Radziwiłowicz, as well as the leader of the first Solidarity, Lech Wałęsa, Wajda tacitly suggests that his narrative is still privileged; if it is not a 'master-narrative' then it at least remains a 'father narrative'.

The majority of the episodes are set in the present and take issue with the legacy of the events of 1980 and 1981. Paradoxically, older directors, such as Robert Gliński, Ryszard Bugajski, Jacek Bromski and even Andrzej Wajda, tend to be dismissive about the fruits of the Solidarity revolution. In Bugajski's episode, which takes the form of a music video, the veteran of Polish rock, Ryszard Markowski, sings about Polish history, beginning in the year 1968 and finishing in 2005. His narrative acknowledges the victory of Solidarity, but also the erosion of its ethos post-1989, especially the disappearance of solidarity from Polish life. In Wajda's episode the director of *Man of Iron* interviews Lech Wałęsa, who admits that the early 1980s was the last moment of Polish history when the working class mattered in Poland and, by extension, in the whole of Eastern Europe. This was because its importance relied on the Soviet Union's demand for the products of heavy industry, provided by Poland and other 'satellite' countries. Once this demand diminished, the working class declined, as the capitalist West does not want Polish coal or ships. We can conclude that the West, which in *Man of Iron* functioned as the chief ally of Polish workers struggling to overcome state socialism, ultimately proved a false friend.

The conclusion that Solidarity did not do the shipyard workers any good is evinced in the episode by Robert Gliński, who through the medium of Japanese tourists takes us on a tour of the old shipyard in Gdańsk, where the famous strike began. The yard is now derelict, looking like a ghost town, a clear metaphor for the decline of the working class in Poland. The workforce in the Gdańsk shipyard, which was about 20,000 strong at the time Wajda and Zajączkowski shot their films, was after 1989 reduced to about 2,000, labouring in over seventy different private companies. Decimated, fragmented and threatened with unemployment, this workforce has little chance of attracting attention to their plight, not least because they now work in a democratic country. Once famous for its ships and the political engagement of the workers, today the shipyard is better known as a destination for tourists and musicians. In the mid-2000s Jean-Michel Jarre and David Gilmour performed there to celebrate the Solidarity 'revolution'. It also hosts a lavish 'European Solidarity Centre', a museum and performance space devoted to the memory and heritage of Solidarity. In this sense the trajectory of the Gdańsk shipyard is following in the footsteps of such famous factories as the factory buildings in New York adopted by Andy Warhol for his studio in the 1960s, and in Manchester by Tony Wilson for Factory Records in the 1970s, proving that post-Fordism might be good for the artists and other factory workers, but not for the blue-collar workers.

Notes

1. A similar image appears in *Rosetta* (1998) by Luc and Jean-Pierre Dardenne, whose titular character also catches fish, although using more primitive equipment than Halina.
2. The shift from class politics to identity politics in Solidarity itself constitutes an important motif of David Ost's book, *The Defeat of Solidarity* (2005).

Bibliography

Adamczak, Marcin (2010). *Globalne Hollywood, filmowa Europa i polskie kino po 1989 roku: Przeobrażenia kultury audiowizualnej przełomu stuleci* (Gdańsk: Słowo/ Obraz Terytoria).
——— (2012). 'Rashomon: Kinematografia okresu PRL', *Człowiek i społeczeństwo*, 34, pp. 177–195.
Adorno, Theodor (1991). *The Culture Industry: Selected Essays on Mass Culture* (London: Routledge).
——— and Max Horkheimer (2002). *The Dialectics of Enlightenment – Philosophical Fragments*, trans. E. Jephcott (Stanford: Stanford University Press).
Agamben, Giorgio (1998). *Homo Sacer: Sovereign Power and Bare Life*, trans. Daniel Heller-Roazen (Stanford: Stanford University Press).
Altman, Rick (1987). *The American Film Musical* (Bloomington and Indianapolis: Indiana University Press).
Armatys, Barbara and Leszek (1988). 'Film krótkometrażowy', in Barbara Armatys, Leszek Armatys and Wiesław Stradomski (eds), *Historia Filmu Polskiego*, Volume 2 (Warsaw: Wydawnictwa Artystyczne i Filmowe), pp. 139–203.
Aslund, Anders (1985). *Private Enterprise in Eastern Europe* (London: Macmillan).
Atanasovski, Srdan and Ana Petrov (2015). 'Carnal Encounters and Producing Socialist Yugoslavia', *Studies in Eastern European Cinema*, 1, pp. 21–32.
Augé, Marc (1995). *Non-places: Introduction to an Anthropology of Supermodernity* (London: Verso).
Auslander, Philip (1992). *Presence and Resistance: Postmodernism and Cultural Politics in Contemporary American Performance* (Ann Arbor: University of Michigan Press).
Badiou, Alain (2010). *The Communist Hypothesis*, trans. David Macey and Steve Corcoran (London: Verso).
Bakhtin, Mikhail (1979). 'Laughter and Freedom', in Maynard Solomon (ed.), *Marxism and Art: Essays Classic and Contemporary* (Sussex: Harvester Press), pp. 295–300.
Banaszkiewicz, Władysław (1966). 'Pierwsze lata niepodległości', in *Historia Filmu Polskiego*, Volume 1 (Warszawa: Wydawnictwa Artystyczne i Filmowe), pp. 117–178.
Bardan, Alice (2013). 'The New European Cinema of Precarity: A Transnational Perspective', in Ewa Mazierska (ed.), *Work in Cinema: Labor and the Human Condition* (New York: Palgrave Macmillan), pp. 69–90.
Bartha, Eszter (2013). *Alienating Labour: Workers on the Road from Socialism to Capitalism in East Germany and Hungary* (Oxford: Berghahn).

Bator, Monika (2011). 'Polskie kino popularne okresu dwudziestolecia międzywojennego w oczach miejskiej prowincjonalnej publiczności', in Piotr Zwierzchowski and Daria Mazur (eds), *Polskie Kino Popularne* (Bydgoszcz: Wydawnictwo Uniwersytetu Kazimierza Wielkiego), pp. 36–50.

Bauman, Zygmunt (2005). *Work, Consumerism and the New Poor*, Second Edition (Maidenhead: Open University Press).

Beinek, Justyna (2011). '"There is no such City as London": The Idea of "the West" in Polish Film Pre- and Post-1989', *Warsaw East European Review*, pp. 143–162.

Berardi, Franco 'Bifo' (2009). *Precarious Rhapsody: Semiocapitalism and the Pathologies of the Post-Alpha Generation* (Wivenhoe, New York, Port Watson: Minor Compositions).

Berend, Ivan T. (1996). *Central and Eastern Europe, 1944-1993: Detour from the Periphery to the Periphery* (Cambridge: Cambridge University Press).

Berliner, Joseph S. (2010). 'Conclusion: Reflections on the Social Legacy of Communism', in James R. Millar and Sharon L. Wolchik (eds), *The Social Legacy of Communism* (Cambridge: Cambridge University Press), pp. 379–385.

Bethell, Nicholas (1972). *Gomułka: His Poland and His Communism* (London: Pelican).

Bhabha, Homi K. (1994). *The Location of Culture* (London: Routledge).

Bloch, Ernst (1986) [1959]. *The Principle of Hope* (Cambridge, Massachusetts: MIT Press).

Bocheńska, Jadwiga (1974). 'Film dokumentalny', in Jerzy Toeplitz (ed.), *Historia Filmu Polskiego*, Volume 3 (Warsaw: Wydawnictwa Artystyczne i Filmowe), pp. 366–374.

Bohle, Dorothee and Béla Greskovits (2007). 'Neoliberalism, Embedded Neoliberalism and Neocorporatism: Towards Transnational Capitalism in Central-Eastern Europe', *West European Politics*, 3, pp. 443–466.

Boltanski, Luc and Eve Chiapello (2005) [1999]. *The New Spirit of Capitalism*, trans. Gregory Elliott (London: Verso).

Bonnell, Victoria E. (1997). *Iconography of Power: Soviet Political Posters under Lenin and Stalin* (Berkeley: University of California Press).

Bordwell, David, Janet Steiger and Kristin Thomson (1985). *The Classical Hollywood Cinema: Film Style and Mode of Production to 1960* (London: Routledge).

Bourdieu, Pierre (1986) [1983]. 'The Forms of Capital', in John G. Richardson (ed.), *Handbook of Theory and Research for the Sociology of Education* (New York: Greenwood Press), pp. 241–258.

—— (1990a). *In Other Words: Essays Towards a Reflexive Sociology* (Cambridge: Polity).

—— (1990b). *The Logic of Practice* (Cambridge: Polity).

—— (1998). 'The Essence of Neoliberalism', trans. Jeremy J. Shapiro, *Le Monde diplomatique*, December, http://mondediplo.com/1998/12/08bourdieu. Accessed 12 January 2014.

Brodziński, Bohdan (1971). 'The Polish Economy in the Inter-war and Post-war Years', in Jan Ostaszewski (ed.), *Modern Poland Between East and West* (London: The Polish School of Political and Social Science), pp. 110–122.

Bromke, Adam (1962). 'Nationalism and Communism in Poland', *Foreign Affairs*, http://www.foreignaffairs.com/articles/23431/adam-bromke/nationalism-and-communism-in-poland. Accessed 12 February 2014.
—— (1971). 'Beyond the Gomulka Era', *Foreign Affairs*, http://www.foreignaffairs.com/articles/24249/adam-bromke/beyond-the-gomulka-era. Accessed 20 March 2014.
—— (1981). 'Policy and Politics in Gierek's Poland', in Maurice D. Simon and Roger E. Kanet (eds), *Background to Crisis: Policy and Politics in Gierek's Poland* (Boulder, Colorado: Westview Press), pp. 3–23.
Bryll, Ernest (1962). 'Statek kabotynów', *Współczesność*, 7, p. 5.
Brzostek, Błażej (2002). *Robotnicy Warszawy: Konflikty codzienne (1950-1954)* (Warsaw: Trio).
—— (2006). 'Robotnicy Paryża i Warszawy w połowie XX wieku', in Jerzy Kochanowski (ed.), *Warszawa: W połowie drogi między Paryżem a Kijowem* (Warsaw: Trio), pp. 11–66.
Bunce, Valerie (1999a). *Subversive Institutions: The Design and the Destruction of Socialism and the State* (Cambridge: Cambridge University Press).
—— (1999b). 'The Political Economy of Postsocialism', *Slavic Review*, 4, pp. 754–793.
Burawoy, Michael and János Lukács (1992). *The Radiant Past: Ideology and Reality in Hungary's Road to Capitalism* (Chicago: The University of Chicago Press).
Bürger, Peter (1994). *Theory of the Avant-Garde*, trans. Michael Shaw (Minneapolis: University of Minnesota Press).
Butler, Judith (1999) [1990]. *Gender Trouble: Feminism and the Subversion of Identity* (London: Routledge).
Cękalski, Eugeniusz (1950). 'Jak powstały Dwie Brygady?', *Film*, 14, pp. 8–9.
Chanan, Michael (2009). 'The Space between Fiction and Documentary in Latin American Cinema: Notes toward a Genealogy', in Miriam Haddu and Joanna Page (eds), *Visual Synergies in Fiction and Documentary Film from Latin America* (Basingstoke: Palgrave), pp. 15–26.
Choroszewski, Włodzimierz (1971). 'Poland under the Stalin-Bierut Regime: 1945-1956', in Jan Ostaszewski (ed.), *Modern Poland Between East and West* (London: The Polish School of Political and Social Science), pp. 54–75.
Chyb, Manana (1999). 'Trzeba się pilnować', *Film*, 11, pp. 104–105.
Ciborowski, Tomasz and Grzegorz Konat (2010). 'Między II a III RP. Gospodarka Polski Ludowej', in Jakub Majmurek and Piotr Szumlewicz (eds), *PRL bez uprzedzeń* (Warsaw: Książka i Prasa), pp. 17–49.
Cieśliński, Marek (2006). *Piękniej niż w życiu: Polska Kronika Filmowa 1944-1994* (Warsaw: Trio).
Clark, Katerina (1981). *The Soviet Novel: History as Ritual* (Chicago: University of Chicago Press).
Coates, Paul (1999). 'Kieślowski and the Crisis of Documentary', in Paul Coates (ed.), *Lucid Dreams: The Films of Krzysztof Kieslowski* (Trowbridge: Flicks Books), pp. 32–53.
—— (2005). *The Red and the White: The Cinema of People's Poland* (London: Wallflower).

—— (2008). 'Ideologie sacrum i profanum: "Europa" oraz "wieś i miasto" w kinie polskim po 1989 roku', in Konrad Klejsa and Ewelina Nurczyńska-Fidelska (eds), *Kino polskie: Reinterpretacje. Historia-Ideologia-Polityka* (Kraków: Rabid), pp. 287–295.

—— (2014). 'Kieślowski and Kafka at the Office: Realism and/as Modernism', *Short Film Studies*, 1, pp. 41–44.

Comolli, Jean-Luc and Jean Narboni (1992) [1969]. 'Cinema/Ideology/Criticism', in Gerald Mast, Marshall Cohen and Leo Braudy (eds.), *Film Theory and Criticism*, Fourth Edition (Oxford: Oxford University Press), pp. 682–689.

Crampton, R.J. (1997). *Eastern Europe in the Twentieth Century – And After*, Second Edition (London: Routledge).

Crowley, David (2002). 'Warsaw Interiors: The Public Life of Private Spaces, 1949-65', in David Crowley and Susan E. Reid (eds), *Socialist Spaces: Sites of Everyday Life in Eastern Bloc* (Oxford: New York), pp. 181–206.

Dabert, Dobrochna (2003). *Kino moralnego niepokoju: Wokół wybranych problemów poetyki i etyki* (Poznań: Wydawnictwo Naukowe AUM).

Dalecki, Mieczysław (1971). 'October 1956 and after', in Jan Ostaszewski (ed.), *Modern Poland Between East and West* (London: The Polish School of Political and Social Science), pp. 76–109.

Davies, Norman (2005) [1979]. *God's Playground: A History of Poland*, Volume II, 1975 to the Present, Revised Edition (Oxford: Oxford University Press).

de Certeau, Michel (2002). 'General Introduction to *The Practice of Everyday Life* (1980)', in Ben Highmore (ed.), *The Everyday Life Reader* (London: Routledge), pp. 63–75.

Detka, Janusz (2006). 'Socrealizm jako cudze słowo (przykład Hłasko)', in Krzysztof Stępnik and Magdalena Piechota (eds), *Socrealizm; Fabuły – Komunikaty – Ikony* (Lublin: Wydawnictwo Uniwersytetu Marii Curie-Skłodowskiej), pp. 103–114.

Djilas, Milovan (1965). 'The New Class', in Arthur B. Mendel (ed.), *Essential Works of Marxism* (New York: Bantam), pp. 319–346.

Doane, Mary-Ann (2003). 'The Close-Up: Scale and Detail in the Cinema', *Differences*, 3, pp. 88–112.

Drozdowski, Bogumil (1985). 'Film Dokumentalny', in Rafal Marszalek (ed.), *Historia Filmu Polskiego*, Volume 5 (Warsaw: Wydawnictwa Artystyczne i Filmowe), pp. 118–133.

Dyer, Richard (1998). 'Resistance through Charisma', in E. Ann Kaplan (ed.), *Women in Film Noir*, New Edition (London: BFI), pp. 115–122.

—— (2002). *Only Entertainment*, Second Edition (London: Routledge).

Eagleton, Terry (2006). 'Preface', to Pierre Macherey, *A Theory of Literary Production* (London: Routledge), pp. vii–xiv.

Eberhardt, Konrad (1967). 'Komedia pomyłek i jej aktorzy', *Kino*, 7, p. 13.

Elsaesser, Thomas (1987). 'Tales of Sound and Fury: Observations on the Family Melodrama', in Christine Gledhill (ed.), *Home Is Where the Heart Is: Studies in Melodrama and the Woman's Film* (London: British Film Institute), pp. 43–69.

Engels, Frederick (1902). *The Origin of the Family, Private Property and the State* (Chicago: Kerr and Company).

Falkowska, Janina (1996). *The Political Films of Andrzej Wajda: Dialogism in Man of Marble, Man of Iron, and Danton* (Oxford: Berghahn).
Farocki, Harun (2002). 'Workers Leaving the Factory', trans. L. Faasch-Ibrahim. *Senses of Cinema*, 21, July, http://sensesofcinema.com/2002/21/farocki_workers/. Accessed 12 December 2013.
Fidelis, Malgorzata (2010). *Women, Communism, and Industrialization in Postwar Poland* (Cambridge: Cambridge University Press).
'Film amatorski' (1962), in Jerzy Chociłowski (ed.), *Współczesna Kinematografia Polska* (Warsaw: Polonia), pp. 113–120.
Firlit, Elżbieta and Jerzy Chłopecki (1992). 'When Theft is Not Theft', in Janine R. Wedel (ed.), *The Unplanned Society: Poland During and After Communism* (New York: Columbia University Press), pp. 95–109.
Fortuna, Piotr (2015). 'Muzykol – kulturowa metafora PRL', *Kwartalnik Filmowy*, 91, pp. 121–140.
Geyer, Michael and Sheila Fitzpatrick (2009). 'Introduction: After Totalitarianism – Stalinism and Nazism Compared', in Michael Geyer and Sheila Fitzpatrick (eds), *Beyond Totalitarianism: Stalinism and Nazism Compared* (Cambridge: Cambridge University Press), pp. 1–37.
Gierszewska, Barbara (2006). *Kino i film we Lwowie do 1939 roku* (Kielce: Wydawnictwo Akademii Świętokrzyskiej).
―― (2010). 'Artystyczne (awangardowe?) ambicje ekipy Eugeniusza Cękalskiego zrealizowane w filmie Strachy (1938)', in Krzysztof Jaworski and Piotr Rosiński (eds), *Między retoryką manifestów a nowoczesnością. Literatura-Sztuka-Film* (Kielce: Wydawnictwo UJK), pp. 49–64.
―― (2011). 'Filmowa kariera Tadeusza Dołęgi-Mostowicza', in Piotr Zwierzchowski and Daria Mazur (eds), *Polskie Kino Popularne* (Bydgoszcz: Wydawnictwo Uniwersytetu Kazimierza Wielkiego), pp. 11–25.
Barbara Lena Gierszewska (2012) (ed.). *Polski Film Fabularny 1918–1939: Recenzje* (Kraków: Księgarnia Akademicka).
Głowa, Jadwiga (1996). 'Bohater indywidualny – obywatel PRL-u', in Mariola Jankun-Dopartowa i Mirosław Przylipiak (eds), *Człowiek z ekranu. Z antropologii postaci filmowej* (Kraków: Arcana), pp. 205–219.
Górski, Artur (1980). '*Znachor* i *Profesor Wilczur* – przedwojenne melodramaty filmowe', in Zbigniew Wyszyński (ed.), *Polskie kino lat 1918-1939 (Zagadnienia wybrane)* (Kraków: Wydawnictwo Uniwersytetu Jagiellońskiego), pp. 54–69.
Grant, Barry Keith (2003). 'Introduction' to Barry Keith Grant (ed.), *Filme Genre Reader III* (Austin: University of Texas Press), pp. xv–xx.
Gregg, Melissa (2011). *Work's Intimacy* (Cambridge: Polity).
Greenberg, Clement (1973). *Art and Culture* (London: Thames and Hudson).
Grodź, Iwona (2009). *Zaszyfrowane w obrazie: O filmach Wojciecha Jerzego Hasa* (Gdańsk: Słowo/ Obraz Terytoria).

Groys, Boris (1992). *The Total Art of Stalinism: Avant-Garde, Aesthetic Dictatorship, and Beyond*, trans. Charles Rougle (Princeton: Princeton University Press).

Guzek, Mariusz (2011). 'O czym się nie mówi: Obraz prostytucji w kinie popularnym dwudziestolecia międzywojennego', in Piotr Zwierzchowski and Daria Mazur (eds), *Polskie Kino Popularne* (Bydgoszcz: Wydawnictwo Uniwersytetu Kazimierza Wielkiego), pp. 26–35.

Hakim, Catherine (2011). *Honey Money: The Power of Erotic Capital* (London: Allen Lane).

Hall, Stuart (1978). 'The Hinterland of Science: Ideology and the "Sociology of Knowledge"', in Centre for Contemporary Cultural Studies (eds), *On Ideology* (Hutchinson of London), pp. 9–32.

Haltof, Marek (2002). *Polish National Cinema* (Berghahn: Oxford).

Hanáková, Petra (2005). 'Voices from Another World: Feminine Space and Masculine Intrusion in *Sedmikrásky* and *Vražda ing. Čerta*', in Anikó Imre (ed.), *East European Cinemas* (London: Routledge), pp. 63–77.

—— (2011). 'From Mařka the Bricklayer to Black and White Sylva: Images of Women in Czech Visual Culture and the Eastern European Visual Paradox', *Studies in Eastern European Cinema*, 2, pp. 145–160.

Hankiss, Elemér (1990). *Eastern European Alternatives* (Oxford: Clarenden Press).

Hanson, Stephen. E. (1997). *Time and Revolution: Marxism and the Design of Soviet Institutions* (Chapel Hill: The University of North Carolina Press).

Hardt, Michael and Antonio Negri (2006). *Multitude: War and Democracy in the Age of Empire* (London: Penguin).

Harvey, David (1990). *The Condition of Postmodernity* (Oxford: Blackwell).

—— (2005a). *A Brief History of Neoliberalism* (Oxford: Oxford University Press).

—— (2005b). *The New Imperialism* (Oxford: Oxford University Press).

—— (2010a). *A Companion to Marx's Capital* (London: Verso).

—— (2010b). *The Enigma of Capital and the Crises of Capitalism* (London: Profile Books).

—— (2011). 'Feral Capitalism Hits the Streets', *Reading Marx's Capital with David Harvey* (David Harvey blog), http://davidharvey.org/2011/08/feral-capitalism-hits-the-streets. Accessed 22 August 2011.

—— (2012). *Rebel Cities: From the Right to the City to the Urban Revolution* (London: Verso).

Havel, Václav (1985). 'The Power of the Powerless', in John Keane (ed.), *The Power of the Powerless* (London: Hutchinson), pp. 23–96.

Heath, Stephen (1976). 'Narrative Space', *Screen*, 3, pp. 68–112.

Heilman, Robert Bechtold (1968). *Tragedy and Melodrama: Versions of Experience* (Seattle: University of Washington Press).

Hendrykowska, Małgorzata (2007a). *Smosarska* (Poznań: Wydawnictwo Naukowe UAM).

—— (2007b). 'Marek Piwowski wyrusza w *Rejs*', in Tadeusz Lubelski and Konrad J. Zarębski (eds), *Historia kina polskiego* (Warsaw: Fundacja Kino), pp. 155–157.

—— (2009). 'Pomiędzy Wielką Wojną a przełomem dźwiękowym: kinematografia polska w latach 1914-1930', in Grażyna M. Grabowska (ed.), *Sto lat polskiego filmu. Kino wielkiego niemowy. Część Druga: Od Wielkiej Wojny po erę dźwięku* (Warsaw: Filmoteka Narodowa), pp. 9–43.

—— (ed.) (2015). *Historia polskiego filmu dokumentalnego* (Poznań: Wydawnictwo Uniwersytetu im. Adama Mickiewicza).

Hendrykowski, Marek (2002). 'Paradoksy poetyki socrealizmu w filmie polskim', *Blok*, 1, pp. 120–138.

Highmore, Ben (2002). 'Introduction: Questioning Everyday Life', in Ben Highmore (ed.), *The Everyday Life Reader* (London: Routledge), pp. 1–34.

Hill, John (1986). *Sex, Class and Realism: British Cinema 1956–1963* (London: BFI).

Hobsbawm, Eric (1995). *Age of Extremes: The Short Twentieth Century 1914–1991* (Abacus: London).

Hodgin, Nick (2014). 'Cannibals, Carnival and Clowns: the Grotesque in German Unification Films', *Studies in Eastern European Cinema*, 2, pp. 124–138.

—— (2015). '"Only One Noble Topic Remained: the Workers". Sympathy, Subtlety and Subversion in East German Documentary Films', *Studies in Eastern European Cinema*, 1, pp. 49–63.

Hučková, Jadwiga (2015). 'Opowieści naocznego świadka. Kino pomiędzy wiosnami Solidarności', in Małgorzata Hendrykowska (ed.), *Historia polskiego filmu dokumentalnego* (Poznań: Wydawnictwo Uniwersytetu im. Adama Mickiewicza), pp. 361–469.

Imre, Anikó (2005). 'Introduction: East European Cinemas in New Perspectives', in Anikó Imre (ed.), *East European Cinemas* (London: Routledge), pp. xi–xxvi.

Iordanova, Dina (2003). *Cinema of the Other Europe: The Industry and Artistry of East Central European Film* (London: Wallflower).

Irzykowski, Karol (1982) [1924]. *Dziesiąta Muza oraz Pomniejsze pisma filmowe* (Kraków: Wydawnictwo Literackie).

Jackiewicz, Aleksander (1954). *Przegląd Kulturalny*, 52/52, p. 9.

—— (1964). 'Żona z Cepelii', *Życie Literackie*, 25, p. 12.

—— (1968). *Film jako powieść XX wieku* (Warsaw: Wydawnictwa Artystyczne i Filmowe).

Jagielski, Sebastian (2013). *Maskarady męskości: Pragnienie homospołeczne w polskim kinie fabularnym* (Kraków: Universitas).

Jałoszewski, Mariusz (2002). 'Film o Amwayu zakazany', *Gazeta Wyborcza*, 28/10, p. 16.

Jameson, Fredric (1992). *Signatures of the Visible* (London: Routledge).

Janicka, Bożena and Andrzej Kołodyński (eds) (2000). *Chełmska 21: 50 lat Wytwórni Filmów Dokumentalnych i Fabularnych w Warszawie* (Warsaw: WFDiF).

Jankun-Dopartowa, Mariola (1996). 'Fałszywa inicjacja bohatera: Młode kino lat siedemdziesiątych wobec założeń programowych Młodej Kultury', in Mariola Jankun-Dopartowa and Mirosław Przylipiak (eds), *Człowiek z ekranu. Z antropologii postaci filmowej* (Kraków: Arcana), pp. 89–121.

Jaworska, Justyna (2014). 'Kłir sułtański w Dziewczynach do wzięcia', *Widok: Teorie i praktyki kultury wizualnej*, http://pismowidok.org/index.php/one/article/view/161/274. Accessed 9 August 2014.
Jazdon, Mikołaj (2000). 'Czarne filmy posiwiały. „Czarna seria" polskiego dokumentu 1956-1958', in Małgorzata Hendrykowska (eds), *Widziane po latach: Analizy i interpretacje filmu polskiego* (Poznań: Wydawnictwo Uniwersytetu Poznańskiego), pp. 47-59.
—— (2008). 'Irena Kamieńska' (Booklet added to a DVD box of the films of Polish female documentary filmmakers) (Warsaw: Polskie Wydawnictwa Audiowizualne).
—— (2009). *Kino dokumentalne Kazimierza Karabasza* (Poznań: Wydawnictwo Naukowe UAM).
Jensen, Kirsten and Bartholomew F. Bland (2013). *Industrial Sublime: Modernism and the Transformation of New York's Rivers 1990-1940* (New York: Fordham University Press).
Jovanović, Nebojša (2015). *Gender and Sexuality in the Classical Yugoslav Cinema, 1947-1962*, PhD Thesis, defended at the Gender Department, Central European University, Budapest.
Kalb, Don (2002). 'Globalism and Postsocialist Prospects', in C.M. Hann (ed.), *Postsocialism: Ideals, Ideologies and Practices in Eurasia* (London: Routledge), pp. 317-334.
Kałużyński, Zygmunt (1976). *Wenus automobilowa: Obyczaje współczesne na ekranie* (Warsaw: Państwowy Instytut Wydawniczy).
Kapica, Tomasz (2012). 'Prostytutki Made in Poland. Tysiące wywieziono do burdeli', http://www.nto.pl/apps/pbcs.dll/article?AID=/20120929/REPORTAZ/120929495. Accessed 16 March 2014.
Karbowiak, Małgorzata (1984). 'Godność', *Głos Robotniczy*, 15/11, p. 9.
Kenez, Peter (2001). *Cinema and Soviet Society: From the Revolution to the Death of Stalin* (London: I. B. Tauris).
Kickasola, Joseph G. (1996). *The Films of Krzysztof Kieślowski: The Liminal Image* (New York: Continuum).
Kideckel, David A. (2002). 'The Unmaking of an East-Central European Working Class', in C.M. Hann (ed.), *Postsocialism: Ideals, Ideologies and Practices in Eurasia* (London: Routledge), pp. 114-132.
Kienzler, Iwona (2015). *Życie w PRL: I Strasznie, I Śmiesznie* (Warsaw: Bellona).
Klaczyński, Zbigniew (1964). 'Adam i dwie Ewy', *Trybuna Ludu*, 32, p. 14.
Klejsa, Konrad (2007). 'Stanisław Bareja – nadrealizm socjalistyczny', in Grażyna Stachówna and Bogusław Zmudziński (eds), *Autorzy kina polskiego*, Volume 2 (Kraków: Wydawnictwo Uniwersytetu Jagiellońskiego), pp. 79-128.
Kligman, Gail (1994). 'The Social Legacy of Communism: Women, Children, and the Feminization of Poverty', in James R. Millar and Sharon L. Wolchik (eds), *The Social Legacy of Communism* (Cambridge: Woodrow Wilson Center Press and Cambridge University Press), pp. 252-270.
Kłopotowski, Krzysztof (1981). 'Bez wyczucia', *Literatura*, 2, p. 8-14.

Konwicki, Tadeusz (1950). '2 brygady – jedna sprawa', *Film*, 14, p. 4.
Korczyński, Józef (2012) [1938]. 'Ludzie Wisły', in Barbara Lena Gierszewska (eds), *Polski Film Fabularny 1918-1939: Recencje* (Kraków: Księgarnia Akademicka), p. 292–293.
Kornacki, Krzysztof (2007). 'Ewa i Czesław Petelscy – w krainie PRL-u', in Grażyna Stachówna and Bogusław Zmudziński (eds), *Autorzy kina polskiego*, Volume 2 (Kraków: Wydawnictwo Uniwersytetu Jagiellońskiego), pp. 43–78.
Kornatowska, Maria (1990). *Wodzireje i amatorzy* (Warsaw: Wydawnictwa Artystyczne i Filmowe).
Koryś, Piotr (2007). 'Idea nowoczesności w działaniach i planach partii komunistycznej w Polsce 1945-1980. Przegląd problematyki', in Elżbieta Kościk and Tomasz Głowiński (eds), *Gospodarka i społeczeństwo w czasach PRL* (Wrocław: GAJT), pp. 440–455.
Kosińska, Karolina (2009). 'Manewry tożsamościowe. Kobieta jako mężczyzna i mężczyzna jako kobieta w przedwojennym polskim kinie komediowym', in Sebastian Jagielski and Agnieszka Morstin-Popławska (eds), *Ciało i seksualność w polskim kinie* (Kraków: Wydawnictwo Uniwersytetu Jagiellońskiego), pp. 13–23.
—— (2011). 'Style and Attitude: Social(ist) Realism in the Polish Black Series and British Free Cinema', *Studies in Eastern European Cinema*, 2, pp. 193–209.
Kracauer, Siegfried (2004) [1947]. *From Caligari to Hitler: A Psychological History of the German Film*, Revised Edition (Princeton: Princeton University Press).
Kuhn, Annette and Susannah Radstone (eds) (1990). *The Women's Companion to International Film* (London: Virago).
Kuron, Jacek and Karol Modzelewski (1982) [1965]. *Solidarność: The Missing Link? The Classic Open Letter to the Party by Jacek Kuron and Karol Modzelewski* (London: Bookmarks).
Kurz, Iwona (2005). *Twarze w tłumie: Wizerunki bohaterów wyobraźni zbiorowej w kulturze polskiej lat 1955—1969* (Izabelin: Świat Literacki).
—— (2008a). 'Gospodarka wyłączona', in Małgorzata Szpakowska (ed.), *Obyczaje polskie: Wiek XX w krótkich hasłach* (Warsaw: W.A.B.), pp. 87–99.
—— (2008b). 'Not Having to Stick to the Point: The Fly Killer by Marek Piwowski', in Łukasz Ronduda and Barbara Piwowarska (eds), *Polish New Wave: The History of a Phenomenon that Never Existed* (Warsaw: Instytut Adama Mickiewicza, CSW Zamek Ujazdowski), pp. 96–99.
—— (2009). 'Trędowata albo qui pro quo, czyli ciało w kulturze filmowej dwudziestolecia międzywojennego', in Sebastian Jagielski and Agnieszka Morstin-Popławska (eds), *Ciało i seksualność w polskim kinie* (Kraków: Wydawnictwo Uniwersytetu Jagiellońskiego), pp. 13–23.
—— (2011). 'Jajko a la Czereśniak', *Dialog*, 5, pp. 23–28.
Ladegaard, Jakob (2014). 'Laughing Matters: Four Marxist Takes on Film Comedy', in Ewa Mazierska and Lars Kristensen (eds), *Marx at the Movies: Revisiting History, Theory and Practice* (Houndmills, Basingstoke: Palgrave), pp. 102–122.
Landau, Zbigniew and Jerzy Tomaszewski (1985). *The Polish Economy in the Twentieth Century*, trans. Wojciech Roszkowski (London: Croom Helm).

Lazzarato, Maurizio (2012). *The Making of the Indebted Man: An Essay on the Neoliberal Condition*, trans. Joshua David Jordan (Amsterdam: Semiotext(e)).

Lefebvre, Henri (1991). *The Production of Space* (Oxford: Blackwell).

—— (2002). 'Work and Leisure in Everyday Life [1958]', in Ben Highmore (ed.), *The Everyday Life Reader* (London: Routledge), pp. 225-236.

Lemann-Zajiček, Jolanta (2008). 'Marzec '68 w szkole filmowej w Łodzi. Wydarzenia i konsekwencje', in Konrad Klejsa and Ewelina Nurczyńska-Fidelska (eds), *Kino polskie: reinterpretacje. Historia – ideologia – polityka* (Kraków: Rabid), pp. 47-58.

Lenin, V.I. (1989) [1902]. *What Is To Be Done?*, trans. Joe Fineberg and George Hanna (London: Penguin).

Lennon, John and Malcolm Foley (2010). *Dark Tourism* (Andover, Hampshire: Cengage Learning).

Leszczyński, Adam (2000). *Sprawy do załatwienia: Listy do 'Po Prostu' 1955-57* (Warsaw: Trio).

Levy, Frank and Richard J. Murnane (2004). *The New Division of Labor: How Computers Are Creating the Next Job Market* (Princeton: Princeton University Press).

Lifshitz, Mikhail (1973) [1933]. *The Philosophy of Art of Karl Marx*, trans. Ralph B. Winn (London: Pluto).

Lisowski, Tomasz (1997). 'Psy szczekają. O języku *Psów* Władysława Pasikowskiego', in Marek Hendrykowski (ed.), *Poloniści o filmie* (Poznań: Instytu Filologii Polskiej UAM), pp. 231-239.

Long, Kristi S. (1996). '*Man of Iron*: Representing and Shaping Historical Consciousness through Film – A Polish Case', *The Journal of Popular Culture*, 1, pp. 163-177.

Löwy, Michael (2009). *Morning Star: Surrealism, Marxism, Anarchism, Situationism, Utopia* (Austin: University of Texas Press).

Lubelski, Tadeusz (1999). 'From *Personnel* to *No End*: Kieślowski's Political Feature Films', in Paul Coates (ed.), *Lucid Dreams: The Films of Krzysztof Kieslowski* (Trowbridge: Flicks Books), pp. 54-76.

—— (2007). 'Krzysztof Krauze – młodszy brat kina moralnego niepokoju', in Grażyna Stachówna and Bogusław Zmudziński (eds), *Autorzy Kina Polskiego*, Volume 3 (Kraków: Wydawnictwo Uniwersytetu Jagiellońskiego), pp. 195-219.

—— (2009a). *Historia kina polskiego: Twórcy, filmy, konteksty* (Katowice: Videograf II).

—— (2009b). 'Nasza komedia narodowa', *Kwartalnik Filmowy*, 67-8, pp. 286-303.

Lukowski, Jerzy and Hubert Zawadzki (2001). *A Concise History of Poland* (Cambridge: Cambridge University Press).

Łuczak, Maciej (2007). *Miś czyli świat według Barei* (Warsaw: Prószyński i S-ka).

Machalica, Bartosz (2010). 'Polityka historyczna PRL-u. Tezy o zmienności i niezmienności', in Jakub Majmurek and Piotr Szumlewicz (eds), *PRL bez uprzedzeń* (Warsaw: Książka i Prasa), pp. 89-101.

Madej, Alina (1994). *Mitologie i konwencje. O polskim kinie fabularnym dwudziestolecia międzywojennego* (Kraków: Universitas).

―――― (1997). 'Zjazd filmowy w Wiśle, czyli dla każdego coś przykrego', *Kwartalnik Filmowy*, 18, pp. 207–214.

Majmurek, Jakub (2010). 'PRL jako projekt modernizacji peryferyjnej', in Jakub Majmurek and Piotr Szumlewicz (eds), *PRL bez uprzedzeń* (Warsaw: Książka i Prasa), pp. 89–101.

―――― and Piotr Szumlewicz (2010). 'Fakty i mity o PRL-u', in Jakub Majmurek and Piotr Szumlewicz (eds), *PRL bez uprzedzeń* (Warsaw: Książka i Prasa), pp. 7–16.

Malatyńska, Maria (1998). 'Jak po mydle...Rzecz o przygodzie Henryka Dederki', *Kino*, 1, p. 3.

Margolit, Evgenii (2001). 'Landscape, with Hero', in Alexander Prokhorov (ed.), *Springtime for Soviet Cinema: Re/Viewing the 1960s* (Pittsburgh: Pittsburgh Russian Film Symposium), pp. 29–50.

Marody, Mira (2010). 'Homo Sovieticus and the Change of Values: The Case of Poland', in Heinrich Best and Agnieszka Wenninger (eds), *Landmark 1989: Central and Eastern European Societies Twenty Years After the System Change* (Berlin: Lit Verlag), pp. 80–90.

Maron, Marcin (2011). 'Złoto Wojciecha Hasa – ironiczna gra z konwencją produkcyjniaka', in Piotr Zwierzchowski and Daria Mazur (eds), *Polskie Kino Popularne* (Bydgoszcz: Wydawnictwo Uniwersytetu Kazimierza Wielkiego), pp. 111–120.

Marszałek, Rafał (2006). *Kino rzeczy znalezionych* (Gdańsk: Słowo/ Obraz Terytoria).

Marx, Karl (1963) [1847]. *The Poverty of Philosophy* (New York: International Publishers).

―――― (1965) [1887]. *Capital: A Critical Analysis of Capitalist Production*, Volume 1 (Moscow: Progress Publishers).

―――― (1967) [1885]. *Capital: A Critique of Political Economy*, Volume 2: The Process of Circulation of Capital (Moscow: Progress Publishers).

―――― (1969). *Theories of Surplus Value* (London: Lawrence and Wishart).

―――― (1974) [1894]. *Capital: A Critique of Political Economy*, Volume 3: The Process of Capitalist Production as a Whole (London: Lawrence & Wishart).

―――― (1975). *Early Writings*, trans. Rodney Livingstone and Gregor Benton (London and New York: Penguin Books).

―――― (1977). *Economic and Philosophic Manuscripts of 1844* (Moscow: Progress Publishers).

―――― (1978) [1852]. 'The Eighteenth Brumaire of Louis Bonaparte', in Robert C. Tucker (ed.), *The Marx-Engels Reader*, Second Edition (New York: W. W. Norton & Company), pp. 595–617.

―――― (2009) [1871]. 'The Civil War in France', *Marx-Engels Internet Archive*, https://www.marxists.org/archive/marx/works/1871/civil-war-france/. Accessed 20 August 2014.

―――― and Frederick Engels (1947). *The German Ideology, Parts I and III* (New York: International Publishers).

―――― and Friedrich Engels (2008) [1848]. *The Communist Manifesto* (London: Pluto).

Maśnicki, Jerzy and Kamil Stepan (2007). 'Aleksander Hertz obchodzi jubileusz', in Tadeusz Lubelski and Konrad J. Zarębski (eds), *Historia kina polskiego* (Warsaw: Fundacja Kino), pp. 24–26.

Mazierska, Ewa (2002a). 'The Exclusive Pleasures of Being a Second Generation Inteligent: Representation of Social Class in the Films of Andrzej Wajda', *Canadian Slavonic Papers*, 3–4, pp. 233–249.

―――― (2002b). 'Agnieszka and Other Solidarity Heroines of Polish Cinema', *Kinema*, 17, pp. 17–36.

―――― (2007). *Polish Postcommunist Cinema: From Pavement Level* (Oxford: Peter Lang).

―――― (2008a). *Masculinities in Polish, Czech and Slovak Cinema: Black Peters and Men of Marble* (Oxford: Berghahn).

―――― (2008b). 'The Politics of Space in Polish Communist Cinema', in Eva Näripea and Andreas Trossek (eds), *Via Transversa: Lost Cinema of the Former Eastern Bloc* (Tallinn: Eesti Kunstiakadeemia), pp. 229–245.

―――― (2011). *European Cinema and Intertextuality: History, Memory and Politics* (Houndmills, Basingstoke: Palgrave).

―――― (ed.) (2012a). 'Dossier: Working Life Now and Then', *Framework*, 1, pp. 147–227.

―――― (2012b). 'Polish Postcommunist Cinema and the Neoliberal Order', *Images*, 20, pp. 53–63.

―――― (2012c). 'International Co-productions as Productions of Heterotopias', in Aniko Imre (ed.), *A Companion to Eastern European Cinemas* (Oxford: Wiley-Blackwell), pp. 483–503.

―――― (2012d). 'What Happened to the Polish Multitude? Representation of Working People in Polish Postcommunist Cinema', *Framework*, 1, pp. 207–227.

―――― (2013a). 'Existentialism and Socialist Realism in the Early Films of Wojciech Has', *Studies in Eastern European Cinema*, 1, pp. 9–27.

―――― (2013b). 'From Fordism to Post-Fordism: Representation of Work in the Films about Nazi Concentration Films', *Kinema*, Fall, http://www.kinema.uwaterloo.ca/article.php?id=544&feature. Accessed 11 July 2014.

―――― (2014a). 'Polski film za granicą: getto, przedsionek salonu czy uniwersalna niewidzialność', *Czas Kultury*, 4, pp. 8–17.

―――― (2014b). 'The Office Polish Style in *The Office*', *Short Film Studies*, 1, pp. 37–40.

―――― (2015a). *From Self-Fulfilment to Survival of the Fittest: Work in European Cinema from the 1960s to the Present* (Oxford: Berghahn).

―――― (2015b). 'Aleksander Jackiewicz – publiczny intelektualista PRL-u', in Barbara Giza and Piotr Zwierzchowski (eds), *Aleksander Jackiewicz* (Warsaw: Scholar), pp. 85–101.

―――― and Michael Goddard (2014). 'Introduction: Polish Cinema beyond Polish Borders', in Ewa Mazierska and Michael Goddard (eds), *Polish Cinema in a Transnational Context* (Rochester, NY: University of Rochester Press), pp. 1–20.

―――― and Elżbieta Ostrowska (2006). *Women in Polish Cinema* (Oxford: Berghahn).

Mazurek, Małgorzata (2005). *Socjalistyczny zakład pracy: Porównanie fabrycznej codzienności w PRL i NRD u progu lat sześćdziesiątych* (Warszawa: Trio).

―――― (2012). 'Keeping It Close to Home: Resourcefulness and Scarcity in Late Socialist and Postsocialist Poland', in Paulina Bren and Mary Neuberger (eds), *Communism Unwrapped: Consumption in Cold War Eastern Europe* (Oxford: Oxford University Press), pp. 298–320.
―――― (2013). 'Moralities of Consumption in Poland across the Short Twentieth Century', *Annales. Histoire et Sciences Sociales*, Spring, http://www.cairn-int.info/load_pdf.php?ID_ARTICLE=E_ANNA_682_0499. Accessed 26 May 2014.
Mąka-Malatyńska, Katazyna (2006). 'Wanda Gościmińska – włókniarka – demontaż filmowej nowomowy', in Marek Hendrykowski (ed.), *Wojciech Wiszniewski* (Łódź: Państwowa Wyższa Szkoła Filmowa, Telewizyjna i Teatralna im. Leona Schillera w Łodzi), pp. 109–120.
Meiksins Wood, Ellen (1986). *The Retreat from Class: A New 'True' Socialism* (London: Verso).
Merz, Irena (1954). 'Jeszcze jedna komedia warszawska', *Trybuna Ludu*, 28.
Michałek, Bolesław (1962). 'Sztuczne serca', *Nowa Kultura*, 12, p. 8.
―――― (1970). *Marzenia i rzeczywistość* (Warsaw: Wydawnictwa Artystyczne i Filmowe).
―――― (1981). *Notes filmowy* (Wydawnictwa Artystyczne i Filmowe).
―――― and Frank Turaj (1988). *The Modern Cinema of Poland* (Bloomington and Indianapolis: Indiana University Press).
Millington, Nate (2013). 'Post-Industrial Imaginaries: Nature, Representation and Ruin in Detroit', *International Journal of Urban and Regional Research*, 1, pp. 279–296.
Morawski, St. (1954). 'Przygoda na Mariensztacie', *Gazeta Krakowska*, 28.
Morawski, Wojciech (2007). 'Poglądy gospodarcze Władysława Gomułki', in Elżbieta Kościk and Tomasz Głowiński (eds), *Gospodarka i społeczeństwo w czasach PRL-u* (Wrocław: GAJT), pp. 326–332.
Morrey, Douglas (2005). *Jean-Luc Godard* (Manchester: Manchester University Press).
Mroz, Matilda (2007). 'Fracturing the Marble Façade: Visceral Excavation in Andrzej Wajda's *Man of Marble*', *Senses of Cinema*, 43, http://www.sensesofcinema.com/2007/feature-articles/man-marble-wajda/. Accessed 3 April 2011.
Mruklik, Barbara (1974). 'Film fabularny', in Jerzy Toeplitz (ed.), *Historia Filmu Polskiego*, Volume 3 (Warsaw: Wydawnictwa Artystyczne i Filmowe), pp. 223–259.
Näripea, Eva (2008). 'A View from the Periphery. Spatial Discourse of the Soviet Estonian Feature Film: The 1940s and 1950s', in Eva Näripea and Andreas Trossek (eds), *Via Transversa: Lost Cinema of the Former Eastern Bloc* (Tallinn: Eesti Kunstiakadeemia), pp. 193–210.
―――― (2014). 'Postcolonial Heterotopias: A Paracinematic Reading of Marek Piestrak's Estonian Coproductions', in Ewa Mazierska and Michael Goddard (eds), *Polish Cinema in a Transnational Context* (Rochester, NY: University of Rochester Press), pp. 115–133.
Narojek, Winicjusz (1991). *Socjalistyczne 'welfare state'* (Warsaw: Wydawnictwo Naukowe PWN).

Neale, Steve (2002). 'Art Cinema as Institution', in Catherine Fowler (ed.), *The European Cinema Reader* (London: Routledge).
Nichols, Bill (2001). *Introduction to Documentary* (Bloomington and Indianapolis: Indiana University Press).
Norman, Daniel (1955). *Marx and Soviet Reality* (London: Batchworth Press).
Nowak, Maciej (2011). '*Arizona* Ewy Borzęckiej, czyli notatki z buszu', in Agnieszka Wiśniewska (ed.), *Polskie kino dokumentalne 1989-2009. Historia polityczna* (Warsaw: Wydawnictwo Krytyki Politycznej), pp. 45–50.
Nowell-Smith, Geoffrey (1987). 'Minnelli and Melodrama', in Christine Gledhill (ed.), *Home Is Where the Heart Is: Studies in Melodrama and the Woman's Film* (London: British Film Institute), pp. 70–74.
Nurczyńska-Fidelska, Ewelina (1982). *Andrzej Munk* (Kraków: Wydawnictwo Literackie).
—— (2003). 'Andrzej Wajda's Vision of *The Promised Land*', in John Orr and Elżbieta Ostrowska (eds), *The Cinema of Andrzej Wajda: The Art of Irony and Defiance* (London: Wallflower), pp. 146–159.
Ociepa, Krzysztof (2003). 'Strategie autorskie Krzysztofa Krauzego (na przykładzie *Gier ulicznych* i *Długu*)', in Konrad Klejsa and Tomasz Kłys (eds), *Film: Fabryka Emocji* (Kraków: Rabid), pp. 47–67.
O'Shaughnessy, Martin (2007). *The New Face of Political Cinema: Commitment in French Film Since 1995* (Oxford: Berghahn).
—— (2012). 'Film and Work: The Work Done by Work-Centered Films', *Framework*, 1, pp. 155–171.
Ost, David (2005). *The Defeat of Solidarity: Anger and Politics in Postcommunist Europe* (Ithaca, NY: Cornell University Press).
Ostrowska, Dorota (2012). 'An Alternative Model of Film Production: Film Units in Poland after World War Two', in Anikó Imre (ed.), *A Companion to Eastern European Cinemas* (Oxford: Wiley, Blackwell), pp. 453–465.
Ostrowska, Elżbieta (2006a). 'Polish "Superwoman": a Liberation or Victimisation', in Ewa Mazierska and Elżbieta Ostrowska, *Women in Polish Cinema* (Oxford: Berghahn), pp. 55–74.
—— (2006b). 'Agnieszka Holland: A Sceptic', in Ewa Mazierska and Elżbieta Ostrowska (eds), *Women in Polish Cinema* (Oxford: Berghahn), pp. 185–204.
—— (2016). 'The Power of Love: Polish Postcommunist Popular Cinema', in Dorota Ostrowska, Francesco Pitassio and Zsusanna Varga (eds), *Popular Cinemas in Central Europe: Film Cultures and Histories* (London: I. B. Tauris), forthcoming.
—— and Adam Wyżyński (2006). 'Obrazy Rosjan w kinie polskim', in Andrzej de Lazari (ed.), *Katalog wzajemnych uprzedzeń Polaków i Rosjan* (Warsaw: Polski Instytut Spraw Międzynarodowych), pp. 303–327.
Parvulescu, Constantin (2015). *Orphans of the East: Postwar Eastern European Cinema and the Revolutionary Subject* (Bloomington and Indianapolis: Indiana University Press).

Pawlik, Wojciech (1992). 'Intimate Commerce', in Janine R. Wedel (ed.), *The Unplanned Society: Poland During and After Communism* (New York: Columbia University Press), pp. 78–94.

Pawlukiewicz, Marek (1987). 'Potrzebny spokój...', *Film*, 10, p. 9.

Peiper, Tadeusz (1972). *Tędy. Nowe Usta* (Kraków: Wydawnictwo Literackie).

Pełczyński, Grzegorz (2002). *Dziesiąta muza w stroju ludowym: O wizerunkach kultury chłopskiej w kinie PRL* (Poznań: Wydawnictwo Naukowe UAM).

Perec, Georges (2002). 'Approaches to What? [1973]', in Ben Highmore (ed.), *The Everyday Life Reader* (London: Routledge), pp. 176–178.

Piątek, Tomasz (2011). 'Witajcie w życiu! Henryka Dederki, czyli kapitalizm jako towar', in Agnieszka Wiśniewska (ed.), *Polskie kino dokumentalne 1989-2009. Historia polityczna* (Warsaw: Wydawnictwo Krytyki Politycznej), pp. 51–58.

Pietrasik, Zdzisław (1999). 'Swobodny buntownik', *Polityka*, 35, p. 46.

Pietrzak, Jarosław (2011). '*Bar na Victorii* Leszka Dawida, czyli emigracja jako druga strona transformacji', in Agnieszka Wiśniewska (ed.), *Polskie kino dokumentalne 1989-2009. Historia polityczna* (Warsaw: Wydawnictwo Krytyki Politycznej), pp. 99–108.

Piper, Franciszek (2002). *Auschwitz Prisoner Labor* (Oświęcim: Auschwitz-Birkenau State Museum).

Płażewski, Jerzy (1953). 'Sprawy do załatwienia', *Życie Literackie*, 37, p. 8.

Pobłocki, Kacper (2012). '"Knife in the Water": The Struggle over Collective Consumption in Urbanizing Poland', in Paulina Bren and Mary Neuberger (eds), *Communism Unwrapped: Consumption in Cold War Eastern Europe* (Oxford: Oxford University Press), pp. 68–86.

Polanyi, Karl (2001) [1944]. *The Great Transformation: The Political and Economic Origins of Our Time* (Boston: Beacon Press).

Preizner, Joanna (2007). 'Feliks Falk – cena sukcesu', in Grażyna Stachówna and Bogusław Zmudziński (eds), *Autorzy kina polskiego*, Volume 3 (Kraków: Wydawnictwo Uniwersytetu Jagiellońskiego), pp. 87–109.

Przylipiak, Mirosław (1984). 'Od konkretu do metafory: Zarys przemian polskiego filmu dokumentalnego w latach siedemdziesiątych', *Kino*, 1, pp. 13–16.

—— (2008a). 'Wojciech Wiszniewski' (Booklet added to a DVD box of Wiszniewski's films) (Warsaw: Polskie Wydawnictwa Audiowizualne).

—— (2008b). 'Refleksja nad dokumentalizmem w filmach fabularnych Andrzeja Wajdy', in Konrad Klejsa and Ewelina Nurczyńska-Fidelska (eds), *Kino polskie: Reinterpretacje. Historia-Ideologia-Polityka* (Kraków: Rabid), pp. 97–118.

—— (2015). 'Dokument polski lat 90tych', in Małgorzata Hendrykowska (ed.), *Historia polskiego filmu dokumentalnego* (forthcoming).

—— and Jerzy Szyłak (1999). *Kino najnowsze* (Kraków: Znak).

Rancière, Jacques (2013) [2010]. *Dissensus: On Politics and Aesthetics*, trans. Steven Corcoran (London: Bloomsbury).

Ray, Nilanjana (2006). 'Looking at Trafficking through a New Lens', *Cardozo Journal of Law & Gender*, 12, pp. 909–929.

Replewicz, Maciej (2009). *Stanislaw Bareja: Król krzywego zwierciadła* (Poznań: Zysk i Spółka).
Ross, Andrew (2008). 'The New Geography of Work: Power to the Precarious?', *Theory, Culture & Society*, 7–8, pp. 31–49.
Roszkowska, Dorota (1992). 'Człowiek z drugiej strony: Kobiety w filmach Wajdy', in Sławomira Walczewska (ed.), *Głos mają kobiety* (Kraków: Convivium), pp. 78–94.
Rowbotham, Sheila and Huw Beynon (2001). 'Handing on Histories', in Sheila Rowbotham and Huw Beynon (eds), *Looking at Class: Film, Television and the Working Class in Britain* (London: Rivers Oram), pp. 2–24.
Różewicz, Tadeusz (1986) [1962]. *Świadkowie, albo Nasza mała stabilizacja* (Kraków: Wydawnictwo Literackie).
Ruiz, Raul (2005). *Poetics of Cinema*, trans. Brian Holmes (Paris: Editions Dis Voir).
Sadowska, Maria (2013). 'Dzień kobiet to western', *Trójka: Polskie Radio*, http://www.polskieradio.pl/9/396/Artykul/799193,Maria-Sadowska-Dzien-kobiet-to-western. Accessed 15 July 2014.
Sadowski, Marek (1987). 'Wyzwanie', *Rzeczpospolita*, 28/02–1/03, p. 10.
Scott, Hilda (1976). *Women and Socialism: Experiences from Eastern Europe* (London: Alison and Busby).
Scribner, Charity (2005). *Requiem for Communism* (Cambridge, Massachusetts: The MIT Press).
Seidman, Gay (2007). 'Looking in from Outside', *Labor History*, 1, pp. 96–103.
Serafin, Krzysztof (2000). 'Żywe roboty. Rozmowa z Ireną Kamieńską', in Bożena Janicka and Andrzej Kołodyński (eds), *Chełmska 21: 50 lat Wytwórni Filmów Dokumentalnych i Fabularnych w Warszawie* (Warsaw: WFDiF), pp. 260–269.
Siatkowski, Zbigniew (1980). 'Wokół *Strachów* Cękalskiego. Mechanizm literackości filmu', in Zbigniew Wyszyński (ed.), *Polskie kino lat 1918-1939* (Zagadnienia wybrane) (Kraków: Wydawnictwo Uniwersytetu Jagiellońskiego), pp. 54–69.
Siebers, Johan (2014). 'The Utopian Function of Film Music', in Ewa Mazierska and Lars Kristensen (eds), *Marx at the Movies: Revisiting History, Theory and Practice* (Houndmills, Basingstoke: Palgrave), pp. 46–61.
Skaff, Sheila (2008). *The Law of the Looking Glass: Cinema in Poland, 1896-1939* (Athens: Ohio University Press).
Skotarczak, Dorota (2004). *Obraz społeczeństwa PRL w komedii filmowej* (Poznań: Wydawnictwo Naukowe UAM).
Skrodzka-Bates, Aga (2011). 'Clandestine Human and Cinematic Passages in the United Kingdom: The Polish Plumber and Kieślowski's Hairdresser', *Studies in Eastern European Cinema*, 1, pp. 75–90.
Skwara, Anita (1992). 'Film Stars Do Not Shine in the Sky Over Poland: The Absence of Popular Cinema in Poland', in Richard Dyer and Ginette Vincendeau (eds), *Popular European Cinema* (London: Routledge), pp. 220–231.
Słonimski, Antoni (2012) [1925]. 'Iwonka', in Barbara Lena Gierszewska (ed.), *Polski Film Fabularny 1918-1939: Recenzje* (Kraków: Księgarnia Akademicka), pp. 72–74.

Sobolewski, Tadeusz (1987a). 'Czas nadziei', *Tygodnik Powszechny*, 10, p. 12.
—— (1987b). 'Partia domina', *Kino*, 10, pp. 7–11.
—— (1998). 'Napij się arizony', *Kino*, 7–8, p. 70.
—— (1999). 'Ultimate Concerns', in Paul Coates (ed.), *Lucid Dreams: The Films of Krzysztof Kieslowski* (Trowbridge: Flicks Books), pp. 19–31.
—— (2012) [1939]. 'Włóczęgi', in Barbara Lena Gierszewska (ed.), *Polski Film Fabularny 1918-1939: Recenzje* (Kraków: Księgarnia Akademicka), p. 316.
Sobotka, Kazimierz (1985). 'Robotnik na ekranie czyli o tak zwanym "filmie produkcyjnym"', in Bronisława Stolarska (ed.), *Szkice o filmie polskim* (Łódź: Łódzki Dom Kultury), pp. 25–70.
—— (1987). 'Między samotnością a karierą, czyli o człowieku pracy w filmie polskim lat siedemdziesiątych', in Kazimierz Sobotka (ed.), *Film polski: Twórcy i mity* (Łódź: Łódzki Dom Kultury), pp. 19–43.
Sokołowski, Jerzy (1953). 'Sprawa do załatwienia', *Po prostu*, 40, p. 20.
Sørenssen, Bjørn (2012). 'The Polish Black Series Documentary and the British Free Cinema Movement', in Anikó Imre (ed.), *A Companion to Eastern European Cinemas* (Oxford: Wiley, Blackwell), pp. 183–200.
'Spotkanie z twórcami filmu *Godność*' (1984). *Rzeczpospolita*, 18/12, p. 8.
Stachówna, Grażyna (1987). '*Nóż w wodzie* Romana Polańskiego czyli: jak debiutować w kinie', *Kino*, 8, pp. 4–7 and 24–26.
—— (2008). 'Socjalistyczne romanse, czyli gorzko-słodkie losy melodramatu w PRL-u', in Konrad Klejsa and Ewelina Nurczyńska-Fidelska (eds), *Kino polskie: Reinterpretacje. Historia-Ideologia-Polityka* (Kraków: Rabid), pp. 353–364.
Stalin, Joseph (1961). 'The Foundations of Leninism', in Arthur B. Mendel (ed.), *Essential Works of Marxism* (New York: Bantam), pp. 209–296.
Stam, Robert (2000). 'Beyond Fidelity: The Dialogics of Adaptation', in James Naremore (ed.), *Film Adaptation* (London: The Athlone Press), pp. 54–76.
Staniszkis, Jadwiga (1992). *The Ontology of Socialism*, trans. Peggy Watson (Oxford: Clarendon Press).
Starski, Stanislaw (1982). *Class Struggle in Classless Poland* (Boston: South End Press).
Stepan, Kamil (2009). 'Wiktor Biegański – próba kina autorskiego', in Grażyna M. Grabowska (ed.), *Sto lat polskiego filmu. Kino wielkiego niemowy. Część Druga: Od Wielkiej Wojny po erę dźwięku* (Warsaw: Filmoteka Narodowa), pp. 45–51.
Stok, Danusia (ed.) (1993). *Kieślowski on Kieślowski* (London: Faber and Faber).
Stradomski, Wiesław (1988). 'Drugi oddech polskiego kina', in Barbara Armatys, Leszek Armatys, Wiesław Stradomski (eds), *Historia Filmu Polskiego*, Volume 2 (Warsaw: Wydawnictwa Artystyczne i Filmowe), pp. 13–107.
Swader, Christopher S. (2010). 'Homo Sovieticus in Interpersonal Relationships Before and After the Collapse of Communism', in Heinrich Best and Agnieszka Wenniger (eds), *Landmark 1989: Central and Eastern European Societies Twenty Years After the System Change* (Berlin: Lit Verlag), pp. 62–79.

Szcześniak, Magda (2012). 'Od Umy do Pumy – od roli podróbki w polskiej transformacji', *Widok: Teorie i praktyki kultury wizualnej*, http://pismowidok.org/index.php/one/article/view/13/30. Accessed 10 October 2014.

Szpakowska, Małgorzata (ed.) (2008). *Obyczaje polskie: Wiek XX w krótkich hasłach* (Warsaw: W.A.B.).

Szumlewicz, Piotr (2010). 'Chadecko-socjalistyczna polityka społeczna', in Jakub Majmurek and Piotr Szumlewicz (eds), *PRL bez uprzedzeń* (Warsaw: Książka i Prasa), pp. 51–64.

Szyma, Tadeusz (1985). 'Godność', *Tygodnik Powszechny*, 5, p. 12.

―― (2005). 'O "Solidarności" – po latach', *Kino*, 10, pp. 54–55.

Śliwińska, Anna (2006). 'W świecie paradoksów (Opowieść o człowieku, który wykonał 552% normy, i Sztygar na zagrodzie...)', in Marek Hendrykowski (ed.), *Wojciech Wiszniewski* (Łódź: Państwowa Wyższa Szkoła Filmowa, Telewizyjna i Teatralna im. Leona Schillera w Łodzi), pp. 79–96.

Świda-Ziemba, Hanna (1998). *Człowiek wewnętrznie zniewolony: Problemy psychosocjologiczne minionej formacji* (Warsaw: Wydawnictwa Uniwersytetu Warszawskiego).

Talarczyk-Gubała, Monika (2007). *PRL się śmieje: Polska komedia filmowa lat 1945-1989* (Warsaw: Trio).

―― (2013). *Wszystko o Ewie: Filmy Barbary Sass a kino kobiet w drugiej połowie XX wieku* (Szczecin: Wydawnictwo Naukowe Uniwersytetu Szczecińskiego).

―― (2015). *Wanda Jakubowska od nowa* (Warsaw: Wydawnictwo Krytyki Politycznej).

Tambor, Konrad (2013). 'Supermarket', *Kino*, 1, pp. 67–68.

Taylor, Richard (1983). 'A "Cinema for the Millions": Soviet Socialist Realism and the Problem of Film Comedy', *Journal of Contemporary History*, 3, pp. 439–461.

Thompson, Kristin and David Bordwell (1976). 'Space and Narrative in the Films of Ozu', *Screen*, 2, pp. 41–73.

Tischner, Józef (2005). *Etyka solidarności oraz homo sovieticus* (Kraków: Znak).

Toeplitz, Jerzy (1950). 'Teatr Film Życie', *Film*, 17, p. 9.

―― (1964). 'Tradycja i perspektywy: Sztuka filmowa dwudziestolecia Polski Ludowej', *Kwartalnik Filmowy*, 1–2, pp. 3–19.

Toniak, Ewa (2008). *Olbrzymki: Kobiety i socrealizm* (Kraków: Ha! Art).

Toporek, Marian (1999). *Historia Polski 1945-1999* (Kraków: Małopolska Oficyna Wydawnicza Korona).

Torańska, Teresa (1989). *Oni* (Warsaw: Omnipress).

Trotsky, Leon (2002) [1923]. 'Habit and Custom', in Ben Highmore (ed.), *The Everyday Life Reader* (London: Routledge), pp. 85–90.

Tumiłowicz, Bronisław (2010). 'Piwowski wyrusza w kolejny *Rejs*', *Przegląd*, 42, http://www.tygodnikprzeglad.pl/piwowski-wyrusza-kolejny-rejs/. Accessed 16 September 2013.

Tym, Stanisław (2000). 'Jeszcze raz o *Rejsie*', *Gazeta Wyborcza*, 171, p. 14.

Tyrmand, Leopold (1989). *Dziennik 1954* (Warsaw: Res Publica).

'Uchwała Sekretariatu KC w sprawie kinematografii' (1994), in Tadeusz Miczka and Alina Madej (eds), *Syndrom konformizmu: Kino polskie lat sześćdziesiątych* (Katowice: Wydawnictwo Uniwersytetu Śląskiego), pp. 27–34.

Ventsel, Aimar (2016). 'Estonian Invasion as Western Ersatz-pop', in Ewa Mazierska (ed.), *Popular Music in Eastern Europe: Breaking the Cold War Paradigm* (London: Palgrave), forthcoming.

Wallerstein, Immanuel (1984). *The Politics of the World-Economy: The States, the Movements and the Civilizations* (Cambridge: Cambridge University Press).

Wasilewski, Jacek (1995). 'The Forming of the New Elite: How Much Nomenklatura is Left?', *Polish Sociological Review*, 2, pp. 113–123.

Wayne, Mike (2014). 'The Dialectical Image: Kant, Marx and Adorno', in Ewa Mazierska and Lars Kristensen (eds), *Marx at the Movies: Revisiting History, Theory and Practice* (Houndmills, Basingstoke: Palgrave), pp. 27–45.

Wedel, Janine R. (ed.) (1992). *The Unplanned Society: Poland During and After Communism* (New York: Columbia University Press).

Werner, Andrzej (1985). 'Film Fabularny', in Rafal Marszalek (ed.), *Historia Filmu Polskiego*, Volume 5 (Warsaw: Wydawnictwa Artystyczne i Filmowe), pp. 19–117.

Williams, Linda (2000). 'Film Bodies: Gender, Genre, and Excess', in Robert Stam and Toby Miller (eds), *Film and Theory: An Anthology* (Oxford: Blackwell), pp. 207–221.

Williams, Raymond (2002) [1958]. 'Culture is ordinary', in Ben Highmore (ed.), *The Everyday Life Reader* (London: Routledge), pp. 91–100.

Winston, Brian (2008). *Claiming the Real II: Documentary: Grierson and Beyond* (Houndmills, Basingstoke: Palgrave).

Wiśniewski, Cezary (1973). 'Komedia grozy obyczajowej', *Kino*, 7, pp. 12–16.

Witczak, Witold (1966). 'Filmy dokumentalne i oświatowe, krótki metraż (1923–1929)', in *Historia Filmu Polskiego*, Volume 1 (Warsaw: Wydawnictwa Artystyczne i Filmowe), pp. 210–212.

Władyka, Władysław (2009). 'Śmierć ideologii (lata 1957-1966)', in Andrzej Brzeziecki (ed.), *Lekcje historii PRL w rozmowach* (Warsaw: W.A.B.), pp. 106–131.

Wyżyński, Adam (2008). 'Filmowe świadectwa narodzin "Solidarności" i ich trudna droga na ekran', in Konrad Klejsa and Ewelina Nurczyńska-Fidelska (eds), *Kino polskie: Reinterpretacje. Historia-Ideologia-Polityka* (Kraków: Rabid), pp. 219–235.

—— (2009). 'Narodziny dźwięku', in Grażyna M. Grabowska (ed.), *Sto lat polskiego filmu. Kino wielkiego niemowy. Część Druga: Od Wielkiej Wojny po erę dźwięku* (Warsaw: Filmoteka Narodowa), pp. 95–105.

Zahorska, Stefania (1928). 'Film w naftalinie', *Wiex XX*, 3, p. 4.

—— (2012a) [1938]. 'Nareszcie polski film. *Strachy*', in Barbara Lena Gierszewska (ed.), *Polski Film Fabularny 1918-1939: Recencje* (Kraków: Księgarnia Akademicka), p. 303–304.

—— (2012b) [1938]. 'Kobiety nad przepaścią', in Barbara Lena Gierszewska (ed.), *Polski Film Fabularny 1918-1939: Recencje* (Kraków: Księgarnia Akademicka), p. 285.

―――― (2012c) [1938]. 'Nareszcie polski film. *Granica*', in Barbara Lena Gierszewska (ed.), *Polski Film Fabularny 1918-1939: Recencje* (Kraków: Księgarnia Akademicka), p. 299–300.

Zajiček, Edward (1992). *Poza ekranem: Kinematografia Polska 1918-1991* (Warsaw: Filmoteka Narodowa).

Zaremba, Marcin (2009). 'Liberał w kontekście', in Andrzej Brzeziecki (ed.), *Lekcje historii PRL w rozmowach* (Warsaw: W.A.B.), pp. 178–211.

Zawiśliński, Stanisław (2005). *Kieślowski. Ważne, zeby iść...* (Izabelin: Skorpion).

Zbieg, Agata (2012). 'Mija 30 lat od aktorskiego bojkotu radia i tv w stanie wojennym', *Dzieje.pl*, http://dzieje.pl/kultura-i-sztuka/mija-30-lat-od-aktorskiego-bojkotu-radia-i-tv-w-stanie-wojennym. Accessed 20 July 2014.

Zielinski, Janusz G. (1973). *Economic Reforms in Polish Industry* (Oxford: Oxford University Press).

Zinoviev, Alexander (1985). *Homo Sovieticus*, trans. Charles Janson (London: Victor Gollancz).

Zusi, Peter A. (2004). 'Echoes of the Epochal: Historicism and the Realism Debate', *Comparative Literature*, 3, pp. 207–226.

Zwierzchowski, Piotr (2000). *Zapomniani bohaterowie: O bohaterach filmowych polskiego socralizmu* (Warsaw: Trio).

―――― (2005). *Pęknięty monolit: Konteksty polskiego kina socrealistycznego* (Bydgoszcz: Wydawnictwo Uniwersytetu Kazimierza Wielkiego).

―――― and Daria Mazur (eds) (2011). *Polskie kino popularne* (Bydgoszcz: Wydawnictwo Uniwersytetu Kazimierza Wielkiego).

―――― and Krzysztof Kornacki (2014). 'Metodologiczne problemy badania kina PRL-u', *Kwartalnik Filmowy*, 85, pp. 28–39.

Žižek, Slavoj (1997). 'Multiculturalism, Or the Cultural Logic of Multinational Capitalism', *New Left Review*, 1, pp. 28–51.

―――― (2001a). *The Fright of Real Life: Krzysztof Kieslowski between Theory and Post-Theory* (London: British Film Institute).

―――― (2001b). *Did Somebody Say Totalitarianism: Five Interventions in the (Mis)Use of a Notion* (London: Verso).

―――― (2006). 'The Lesson of Rancière', in Jacques Rancière, *The Politics of Aesthetics*, trans. Gabriel Rockhill (London: Continuum), pp. 69–79.

―――― (2011). *Living in the End Times* (London: Verso).

Index

A

Adam's Two Ribs (Dwa żebra Adama), 171
Adorno, Theodor, 33, 48–9, 114, 163, 309
Adventure at Marienstadt, An (Przygoda na Mariensztacie), 106, 114–22, 154
Agamben, Giorgio, 281, 309
Aktorzy prowincjonalni (Provincial Actors), 195
Amator (Camera Buff), 195, 202–5
Angst essen Seele auf (Fear Eats the Soul), 68
Antonioni, Michelangelo, 160
Arizona, 280–84
Article Zero (Paragraf Zero), 138–40
Ashes and Diamonds (Popiół i diament), 137, 354
Austen, Jane, 49

B

Badiou, Alain, 25, 309
Bad Luck (Zezowate szczęście), 141
Bailiff (Komornik), 293–97
Bajon, Filip, 265
Bakhtin, Mikhail, 47–8, 309
Balanga (Party), 270
Balcerowicz, Leszek, 230, 258, 260
Ballet Mécanique, 40
Battleship Potemkin (Bronenosets Potemkin), 37
Bareja, Stanisław, 15, 141, 163–70, 173–74, 180, 187, 192, 194, 202, 219–20, 222, 243–47, 254, 269, 271, 299
Bar at Victoria Station, A (Bar na Viktorii), 301, 305
Bar na Viktorii (A Bar at Victoria Station), 301, 305
Barszczewska, Elżbieta, 63, 65–6
Bartek the Winner (Bartek Zwycięzca), 37
Bartek Zwycięzca (Bartek the Winner), 37
Barwy ochronne (Camouflage), 97
Baza ludzi umarłych (The Depot of the Dead), 109, 134–38, 143, 151, 154
Bazin, André, 15
Becker, Wolfgang, 266
Bednarczyk, Antoni, 36
Będzie lepiej (Things Will Get Better), 55–8

Behind a Curtain (Za zasłoną), 78
Benita, Ina, 71
Benjamin, Walter, 16
Better to Be Beautiful and Rich (Lepiej być piękną i bogatą), 265
Bez miłości (Without Love), 244, 249–51
Biegański, Wiktor, 33
Bielawska, Karolina, 305–7
Bierut, Bolesław, 87, 89, 104, 109, 116, 134, 140, 144–45, 213, 225
Bilet powrotny (Return Ticket), 167, 220–21, 247
Birth and Life of a Newspaper, The (Narodziny i życie gazety), 70
Birth of a Robot, The (Narodziny robota), 70
Blackmail, 34
Bloch, Ernst, 48–9, 58, 274, 310
Blonde in Love, A (Lásky jedné plavovlásky), 191
Bobrowski, Czesław, 103
Bodo, Eugeniusz, 29, 53
Bohater roku (Hero of the Year), 244, 251–53, 266, 293
Bolesławski, Ryszard, 3, 35
Border, The (Granica), 65–6
Borowczyk, Walerian, 97, 194
Borowik, Włodzimierz, 138
Borzęcka, Ewa, 280–84
Böttcher, Jürgen, 180
Bourdieu, Pierre, 2, 258, 310
Boyle, Danny, 284
Brassed Off, 279
Brezhnev, Leonid, 183, 225
Bricklayer, The (Murarz), 206, 209–11, 241, 253
Britten, Benjamin, 133
Bromski, Jacek, 307
Bronenosets Potemkin (Battleship Potemkin), 37
Bruegel, Pieter, 284
Brunet wieczorową porą (Brunet Will Call), 187, 192–93, 298
Brunet Will Call (Brunet wieczorową porą), 187, 192–93, 298

Brzeski, Janusz Maria, 70
Buczkowski, Leonard, 106, 114–16, 120
Bugajski, Ryszard, 307
Bugdol, Bernard, 206, 209, 212, 217, 242

C

Cabinet of Dr Caligari. The (Das Kabinett des Dr. Caligari), 40
Camera Buff (Amator), 195, 202–5
Camouflage (Barwy ochronne), 97
Capital, or How to Make Money in Poland (Kapitał, czyli jak zrobić pieniądze w Polsce), 265–69, 286
Carry On, 187
Catch Me If You Can, 188
Cavalcanti, Alberto, 133
Cękalski, Eugeniusz, 61, 72–3, 98, 111–12, 125, 311
Chaberski, Emil, 36, 66
Chamiec, Krzysztof, 155
Chaplin, Charles, 48, 56, 151, 277
Chęciński, Sylwester, 163
Children Must Laugh (Droga Młodych), 70
Chłopi (The Peasants), 33
Chmielewski, Tadeusz, 163
Chodakowski, Andrzej, 226, 232
Chwalibóg, Maria, 195
Chyra, Andrzej, 295
Chytilová, Věra, 179
Chrzanowski, Tadeusz, 78
Citizen Kane, 142, 207
City Lights, 48, 277
Coal Face, 133
Co mi zrobisz, jak mnie złapiesz (What Will You Do When You Catch Me?), 219
Co mój mąż robi w nocy? (What Is My Husband Doing at Night?), 76
Comolli, Jean-Luc, 16–7, 110, 136, 312
Conductor (Dyrygent), 195
Čovek nije tica (Man Is Not a Bird), 137
Cranes are Flying, The (Letyat zhuravli), 64
Cruise (Rejs), 187–92, 194, 221, 244, 247
Cud nad Wisłą (The Miracle on the Vistula), 3, 35
Cudowne miejsce (Miraculous Place), 280
Cult of the Body, The (Kult ciała), 38, 41
Cybulski, Zbigniew, 99
Czas nadziei (Time of Hope), 234–38

Człowiek na torze (Man on the Tracks), 100, 120, 141–42, 207
Człowiek z marmuru (Man of Marble), 97, 135, 142, 195, 206, 211–14, 230–32, 251
Człowiek z żelaza (Man of Iron), 213–14, 226, 229–32, 234–35, 239–240, 244, 307–8
Czterdziestolatek (Forty Years Old), 188
Czy Lucyna to dziewczyna? (Is Lucyna a Woman?), 50–1, 53
Czyżewska, Elżbieta, 99

D

Dąbrowska, Maria, 90
Dance Leader (Wodzirej), 195, 199–200, 216, 251–53, 266, 293
Daisies (Sedmikrásky), 179
Dardenne, Luc and Jean-Pierre, 308
Dawid, Leszek, 301, 305
Day after Day (Dzień za dniem), 240–44
Debt (Dług), 290–93, 295–97, 300, 302
de Certeau, Michel, 11, 312
Dederko, Henryk, 284–86
Dejmek, Kazimierz, 146
Deluge, The (Potop), 186
Depot of the Dead, The (Baza ludzi umarłych), 109, 134–38, 143, 151, 154
Deux ou trois choses que je sais d'elle, 219
Difficult Love (Trudna miłość), 125
Dignity (Godność), 234–38, 244
Djilas, Milovan, 88–9, 312
Dla Ciebie, Polsko (For You, Poland), 36
Dług (Debt), 290–93, 295–97, 300, 302
Dmowski, Roman, 27
Dobrowolski, Tomasz, 279
Doctor Murek (Doktór Murek), 39, 68–9, 76
Dogs (Psy), 287–90, 297
Doktór Murek (Doctor Murek), 39, 68–9, 76
Dołęga-Mostowicz, Tadeusz, 32, 68
Dom na pustkowiu (The Lonely House), 106
Droga Młodych (Children Must Laugh), 70
Dusze w niewoli (Souls in Bondage), 38, 41–3
Dutkiewicz, Maciej, 270, 273
Dwa żebra Adama (Adam's Two Ribs), 171
Dwie brygady (Two Teams), 111–14, 121, 197
Dymsza, Adolf, 122–23
Dyrygent (Conductor), 195

Dziady (Forefathers' Eve), 146
Dzieje grzechu (The Story of Sin), 194
Dzień kobiet (Women's Day), 297–301
Dzień za dniem (Day after Day), 240–44
Dziewczęta z Nowolipek (Girls from Nowolipki), 61, 63–6, 79, 272
Dziewczyny do wzięcia (Girls to Pick Up), 187, 190–93, 216
Dziki, Waldemar, 270, 273–76

E
Eberhardt, Konrad, 163–64, 312
Edi, 78
Eisenstein, Sergei, 37
Elsaesser, Thomas, 61
End of the Epoch of Coal, The (Koniec epoki węgla kamiennego), 279
Engels, Frederick, 5, 7, 19–20, 50, 62, 67, 117, 137, 257

F
Fair Cornfields (Jasne łany), 125
Falk, Feliks, 187, 195, 199–202, 244, 251, 254, 265–69, 293–96
Faraon (Pharaoh), 99
Farewell to Devil (Pożegnanie z diabłem), 125
Farocki, Harun, 24, 313
Fassbinder, Rainer Werner, 68
Fear Eats the Soul (Angst essen Seele auf), 68
Fethke, Jan, 106, 121–24
First Million (Pierwszy million), 270, 273–76, 292
Fog (Mgła), 280–81
Forbidden Songs (Zakazane piosenki), 106
Ford, Aleksander, 14, 70–1, 98, 148
Forefathers' Eve (Dziady), 146
Foreman on a Farm..., (Sztygar na zagrodzie...), 217–18
Forman, Miloš, 191
Forty Years Old (Czterdziestolatek), 188
For You, Poland (Dla Ciebie, Polsko), 36
Fourier, Charles, 7
Friedman, Milton, 258
Fuks (Stroke of Luck), 270–73

G
Gangsters and the Philanthropists, The (Gangsterzy i filantropi), 172–74
Gangsterzy i filantropi (The Gangsters and the Philanthropists), 172–74
Gardan, Juliusz, 39, 50–1, 61, 65, 68
Generation, A (Pokolenie), 109
Geremek, Bronisław, 233
Ghosts, The (Strachy), 61, 67, 72–4, 79, 112
Gierek, Edward, 88, 90, 99, 143, 147, 180–86, 189, 193–97, 209, 213–14, 216–21, 223, 225, 243, 246, 257
Girls from Nowolipki (Dziewczęta z Nowolipek), 61, 63–6, 79, 272
Girls to Pick Up (Dziewczyny do wzięcia), 187, 190–93, 216
Gliński, Robert, 307–8
Gniazdowski, Zbigniew, 33
Godard, Jean-Luc, 14, 16, 79, 219, 301
Godność (Dignity), 234–38, 244
Gojawiczyńska, Pola, 62–3, 79
Gold (Złoto), 109, 143, 149–5, 157–61, 171
Gold Rush, The, 151
Gomułka, Władysław, 27–8, 82, 87–9, 91–2, 99, 104, 144–47, 151, 154, 157, 163, 171, 181, 185, 187, 189, 213, 221
Good Bye Lenin!, 266
Gorbachev, Mikhail, 86
Gorczyńska, Maria, 69, 154
Goździk, Lechosław, 180
Grabski, Władysław, 29
Granica (The Border), 65–6
Grant, Barry Keith, 13
Greenberg, Clement, 33, 313
Grierson, 44, 121
Grodzieński, Stefan, 44
Gromada (The Village Mill), 125–26
Groys, Boris, 107–8, 111, 120, 128, 285, 314
Gwiazda, Andrzej, 233–34
Gwiazdy muszą płonąć (The Stars Must Burn), 129–33

H
Hamer, Robert, 54
Hands Up (Ręce do góry), 97, 301

Harvey, David, 2, 6–7, 30, 62–3, 84, 255–56, 258, 261, 270, 280, 300, 304, 314
Has, Wojciech, 14, 96, 99, 109, 143, 149, 151–55, 158, 160, 227
Havel, Václav, 185, 314
Hearts of Steel (Stalowe serca), 109
Heather (Wrzos), 61, 75, 77
Heilman, Robert Bechtold, 61–2, 69, 299, 314
Hendrykowska, Małgorzata, 26, 31–3, 53, 190, 314
Herman, Mark, 279
Hero of the Year (Bohater roku), 244, 251–54, 266, 293
Hertz, Aleksander, 31, 33
Highmore, Ben, 4, 9
His Excellency the Shop Assistant (Jego ekscelencja subiekt), 53–5
His Highness the Chauffeur (Jaśnie pan szofer), 53–4, 59
Hitchcock, Alfred, 34
Hitler, Adolf, 29, 39
Hłasko, Marek, 134–35, 137
Hobsbawm, Eric, 84, 183, 315
Hoffman, Jerzy, 3, 172, 174, 186, 263
Holland, Agnieszka, 96–7, 187, 195, 226, 239–40, 243–44, 290
Holoubek, Gustaw, 173
Huk, Tadeusz, 195
Husband of His Wife, A (Mąż swojej żony), 164–66, 245
Huston, John, 275

I

Irena do domu! (Irena Go Home), 106
Irena Go Home (Irena do domu!), 106
Irzykowski, Karol, 36
Is Lucyna a Woman? (Czy Lucyna to dziewczyna?), 50–1, 53
Ivens, Joris, 203
Iwonka, 36

J

Jackiewicz, Aleksander, 14, 44–5, 167, 315
Jadzia, 51–3, 57, 75
Jagielski, Mieczysław, 232
Jakubowska, Wanda, 96, 98, 106, 125, 148, 298
Janda, Krystyna, 99, 307
Januszewski, Stanisław, 109
Jaruzelski, Wojciech, 224, 237–38
Jasne łany (Fair Cornfields), 125
Jaśnie pan szofer (His Highness the Chauffeur), 53–4, 59
Jego ekscelencja subiekt (His Excellency the Shop Assistant), 53–5
John Paul II, 223
Jurandot, Jerzy, 165

K

Kabinett des Dr. Caligari, Das (The Cabinet of Dr Caligari), 40
Kaczyński, Lech, 291
Kalatozov, Mikhail, 63
Kamieńska, Irena, 240–44, 280–81, 283
Kania, Stanisław, 223
Kapitał, czyli jak zrobić pieniądze w Polsce (Capital, or How to Make Money in Poland), 265–69, 286
Karabasz, Kazimierz, 15, 138, 175–77, 209, 215–16, 302, 305–6
Kasprzyk, Ewa, 79
Kawalerowicz, Jerzy, 14, 96, 98–9, 125, 127, 148, 226, 238, 263
Kazejak-Dawid, Anna, 302–4
Kieślowski, Krzysztof, 14, 96, 141, 177–79, 187, 195–98, 201–2, 204–6, 209–11, 214, 241, 253, 276–78, 290
Kind Hearts and Coronets, 54
King, Queen, Knave, 79
Khruschchev, Nikita, 144
Kiler, 265
Kilerów dwóch (Two Kilers), 265
Kłamstwo Krystyny (Krystyna's Lie), 61, 65, 74–5, 272
Knife in the Water (Nóż w wodzie), 161–63, 179, 187
Kobieta samotna (A Woman Alone), 239–40, 243
Kobiety nad przepaścią (Women on the Abyss), 42–3, 66, 77
Kobiety naszych dni (Women of Our Days), 133
Kolejarskie słowo (A Railwayman's Word), 129–31, 133, 141
Kolski, Jan Jakub, 280
Komasa, Jan, 302

Komornik (Bailiff), 293–97
Kondratiuk, Janusz, 15, 187, 191
Koniec epoki węgla kamiennego (The End of the Epoch of Coal), 279
Kornacki, Krzysztof, 3
Konwicki, Tadeusz, 112, 317
Kornhauser, Julian, 194, 198
Kossobudzka, Wanda, 172
Kostenko, Andrzej, 219
Koterski, Marek, 222
Kracauer, Siegfried, 39
Krauze, Krzysztof, 290–93, 296, 300
Krawicz, Mieczysław, 38, 43, 51–2, 55, 61, 67, 78
Krenz, Jan, 133
Krystyna M., 215–16, 305
Krystyna's Lie (Kłamstwo Krystyny), 61, 65, 74–5, 241, 272
Kucharski, Jan, 33
Kuczkowski, Feliks, 33
Kult ciała (The Cult of the Body), 38, 41
Kurek, Jalu, 45
Kuroń, Jacek, 300, 317
Kwaśniewski, Aleksander, 255, 291

L

Ladykillers, The, 173
Lang, Fritz, 40
L'Année dernière à Marienbad (The Last Year in Marienbad), 45
Łapicki, Andrzej, 134
Lásky jedné plavovlásky (A Blonde in Love), 191
Last Stage, The (Ostatni etap), 106, 298
Last Year in Marienbad, The (L'Année dernière à Marienbad), 45
Latałło, Stanisław, 195
Laurel and Hardy, 55
Lee, Bruce, 227
Lefebvre, Henri, 4, 11–2, 160, 318
Léger, Fernand, 40
Lejtes, Józef, 14, 61, 63–5, 78
Lenin, V.I., 8, 171, 260
Leper, The (Trędowata), 61, 65
Lepiej być piękną i bogatą (Better to Be Beautiful and Rich), 265
Lesiewicz, Witold, 131
Leszczyński, Witold, 219

Letyat zhuravli (The Cranes are Flying), 64
Linda, Bogusław, 263
Lipman, Jerzy, 149
Lis, Bogdan, 233
Little Town (Miasteczko), 138, 140–41, 178
Łódź – miasto pracy (Łódź – The City of Work), 44
Łódź – The City of Work (Łódź – miasto pracy), 44
Lonely House, The (Dom na pustkowiu), 106
Łopacka, Bożena, 297
Lubelski, Tadeusz, 25, 31–3, 35–6, 46, 62, 110, 114, 141–42, 164, 194, 198, 227, 244, 291, 318
Ludzie Wisły (The People of the Vistula), 70–1
Ludzie z pustego obszaru (People from an Empty Zone), 138–39
Lukacs, Georg, 107
Lumiere Brothers, 24

M

Macherey, Pierre, 20, 24
Machulski, Juliusz, 98, 265
Mackendrick, Alexander, 173
Madej, Alina, 31–2, 36, 46, 60, 62, 109
Maetzig, Kurt, 108, 142
Majmurek, Jakub, 20, 84, 86
Makavejev, Dušan, 137–38, 143, 286
Maklakiewicz, Zdzisław, 190
Małżeństwo z rozsądku (Marriage of Convenience), 165, 167–70, 174
Man Is Not a Bird (Čovek nije tica), 137
Man of Iron (Człowiek z żelaza), 213–14, 226, 229–32, 234–35, 239–40, 244, 307–8
Man of Marble (Człowiek z marmuru), 97, 135, 142, 195, 206, 211–14, 230–32, 252
Man on the Tracks (Człowiek na torze), 100, 120, 141–42, 207
Marcuse, Herbert, 114
Markowski, Ryszard, 307
Marriage of Convenience (Małżeństwo z rozsądku), 165, 167–70, 174
Marx, Karl, 5–6, 19–20, 25, 50, 59, 67, 74–5, 85, 117, 120, 137, 160, 211, 217, 225, 231, 234, 256–57, 264, 266, 269, 273, 277, 294, 319
Mat (Mother), 238
Matter to Be Settled (Sprawa do załatwienia), 106, 121–24, 142, 167

Mazierska, Ewa, 1, 3, 14, 25, 78, 96, 101, 153, 179–80, 214, 222, 230–31, 247, 264, 282, 294, 298, 320
Mazowiecki, Tadeusz, 225, 233, 258
Mąż swojej żony (A Husband of His Wife), 164–66, 245
Meiksins Wood, Ellen, 1
Metropolis, 40
Mgła (Fog), 280–81
Miasteczko (Little Town), 138, 140–41, 178
Miasto prywatne (Private City), 270
Michałek, Bolesław, 25, 97–100, 106, 149, 157–58, 162, 321
Michnik, Adam, 225, 260, 289
Mickiewicz, Adam, 146, 171
Migas, Maciej, 302
Mikołajczyk, Stanisław, 87
Minc, Hilary, 104
Miracle on the Vistula, The (Cud nad Wisłą), 3, 35
Miraculous Place (Cudowne miejsce), 280
Miś (Teddy Bear), 170, 244–47
Miss from Poste Restante (Panienka z poste restante), 50–1
Mniszkówna, Helena, 32
Mocny człowiek (The Strong Man), 38–9, 41, 43
Modern Times, 56
Modzelewski, Eugeniusz, 33
Moi rodzice się rozwodzą (My Parents Are Divorcing), 67
Molo (The Pier), 149–50, 157–60, 171
Moonlighting, 244–45, 247, 249
Morawski, Piotr, 278–79
Morgenstern, Janusz, 164, 171, 180
Mother (Mat), 238
Munk, Andrzej, 96, 100, 129–34, 141
Murarz (The Bricklayer), 206, 209–11, 241, 253
Musicians, The (Muzykanci), 175, 177
Muzykanci (The Musicians), 175, 177
My Parents Are Divorcing (Moi rodzice się rozwodzą), 67
Mystery of a Tram Stop, A (Tajemnica przystanku tramwajowego), 33

N
Nałkowska, Zofia, 62, 65
Narodziny i życie gazety (The Birth and Life of a Newspaper), 70
Narodziny robota (The Birth of a Robot), 70
Narutowicz, Gabriel, 28
Na srebrnym globie (On the Silver Globe), 101, 186
Niemirski, Alfred, 38, 43
Night Mail, 131
Noose (Pętla), 160
Nowina-Przybylski, Jan, 50
Nóż w wodzie (Knife in the Water), 161–63, 179, 187

O
Och, Karol!, 228
O czem się nie mówi (What Should Not Be Mentioned), 38, 61, 66–7
Oda do radości (Ode to Joy), 302–4
Ode to Joy (Oda do radości), 302–4
Office (Urząd), 293
Office, The (Urząd), 141, 177–79
Ogniem i mieczem (With Fire and Sword), 263
Olbrychski, Daniel, 99
One Floor Above (Piętro wyżej), 49, 54, 60
On the Silver Globe (Na srebrnym globie), 101, 196
Opania, Marian, 253, 295
Opowieść o człowieku, który wykonał 552% normy (A Story of a Man Who Filled 552% of the Quota), 206–9, 241
Orwell, George, 20, 93–4, 277
Osiecka, Agnieszka, 167
Ostatni etap (The Last Stage), 106, 298

P
Pamiętniki chłopów (Peasants' Memoirs), 129–31, 133
Panienka z poste restante (Miss from Poste Restante), 50–1
Paragraf Zero (Article Zero), 138–40
Party (Balanga), 270
Pasażerka (Passenger), 129
Pasikowski, Władysław, 254, 287–90
Passenger (Pasażerka), 129
Paweł and Gaweł (Paweł i Gaweł), 55
Paweł i Gaweł (Paweł and Gaweł), 55
Peasants' Memoirs (Pamiętniki chłopów), 129–31, 133

Peasants, The (Chłopi), 33
Peiper, Tadeusz, 58
People from an Empty Zone (Ludzie z pustego obszaru), 138–39
People of the Vistula, The (Ludzie Wisły), 70–1
Perec, Georges, 3
Personel (Personnel), 195–99, 204
Personnel (Personel), 195–99, 204
Petelska, Ewa, 167, 220–21, 247
Petelski, Czesław, 109, 134–38, 143, 152, 167, 220–21, 247
Pętla (Noose), 160
Pharaoh (Faraon), 99
Pienkowska, Anna, 232
Pier, The (Molo), 149–50, 157–60, 171
Pierwszy million (First Million), 270, 273–76, 292
Piestrak, Marek, 14, 222
Piętro wyżej (One Floor Above), 49, 54, 60
Piłsudski, Józef, 2, 27–8, 30, 34, 75
Piwowski, Marek, 15, 187–90, 221–22, 247
Pod gwiazdą frygijską (Under the Phrygian Star), 238
Pograbek, 280
Pokolenie (A Generation), 109
Polanski, Roman, 14, 97, 143, 149, 161, 179, 187
Polanyi, Karl, 273, 286, 323
Polish Work at the Sea (Praca Polski na morzu), 44
Popiół i diament (Ashes and Diamonds), 137, 254
Potop (The Deluge), 186
Pożegnanie z diabłem (Farewell to Devil), 125
Praca Polski na morzu (Polish Work at the Sea), 44
Private City (Miasto prywatne), 270
Profesor Wilczur (Professor Wilczur), 44
Professor Wilczur (Profesor Wilczur), 44
Promised Land, The (Ziemia obiecana), 33, 99, 186, 194, 241, 275
Provincial Actors (Aktorzy prowincjonalni), 195
Przybyszewski, Stanisław, 39–40, 46
Przygoda na Mariensztacie (An Adventure at Mariensztadt), 106, 114–22, 154
Pstrowski, Wincenty, 207
Psy (Dogs), 287–90, 297
Puchalski, Edward, 37–8
Pudovkin, Vsevolod, 238
Pulse of Polish Manchester, The (Tętno polskiego Manchesteru), 70

Q
Quack, The (Znachor), 44, 68
Quo Vadis, 263

R
Radziwiłowicz, Jerzy, 307
Railwayman's Word, A (Kolejarskie słowo), 129–31, 133, 141
Rakowski, Mieczysław, 238
Rancière, Jacques, 17–8, 237, 323
Ręce do góry (Hands Up), 97, 301
Rejs (Cruise), 187–92, 194, 221, 244, 247
Rękopis znaleziony w Saragossie (The Saragossa Manuscript), 99
Resnais, Alain, 45
Return Ticket (Bilet powrotny), 167, 220–21, 247
Rewizja osobista (Strip Search), 219
Reymont, Władysław, 33, 275
Rhys, Jean, 72
Robinson warszawski (Warsaw Robinson), 106
Robotnice (Workwomen), 240–41
Robotnicy '80 (Workers 1980), 226, 228, 232–34, 236
Rok Franka W. (The Year of Franek W.), 175, 209, 215
Roman einer jungen Ehe (Story of a Young Couple), 108, 142
Rosetta, 308
Różewicz, Stanisław, 125
Różewicz, Tadeusz, 148, 157, 324
Ruiz, Raul, 16–7, 324
Ruszkiewicz, Julia, 305–7
Rybkowski, Jan, 106, 121–24, 148

S
Sabre from the Commander (Szabla od komendanta), 280
Sadowska, Maria, 297–99
Saragossa Manuscript, The (Rękopis znaleziony w Saragossie), 99
Sass, Barbara, 79, 244, 249–51
Sawicka, Teresa, 195
Scorsese, Martin, 271
Sedmikrásky (Daisies), 179
Shared Room, A (Wspólny pokój), 160
Sienkiewicz, Henryk, 3, 37

Silesia – the Pupil of Poland (Śląsk – źrenica Polski), 44
Skalski, Jacek, 270
Skolimowski, Jerzy, 78, 97, 149–50, 155, 159, 244–45, 247–49, 301
Skórzewski, Edward, 172, 174
Śląsk – źrenica Polski (Silesia – the Pupil of Poland), 44
Ślesicki, Władysław, 138
Słonimski, Antoni, 36, 324
Smosarska, Jadwiga, 53
Sobczuk, Bogusław, 253
Solarz, Wojciech, 149
Solidarity, Solidarity... (Solidarność, Solidarność), 100, 307
Solidarność, Solidarność (Solidarity, Solidarity...), 100, 307
Souls in Bondage (Dusze w niewoli), 38, 41–3
Spielberg, Steven, 188
Sprawa do załatwienia (Matter to Be Settled), 106, 121–24, 142, 167
Stalin, Joseph, 85, 97, 104, 125, 134, 144, 172, 301, 325
Stalińska, Dorota, 251
Stalowe serca (Hearts of Steel), 109
Stars Must Burn, The (Gwiazdy muszą płonąć), 129–33
Stawiński, Jerzy Stefan, 220
Stępowski, Kazimierz Junosza, 75
Stern, Anatol, 45
Story of a Man Who Filled 552% of the Quota, A (Opowieść o człowieku, który wykonał 552% normy), 206–9, 241
Story of Sin, The (Dzieje grzechu), 194
Story of a Young Couple (Roman einer jungen Ehe), 108, 142
Strachy (The Ghosts), 61, 67, 72–4, 79, 112
Strip Search (Rewizja osobista), 219
Stroke of Luck (Fuks), 270–73
Strong Man, The (Mocny człowiek), 38–9, 41, 43
Supermarket, 297, 299–301
Sweet Movie, 286
Świadkowie albo nasza mała stabilizacja (Witnesses or Our Small Stabilisation), 148
Szabla od komendanta (Sabre from the Commander), 280

Szaro, Henryk, 38, 40, 61
Szczepko and Tońko, 55, 59, 78
Szlakiem hańby (A Trail of Disgrace), 38, 42–3, 66
Szmidt, Tadeusz, 119
Szołowski, Karol, 61, 72–3
Sztygar na zagrodzie... (Foreman on a Farm...), 217–18
Szykulska, Ewa, 191

T

Tajemnica przystanku tramwajowego (A Mystery of a Tram Stop), 33
Ta wspaniała praca (This Wonderful Work), 278–79
Teddy Bear (Miś), 170, 244–47
Test of Pilot Pirx, The (Test Pilota Pirxa), 222
Test Pilota Pirxa (The Test of Pilot Pirx), 222
Tętno polskiego Manchesteru (The Pulse of Polish Manchester), 70
Thatcher, Margaret, 95, 280
Things Will Get Better (Będzie lepiej), 55–8
This Wonderful Work (Ta wspaniała praca), 278–79
Time of Hope (Czas nadziei), 234, 236–38
Toeplitz, Jerzy, 106, 109–10, 112, 115, 149, 326
Tout va bien, 301
Trail of Disgrace, A (Szlakiem hańby), 38, 42–3, 66
Trainspotting, 284
Treasure of the Sierra Madre, The, 275–76
Trędowata (The Leper), 61, 65
Trotsky, Leon, 9–11, 94
Trudna miłość (Difficult Love), 125
Trystan, Leon, 38, 42, 49
Trzaskalski, Piotr, 78
Two Kilers (Kilerów dwóch), 265
Two Teams (Dwie brygady), 111–14, 121, 197
Tym, Stanisław, 189, 222, 326

U

Under the Phrygian Star (Pod gwiazdą frygijską), 238
Ukniewska, Maria, 62, 72, 79
Urząd (The Office), 141, 177–79
Urząd (Office), 293
Uspensky, Gleb, 10

V

Vagabonds (Włóczęgi), 55, 57
Village Mill, The (Gromada), 125–26

W

Wajda, Andrzej, 14, 96–8, 101, 109, 137, 142, 186, 194–95, 201, 206, 208, 211–14, 226–33, 239, 241, 246, 249, 254, 275, 307–8
Walentynowicz, Anna, 223, 231, 234
Wałęsa, Lech, 85, 100, 208, 224–26, 233–34, 255, 259, 281, 304, 307
Wałęsa: Człowiek z nadziei (Wałęsa: Man of Hope), 208, 230
Wałęsa: Man of Hope (Wałęsa: Człowiek z nadziei), 208
Walkover (Walkower), 149–50, 155, 157–60, 171
Walkower (Walkover), 149–50, 155, 157–60, 171
Wallerstein, Immanuel, 84, 261, 327
Warhol, Andy, 308
Warsaw Available (Warszawa do wzięcia), 305–7
Warsaw Robinson (Robinson warszawski), 106
Warszawa do wzięcia (Warsaw Available), 305–7
Waszyński, Michał, 32, 38, 43–4, 53, 55–6, 59, 66, 68, 76
Watt, Harry, 131
Weber, Kurt, 149
Wedding, The (Wesele), 157
Welcome to Life! (Witajcie w życiu!), 284–86
Welles, Orson, 142
Wesele (The Wedding), 157
What Is My Husband Doing at Night? (Co mój mąż robi w nocy?), 76
What Should Not Be Mentioned (O czem się nie mówi), 38, 61, 66–7
What Will You Do When You Catch Me? (Co mi zrobisz, jak mnie złapiesz), 219
White, 276–78
Wiene, Robert, 40
Wife for an Australian (Żona dla Australijczyka), 165–66, 219
Williams, Raymond, 11
Wionczek, Roman, 234–38
Wiszniewski, Wojciech, 15, 135, 206–9, 212–14, 217–18, 241
Witajcie w życiu! (Welcome to Life!), 284–86
With Fire and Sword (Ogniem i mieczem), 263
Without Love (Bez miłości), 244, 249–51
Witnesses or Our Small Stabilisation (Świadkowie albo nasza mała stabilizacja), 148
Włóczęgi (Vagabonds), 55, 57
Wodzirej (Dance Leader), 195, 199, 216, 251–53, 266, 293
Wohl, Stanisław, 73
Woman Alone, A (Kobieta samotna), 239–40, 243
Women of Our Days (Kobiety naszych dni), 133
Women on the Abyss (Kobiety nad przepaścią, 42–3, 66, 77
Women's Day (Dzień kobiet), 297–301
Workers 1980 (Robotnicy '80), 226, 228, 232–34, 236
Workwomen (Robotnice), 240–41
Wright, Basil, 131
Wrzos (Heather), 61, 75, 77
Wspólny pokój (A Shared Room), 160
Wylężałek, Łukasz, 270
Wysocka, Stanisława, 71
Wyspiański, Stanisław, 157
Wyszomirski, Włodzimierz, 44
Wyszyński, Stefan, 104

Y

Year of Franek W., The (Rok Franka W.), 175, 209, 215

Z

Zagajewski, Adam, 194, 198
Zahorska, Stefania, 36, 53, 66, 72, 77, 327
Zajączkowski, Andrzej, 232, 308
Zajiček, Edward, 31, 96–7, 148–49, 186, 227
Żak, Maciej, 297–301
Zakazane piosenki (Forbidden Songs), 106
Zaluski, Roman, 228
Zanussi, Krzysztof, 96–8, 226, 228
Zapolska, Gabriela, 66
Zarzycki, Jerzy, 70–1, 106
Za zasłoną (Behind a Curtain), 78
Żelichowska, Lena, 66
Zelnik, Jan, 133–34
Żeromski, Stefan, 32
Zezowate szczęście (Bad Luck), 141
Zhdanov, Andrei, 107
Ziarnik, Jerzy, 138, 140, 163, 178

Ziemia obiecana (*The Promised Land*), 33, 99, 186, 194, 241, 275
Zinoviev, Aleksander, 94, 163, 178–79, 329
Žižek, Slavoj, 237, 249, 259, 288, 329
Złoto (*Gold*), 109, 143, 149–55, 157–61, 171
Zmarz-Koczanowicz, Maria, 293
Znachor (*The Quack*), 44, 68
Żona dla Australijczyka (*Wife for an Australian*), 165–66, 219
Żuławski, Andrzej, 101, 186

www.ingramcontent.com/pod-product-compliance
Lightning Source LLC
Chambersburg PA
CBHW072143100526
44589CB00015B/2067